Protestantism after 500 Years

Protestantism
after
500 Years

Edited by

THOMAS ALBERT HOWARD

AND

MARK A. NOLL

OXFORD
UNIVERSITY PRESS

OXFORD
UNIVERSITY PRESS

Oxford University Press is a department of the University of Oxford. It furthers
the University's objective of excellence in research, scholarship, and education
by publishing worldwide. Oxford is a registered trade mark of Oxford University
Press in the UK and certain other countries.

Published in the United States of America by Oxford University Press
198 Madison Avenue, New York, NY 10016, United States of America.

Library of Congress Cataloging-in-Publication Data

Names: Howard, Thomas Albert, editor. | Noll, Mark A., editor.
Title: Protestantism after 500 years / edited by Thomas Albert Howard and Mark A. Noll.
Description: New York, NY : Oxford University Press, [2016]
Identifiers: LCCN 2015033530| ISBN 9780190264789 (hardback : alk. paper) |
ISBN 9780190264796 (pbk. : alk. paper)
Subjects: LCSH: Reformation. | Protestantism. | Reformation—Anniversaries, etc. |
Reformation—Influence. | Protestantism—Influence.
Classification: LCC BR309 .P95 2016 | DDC 280/.4—dc23 LC record available at
http://lccn.loc.gov/2015033530

1 3 5 7 9 8 6 4 2
Printed by Webcom, Inc., Canada

To Donald A. Yerxa,
who has helped so many to speak historically

Contents

Acknowledgments

WITH THE EXCEPTION of three contributions, the material in this book originated as papers presented at a conference at Gordon College on November 14–16, 2013, sponsored by Gordon's Center for Faith and Inquiry, then directed by Thomas Albert Howard. We are grateful to the many people who provided feedback during that conference. Sponsors of the conference also included the University of Notre Dame, Refo500, and the Boston Theological Institute. The latter was then directed by Rodney Peterson, who took a special interest in promoting this endeavor, for which we are grateful.

Agnes R. Howard provided wonderful editorial (and moral) support at various stages of this project. We also thank Debbie Drost, Ryan Groff, and Susanne McCarron of the Center for Faith and Inquiry at Gordon College—along with many of the Center's student aides and "apprentices," especially Katharine Stephens, Elizabeth Baker, Matthew Reese, Hilary (Sherratt) Yancey, Mary Hierholzer, and Elspeth Currie. Their myriad and selfless efforts contributed immensely to our work. We would also like to thank Lori Franz, Martha Crain, and Anna Appa for their assistance. Some material in chapter 1 appeared under the title, "Remembering the Reformation, 1817 and 1883: Commemorating the Past as Agent and Mirror of Social Change," in Donald Yerxa, ed., *Religion and Innovation: Antagonists or Partners?* (Bloomsbury Academic, 2015). We are grateful to be able to republish this material here.

Both the conference and the book were generously enabled by the Religion and Innovation in Human Affairs (RIHA) initiative of the Historical Society, funded by a major grant from the Templeton Foundation. We are very grateful for this support. In particular, we thank the RIHA project director Donald A. Yerxa, whose wide-ranging interests in the human past are only matched by his largeness of soul and geniality of character. We are very pleased to dedicate this book to him.

List of Contributors

CARLOS EIRE is T. Lawrason Riggs Professor of History and Religious Studies at Yale University. He specializes in the social, intellectual, religious, and cultural history of late medieval and early modern Europe, with a strong focus on both the Protestant and Catholic Reformations; the history of popular piety; and the history of death. He is the author of *War Against the Idols: The Reformation of Worship From Erasmus to Calvin* (Cambridge University Press, 1986); *From Madrid to Purgatory: The Art and Craft of Dying in Sixteenth Century Spain* (Cambridge University Press, 1995); *A Very Brief History of Eternity* (Princeton University Press, 2010); and co-author of *Jews, Christians, Muslims: An Introduction to Monotheistic Religions* (1997). He has also ventured into the twentieth century and the Cuban Revolution in the memoir *Waiting for Snow in Havana* (Free Press, 2003), which won the National Book Award for nonfiction (2003) and has been translated into more than a dozen languages—but is banned in Cuba. His memoir, *Learning to Die in Miami* (Free Press, 2010), explores the exile experience.

TIMOTHY GEORGE has been the Dean of Beeson Divinity School of Samford University since its inception in 1988. Trained in theology and church history at Harvard University, he is the author of more than twenty books, including *Theology of the Reformers* (Broadman Press, 1988; revised edition, 2013), *John Calvin and the Church* (Westminster/J. Knox Press, 1990), *Is the Father of Jesus the God of Muhammad?* (Zondervan, 2002), and *Reading Scripture with the Reformers* (IVP Academic, 2011). He also serves as the general editor of the *Reformation Commentary on Scripture*, a 28-volume series of sixteenth-century exegetical commentary. He serves on the editorial advisory boards of *First Things*, *Christianity Today*, and *Books & Culture*. An ordained minister in the Southern Baptist Convention, he is a life advisory trustee of Wheaton College and a senior fellow of the 21st Century Wilberforce Initiative.

BRAD S. GREGORY is Professor and Dorothy G. Griffin Collegiate Chair of Early Modern European History, as well as the Director of the Institute for Advanced Study at the University of Notre Dame, where he has taught since 2003. From 1996 to 2003, he taught at Stanford University. Gregory specializes in the history of Christianity in Europe during the Reformation era and the long-term influence of the Reformation era on the modern world. His first book, *Salvation at Stake: Christian Martyrdom in Early Modern Europe* (Harvard, 1999) received six book awards. In 2005, he was named the winner of the first annual Hiett Prize in the Humanities from the Dallas Institute of Humanities and Culture, an award given to an outstanding mid-career humanities scholar in the United States. His most recent book is *The Unintended Reformation: How a Religious Revolution Secularized Society* (Belknap, 2012), which has received widespread attention.

PETER HARRISON is an Australian Laureate Fellow and Director of the Institute of Advanced Studies in the Humanities at the University of Queensland. He has published extensively in the area of intellectual history, with a focus on the philosophical, scientific, and religious thought of the early modern period. He was the Idreos Professor of Science and Religion at the University of Oxford from 2007 to 2012, and in 2011, he delivered the Gifford Lectures at the University of Edinburgh. His books include *The Territories of Science and Religion* (Chicago, 2015); *Wrestling with Nature: From Omens to Science* (Chicago, 2011), edited with Ronald Numbers and Michael Shank; *The Cambridge Companion to Science and Religion* (Cambridge, 2010); *The Fall of Man and the Foundations of Science* (Cambridge, 2007); *The Bible, Protestantism, and the Rise of Natural Science* (Cambridge, 1998); and *'Religion' and the Religions in the English Enlightenment* (Cambridge, 1990).

THOMAS ALBERT HOWARD is Professor of History and the Humanities at Valparaiso University, where he also holds the Phyllis and Richard Duesenberg Chair in Christian Ethics. Formerly, he directed the Center for Faith and Inquiry at Gordon College. Professor Howard holds a Ph.D. in European intellectual history from the University of Virginia. He is the author of *Religion and the Rise of Historicism* (Cambridge, 2000); *Protestant*

Theology and the Making of the Modern German University (Oxford, 2006), winner of the Lilly Fellows Program Book Prize for 2007; and *God and the Atlantic: America, Europe and the Religious Divide* (Oxford, 2011), winner of a *Christianity Today* Book of the Year Award. He is also the editor of *The Future of Christian Learning: An Evangelical and Catholic Dialogue* by Mark Noll and James Turner (Brazos Press, 2008) and *Imago Dei: Human Dignity in Ecumenical Perspective* (Catholic University of America Press, 2013). Currently he is completing a project entitled "The Pope and the Professor: Pius IX, Ignaz von Döllinger, and the Quandary of the Modern Age" (Oxford University Press, forthcoming).

PHILIP JENKINS was educated at Cambridge University, where he obtained his doctorate in history. From 1980 through 2011, he taught at Pennsylvania State University, where he held the rank of Edwin Erle Sparks Professor of the Humanities. In 2012, he became a Distinguished Professor of History at Baylor University, where he also serves in the Institute for Studies of Religion. A prolific scholar, he has published twenty-six books, including *The Next Christendom: The Coming of Global Christianity* (Oxford University Press, 2002), *The Lost History of Christianity* (HarperOne, 2008), and *Jesus Wars* (HarperOne, 2010). His most recent book is *The Many Faces of Christ: The Thousand Year Story of the Survival and Influence of the Lost Gospels* (New York: Basic Books, 2015).

MATTHEW LEVERING is Perry Family Foundation Professor of Theology at Mundelein Seminary. He earned an M.T.S. from Duke University Divinity School and a Ph.D. from Boston College. He is the co-editor of the *International Journal of Systematic Theology* and of *Nova et Vetera*. Since 2004, he has been a member of Evangelicals and Catholics Together. He is the author of numerous books, including *Paul in the Summa Theologiae* (Catholic University of America Press, 2014); *The Theology of Augustine* (Baker Academic, 2013); *Jesus and the Demise of Death* (Baylor University Press, 2012); *Predestination* (Oxford University Press, 2011); *Christ and the Catholic Priesthood* (Hillenbrand Books, 2010); *Jewish-Christian Dialogue and the Life of Wisdom* (Continuum, 2010); *Biblical Natural Law* (Oxford University Press, 2008); *Participatory Biblical Exegesis* (University of Notre Dame Press, 2008); *Sacrifice and Community* (Blackwell, 2005); *Scripture and Metaphysics* (Blackwell, 2004); and *Ezra and Nehemiah* (Brazos Press, 2007). He has also co-edited numerous books, including *The Oxford Handbook of the Trinity* (Oxford University Press, 2011); *Reading Romans with St. Thomas Aquinas* (Catholic University of America Press, 2012); and *Vatican II: Renewal within Tradition* (Oxford University Press, 2008). He currently serves as Chair of the Board of the Academy of Catholic Theology.

MATTHEW LUNDIN is Associate Professor of History at Wheaton College, Illinois. His recent book—*Paper Memory: A Sixteenth-Century Townsman Explores His World* (Harvard University Press, 2012)—explores how a Catholic burgher from the German city of Cologne struggled, in private writings, to make sense of a flood of printed information and the "great schism" in religion. He is currently working on a cultural history of Reformation-era debates about memory.

KARIN MAAG is Director of the H. Henry Meeter Center for Calvin Studies and Professor of History at Calvin College in Grand Rapids, Michigan. She began her teaching and administrative career at Calvin College in 1997, after receiving her B.A. from Concordia University in Montreal and her master's and Ph.D. degrees from the University of Saint Andrews in Scotland, where she worked under the supervision of Andrew Pettegree. She is the author of *Seminary or University? The Genevan Academy and Reformed Higher Education, 1560–1620* (Ashgate, 1995), and of over twenty peer-reviewed articles and book chapters. She is the editor or co-editor of five collections of essays, including *Politics, Gender, and Belief: Essays in memory of Robert Kingdon* (Droz, 2014) and the translator of two monographs, including most recently Max Engammare's *On Time, Punctuality, and Discipline in Early Modern Calvinism* (Cambridge, 2010). Her research interests include early modern higher education, the training of clergy in the Reformation era, and church and state issues in the urban Reformation. She is currently preparing a volume of edited primary sources on worship in Calvin's Geneva.

MARK A. NOLL, now emeritus, was the Francis A. McAnaney Professor of History at the University of Notre Dame. Among his books are *Protestantism: A Very Short Introduction* (Oxford, 2011); *Jesus Christ and the Life of the Mind* (Eerdmans, 2011); with Carolyn Nystrom, *Clouds of Witnesses: Christian Voices from Africa and Asia* (InterVarsity Press, 2011); *The New Shape of World Christianity: How American Experience Reflects Global Faith* (InterVarsity Press, 2009); *America's God, from Jonathan*

Edwards to Abraham Lincoln (Oxford, 2002); *The Old Religion in a New World: The History of North American Christianity* (Eerdmans, 2002); (as editor) *Confessions and Catechisms of the Reformation* (Baker, 1991; Regent College Press, 2004); and *The Scandal of the Evangelical Mind* (Eerdmans, 1994).

SUNG-DEUK OAK is Dongsoon Im and Mija Im Associate Professor of Korean Christianity in the Department of Asian Languages and Cultures at the University of California, Los Angeles. His fields of expertise include the history of Korean Christianity and its global connections, especially the localization of Christianity in East Asia, Protestant missionaries, medical/ nursing and educational missions, and Christian print culture. Recently he published *The Making of Korean Christianity: Protestant Encounters with Korean Religions, 1876–1915* (Baylor University Press, 2013). Now he is writing *The History of the Korean Bible Society, volume III, 1945–2010.*

RONALD K. RITTGERS holds the Erich Markel Chair in German Reformation Studies at Valparaiso University, where he also serves as Professor of History and Theology. He received his B.A. from Wheaton College and his M.T.S. from Regent College; his Ph.D. is from Harvard University. Rittgers is the author of two monographs: *The Reformation of the Keys: Confession, Conscience, and Authority in Sixteenth-Century Germany* (Harvard University Press, 2004) and *The Reformation of Suffering: Pastoral Theology and Lay Piety in Late Medieval and Early Modern Germany* (Oxford University Press, 2012). He has recently served as President of the American Society of Church History.

HERMAN J. SELDERHUIS is Professor of Church History at the Theological University Apeldoorn (The Netherlands) and Director of Refo500, an international platform on projects related to the sixteenth century. He is the author and editor of several books, including *John Calvin: A Pilgrim's Life* (IVP Academic, 2009). He also is Director of the Reformation Research Consortium (RefoRC), President of the International Calvin Congress, and Curator of Research at the John Lasco Library (Emden, Germany).

SARAH HINLICKY WILSON is a graduate of Lenoir-Rhyne College and Princeton Theological Seminary, where she earned her Ph.D. in Systematic Theology. Her dissertation, now published by T & T Clark, is entitled *Woman, Women, and the Priesthood in the Trinitarian Theology of*

Elisabeth Behr-Sigel (2013). In 2006 she was ordained a pastor in the Slovak Zion Synod of the Evangelical Lutheran Church in America and served a congregation in Trenton, New Jersey, for two years. Since 2007, she has been the editor of *Lutheran Forum*, the largest independent theological quarterly in American Lutheranism. In 2008, she moved to Strasbourg, France, to take up a position as Assistant Research Professor at the Institute for Ecumenical Research, which works on behalf of the Lutheran World Federation toward the ecumenical reconciliation of Lutherans with other Christian churches. Her specialties include Eastern Orthodoxy and Pentecostalism. In 2010, she and her husband Andrew Wilson re-created Martin Luther's 1510 pilgrimage from Germany to Rome in order to draw attention to Lutheran-Catholic rapprochement (www.hereiwalk. org). She has published over 100 articles in both popular and scholarly journals on theological topics.

JOHN WITTE JR. is Robert W. Woodruff Professor of Law, Alonzo L. McDonald Distinguished Professor, and Director of the Center for the Study of Law and Religion Center at Emory University. A specialist in legal history, marriage law, and religious liberty, he has published 220 articles, 15 journal symposia, and 27 books, in 15 languages. Recent book titles include *The Reformation of Rights: Law, Religion, and Human Rights in Early Modern Calvinism* (Cambridge University Press, 2007); *Christianity and Law: An Introduction* (Cambridge University Press, 2008); *The Sins of the Fathers: The Law and Theology of Illegitimacy Reconsidered* (Cambridge University Press, 2009); *Christianity and Human Rights: An Introduction* (Cambridge University Press, 2010); *Religion and Human Rights: An Introduction* (Oxford University Press, 2012); *The Western Case for Monogamy over Polygamy* (Cambridge University Press, 2015); and *Religion and the American Constitutional Experiment* (Oxford University Press, 4th ed., 2016).

Protestantism after 500 Years

Introduction

Thomas Albert Howard and Mark A. Noll

THE WORLD STANDS before a landmark date: October 31, 2017, the quincentennial of the Protestant Reformation, the conventional date marking Martin Luther's 95 Theses. Countries, social movements, churches, universities, seminaries, and other institutions shaped by Protestantism face a daunting question: How should the Reformation be commemorated 500 years after the fact? Like the American bicentennial in 1976 or the marking of Columbus's voyages in 1992, observation of the year 2017 will bring into public view longstanding scholarly debates and interpretations and their revisions—along with a host of stock historical images, lingering confessional animosities, and more recent ecumenical overtures. For Western Christianity, a moment of historical recollection on this scale has not appeared in recent memory.[1]

But how does one commemorate a historical juggernaut of such immense influences and contested interpretations—one that "impelled the human mind to new courses," to quote one nineteenth-century historian? Protestantism, it should be remembered, has not only been credited with restoring essential Christian truth or blamed for disastrous church divisions, but has also been invoked as the cause of modern liberalism, capitalism, religious wars, tolerance, democracy, individualism, subjectivism, nationalism, pluralism, freedom of conscience, modern science, secularism, and so much else. As Brad Gregory, a contributor to this volume, has recently observed: "What transpired five centuries ago continues today profoundly to influence the lives of everyone not only in Europe and North America but all around the world, whether or not they are Christians or indeed religious believers of any kind."[2] The Reformation was "an epochal moment in the history of the Western world," agrees another contributor, Philip Jenkins; it "touched everything. It altered not just the practice of religion but also the nature of society, economics, politics, education, and law."[3]

To underscore the validity of such claims, it is only necessary to remember a number of seminal historical studies and major social scientific investigations from the previous century. Priority of place might well go to Max Weber's well-known *The Protestant Ethic and the Spirit of Capitalism*, which argued that the rise of commercial capitalism could be linked to the Reformation's "this-worldly asceticism" and the predestinarian views of early modern Protestants. While not without its critics, Weber's thesis was modified and expanded in works such as Ernst Troeltsch's *Protestantism and Progress: A Historical Study of the Relation of Protestantism to the Modern World* (1912) and R. H. Tawney's *Religion and the Rise of Capitalism* (1926).[4] More recently, when he considered the economic behavior of converts to Pentecostalism in Latin America, the sociologist of religion Peter Berger humorously opined, "Max Weber is alive and well and living in Guatemala."[5]

But the possible tie between Protestantism and capitalism is only one instance of the Reformation's contested influence. Protestantism has also been linked to the rise of modern science. Variations on this claim can be found in works such as R. F. Jones's *Ancients and Moderns* (1936); Robert Merton's *Science, Technology, and Society in Seventeenth-Century England* (1938); Charles Webster's *The Great Instauration* (1975); and, more recently by another contributor to this book, Peter Harrison's *The Bible, Protestantism, and the Rise of Natural Science* (1998). "The Protestant ethos—especially found in English Puritanism and German Pietism—stimulated scientific research by giving it a religious dimension," as Steven Shapin has written. Quibbles and qualifications notwithstanding, this and similar lines of inquiry have produced unusually fruitful scholarship on the early modern world.[6]

An even larger literature has traced the origins of modern liberalism and democracy back to the Reformation. This view was first advanced by a host of nineteenth-century figures such as Jules Michelet, François Guizot, Thomas Babbington Macaulay, Thomas Carlyle, and James Anthony Froude, among others. While Herbert Butterfield punctured the cheerful progressivism of these writers in his famous *The Whig Interpretation of History* (1931), the idea that modern political liberalism took root in the soil of the Reformation (and its immediate aftermath) has never really gone away. In fact, the idea has received more circumspect, sophisticated treatment in works such as Quentin Skinner's *The Foundations of Modern Political Thought* (1978); Dale Van Kley's *The Religious Origins of the French Revolution* (1996); and Perez Zagorin's *How the Idea of Religious Toleration Came to the West* (2006).[7] Notably, liberal reformers among Muslims today have sometimes been referred to by analogy as "Protestants."[8] "[C]an we expect Islam to undergo its own version of the Reformation, or produce its own Martin Luther?", as a writer in *The Economist* recently phrased an often-posed question.[9]

Of course, the historical significance of Protestantism cannot be confined to its relationship to "modernity." Above all, it has remained an enduring, albeit protean *religious* force in its own right, influencing the lives and communities of countless people in the West and, through missionary endeavors taking off in the eighteenth century, across the globe. The first such European Protestant effort overseas, the so-called Danish-Halle mission, sent the German pietists Bartholomäus Ziegenbalg (1682–1719) and Heinrich Plütschau (1676–1752) to Tranquebar, India, in 1706, financed by the crown of (Lutheran) Denmark.[10] The Protestant mission impulse eventually spread to other parts of Europe, crossing the English Channel and the Atlantic with great consequence in the late eighteenth and early nineteenth centuries.[11] Missionaries such as William Carey (1761–1834), Adoniram Judson (1788–1850), David Livingstone (1813–1873), J. Hudson Taylor (1832–1905), and Mary Slessor (1848–1915) paved the way for the global spread of Protestant Christianity and for myriad patterns of its local indigenization. The world-historical implications of such efforts are suggested by a roster of leaders shaped, at least in part, by missionary educators, including figures such as Sun Yat-Sen, Jomo Kenyatta, and Nelson Mandela. While missionary efforts cannot be easily disentangled from Western colonialism, their results have been far from uniformly negative, especially—and considering only secular outcomes—as they have opened countless avenues of education, health care, self-worth, and liberation from local forms of humiliation and oppression.[12] Globally viewed, as Robert D. Woodberry has argued in a highly decorated article, "conversionary Protestants were a crucial catalyst initiating the development and spread of religious liberty, mass education, mass printing, newspapers, voluntary organizations, and colonial reforms, thereby creating conditions that made stable democracy more likely."[13]

Today, there are an estimated 500 million Protestants in the world and this number is growing. Through such teachings as "the priesthood of all believers" and *sola scriptura*, Protestantism, in the words of Alister McGrath, "from the outset ... was a religion designed for global adap tation and transplantation."[14] The twentieth century has greatly acceler ated this trend: in 1910 an estimated 11 percent of the world's Protestants lived outside of Europe and North America; today that figure stands at 73 percent.[15] The dynamics and implications of this reality have been doc umented by much insightful writing on global Christianity by scholars such as Andrew F. Walls, Philip Jenkins, Dana L. Robert, David Martin, Peter Berger, Friedrich Wilhelm Graf, and Todd Johnson.[16]

Because the Reformation prioritized the role of individual conscience over established authority, divisions *within* Protestantism have constituted one of its telltale legacies. Wherever Protestantism has spread, rifts, rup tures, and new departures among the devout have routinely followed. The first splitting of the trunk occurred before Protestantism was a decade old: first in Zurich, where students of Ulrich Zwingli explained why his teachings demanded the baptism only of adults, only to have these Anabaptists ("Re-baptizers") exiled and executed for advancing such a view; and then only a few years later when at Marburg representatives of German-Lutheran and Swiss-Reformed branches could not agree on a common meaning for the Lord's Supper and thereafter went their sepa rate ways. Subsequently, other limbs branched off in many different direc tions: Anglicans, pietists, Presbyterians, Methodists, Congregationalists, Baptists, Quakers, Plymouth Brethren, Pentecostals, and on and on. And this is to say nothing of other intellectual and religious movements rooted in Protestantism, such as Transcendentalism, Unitarianism, and, not least, Mormonism.[17] *The Atlas of World Christianity*, published in 2009, estimates no fewer than 41,000 Protestant denominations among the some 4,850,000 individual congregations worldwide![18] In these statistics, some have seen conscience-driven variety, while others have lamented the disintegration of the "one holy Catholic and apostolic church." But all can agree that the spread of Protestantism has been accompanied by powerful centrifugal forces of multiplication and division.

Quite apart from divisions and global expansion, the influ ence of Protestantism on modern Western thought and culture has been immense. Simply consider the names of some usual suspects. What would modern theology look like apart from the legacies of Friedrich Schleiermacher, Karl Barth, Dietrich Bonhoeffer, Walter Rauschenbusch, Carl Henry, and Reinhold Niebuhr? Modern philos ophy has as its taproot the thought of figures such as Locke, Berkeley,

Hume, Reid, Leibniz, Kant, Hegel, and Kierkegaard—all figures educated as Protestants before they (often) went on their own ways. Music and hymnody today look back to Bach, Handel, Mendelssohn, Charles Wesley, Fanny Crosby, and John Mason Neale. And who can imagine the shaping of English-language literature apart from John Donne, George Herbert, John Bunyan, John Milton, Samuel Johnson, and Harriet Beecher Stowe? Furthermore, the history of higher education, in the West and across the globe, has been enduringly and diversely marked by Protestant influence.[19]

Finally, social movements such as Abolitionism in the nineteenth century and the civil rights movement in the twentieth can hardly be conceived apart from the reforming energies of figures such as William Wilberforce and Martin Luther King Jr. The crusade against segregation in the American South, as Charles Marsh has shown, was not just a political movement, as so often taught, but also something closer to a "theological drama" informed in fundamental ways by patterns of biblical interpretation, shaped by the experience of slavery, to be sure, but also by the possibility of direct encounters with the narratives of scripture—something enabled centuries beforehand in Wittenberg, Saxony.[20]

But it would be negligent not to recognize Protestantism's darker sides. Extremist polemics and coercive violence against "Papists" and different-thinking Protestants (to say nothing of Jews and Muslims) in the post-Reformation era and a virulent anti-Catholicism in later times have also shaped much of the modern Protestant experience.[21] The visual arts and architecture in many Protestant countries have long suffered from the legacy of iconoclasm, even if Protestant theological accents, as some art historians have argued, opened new avenues of dignifying the ordinary in human experience.[22] Tragically, many German, other European Protestants, and even Chinese Protestants seemed all too eager to cooperate with either Nazi or later communist totalitarianism in the twentieth century.[23] And William Wilberforce and other abolitionists must be viewed next to the numerous Protestant theologians and pastors who defended slavery as biblically sanctioned. Finally, one cannot overlook the reductive biblicism, anti-intellectualism, and eschatological fearmongering that has stunted the imaginations of many sectors of evangelical Protestantism.[24]

If, therefore, the legacies of Protestantism exist through the world and extend to practically every sphere of human endeavor, so too do the searching questions and criticisms that ought to attend those legacies.

Plans for Commemoration in 2017

In light of the significance and global scope of Protestantism, it should come as no surprise that plans to commemorate the Reformation in 2017 have been in the works for some time. As one might expect, Germany, the cradle of the Reformation, has led the way. In the early 2000s, government officials, scholars, and representatives of the German Evangelical Church (EKD) came together to launch "Luther 2017: 500 Years of the Reformation," an ambitious ten-year project, beginning in 2008 (Luther first arrived in Wittenberg in 1508) and culminating in 2017, the year of the iconic 95 Theses. One year was simply not enough to grapple with the impact of the Reformation on history, organizers held, and so they devised the "Luther Decade." Each year leading up to 2017 has had a separate theme, marking something of importance in Luther's life or in the movements associated with his name.[25] Past themes have included "Reformation and Education" (2010), "Reformation and Freedom" (2011), and "Reformation and Music" (2012). In 2015, "Reformations—Visual Arts and the Bible" was the focus, whereas in 2016 it is "The Reformation and the World." In 2017, a dizzying array of conferences, concerts, and symposia will take place.

For this effort, a scholarly advisory board came up with a list of 23 "perspectives" to guide commemorative events. The first indicates the project's scope: "The Reformation is an event of global significance. The epoch-marking changes that it produced had effects across all continents. What proceeded from it is therefore not just of national but of European and world-wide significance." To leave no room for doubt, thesis eleven proclaims that the events of the sixteenth century "penetrated far beyond church and Christendom into the entire Western world, and then even beyond it. This is particularly true of the areas of culture, scholarship and education, law, politics, and economy."[26] The "Luther Decade" has not advanced without criticism; some have charged that it has been too fixated on the person of Luther, insufficiently global in outreach (despite its rhetoric), and/or too complicit in catering to businesses and the government's desires to increase tourist spending in Germany.[27] Even so, it's hard not to be impressed by the breadth of its goals and organization.

Following closely on the heels of the German Luther Decade appeared Refo500, a multi-year commemorative, networking project, seated in the Netherlands and spearheaded by Herman Selderhuis (a contributor to this volume). With over one hundred partners worldwide, Refo500

is self-consciously global in its scope, and it operates in a more intentionally scholarly idiom than "Luther Decade." Its directors describe its
mission as helping people "make a connection between items from the
time of the Reformation and our time, between then and now, between
people and Reformation history." "On the occasion of the 500th anniversary of the Reformation," the project website elaborates, "Refo500
wants to reach a wide audience by giving broad attention to the meaning of the Reformation." It has tagged six particular areas to measure the
Reformation's impact: history, theology, religion, politics, society, and culture. Nine additional paired themes have also been designated for attention: education and learning, confession and conflict, money and power,
doctrine and church, living and dying, art and culture, freedom and
preaching, renewal and piety, and Bible and language.[28]

The Reformation tore Western Christianity asunder. It should not surprise, therefore, that in our age, after the twentieth-century Ecumenical
Movement and the Second Vatican Council (1962–65), commemorative
efforts aimed at 2017 are also focusing on questions of Christian unity
and interfaith dialogue. Exactly which focus depends on a host of institutional, denominational, and geographical factors. But pride of place in
this respect ought to go to the Roman Catholic Church and the Lutheran
World Federation's joint project, launched in 2013, "From Conflict to
Communion: Lutheran-Catholic Common Commemoration of the
Reformation in 2017." Drawing inspiration from their history-making
Joint Declaration on the Doctrine of Justification from 1999,[29] these two
imposing church bodies regard 2017 as an opportunity to deplore past
divisions, engage in self-criticism for opportunities lost, and strive for
greater unity in the future. As Karlheinz Diez (Auxiliary Catholic Bishop
of Fulda, Germany) and Eero Huovien (Lutheran Bishop Emeritus of
Helsinki, Finland) size up the opportunity evocatively:

> In 2017, Catholic and Lutheran Christians will most fittingly look
> back on events that occurred 500 years earlier by putting the gospel
> of Jesus Christ at the center. The gospel should be celebrated and
> communicated to the people of our time so that the world may be-
> lieve that God gives Himself to human beings and calls us into com-
> munion with Himself and His church. Herein lies the basis for our
> joy in our common faith. . . . The true unity of the church can only
> exist as unity in the truth of the gospel of Jesus Christ. The fact
> that the struggle for this truth in the sixteenth century led to the

loss of unity in Western Christendom belongs to the dark pages of church history. In 2017, we must confess openly that we have been guilty before Christ of damaging the unity of the church. This commemorative year presents us with two challenges: the purification of memories and healing of memories, and the restoration of Christian unity in accordance with the truth of the gospel of Jesus Christ.[30]

In light of lingering ecclesiastical divisions that have endured half a millennium, Diez and Huovien announce a lofty goal, to be sure. But perhaps as a pious wag once quipped, the practically impossible should never be granted the chutzpah to impede the theologically necessary.[31] (As this book was going to press, the Vatican announced that Pope Francis will visit Lund, Sweden on October 31, 2016 to participate with the Lutheran World Federation in an ecumenical service to launch a year of activities marking the Reformation's quincentennial.)

This Catholic-Lutheran ecumenical effort is hardly the only one. Looking ahead to 2017, the Evangelical Church in Germany (EKD) has reached out to the German Catholic Bishops' Conference. The Council of Christian Churches in Germany (ACK) plans to organize a week-long prayer for Christian unity in 2017. The World Council of Churches, inspired in part by 2017, has in the works a new Ecumenical Center in Geneva. The Community of Protestant Churches in Europe and the Federation of Swiss Protestant Churches, among other Protestant bodies, plan to reflect on the Leuenberg Agreement (1973), a key postwar document of intra-Protestant unity, while also reaching out to non-Protestants.[32] Finally, numerous seminaries, institutes, colleges, and other institutions of faith and learning have smaller-scale plans in the works, albeit some more ecumenically focused than others.

What to call all these events has posed terminology problems. Since the traditional "celebration" or, in German, "jubilee" (*Jubel*) has seemed to many too triumphalistic, "common remembrance" or simply "commemoration" appear to be the terms of choice at present—even if one might anticipate many triumphalistic elements gathering force as 2017 arrives.

AGAINST THE BACKGROUND of these and other efforts, how does this volume fit in? At one level, we hope simply to expand and enrich an ongoing conversation about the significance of the Reformation—a conversation that really began alongside the sixteenth-century events themselves.[33] More specifically, the contributors to this volume were asked an open-ended question: How ought the Reformation be commemorated in 2017? And then they were enjoined to draw from their respective areas of expertise—principally history and theology—in formulating essays reflecting on the significance of sixteenth-century religious upheavals for Western and global society today. What did the Reformation (or, as some prefer, Reformations) accomplish, in other words, and how ought we to evaluate its (their) influence nearly 500 years after the fact?

Big questions often need qualifying smaller ones. Here is a generous sampler of questions that contributors were also asked to consider:

1. Which changes and innovations in human history can one actually attribute to Protestantism and which are the result of speculation, polemical motivation, or faulty reasoning that mistakenly view cause-and-effect where only a chronological sequence exists?

2. What is the relationship of the numerous forms of Global South Christianity flourishing today to their sixteenth-century forebears, which in creed and praxis often stood closer to faith expressions of the late Middle Ages?

3. What, in fact, is the causal relationship between Protestantism and some of the signature developments of modernity, such as secularism, capitalism, nationalism, pluralism, democracy, science, and religious freedom?

4. What unintended consequences (for better or worse) have arisen from some of the reformers' key theological emphases (*sola scriptura, sola fide*, etc.)?

5. How have "ideas" about and "interpretations" of the Reformation been enlisted in various political and social movements over the centuries?

6. How will, or how ought, the coming centenary differ from past ones, which took place during more confessional eras and before the accelerated "globalization" of Christianity in the twentieth century?

7. How have recent conciliatory overtures between Protestants and Catholics influenced the "memory" of the Reformation, and what developments in history and theology might this new ecumenism betoken?[34]

The responses to at least some of these questions (and others) make up this book. They combine reflections on cultural impact, explorations in Protestant history, and theological reflection, sometimes of a quite personal nature—a mixture of emphases that alert observers in the sixteenth century, we believe, would have recognized as among the most important aspects of the Reformation. At the same time, we renounce any claims to exhaustiveness; to focus on *some* important topics meant that many others of necessity had to be omitted. What is more, the topics that are taken up could, in other hands, be rendered in an entirely different manner. A topic as broad as "Protestantism" chastens intellectual ambition.

Summaries are inevitably poor proxies for the things themselves, but permit us to summarize the individual chapters that follow.

IN AN EFFORT to put 2017 into broader historical perspective, the editor Thomas Albert Howard reflects in chapter 1 on the circumstances and significance of several past Reformation centenary commemorations or "jubilees," particularly as they were marked in German-speaking lands. While he devotes some attention to the first, highly confessional centenary of 1617, more attention is given to those in the modern era, particularly the 300th anniversary jubilee in 1817 and the 400th anniversary of Luther's birthday in 1883. The reality that past centennials have been profoundly colored by their respective historical milieux implicitly raises pressing contemporary questions: What current circumstances will celebrations in 2017 reflect? What ought they to reflect?

In chapter 2, the legal scholar John Witte Jr. of Emory University makes clear that the Lutheran Reformation transformed not only theology and the church but also law and the state. Despite Luther's burning of canon law books and his berating of lawyers as sorry Christians, he soon realized that he needed both law and the legal profession to preserve his theological reforms, and to extend them into the realms of marriage, education, social welfare, and more. Luther and his colleagues ultimately reconciled the new dialectics between gospel and law, church and state through Luther's complex two-kingdoms theory, which remains at the heart of Lutheran thought to this day. More broadly, legal and political forces unleashed during the Reformation have exerted an enduring influence throughout the Western world and beyond.

The historian of early modern Europe, Carlos Eire of Yale University, returning to some of Max Weber's concerns, argues in chapter 3 that the Reformation made possible, at first for Protestants and then for the less devout, an experience of reality distanced from the supernatural. Yet palpable connections between the divine and the human, a hallmark of medieval piety, powerfully continued, and were arguably even amplified, in places shaped by the Catholic Reformation or "Counter-Reformation," as some still prefer.[35] An enduring supernatural divide, we might call it, then and now, forms one of the strongest points of division between Catholics, on the one hand, and Protestants and secularists, on the other.

The intellectual historian Peter Harrison of Queensland University (Australia) considers in chapter 4 some of the ways in which the Protestant Reformation influenced the emergence of modern science in the sixteenth and seventeenth centuries. He reflects on the connections between challenges to prevailing orthodoxies in the spheres of religion and of science; the link between Protestant understandings of original sin and the rise of experimental methods; the possible influence of Protestant ideas and practices on the "desacralization" of nature; and the ways in which the Protestant Reformation contributed, often inadvertently, to the social status and authority of the natural sciences.

Karin Maag, director of the H. Henry Meeter Center for Calvin Studies at Calvin College, focuses attention in chapter 5 on the Reformation and higher education in the early sixteenth and seventeenth centuries. While the initial impact of the Reformation on preexisting universities proved chaotic, as she argues, the movement for religious renewal quickly generated its own momentum in transforming older centers of learning and establishing new ones to meet the Reformation's goals. Chief among these was the need to provide learned pastors, trained in confessionally orthodox settings, for a growing number of congregations. While Reformed and Lutheran areas were largely successful in expanding the number of universities and academies in their territories, they also faced a range of challenges, including financial difficulties, faculty recruitment, and declines in matriculation. Repeated conflicts also took place over the relative merits of doubling down on confessional orthodoxy versus a more broadbased theological outlook.

In chapter 6, Brad Gregory, director of the Notre Dame Institute for Advanced Study, reprises aspects of his much-discussed book, *The Unintended Reformation: How a Religious Revolution Secularized Society*. The long-term effects of the Protestant Reformation on modernity, he argues, have included the formation of powerful, sovereign liberal nation-states that protect individual freedom of religious (and irreligious) belief and practice. A once-dominant liberal-progressive narrative of the Reformation's influence on modernity emphasized the Reformation's discontinuity with the Middle Ages and its continuity with modern rationality, autonomy, and material prosperity. A revisionist-confessionalization narrative of the Reformation's influence, which has been more important in recent decades of scholarship, has stressed ideological continuity with the Middle Ages and discontinuity with secular modernity. By combining aspects of both narratives and historically reintegrating the radical (Anabaptist) Reformation with the magisterial Reformation, Gregory argues, we can see more clearly how the commitment to the principle of *sola scriptura* unintentionally sowed the seeds for the individualization and privatization of "religion" within modern liberal states.

WHILE NOT LEAVING the early modern era behind, the second and third parts of the book focus more explicitly on contemporary matters—on how the Reformation remains relevant for denizens of the twenty-first century—and on matters of constructive and ecumenical theology.

In chapter 7, Matthew Lundin of Wheaton College surveys the recent past and current state of historiography on the Reformation. Ironically, he claims, the more scholars today have examined the legacies of 1517, the less confident they have become to proclaim the Reformation as a decisive turning point in Western history. Specialized studies have made a once familiar Reformation strange, showing just how much early Protestantism was rooted in cultural and social contexts very different from our own. Ethnography has eclipsed historical theology as the primary method of studying early modern Protestantism, and scholars have shifted their attention to the deep structural forces that transformed all variants of early modern religion. His chapter also explores recent attempts at reviving grand narratives of the Protestant Reformation as a "religious revolution." He concludes by arguing that it is only by setting early modern Protestantism fully within its original context—a context in which the church was as powerful and visible a reality as the state or the market are today—that we begin rightly to understand its historical significance. Locating the meaning of the Reformation in its "original context," it should be noted, implicitly calls into question some of the prior contributors' efforts to see the era as one of fundamental discontinuity.

Herman J. Selderhuis (Director of Refo500) examines the challenges and opportunities of commemorating the Reformation in Europe today. While secularization in the Old World has taken its toll on the memory of the Reformation, Selderhuis urges caution before applying the term "post-Christian" to Europe, for religious pockets in society abound, and 2017 presents a welcomed opportunity to expand religious literacy and accurate historical knowledge, and also to raise theological questions. Yet the popular focus on Luther as a funny, beer-drinking monk or as the grandfather of contemporary goods such as tolerance, democracy, and freedom of con-science does a disservice to the memory of the Reformation. Rather, we must dig deeper and understand the Reformation, foremost, as a deeply *religious* development animated by *theological* concerns. Only then, he believes, are moderns in a position to assess the long-term influence of sixteenth-century events and discuss their significance for Europe today.

A leading student of global Christianity, Philip Jenkins of Baylor University insists in chapter 9 that we need to shift our focus from the North Atlantic world if we are to understand what is going on in Christianity today. Once the perspective is shifted, prominent resem-blances between the sixteenth century and our own age become appar-ent: the two eras include a radical new emphasis on the role of scripture, and the massive impact of new forms of media and communication. In both eras, we also see a stark confrontation between forms of religious sensibility, marked by the rejection of holy images, and a consequent ri-valry between (broadly) Protestant and (broadly) Catholic communities. Jenkins asks, further, whether these parallels might even be more ex-tensive, so that the post-Reformation European experience could have, at least to a degree, predictive value for understanding today's new global Christian communities.

A scholar of Korean Christianity at UCLA, Sung-Deuk Oak offers, in chapter 10, a specific case-in-point of global Protestantism by examining missionary efforts in Korea and its indigenization there in the late nine-teenth and early twentieth century, as well as trends in Korean Christianity in recent decades. Although many countries in Asia have been receptive to Protestantism, Korea stands out from a demographic perspective, even if some evidence suggest that this Protestant surge might have tapered off in recent years. One is even tempted to speak of "Korean exceptionalism," in light of this country's initial embrace and indigenization of various forms of Protestantism. Recently, South Korea has taken a leading role in sending Protestant missionaries to other parts of the globe, ranking second only to the United States in the number of missionaries it sends out.[36]

In chapter 11, editor Mark Noll attempts to show that the Protestant emphasis on *sola scriptura*, "the Bible alone," ought to be studied from two different angles. From one angle, the principle of trusting the Bible as supreme religious authority has led to the disputes and divisions that Catholic leaders predicted when they first faulted the reformers for elevat-ing "private judgment" over established authority. Yet from another, it is clear that the consequences of *sola scriptura* have never been as chaotic as Protestant principles might suggest. In making these points, Noll attends to early Reformation history, the use of *sola scriptura* before the Reformation, theological reasons why a considerable measure of cohesion has accompanied much Protestant chaos in interpreting scripture, and the evidence of hymnody as an instance of a cohesive Protestant force. This chapter also enlists examples from recent Bible translations in parts of the world new to the Christian faith to illustrate the Janus-faced legacy of *sola scriptura*.

IN PART III, the book concludes with reflections by three theologians, two Protestants (one Lutheran, one Baptist) and one Catholic. An ordained Lutheran pastor and a scholar at the Institute for Ecumenical Research in Strasbourg, France, Sarah Hinlicky Wilson in chapter 12 argues that appropriate commemoration of 2017 demands concentration on what Luther principally sought to achieve—to call the church back to the gospel—and less about the accretion of caricatures and hagiographies that have arisen around his person over the centuries. While Luther's incendiary comments about Jews, Anabaptists, and others must not be forgotten, the sentiments they expressed are best contravened in light of the charity and justice enjoined by the very gospel he sought to recover. What is more, Wilson surveys the reception of Luther in Lutheran churches across the world, with hope for theological fruit to be harvested from a truly globally interpreted Luther. This in turn leads her to consider the fate of Luther in the Catholic world and the prospects for reconciliation between the divided churches. She concludes with proposals for reconsidering the merits of Lutheran and Catholic theologies apart from the mutual hostility that once divided them, and for undertaking a joint project of historical truth-telling for the sake of repentance and forgiveness.

The Catholic theologian Matthew Levering of Mundelein Seminary begins chapter 13 with the question of whether, five hundred years after sixteenth-century divisions and hostilities, we can still speak of the Church as "holy." In the Nicene Creed, believing Christians—while regarding themselves as sinners in need of grace and redemption—proclaim the church to be holy. Recent theological scholarship, however, has argued that the church's persistence in a state of division and strife simply confirms the obvious fact that the church is not holy and henceforth dissuades Christians from the dubious endeavor of persisting to claim otherwise.[37] Levering, in counterpoint, shows that John Calvin thought it important to confess the holiness of the church, which, in the end, he considered to be a proper title that God *imputes* to the church. A similar position was held earlier by Thomas Aquinas, who even spoke of the church as "immaculate." Drawing, then, from both (Protestant) Calvin and (Catholic) Aquinas, Levering concludes that, although Reformation divisions are deplorable and the behavior of believers often lamentable, Christians of both confessions should recognize God's redemptive work in history by continuing to confess with Calvin and Aquinas the holiness of the church.

In the final chapter, the Baptist theologian and ecumenist Timothy George makes clear that, as in the sixteenth century so also in the twenty-first, matters of great importance are under way in Christian thought and practice. An older reality of acrimony between Protestants and Catholics, on the one hand, and a least-common-denominator ecumenism among Protestants, on the other, have given way to an ecumenism of mutual respect and common cause, most notably seen in relations between Roman Catholics and evangelical Protestants. Although this reality was felt first in the ethical and political arena (where George famously dubbed it an "ecumenism of the trenches"), it has led to far more ambitious efforts of common *theological* purpose. Drawing from his own life experience and face-to-face meetings in the Vatican, George urges that these efforts should go forward, for ours, as he has written elsewhere, "is a time to sew, not a time to rend."[38]

The accomplished Reformation scholar Ronald K. Rittgers of Valparaiso University closes the book with an afterword, in which he, in a theological register, adds a question mark to our title as a way of complicating, but also enriching, the book's contributions as whole.

Conclusion: Still a Tragic Necessity?

In the final analysis, how should the 500th anniversary of the Reformation be commemorated in 2017? The question remains difficult, as possible answers can only be partial and open-ended. Even so, allow us to make a couple of concluding points. The first is applicable to all people who desire to understand the significance of the Reformation today. The second point applies particularly to Western Christians, who continue to experience sixteenth-century divisions at an existentially close range, even as we invite all others to eavesdrop.

First, thinking about the Reformation should help us acknowledge how deeper currents of history—and their interpretations—affect our lives. Too often in our presentist, media-saturated world, appeals to "history" mean going back only as far as, say, the fall of the Berlin Wall or the end of World War II. By contrast, considering the Reformation's many trajectories of influence acknowledges the purchase of the remote past on our lives today; it shows how seemingly distant ideas and events continue to shape not only our social reality but even the lenses through which we experience and make sense of this reality. While we happily admit that no simple causal link can be established between sixteenth-century religious upheavals and "the modern world," all evidence suggests that countless intricate links have wound their way from "their then" to "our now." As a character of William Faulkner's unsurpassingly phrased it, "The past is never dead. It's not even past."

Second, while longstanding divisions between Catholics and Protestants will still be obvious in 2017, it also appears that, alongside this continuing scandal and embarrassment to all believers, the looming anniversary provides a welcomed opportunity to concentrate the mind on some of the best ecumenical impulses of the preceding century, as several contributors to this volume indicate. We conclude by offering suggestions of our own for how steps of rapprochement might proceed.

To start with, we believe that it is *theologically* important to think of the Reformation in historical terms and not strictly as a theological occurence. As should be clear from the chapters in this volume, the Reformation took place as a massively complex, confusing set of historical events, not as a checklist for choosing doctrinal principles that dropped from the sky after 1517. Approaching the Reformation era exclusively from a doctrinal or theological standpoint tempts partisans to regard the conclusions and condemnations from this era as timeless and above criticism and to construct oversimplified stories of this period's place in church history that conveniently lends credence to one's own religious standpoint. By contrast, we believe that appraising the Reformation's contingency and messiness, the unexpected sources and ironic outcomes, helps us take a step back, gain perspective, and view the conclusions of this era, however important, not as set in stone.

Attention to the historical circumstances of the Reformation—particularly attention to the fact that many of the condemnations and doctrinal statements of this era, whether Protestant or Catholic, issued from a highly propagandistic, polemical, and political atmosphere—has been one of the key factors allowing for significant ecumenical progress in recent years, creating space for communication and understanding where almost none existed beforehand. In an important ecumenical project from some years ago in Germany, the Catholic Archbishop of Mainz Karl Lehmann and the Protestant theologian Wolfhart Pannenberg thus concluded:

> It has been generally accepted that doctrinal differences were the essential reason for the disintegration of the Western Church into different denominations. At the same time, it must be pointed out that other elements contributed to the division of the churches in the sixteenth century, not differences of doctrine alone. Political, cultural, social, and economic factors were involved, as well as the laws that go to maintain any already existing institution. Nor must we forget the part played by individual human characteristics.[39]

Finally, we believe that words from the late church historian Jaroslav Pelikan continue to merit serious consideration. For the interests of truth and conciliation to be served in remembering the Reformation, Pelikan once wrote, Protestants and Catholics should think of the Reformation as a "tragic necessity." Partisans on both sides, he elaborated, will have difficulty acknowledging this: "Roman Catholics agree that it was tragic, because it separated many millions from the true church; but they cannot see that it was really necessary. Protestants agree that it was necessary, because the Roman church was so corrupt; but they cannot see that it was such a tragedy after all."[40] In light of 2017, it seems to us that Protestants are duty-bound to try to understand the tragic dimensions of the Reformation. As the theologian Stanley Hauerwas has put it, "If we no longer have broken hearts at the church's division, then we cannot help but unfaithfully celebrate [the] Reformation."[41] At the same time, Catholics should make the effort to grasp why Protestants, then and now, felt that the Reformation was necessary.

Admittedly, "tragic necessity" might not constitute the final word on the Reformation—a point the afterword makes clear. But, five hundred years on, it still does not seem a bad place to start. Even if we concede that ecumenical goals are often difficult and elusive, the foundational Christian necessity to pursue truth and serve as peacemakers remains inviolate. It is our hope that the inquiries in this volume serve both truth and peace, and neither at the expense of the other.

Notes

1. For a sampling of preparations already under way, see *Ratlos vor dem Reformationsjubiläum 2017?*, a special volume of the *Berliner Theologische Zeitschrift* 28, no. 1 (2011). Cf. Thomas Albert Howard, "Preparing for 2017," *Books & Culture* 18 (March/April 2012): 16–17.

2. Brad S. Gregory, *The Unintended Reformation: How a Religious Revolution Secularized Society* (Cambridge, MA: Belknap Press of Harvard University Press, 2012), 1.

3. Philip Jenkins, "The Next Christianity," *Atlantic Monthly* 290, no. 3 (October 2002): 53.

4. For criticism of Weber's thesis, see H. M. Roberston, *Aspects of the Rise of Economic Individualism: A Critique of Max Weber and his School* (Cambridge: Cambridge University Press, 1933). Cf. William H. Swatos and Lutz Kaelber, eds., *The Protestant Ethic Turns 100: Essays on the Centenary of the Weber Thesis* (Boulder, CO: Paradigm, 2005).

5. Charles T. Matthews, "An Interview with Peter Berger," *Hedgehog Review* 8 (Spring/Summer 2006): 158.

6. Stephen Shapin, "Understanding the Merton Thesis," *Isis* 79 (1988): 594–605. Cf. Francis Oakley, "Christian Theology and the Newtonian Science," *Church History* 30 (1961): 433–57; and Ted Peters, "Protestantism and the Sciences," in *The Blackwell Companion to Protestantism*, eds. Alister McGrath and Darren C. Marks (Oxford: Blackwell, 2004), 306–21.

7. For the early American liberal tradition, see Thomas S. Engeman and Michael P. Zuckert, eds., *Protestantism and the American Founding* (Notre Dame, IN: University of Notre Dame Press, 2004).

8. Mustafa Akyol, *Islam without Extremes: A Muslim Case for Liberty* (New York: Norton, 2011), 38.

9. *The Economist*, www.economist.com/blogs/erasmus/2015/01/reforming-islam. Cf. Rouila Khalaf, "The Search for a Muslim Martin Luther," *Financial Times*, January 15, 2015.

10. Daniel Jeraraj, *Bartholomäus Ziegenbalg: The Father of Modern Protestant Missions* (Delhi: Indian Society for Promoting Christian Knowledge, 2006).

11. On the broad transatlantic influence of German Pietism, see Jonathan Strom, ed., *Pietism and Community in Europe and North America, 1650–1850* (Leiden: Brill, 2010). We might also consider the Puritan John Eliot's efforts to convert Native Americans as a beginning point of Protestant missions. See Richard W. Cogley, *John Eliot's Mission to the Indians before King Phillip's War* (Cambridge, MA: Harvard University Press, 1999).

12. Stephen Neill, *A History of Christian Missions*, 2nd ed. (New York: Penguin, 1986), 187ff.; and Mark Noll, *Turning Points: Decisive Moments in the History of Christianity*, 2nd ed. (Grand Rapids, MI: Baker Academic, 2000), 276–94. Cf.

Lamin O. Sanneh, *Encountering the West: Christianity and the Global Process, the African Dimension* (Marynoll, NY: Orbis, 1993); and A. N. Porter, *Religion versus Empire: British Protestant Missionaries and Overseas Expansion, 1700–1914* (New York: Manchester Press, 2004).

13. Robert D. Woodberry, "The Missionary Roots of Liberal Democracy," *American Political Science Review* 106 (May 2012): 244.

14. Alister McGrath, *Christianity's Dangerous Idea: The Protestant Revolution—A History from the Sixteenth Century to the Twenty-First* (New York: HarperOne, 2007), 2.

15. Mark A. Noll, *Protestantism: A Very Short History* (New York: Oxford University Press, 2011), 8.

16. See Andrew F. Walls, *The Missionary Movement in Christian History: Studies in Transmission of Faith* (Marynoll, NY: Orbis Books, 1996); David Martin: *Tongues of Fire: The Explosion of Protestantism in Latin America* (Oxford: Blackwell, 1990); Philip Jenkins, *The Next Christendom: The Coming of Global Christianity*, 3rd ed. (Oxford: Oxford University Press, 2011); and Peter Berger, ed., *The Desecularization of the World: Resurgent Religion and World Politics* (Grand Rapids, MI: Eerdmans, 1999); Dana L. Robert, "Shifting Southward: Global Christianity since 1945." *International Bulletin of Missionary Research* 24, no. 2 (2000): 50–58; Todd M. Johnson and Cindy M. Wu, *Our Global Families: Christians Embracing Common Identity in a Changing World* (Grand Rapids, MI: Barker Academic, 2015); F. W. Graf, *Götter global: wie die Welt zum Supermarkt der Religionen wird* (Munich: C. H. Beck, 2014).

17. Nathan Hatch, "Sola Scriptura and Novus Ordo Seculorum," in Nathan Hatch and Mark Noll, eds., *The Bible in America* (New York: Oxford University Press, 1982), 59–78. Cf. Richard Lyman Bushman, *Mormonism: A Very Short Introduction* (Oxford: Oxford University Press, 2008), 6–13.

18. Todd M. Johnson et al., eds., *The Atlas of Global Christianity, 1910–2010* (Edinburgh: University of Edinburgh Press, 2009), 68.

19. Thomas Albert Howard, *Protestant Theology and the Making of the Modern German University* (Oxford: Oxford University Press, 2006); and George Marsden, *The Soul of the American University: from Protestant Establishment to Established Nonbelief* (New York: Oxford University Press, 1994).

20. Charles Marsh, *God's Long Summer: Stories of Faith and Civil Rights* (Princeton, NJ: Princeton University Press, 1997), 3.

21. Ray Allen Billington, *The Protestant Crusade, 1800–1860: A Study of the Origins of American Nativism* (Chicago: Quadrangle Books, 1964); and Mark S. Massa, *Anti-Catholicism: The Last Acceptable Prejudice* (New York: Crossroad, 2003). On the Reformation and Judaism, see David Nirenberg, *Anti-Judaism: The Western Tradition* (New York: Norton, 2013), 246–68. On Protestants and Muslims, see Thomas S. Kidd, *American Christians and Islam: Evangelical Culture and Muslims from the Colonial Period to the Present* (Princeton, NJ: Princeton University Press, 2009).

22. Carlos Eire, *The War Against the Idols: The Reformation of Worship from Erasmus to Calvin* (Cambridge: Cambridge University Press, 1984). Cf. David Morgan, "The Protestant Struggle with the Image," *Christian Century* 106 (1989): 308–11; and Werner Hofmann, ed., *Luther und die Folgen für die Kunst* (Munich: Prestel-Verlag, 1983).

23. See Doris Bergen, *Twisted Cross: The German Christian Movement in the Third Reich* (Chapel Hill: University of North Carolina Press, 1996); Susannah Heschel, *The Aryan Jesus: Christian Theologians and the Bible in Nazi Germany* (Princeton, NJ: Princeton University Press, 2008); Gregory Baum, *The Church for Others: Protestant Theology in Communist East Germany* (Grand Rapids, MI: Eerdmans, 1996); and Merle Goldman, "Religion in Post-Mao China," *Annals of the Academy of Political and Social Science* 483 (January 1986): 146–56.

24. Mark A. Noll, *The Scandal of the Evangelical Mind* (Grand Rapids, MI.: Eerdmans, 1994).

25. For a listing of events, see www.luther2017.de.

26. www.luther2017.de/sites/default/files/downloads/perspectives_for_the_reformation_jubilee_2017_.pdf.

27. See Hartmut Lehmann, "Unterschiedliche Erwartungen an das Reformationsjubiläum 2017," in *Ratlos vor dem Reformationsjubiläum 2017?*, 16–27.

28. See the Refo500 website www.refo500.nl/en/news/6.

29. www.vatican.va/roman_curia/pontifical_councils/chrstuni/documents/rc_pc_chrstuni_doc_31101999_cath-luth-joint-declaration_en.html.

30. See *From Conflict to Communion: Lutheran-Catholic Common Commemoration of the Reformation in 2017: Report of the Lutheran-Roman Catholic Commission on Unity* (Leipzig: Evangelische Verlagsanstalt/Paderborn: Bonifatus, 2013), 7.

31. For some additional initiatives focused on 2017, see the Lutheran World Federation's "Reformation 2017" site at www.lutheranworld.org/reformation-2017.

32. On the Leuenberg Agreement, see Wilhelm Neuser, *Die Entstehung und theologische Formung der Leuenberger Konkordie 1971 bis 1973* (Münster: Lit, 2003).

33. On the history of interpretations of the Reformation, see A. G. Dickens and J. M. Tonkin, *The Reformation in Historical Thought* (Cambridge, MA: Harvard University Press, 1985).

34. Thomas Oden, *The Rebirth of Orthodoxy: New Signs of Life in Christianity* (San Francisco: Harper, 2003). Cf. Jeremy Morris and Nicholas Sagovsky, eds., *The Unity We Have and the Unity We Seek: Ecumenical Prospects for the Third Millennium* (London: T&T Clark, 2003).

35. On the "Counter-Reformation" as a historiographical concept, see the essays in Alexandra Bamjii et al. eds., *The Ashgate Research Companion to the Counter-Reformation* (Burlington, VT: Ashgate, 2013).

36. Steve Moon, "The Recent Korean Missionary Movement." *International Bulletin of Missionary Research* 27, no. 1 (2003): 11ff.

37. Ephraim Radner, *A Brutal Unity: The Spiritual Politics of the Christian Church* (Waco, TX: Baylor University Press, 2012).

38. Timothy George, "Between the Pope and Billy Graham," in *Pilgrims on the Sawdust Trail: Evangelical Ecumenism and the Quest for Christian Identity*, ed. Timothy George (Grand Rapids, MI: Baker Academic, 2004), 137.

39. Karl Lehmann and Wolfhart Pannenberg, eds., *The Condemnations of the Reformation Era—Do They Still Divide?*, trans. Margaret Kohl (Minneapolis, MN: Fortress Press, 1990), 2.

40. Jaroslav Pelikan, *The Riddle of Roman Catholicism* (New York: Abingdon Press, 1949), 46.

41. Stanley Hauerwas, "Sermon on Reformation Sunday" at www.calledtocommunion.com/2009/10/stanley-hauerwas-on-reformation-sunday.

PART I

Looking Back

I

Remembering the Reformation, 1617, 1817, and 1883

COMMEMORATION AS AN AGENT OF CONTINUITY AND CHANGE

Thomas Albert Howard

THE QUINCENNTENIAL OF the Reformation in 2017 invites curiosity about how past commemorations of the Reformation have been observed. In Protestant German-speaking lands, a rich tradition of publicly remembering the Reformation stretches back to the first-centenary "Reformation jubilee" (*Reformationsjubiläum*) in 1617.[1] Martin Luther's birth and death dates, respectively 1483 and 1546, have also been ritualistically and ceremoniously commemorated over the centuries, in German-speaking lands and beyond.

In the sprawling literature on commemoration and social memory, one frequently encounters the refrain that acts of public remembrance have as a principal aim the stabilization of group identity. The retrospective gaze helps a group (in our case, German Protestants) remember who they are and extend their identity into the future. As John Gillis writes, "The core meaning of any individual or group identity, namely, a sense of sameness over space and time, *is sustained by remembering and what is remembered is defined by the assumed identity*" (emphasis added).[2]

Put differently, acts of commemoration seek to shore up collective identities, to "stop time" to ensure appropriate uniformity between past and present.[3] Without shared referents in the past, group identities would be fleeting or nonexistent. Identities, in other words, must be continually activated by rituals of memory and commemoration, or else they will peter out and the past that once gave substance and energy to identity will become what the great memory theorist Maurice Halbwachs once called "dead memory."[4]

In many cases, such motivations for commemorations are no doubt accurate. And I believe they generally hold true for the first Reformation jubilee of 1617, which is treated in this chapter. But commemorative occasions can also serve as powerful catalysts and shapers of social innovation and change in history. This point will be made by examining two later jubilees: (1) the 300th anniversary of the Reformation in 1817 as commemorated in the states of the newly formed German Confederation (1815), and (2) the 400th anniversary of Luther's birth in 1883 as commemorated in the newly founded German Empire (1871).

Commemorations in the seventeenth and eighteenth centuries took place as profoundly religious events in the confessionally divided Holy Roman Empire. But in the wake of the Enlightenment in the late eighteenth century and the disruptive revolutionary-Napoleonic years (1789–1815), new, distinctly modern historical forces took root and grew in central Europe—namely, liberalism, nationalism, and a new historical consciousness often designated with the umbrella term "historicism."[5] These new forces did not wholly displace older religious motives for commemoration; what is interesting in fact is precisely how powerful religious elements retain their salience in nineteenth-century commemorations, while at the same time mutating in ways that accommodate, and even foster, innovative, modern idea and sensibilities.

1617: The First Reformation Centennial Jubilee

In order to observe how nineteenth-century jubilees contrasted with earlier ones, we must first turn our gaze on 1617. Not surprisingly, in a time of divided religious confessions across Europe, matters of religious identity stood at the center of commemorations: questions of biblical exegesis, theological polemics, and eschatological speculation pervade the events of this year. What is more, in the complex realities of the Holy Roman Empire, the line between religion and politics blurred greatly, and we might do better to think of the events of 1617 as religio-political in character.[6]

Commemorating the Reformation in 1617 did not take place without precedents. In the late sixteenth century, a patchwork of different dates had been set aside for annual remembrance. The vast majority of commemorations prior to 1617, however, either focused on the birth, baptism, or death of Luther or on a date marking a territory's embrace of Protestantism. The date of October 31, 1517, and the "posting of the 95 Theses" (the *Thesenanschlag* in German) played virtually no role in the earliest commemorations.[7] In fact, the only known mention in the sixteenth century of the posting of the 95 Theses—which later became the major focus of commemorations—came in a brief *vita* of Luther penned in 1547 by Philip Melanchthon and published in the first collected edition of Luther's writings.[8]

The circumstances and events of 1617, however, hoisted 1517 into the historical limelight, where it has stayed ever since. As the seventeenth century dawned, Protestant territories within the Holy Roman Empire were confronted by several realities that would shape the memory of the Reformation. The first was the threat of an increasingly assertive Tridentine Catholic Church; the second, division in their own ranks between Lutheran and Calvinist-Reformed areas. Finally, there existed divisions *within* Lutheranism—between stricter traditionalists and more moderate (named "Philippist" after Philipp Melanchthon) voices, who sought greater conciliation with their Reformed counterparts. These confessional dynamics fundamentally structured the social environment of 1617.[9]

In 1607, with other Catholic territories nodding approval, Maximillian I of Bavaria re-imposed the Catholic faith on the small city of Donauwörth, stirring alarm in many Protestant quarters. This act precipitated in short order the formation in 1608 of the so-called Protestant Union under the (Reformed) leadership of Elector Friedrich V of the Rhineland Palatinate.[10] In the years leading up to 1617, leaders and representatives from several Protestant territories, Lutheran and Reformed, thereafter met annually to discuss the Catholic threat along with other matters.

Among the first known calls for a centenary celebration came in 1617 in a New Year's sermon given in Heidelberg by the royal chaplain, one Abraham Scultetus (1566–1625), who opined that one hundred years ago "the eternal, all-powerful God has looked upon us graciously and delivered us from the horrible darkness of the papacy" (*schrecklichen finsternuß deß Bapstthumbs*) and led [us] into the bright light of the Gospel."[11] In April 1617 at the Protestant Union's annual meeting in Heilbronn, Friedrich V followed up by suggesting that commemorations take place between October 31 and November 2 to mark the beginnings of the Reformation. The driving force behind the initiative was the desire to reduce tension between Lutheran and Calvinist members of the Union. At this time, the latter were not legally recognized in the Holy Roman Empire and, in light of the Catholic threat, desired to build bridges to their Protestant co-religionists, differences and acrimony notwithstanding. Exactly what commemorative events were to take place was left up to the individual territories, but in a joint resolution from April 23, 1617, the signatories affirmed that during the celebrations all bitterness and personal attacks among Protestants should be suspended and a general thanksgiving offered to God for the recovery and maintenance of the true evangelical faith some one hundred years ago.[12]

But the Calvinist-Lutheran rupture could not be muted so easily. As the conciliatory plans of the Protestant league were being hatched, scholars in Saxon Wittenberg concurrently had seized upon the moment to assert their own custodial leadership of Lutheran orthodoxy and rally together the "pure" territories—those that had officially accepted the Augsburg Confession (1530) and the Formula of Concord (1577), the benchmarks of confessional Lutheranism.[13] Already in November of 1616 and again in April of 1617, the dean of the philosophical faculty at Wittenberg, Erasmus Schmidt, made reference to a "jubilee year" (*Jobeljahr*) or "celebratory year" (*Halljahr*) year in 1617, recognizing one hundred years since Luther's initial actions.[14]

On April 22, 1617, Wittenberg's theological faculty wrote to Georg I, elector of Saxony, requesting that "the first Luther jubilee" (*primus Jubilaeus Lutheranus*) be "celebrated with festive and heartfelt worship."[15] The elector heartily approved and the decision was supported by church authorities in Dresden, who enjoined all other orthodox Lutheran territories in the Empire to observe the centenary.

Wittenberg's theologians requested that Georg I issue an official "Instruction and Order" to set things in motion. This transpired on August 12, 1617 when the elector called for the first centennial *evangelisches Jubel-Fest* and outlined the time and place of the celebrations, including a list of biblical texts on which the sermons over three days (October 31–November 2) were to be based.[16] Deeming many preachers ill-fit to reckon adequately with the significance of the occasion, the Dresden court preacher Matthias Hoë von Hoënegg (1580–1645) published exegetical guidelines of the biblical passages deemed appropriate for the occasion.[17]

Printed copies of Georg's "Instruction and Order" and other directives were sent out to Lutheran territories. Clearly, Saxony saw 1617 as an opportunity to shore up its authority both against the Catholic threat and against the dilution of the Protestant faith by Calvinists and by the Lutherans who had rebuffed the Formula of Concord. As sermons and pamphlets indicate in the preparation before and during the events between October 31 and November 2, the first evangelical jubilee was conceived as a commemoration of corrected faith—in contrast to the putatively false beliefs and superseded jubilees of the Jews and the Catholics. Rome was the corrupting innovator, it was repeatedly maintained; Luther had only returned things to the way they were supposed to be.

Neither Catholic territories within the empire nor Rome took Protestant developments in 1617 kindly. The Protestant appropriation of the term "jubilee" proved especially vexing. In 1300, the first Catholic jubilee had taken place at the instigation of Pope Boniface VIII.[18] Originally, these were to take place every hundred years, later that was reduced to fifty years following the biblical example of the Jewish jubilee in Leviticus 25. Then, in 1470, it was officially reduced to every twenty-five years. Prior to 1617, highly triumphalist, Tridentine jubilees had been celebrated in 1575 and 1600; the next was scheduled for 1625.[19] But faced with the specter of a Protestant jubilee, an indignant Pope Paul V declared on June 12, 1617, that the remainder of the year was going to be observed as a year of extraordinary jubilee for the Catholic Church.[20]

Alas, the Catholic jubilee must fall outside the scope of this chapter. But what actually happened in Protestant lands between October 31 and November 2, 1617? And what is the general significance of these events for subsequent Reformation jubilees? A trove of evidence has been left behind in the form of official ordinances and reports, sermons, academic addresses, debates, poems, plays, prayers, pamphlets, woodcuts, and commemorative coins and medals. While the ordinances and records are mostly prescriptive in character, telling us little about how ordinary people experienced the jubilee, they do have much to tell us about how elites planned and orchestrated the celebrations and what they hoped to accomplish through them.

The instructions (*Verzeichnus*) for the Lutheran imperial city of Ulm are representative of the larger phenomenon; these are particularly important, in fact, as the published version recounts some retrospective details of what actually took place—and these in fact do give at least some sense of the experience. As was the case in other areas, the jubilee in Ulm was celebrated over a three-day period, from October 31 to November 2. A few days prior, however, on October 26, the ecclesiastical superintendent of Ulm, one Conrad Dieterich (1575–1635), informed the town's citizens that for the coming jubilee they were to comport themselves as virtuous Christians, and not be found drinking, disturbing the peace, or in any other disorderly behavior. Instead, they were to listen to sermons, pray, partake of the Eucharist, and reflect on God's grace for bringing the purified faith to their city. The focal sites of the jubilee were Ulm's main parish cathedral, the Münster, and the Spitalkirche, or the Hospital or Trinity Church. Because of the expected large number of participants, additional clergy were brought in from the countryside.[21]

The entire period was to be treated as a time of high feast: bells were rung before and after services; a full choir with organ was employed during services. The sermon delivered on October 31 at the city cathedral recalled and derided the indulgence trade, while the one on November 1 proclaimed the proper purpose of worship and inveighed against the papal abuse of the mass. Three sermons were delivered on Sunday, November 2, all making connections between biblical passages and Reformation events.[22]

The official instructions for Ulm indicate that similar services with the same biblical texts took place at the Spitalkirche and in all rural parishes under the supervision of the Ulm church council; children in even the smallest villages were given a keepsake medal. The jubilee trickled into the week following. On Monday, the rector of the Latin school read a poem on the life of Martin Luther, composed for the occasion. On Tuesday, the rector's assistant delivered an oration on Luther and the Reformation. Later in the week, several orations in Latin were delivered by students, focusing on turning points in Luther's life.[23]

The record from Ulm provides a glimpse into what took place in other Protestant territories, although differences in detail abounded.[24] Again, most of the records are prescriptive or else homiletic, illustrating more what elites intended for the jubilee than how commoners experienced it. Nonetheless, several common themes thread the celebrations.

First, and not surprisingly, the person of Martin Luther takes center stage in both the written and visual artifacts from 1617; he emerges as the undisputed hero of the Reformation. Like Moses, he was interpreted to be a chosen messenger, God's man or instrument (*Gottesman, Gottes Werkzeug*), to liberate the faithful from the bondage of "Egypt"—that is, the papalist false church. Luther's image appeared on broadsheets and commemorative medals and coins, and countless references to him occur in sermons from 1617. Mirroring medieval hagiographies of saints, sermons and images recounted key turning points in Luther's life, such as his decision to become a monk, his burning of Pope Leo X's bull condemning him, his defiant appearance in 1521 before Charles V at the Diet of Worms, his translation of scripture at the Wartburg castle, his marriage to Katherina von Bora, and his death and burial. Much was made of the disparity between Luther's stature—"one little monk"—and the bloated, corrupt papalist system that he attacked. The disparity in fact was regularly seen as prima facie evidence that only God could have been behind an occurrence of such implausibility.[25]

Second, and related, symbols already associated with Luther in the sixteenth century received wide circulation in the jubilee festivities of 1617, influencing subsequent commemorations and shaping Protestant historical consciousness more generally. Three are particularly noteworthy. The first is the so-called Luther rose, an open white rose on a blue field, at the center of which was a red heart emblazoned with a black cross. Luther himself had devised this symbol, adapting it from his family's coat of arms, and had given it a theological interpretation. The black cross signified death and suffering; the red heart, life; the white rose, peace through justification; and the blue field, heavenly joy. Already in wide circulation in the sixteenth century, the Luther rose appeared on numerous broadsheets, coins, and medals in 1617.[26] The second image is that of a swan. During the heady 1520s and 1530s, the story gained wide currency that the Bohemian reformer Jan Hus from his prison cell had said that, although he might be a weak goose, a more powerful bird would come after him to reform the church. In his funeral sermon for Luther, Wittenberg's Johannes Bugenhagen made the coming bird a swan and attributed this line to Hus: "You may burn the goose, but in a hundred years will come a swan you will not be able to burn."[27] The third symbol was the image of a lamp or light derived from Matthew 5:14–16: "You are the light of the world.... Men do not light a lamp and put it under a bushel, but on a stand, and it gives light and life to all in the house." Frequently, in jubilee artifacts from 1617, the two symbols, swan and light, are joined.[28]

Finally, a firm link between theological and political authority recurred as a motif in 1617. Absent the Catholic hierarchy in Lutheran lands, the prince came to function first as an "emergency bishop" (*Notbischof*) and then as the *summus episcopus*, the titular head of the church and its armed protector.[29] In Saxony, a direct connection was made between the past support and protection offered to Luther by Elector Friedrich the Wise and the current protection of the Church by the elector in 1617, Georg I. A striking example of this relationship appears in an etching done by Balthasar Schwan, as part of a series of broadsheets published in Nuremberg in 1617. Luther and his key ally, Philip Melanchthon, both stand by an altar with Luther pointing to the open Bible with the phrase, "The Word of God remains forever." The two reformers are flanked by Friedrich the elector on the left with his sword resting on the altar, a sign of his past protection of the pure faith, and by Georg I on the right, his sword raised in the air, symbolizing his ongoing protection in the present. Variations on this etching were frequently produced for 1617; numerous coins and medals show Friedrich the Wise on one side and Georg I or another Protestant territorial prince on the other.[30] As Charles Zika has summed up, "The *Jubeljahr* links and legitimates the unity of political and religious purpose which is characteristic of the confessional states of the seventeenth century. It is a theme which . . . [became] even more pronounced in the verbal and visual images used in the centenary celebrations of the later seventeenth and eighteenth centuries."[31]

1817: The First Modern Centennial of the Reformation

After 1617 and prior to its collapse in 1806, the Holy Roman Empire witnessed numerous additional commemorations of key Reformation events. In 1717, Luther's attack against indulgences was marked again; in 1630 and 1730, the Augsburg Confession (1530) was remembered.[32] And all along, the birth and death dates of Luther and other key reformers received wide, public ceremonial attention. While differences in these events abound, their commonalities are most striking. They were planned and experienced as profoundly religious events expressing the realities of the confessionally divided nature of the Empire. Prior to the nineteenth century, in other words, Reformation jubilees were by and large confessional affairs, promoted by state churches for the primary purpose of reflecting on Luther's recovery of religious truth and the political protection of that truth given by the arm of the various states in the Holy Roman Empire.[33]

By 1817, however, important changes were afoot that affected Reformation commemorations; these changes did not vitiate their religious element, but enabled their retrospective gaze concurrently to incubate and transmit distinctly modern social and intellectual currents. These changes did not happen overnight, but it is fair to generalize that

a number of developments and events in the eighteenth century precipitated a metamorphosis in the memory of the Reformation. Some of these
changes can be attributed to the revolutionary-Napoleonic watershed years
after 1789, to be sure, and with them the turbulent rise of a novel, bourgeois ethos. But others go back to developments earlier in the eighteenth
century. Four developments, in particular, gaining momentum prior to
1817, merit spotlighting.

First, the trickle of Enlightenment sensibilities, some already evident in the 1717 commemorations, had become a gushing stream by 1817,
greatly affecting views of the Reformation. While Enlightenment figures
(*Aufklärer*) certainly did not speak with one voice, many converged on a
stadial view of human history—the view that history was not simply the
arena of sin, death, and salvation, but a forward-moving enterprise, capable
of discernable development and progress.[34] For those who subscribed to
such views, Luther could still be regarded as the restorer of proper religion, but in doing so he also became a catalyzing agent advancing the
human story away from superstition and darkness (medieval Catholicism)
toward reason and light (modern Protestantism). In scholars such as
Johann Lorenz von Mosheim (1694–1755) and Johann Salomo Semler
(1725–1791), moreover, the stirrings of a less confessional, more objective or
scientific (*wissenschaftlich*) approach to the Reformation became more pronounced.[35] For such men, the creedal correctness of Lutheranism might
not be beside the point, but they emphasized the form, not the content, of
Luther's challenge to the papacy. Just as Luther had taken on the authorities of his day, so contemporary scholars should challenge authorities—
indeed, even orthodox Lutheran ones—if they were beholden to tradition
bereft of reason's illumination. "The true Lutheran," as Gotthold Ephraim
Lessing captured this sentiment, "does not take refuge in Luther's writings, but in Luther's spirit," equating it with conscience and reason and
pitting it, when necessary, against the "yoke of tradition."[36]

Second, the evangelical renewal movement of pietism exerted a significant influence on assessments of the Reformation throughout the eighteenth century—indeed, it was among Pietists that the word *Reformation*
first began to designate a discrete period of church history. While one
rightly resists making an overly sharp distinction between Lutheranism
and pietism (as well as between pietism and *Aufklärung*) in the eighteenth century, Pietists were less inclined to confessional rigidity when
interpreting the Reformation and more open to thinking about its ethical
and affective aspects. Leading Pietist scholars focused attention on the

vital, introspective piety of Luther and contrasted that to the doctrinal rigidity and state control of the Lutheran churches of their times. Many also
made distinctions *within* Luther's own life, extolling the young Luther as
"liberator" and pitting that image against the mature, wizened Luther as
"statesman and church builder."[37] Pietist-inflected interpretations and
evocations of the Reformation, radiating especially from the university
town of Halle, gained ground throughout the eighteenth century.[38]

Third, the late eighteenth and early nineteenth centuries are well
known as the crucible period during which historicism (*Historismus*) was
born. Historicism is a notoriously difficult concept to get a handle on,
in part no doubt because scholars have used it as shorthand to signify
such a massive and multifaceted shift in modern German and Western
thought—what Friedrich Meinecke called "one of the greatest intellectual
revolutions that has ever taken place in human thought."[39] Its representative figures, such as the philologist Friedrich August Wolf, the jurist
Friedrich Carl von Savigny, or the historian Leopold von Ranke, looked
primarily to the past and to the category of "development" (*Entwicklung*)
to understand any human phenomena—not least the French Revolution,
which had given practically all Europeans an acute sense of historical
rupture and change.[40] The "turn to history" in German thought brought
with it renewed and copious attention to the Reformation as a watershed
moment in the not-too-distant past. What is more, a causal link existed,
many scholars felt, between the Reformation's challenge to authority
in the sixteenth century and the liberal, modernizing impulses of their
present.

Finally, early currents of German nationalism influenced assessments of the Reformation in the nineteenth century. Incubating in the
thought of a few eighteenth-century thinkers and popularized as a result
of the French Revolution and Napoleonic Wars, nationalism had a marked
impact on the jubilee of 1817 and, indeed, on practically all commemorations during the nineteenth century. Johann Gottfried Herder (1744–1803)
portrayed Luther as a German hero, the repository of a noble past and
the herald of a bright future for the German-speaking peoples of central
Europe. "Become once more [Luther] the Teacher of thy nation, its Prophet,
its Pastor," Herder exclaimed.[41] With a handful of others, Herder inspired
the idealist-romantic notion that each nation possessed a "soul" or "spirit"
(*Geist*), which at times manifested itself in a "great man"—larger-than-life
geniuses who embody this spirit in their very being, and through national
means contribute to the commonweal of humanity. For the English, it was

Shakespeare; for Italians, Dante; and, for Germans, Luther.[42] The image of Luther as the harbinger of the German nation stirred to life toward the end of the eighteenth century, and became more broadly popular after the Battle of Nations near Leipzig in October 1813—an event that effectively threw off the Napoleonic yoke and intensified nationalist sentiment, especially among the young and educated classes.[43]

THE INTERTWINED FATE of Napoleon and the German people, in fact, provides the crucial, immediate context for understanding the Reformation commemorations of 1817. As Thomas Nipperdey has famously written, "In the beginning was Napoleon. His influence upon the German people, their lives and experiences was overwhelming at a time when the initial foundations of a modern German state were being laid."[44] In his quest for European mastery, Napoleon's actions had precipitated the massive reorganization of ecclesiastical and political arrangements, resulting in the humiliation of Prussia at the Battle of Jena in 1806 and the cessation of the Holy Roman Empire in the same year. Under Napoleon's yoke, currents of liberalism and nationalism fanned to life, reaching a crescendo as a consequence of the aforementioned Battle of Nations. Regrettably, however, in the view of nationalists, no robust, pan-German state emerged after Napoleon's defeat. Instead, the German people had foisted upon them the unwieldy "German Confederation," a sop to nationalist sentiment but in reality an integral part of the reactionary scheme hatched by Count Metternich and other architects of Restoration at the Congress of Vienna (1814–15). In short, the peace settlement of Vienna sought to put a lid on German liberalism and nationalism and to restore the *Ancien-Régime* principles of Throne and Altar.[45]

But neither liberalism nor nationalism complied. In fact, they dramatically burst onto the scene in October 1817 when German students from eleven different universities convened at Wartburg Castle to commemorate the fourth anniversary of the Battle of Nations *and* the 300th anniversary of the Protestant Reformation. This was one of two defining events of 1817. The other was the establishment of the Prussian Union Church (*Unionskirche*), a government-orchestrated effort to merge the Lutheran and Reformed churches in Prussian lands in an effort to create one harmonious, Reformation-heritage (*evangelisch*) church—an example imitated by other territorial churches. Examining more closely the Wartburg student rally and the Prussian Union Church, followed by sampling the content of celebratory addresses and sermons (*Festpredigten*) from October

31 to November 2, 1817, will shed broader perspective on the 300th anniversary of the Reformation as a departure from past centenaries and as agent of historical change.

Frustrated by the conservative settlement at Vienna in 1815, nearly five hundred young men—all members of university "fraternities" of *Burschenschaften*—met at the Wartburg castle on October 18 and 19, 1817. Many had fought in the wars again Napoleon and they desired to rekindle the exalted nationalist-liberal sentiment that they had felt in 1813. In the "Wartburg Rally Declarations," the students summarized their aims: national unity, constitutional freedom, a liberal pan-German government, and the elimination of the vestiges of feudalism.[46] The site where Luther translated the New Testament into German in 1521–22 seemed an apt symbolic location for such a gathering. Amid the drinking, singing, and nostalgia for the recent past, speeches were given in which students exhorted one another to long for the German nation, to love freedom, to transcend particularism, and to defy the reactionary political climate. With reference to Luther's setting fire to the papal bull condemning him, students staged a book burning of works deemed "un-German" by their ideological standards. At root, the enthusiasms of the Wartburg rally reflected the students' sense of betrayal; the nationalist-liberal longings of 1813 had been stifled by the political settlement of 1815, and the students desired to use the Reformation's tercentenary of 1817 to bring the spirit of 1813 back to life. "Four long years have gone by since the battle," one student exclaimed; "[t]he German people entertained bright hopes, but they have all come to nothing; everything is different from what we expected."[47]

For those who experienced Wartburg, it was an intoxicating event, and in the judgment of historians, a key moment in shaping German national sentiment.[48] A heady blend of nationalist hopes, historical awareness, and Protestant conviction permeated the rally. As one popular song put it: "In our own manner, we want / to observe the great festival day. / Today is Doctor Luther's day, / [Thus] above all, everyone must sing / long live doctor Luther!"[49] But Luther was not just tied to the "nation." In the judgment of the Wartburg celebrants, the Reformation had also inaugurated an expansive understanding of spiritual freedom (*Geistesfreiheit*) and inwardness (*Innerlichkeit*). Just as the Prussian General Gebhard von Blücher had defeated Napoleon in 1813, so Luther had earlier defeated papal tyranny and superstition—longstanding impediments to freedom. The freedom envisioned by the students, however, was not the license often associated with Western liberalism, but a freedom that manifested itself in the hope for the progressive national unity and statehood of the German people. This sensibility pervaded the *Jubelfeier* of 1817.[50]

The ruling elite of Prussia envisioned a different sort of unity, but one that nonetheless dovetailed with nationalist sentiments and goals: the unity of the two Protestant confessions into one united evangelical church, or *Unionskirche*—something unthinkable in earlier, more confessional epochs. In part, the drive toward union arose from the king's personal religious motivations. In the years preceding the union, Friedrich Wilhelm III (r. 1797–1840) had taken an interest in the episcopal structure of the Church of England and in the liturgies of the Orthodox and Catholic churches. In comparison, his churches in Prussia seemed poorly organized and liturgically too variegated. What is more, the Reformed king had previously married a Lutheran wife from Mecklenburg, and had found it frustrating that they could not share communion together.[51]

Yet the decision for union did not emanate from the king's whims alone; other intellectual and political exigencies came into play. To a number of Prussian ministers, the Church Union represented a welcomed opportunity to overcome confessionalism and thus achieve a more progressive understanding of religion, one more in line with the outlook of the Enlightenment and German idealist philosophy. Furthermore, the union was recognized as a matter of raison d'état, of bringing religion "into harmony with the direction of the state," as Minister Karl von Altenstein put it.[52] In turn, a single Protestant church organically connected to the state would present a "united front" against the sizable Catholic minority and the smaller Jewish one.

The dual goals of diminishing intra-Protestant confessionalism and consolidating (Prussian) national unity gained wide support, not least from the likes of the philosopher Hegel and the theologian Friedrich Schleiermacher, who energetically advocated for union.[53] The actual process of church union fully got under way in September 1817.[54] In anticipation of the tercentenary celebration of the Reformation in October, the king issued a proclamation on September 27, 1817, in which he deplored Protestant divisions, argued that only externals still divided the two churches, and commended reunification as an act of deep religious significance. The king made clear that the Reformed did not have to become Lutheran, nor Lutheran Reformed, but that from their separate identities a new "evangelical" church would develop.[55] A medal to mark the event was minted: Luther and Calvin graced one side, and on the other a symbol of Mother Church appeared clutching her two sons to her bosom.[56]

The drive toward Protestant union was not limited to Prussia but spread to other German states as well.[57] A variety of particular circumstances accompanied these unions, but practically all drew inspiration from the lofty rhetoric of the Reformation's tercentenary and the example of Prussia. What is more, practically all were "top-down" affairs, influenced and orchestrated by church and state bureaucracies and carried out under the banner of "national interest."

Not everyone was pleased with this arrangement. In the judgment of more tradition-minded Lutherans, the top-down, coerced unity by the state was anathema—a betrayal of what Luther desired, not its fulfillment. No one evinced greater displeasure than the Kiel pastor Claus Harms (1778–1855), who took it upon himself in 1817 to pen his own 95 theses against the Prussian union, publishing them alongside Luther's original 95, which he called the "cradle and diapers in which our Lutheran church lay." As a diehard confessional Lutheran, Harms's exasperation with the direction of events in 1817 offers strong testimony about how this jubilee departed from previous ones. Harms interpreted "unionism" as a worrisome manifestation of various eighteenth-century currents of thought, which he grouped under the catchall rubric "rationalism." In his judgment, such rationalism had pitted progress, the autonomous conscience, and the imperatives of theological conciliation against the time-tested truths of an older, creedal Lutheranism. A sampling of Harms's theses provides a window onto his concerns:

> 3. With the idea of a progressive reformation (*fortshreitenden Reformation*)—as this idea is defined and how it is brought up— one reforms Lutheranism into paganism and Christianity out of the world.
> 43. When reason touches on religion, it throws out the pearls and plays with the husks, the empty words.
> 77. To say that time has abolished the dividing wall between Lutherans and Reformed is not clear talk. At issue is: who has fallen away from the faith of their church, the Lutherans or the Reformed? Or perhaps both?[58]

The publication of Harms's theses on October 31, 1817, lit a tinderbox of controversy; over sixty pamphlets appeared weighing in for or against him.[59] In the ensuing decades, the controversy did not die down. In fact, an attempt to impose a new uniform liturgical book (*Agenda*) throughout

Prussia resulted in the further disaffection of large numbers of so-called Old Lutherans, led by the Silesian pastor Johannes G. Scheibel (1783–1843), many of whom decided to emigrate rather than face what they deemed an intolerable situation.[60]

In the celebratory sermons and addresses of 1817, themes of bourgeois liberalism and nationalism crop up repeatedly. Again, these did not entirely displace older confessional themes, but the disparity between 1617 (and 1717), on the one hand, and 1817, on the other, is striking.

The Enlightenment theme of historical progress in particular stands out in 1817. The Reformation might have been a religious event that sought to return Christianity to its sources, but the net salutary effect of this retrospective vision was to inaugurate a new vision of historical progress and freedom. The Reformation, thus understood, became a stepping stone (*Vorstufe*) to the modern world, a premonition (*Vorboten*) of modern enlightenment. In this vision, Roman Catholicism was less a false church (though perhaps that, too) than a massive impediment to historical progress.

A pastor from Bayreuth, Johann Gottlieb Reuter (1765–1831), aptly illustrates this outlook in a sermon from 1817. The Reformation served all of humanity because it brought with it "enlightenment and morality" (*Aufklärung und Sittlichkeit*). He elaborated: "The Christian peoples, who sat enveloped in lamentable darkness, saw in the Reformation a welcomed, bright light, which awakened their spirits to a new active life. The chains that previously held the free development of all thinking minds were loosened. The free spirit of inquiry was aroused and one no longer could be satisfied with holy errors maintained by custom and superstition."[61]

In Berlin, both Friedrich Schleiermacher and the pastor August Ludwig Hanstein (1761–1821) made similar arguments, interpreting the Reformation as modern humanity's collective step in the right direction. As dean of Berlin's theological faculty, Schleiermacher gave an address on November 3, 1817, in which he praised the Reformation for introducing the critical spirit into theology, without which it would slip back into Catholic dogmatism, itself a species of "Jewish" priest craft.[62] Luther's acts in the sixteenth century represented for Schleiermacher "the complete overthrow of the superstition of arbitrary works and external merit." While Catholic universities fell prey to papal authority, Protestant universities "were ennobled by freedom of teaching and learning."[63] In a series of before-and-after scenarios, Hanstein made his case for the progressive character of the Reformation. "The Reformation brought instead of the word of man, the word of God; instead of constrained interpretation, free inquiry into the Holy Scripture; instead of dark, blind faith, the rational clarity of free conviction; instead of the coercion of conscience under priestly power, the freedom of the spirit and heart under a conscience under God's power."[64]

Indeed, numerous homilies and orations in 1817 sought to connect the Reformation with the birth pangs of modern reason, political liberalism, and/or bourgeois society. It was frequently pointed out that all of the major reformers—Luther, Melanchthon, Zwingli, and others—hailed not from aristocratic but from middle-class backgrounds.[65] K. H. L. Pölitz of the University of Leipzig captured a broadly felt sentiment in the title of an address he gave on October 30, 1817: "the similarity between the fight for civic and political freedom in our age and the fight for religious and ecclesiastical freedom in the age of the Reformation."[66] The Berlin biblical scholar Wilhelm Martin Leberecht de Wette (1780–1849) went further still, contending that the Reformation contained the seeds of practically every sort of modern freedom, "The spirit of Protestantism," he opined, "necessarily brings the spirit of freedom and the independence of the people (das Volk); Protestant freedom leads necessarily to political freedom."[67]

But not only did the Reformation anticipate modern political ideals: its influence also had improved the material and social circumstances of life. In contrast to Catholicism, which conduced society to accept autocracy, sloth, and social squalor, Protestantism—so many argued—encouraged civic virtue, domestic manners, and bourgeois respectability. Adumbrating Max Weber's notion of a "Protestant ethic," Gottfried Erdmann Petri of Zittau, for example, argued that the Reformation by reshaping everyday habits led to overall improved social and moral conditions. "Wherever Protestantism triumphs," he proclaimed, "the conditions of ethics, of the industry of businesses, and of domestic life receive a better form." The Erlangen pastor Carl Georg Friedrich Goes (1762–1836) reasoned similarly: "A good [Protestant] Christian [is] a good citizen (Bürger)," he contended. A sense of "vocation and duty" (Beruf und Pflicht) followed in the wake of the Reformation; through its influence, the Lord brought "blessing and prosperity to bourgeois life and activity."[68]

Significantly, it was only around the time of the tercentenary that images of the 95 Theses being posted on the castle church door in Wittenberg "went viral," as we might say today. The image had several variations. Often the artist depicted a young student proxy posting the theses while Luther and other scholars in the foreground led a theological discussion. Sometimes Luther was portrayed posting the theses himself; this now iconic image appeared in print for the first time in 1817, in a cycle of Luther's life by the artist Georg Paul Buchner. Alongside the image of the reformer burning his bull of excommunication and his defiance of Charles V at Worms in 1521, the image of the 95 Theses formed a kind of mental tryptich for the post-Enlightenment liberal spirit of the times: Luther had first shown that reason cannot always trust tradition and authority.[69]

To say that themes of bourgeois respectability, liberalism, nationalism, or historical progress permeated the tercentenary jubilee is not to say that older confessional themes vanished. As we have already seen, the orthodox pastor Claus Harms took strong exception in 1817 to the "rationalism" and "unionism" that he felt was subverting Luther's pure religious teachings. And he was not alone.[70] Channeling the stricter orthodoxy of the early modern era, but also in touch with the religious piety and the political conservatism of their day, such voices sought to focus on doctrinal purity above all else—and on Luther's teachings on justification and the Eucharist in particular.[71] Nonetheless, the fact that such voices were perceived and regularly perceived themselves as a protest movement against more dominant trends suggests that the Reformation centenary of 1817 no longer functioned strictly as an effort to stabilize confessional Protestant identities. It had become the vehicle through which newer ideologies, alongside the modification of older ones, could express themselves and, through the power of public memory, shape the future course of German history.

1883: Martin Luther and the German Empire

The tercentenary celebration of 1817 set in motion a century of Reformation commemorations—what one scholar has called the nineteenth century's "epidemic" of commemorations. Leaving aside the birth and death dates of key reformers besides Luther, mention ought to be made of the 300th anniversary of the Augsburg Confession in 1830, the 300th anniversary of Luther's death in 1846, the 200th anniversary of the Peace of Westphalia in 1848, the 300th anniversary of the Peace of Augsburg in 1855, and the 350th anniversary of Luther's challenge to indulgences in 1867.[72] The nineteenth century also witnessed the designing and erection of numerous monuments (*Denkmäler*) to Luther and the Reformation. The foundation stone for the first of many Luther statues was laid in Wittenberg in 1817 by no less a person than Prussia's king Friedrich Wilhelm III. His successor, Friedrich Wilhelm IV, used the occasion of the renovation of the Castle Church there in 1856–57 to put up bronze doors engraved with Luther's 95 Theses.

But such actions were mere prelude to 1883: the 400th anniversary of Luther's birth, an epic jubilee, the first after the founding of the German Empire in 1871. As was true in 1817, religious and particularly Protestant-confessional motivations and motifs were by no means absent in 1883. But what strikes one is how the memory of Luther at this time was put into the service of newer movements and developments: in a major key imperialist nationalism, and in a minor key the new scholarly ethos of historicism. The latter is evidenced in fresh efforts to achieve greater historical under-standing of Luther and the Reformation. The former is seen in the fact that the Luther remembered in 1883 frequently comes across less as a re-storer of religious truth than as *the* hero of the German nation, indeed the quintessential, primal German man—a liberator of the "Teutonic mind" from Rome, the author of practically every major German achievement, and no less the creator of a new ideal of humanity.[73] The Luthermania of 1883, as the historian Thomas A. Brady once quipped, amounted to a "be-lated birthday for the new German Reich."[74]

The tone of the Luther jubilee of 1883 was set from above. Emperor Wilhelm I issued an order on May 21, 1883, encouraging all churches in the German Empire festively to mark the 400th anniversary of Luther's birth. The selected dates were November 9, 10, and 11, a Friday through Sunday (November 10 was his actual birthday). On Friday, church bells were to be rung; on Saturday, activities in educational institutions should take place; and on Sunday, special commemorative worship services were to be held.[75]

In cities and towns across Protestant Germany, a spate of events took place during these dates. These included parades and torch-lit proces-sions; academic orations; the distribution of commemorative medals and medallions; the singing of hymns, particularly "A Mighty Fortress"; the unveiling of monuments and busts of Luther; the publication of pam-phlet and histories; encomiums to secular powers for their past and pre-sent protection of Protestantism; the laying of foundation stones for new churches; and of course countless sermons reflecting on Luther's life and the broader significance of the Reformation.[76] To be sure, a jumble of themes and emphases are apparent in these events. But, again, among the most conspicuous in 1883 was the refrain that Luther was a German hero, a powerful early manifestation of German culture and national identity, which, finally, had rendezvoused with political destiny in 1871. German Protestants in 1883, as Hartmut Lehmann has written, collectively felt that "Luther's heritage demanded ... nothing less than the completion of Germany's unification."[77] The year 1871 made good, in other words, on potentialities unleashed in 1517, which, in turn, were celebrated in 1883.

Such a triumphalist, nationalist sentiment appeared nowhere clearer than in an address, "Luther and the German Nation," given in Darmstadt by the Prussian historian Heinrich von Treitschke. Bewailing the fact that German Catholics, still reeling from Bismarck's *Kulturkampf*, could not rightly appreciate Luther's legacy, Treitschke identified the Wittenberg reformer as "the pioneer of the whole German nation," as a man possessing "the power of independent thought that typifies the German character," and as someone "with all the native energy and unquenchable fire of German defiance."[78]

An untiring champion of German political unification under Prussian leadership, Treitsckhe praised Luther for liberating the state from "ecclesiastical despotism" and setting in motion the possibility of state sovereignty. Luther's "two kingdoms" political teachings, in particular, merited Treitschke's commendation:

> Luther first smashed into ruins the dictum behind which the Romanists entrench themselves: he denied that "spiritual power is higher than temporal power," and taught that the State is itself ordained of God, and that it is justified in fulfilling and indeed pledged to fulfill, the moral purposes of its existence independently of the Church.[79]

The consequences of this teaching, according to Treitschke, were especially salutary for the future of Germany: "The emancipation of the State from the tyranny of church control nowhere brought with it so rich and lasting a blessing than in Germany."[80]

With many others in 1883, Treitschke traced the achievements of the German language, literature, and education back to the "little monk" of Wittenberg. "Goethe alone has rivaled him in his command over language," Treitschke noted; "but, notwithstanding this eloquence, [Luther] remains the most 'popular' of all our writers." In translating the New

Testament at the Wartburg Castle, "we received our literary language at a definite moment of time and at the hands of a single man." In doing so, Luther allowed "that God might speak German to the German nation."[81]

What was good for language was good for education. By dignifying the vernacular and allowing conscience to trump traditional authorities, Luther had set in motion forces salutary for German higher education. These forces bore fruit especially in the eighteenth-century Enlightenment at the reform university of Halle, epitomized there by the polymath Christian Thomasius, the first scholar to lecture in the vernacular and one keen to appeal to conscience over custom in championing an enlightened cosmopolitan. But whether at Halle or elsewhere, Treitschke emphasized, "all the leaders of this new learning were Protestants."[82]

In short, the German Empire in 1883 possessed a historical hero worthy of its present-day aspirations. But not only that. Luther in fact towered above other national heroes. There was something primal, commanding, awe-inspiring about this determined monk. In breaking with the church, he had unwitting and incipiently forged "Germania." The nation, the *Volksgeist*, first became personified in his person:

> No other modern nation can boast of a man who was the mouthpiece of his countrymen in quite the same way, and who succeeded as fully in giving expression to the deepest essence of his nation.... "Here speaks our own blood." From the deep eyes of this uncouth son of a German farmer flashed the ancient and heroic courage of the Germanic races—a courage that does not flee from the world, but rather seeks to dominate it by strength of its moral purpose.[83]

IF A PUNGENT imperialist nationalism was one aspect of Treitschke's talk, the Prussian historian also gave indication, less ominously, of the new scholarly historicism of the nineteenth century. Great strides in "historical science," he observed, had made possible a more penetrating understanding of Luther and the Reformation. Many other addresses from 1883 made this point. The young church historian Adolf Harnack, for example, held an oration on "Martin Luther and his Significance for the History of Scholarship and Education," in which he argued that Luther, although no great scholar himself by modern standards, had through his defiance helped conquer medieval obscurantism and thereby paved the way for the rise of "free inquiry."[84] Two other influential examples from

1883 will underscore the significance of this anniversary for historical scholarship.

First, the 1883 anniversary witnessed the launch of the monumental "Weimarer Ausgabe" of Luther's works.[85] While there had been earlier collected editions, the editors deemed these insufficiently based on "scholarly research" (*wissenschaftliche Forschung*); therefore, a genuinely critical collection of Luther's works had become "an urgent necessity." In light of the "upcoming Luther jubilee," as recounted in the preface to volume one, the Consistorial Counselor of Halle, Julius Köstlin, approached the Prussian Ministry of Culture about the need for such a project. Since his proposal was also supported by the prestigious Berlin Academy of Science, a "large sum" was granted by the emperor "to secure and set in motion the scholarly preparation of the edition."[86] Publication began in 1883 by the publisher Hermann Böhlau and, with various twists and turns, continued through 121 volumes until 2009!

Another major scholarly effort tied to the Luther jubilee and launched on February 13, 1883, was that of the Society for the History of the Reformation (*Verein für Reformationsgeschichte*). Seated at first in Magdeburg and initially directed by Julius Köstlin, it set as its original goal "to spread broadly the results of completed research about the emergence of the Protestant Church, about the personalities and facts of the Reformation, and about [its] effects in all areas of the life of the people." Mainly through conferences and publications, the society pursued its ends, notably launching a series of publications in 1883 that has resulted in two hundred volumes. Research impulses, however, blended freely with religious ones, for the society sought, too, "to solidify and strengthen Protestant consciousness through immediate contact with the history of our church."[87] Such religious objectives blended worrisomely with nationalist ones in the late nineteenth century through the Nazi period. But since then, the society has reoriented itself toward more strictly scholarly aims and today plays a leading international role in promoting knowledge of the sixteenth century, not least through its journal *Archiv für Reformationsgeschichte*.

Conclusion

As the example of the Society for the History of the Reformation makes clear, it is not always easy to disentangle religious elements from other aspects of nineteenth-century commemorations. The powerful inertia of older confessional realities certainly persists in 1817 and 1883, and indeed, in practically all of the many commemorative occasions of the nineteenth century.

At the same time, if one compares the activities and events of these two jubilees with earlier ones, not least with that of 1617, it is clear that far from simply seeking to reify older confessional ideas and identities, the commemorations of the nineteenth century stand out as mirrors and agents of newer developments—particularly, as I have argued, of liberalism, nationalism, and historicism, among the defining ideologies of the nineteenth century.

Thus understood, we need to take with a grain of salt the claim that acts of commemoration aim at stabilizing identity and/or seeking to preserve continuity between past and present. That is certainly true—and perhaps more often true than not. But the Reformation of jubilees of both 1817 and 1883, in contrast to their pre-modern counterparts, also indicate that acts of commemoration can be enlisted to reflect, shape, and introduce novel forces into history. These were not simply conduits or transmitters of the old, but definers and harbingers of the new. In this sense, we might view these jubilees not unlike the sixteenth-century Reformation itself: a series of acts motivated by the desire for retrieval and restoration that, in the final analysis, left a legacy of profound change, disruption, and innovation in human history.

Insofar as the past is often prologue to the present, we should anticipate similar patterns in 2017.

Notes

1. D. E. Kennedy, ed., *Authorized Pasts: Essays in Official History* (Melbourne: University of Melbourne, History Department, 1995), 75ff. Cf. Winfried Müller, "Das historische Jubiläum. Zur Geschichtlichkeit einer Zeitkonstruktion," in *Das historische Jubiläum. Genese, Ordungsleistung, und Inszenierungsgeschichte eines institionellen Mechanismus*, ed. Winfried Müller (Münster: Lit, 2004), 1–75.

2. John R. Gillis, ed., *Commemorations: The Politics of National Identity* (Princeton, NJ: Princeton University Press, 1994), 3.

3. Pierre Nora, ed., *Realms of Memory: Rethinking the French Past*, trans. Arthur Goldhammer (New York: Columbia University Press, 1996), x, 6.

4. Jeffry K. Olick et al., eds., *The Collective Memory Reader* (Oxford: Oxford University Press, 2011), 177.

5. On the term historicism, see Georg Iggers, "Historicism: The History and Meaning of the Term," *Journal of the History of Ideas* 56 (Spring 1995): 129–52.

6. R. J. W. Evans et al., eds., *The Holy Roman Empire, 1495–1806* (Oxford: Oxford University Press, 2011), 8–11. On confessionalization in general, see Heinz Schilling, *Konfessionalisierung und Staatsinteressen* (Paderborn: Schöningh, 2007).

7. Hans-Jürgen Schönstadt, "Das Reformationsjubiläum 1617: Geschichtliche Herkunft und geistige Prägung," *Zeitschrift für Kirchengeschichte* 93 (1982): 5–6.

8. See C. G. Bretschneider, ed., *Philippi Melanchthonis Opera* in *Corpus Reformatorum* (Halle, 1839), 6:161.

9. For an overview of the confessional situation in the late sixteenth and early seventeenth centuries, see Thomas A. Brady, *German Histories in the Age of the Reformation, 1400–1650* (Cambridge: Cambridge University Press, 2009), 259–318.

10. Catholic territories founded their own Catholic League in retaliation in 1609. On the founding of the Protestant Union and Catholic League, see Axel Gotthard, "Protestantische 'Union' und katholische 'Liga'—subsidäre Strukturelemente oder Alternativentwürfe," in *Alternativen zur Reichsverfassung in der Frühen Neuzeit?*, ed. Volker Press (Munich: R. Oldenbourg, 1995), 81–112.

11. Quoted in Gustav Benrath, *Reformierte Kirchengeschichtsschreibung an der Universität Heidelberg im 16. und 17. Jahrhundert* (Speyer: Veröffentlichung des Vereins für Pfälzische Kirchengeschichte, 1963), 37f.

12. Hans-Jürgen Schönstädt, *Antichrist, Weltheilsgeschehen und Gottes Werkzeug. Römische Kirche, Reformation und Luther im Spiegel des Reformationsjubiläum 1617* (Wiesbaden: Steiner, 1978), 13–15.

13. In effect, this meant the desire to exclude not only Reformed territories, but those, such as the cities of Nuremberg and Strasbourg, which had not signed on to the Book of Concord. See Eric W. Gritsch, *A History of Lutheranism*, 2nd ed. (Minneapolis: Fortress Press, 2010), 91ff.

14. Schmidt's utterances are the first known evidence of awareness of the historical significance of 1617. See Schönstädt, *Antichrist*, 12–13.

15. Quoted in Schönstädt, *Antichrist*, 16. Cf. Friedrich Loofs, "Die Jahrhundertfeier der Reformation an den Universitäten Wittenberg und Halle 1617, 1717, 1917," *Zeitschrift des Vereins für Kirchengeschichte in der Provinz Sachsen* 14 (1917): 5.

16. Quoted in Schönstädt, *Antichrist*, 18.

17. On Hoënegg and his role during 1617, see Wolfgang Sommer, *Die lutherische Hofprediger in Dresden: Grundzüge ihrer Geschichte und Verkündigung im Kurfürstentum Sachsen* (Stuttgart: Franz Steiner Verlag, 2006), 137ff.

18. Joseph Stricher, "L'annee jubilaire et la tradition catholique," *Foi et Vie* 99 (2000): 73–86.

19. Barbara Witsch, "The Roman Church Triumphant: Pilgrimage, Penance, and Processions. Celebrating the Holy Year of 1575," in *Art and Pageantry in the Renaissance and Baroque*, ed. Barbara Witsch and Susan Scott Munshower (University Park, PA: Pennsylvania University Press, 1990), 82–117.

20. See Ruth Kastner, *Geistlicher Rauffhandel: Form und Funktion der illustrerten Flugblätter zum Reformationsjubiiläum in ihrem historischen und publizistischen*

Kontext (Frankfurt am Main: Peter Lang, 1982), 30–33; and Charles Zika, "The Reformation Jubilee of 1617: Appropriating the Past through Centenary Celebration," in *Authorized Pasts: Essays in Official History*, ed. D. E. Kennedy (Melbourne, 1995), 84.

21. See the *Verzeichnus wie auf christliche anordnung eines Ersamen Raths das Evangelische Jubelfest allhier zu Ulm 1617.2 Novemb. Freylich begangen*, in Conrad Dieterich, *Zwo Ulmische Jubel und Danckpredigten* (Ulm, 1618). Cf. Schönstädt, *Antichrist*, 64–67.

22. Dieterich, *Zwo Ulmische Jubel und Danckpredigten*, 9ff. Cf. Kastner, *Geistlicher Rauffhandel*, 62–63.

23. Zika, "The Reformation Jubilee of 1617," 86.

24. Schönstadt, *Antichrist*, 20–85; and Kastner, *Geistlicher Rauffhandel*, 34–102.

25. Zika, "The Reformation Jubilee of 1617," 96.

26. Kastner, *Geistlicher Rauffhandel*, 183.

27. Quoted in Robert Scribner, *Popular Culture and Popular Movements in Reformation Germany* (London: Hambledon Press, 1987), 327.

28. Heinrich Gottlieb Kreussler, *Luthers Andenken in Jubel-Münzen* (Leipzig, 1818), plate 2; and Scribner, *Popular Culture and Popular Movements in Reformation Germany*, 342–43.

29. Lewis Spitz, "Luther's Ecclesiology and his Concept of the Prince at *Notbischof*," *Church History* 22 (1953): 113–41.

30. John Roger Paas, *The German Political Broadsheet: 1600–1700* (Wiesbaden: O. Harrassowitz, 1986), 2:111 (plate 302).

31. Zika, "The Reformation Jubilee of 1617," 99.

32. On 1717, see Harm Cordes, *Hilaria evangelica academia: Das Reformationsjubiläum von 1717 an den deutschen lutherischen Universitäten* (Göttingen: Vandenhoeck & Ruprecht, 2006).

33. Klaus Tanner, ed., *Konstruktion von Geschichte: Jubelrede, Predigt, Protestantische Historiographie* (Leipzing: Evangelische Verlagsanstalt, 2012), 15ff.

34. On the idea of progress in the German Enlightenment, see Sophie Bourgault and Robert Sparkling, *A Companion to Enlightenment Historiography* (Leiden: Brill, 2013), 55–56.

35. John Tonkin, "Reformation Studies," in *Oxford Encyclopedia of the Reformation*, ed. Hans J. Hillerbrand (New York: Oxford University Press, 1996), 3:403–05.

36. Quoted in Ernst Walter Zeeden, *The Legacy of Luther*, trans. Ruth Mary Bethell (London: Hollis & Carter, 1954), 137.

37. Tonkin, "Reformation Studies," 403.

38. A. G. Dickens and John Tonkin, *The Reformation in Historical Thought* (Cambridge, MA: Harvard University Press, 1985), 116ff.

39. Friedrich Meinecke, *Historism: The Rise of a New Historical Outlook*, trans. J. E. Anderson (New York: Herder and Herder, 1972), liv.

40. See Thomas Nipperdey's very helpful discussion of the "revolution of historicism," in *Germany from Napoleon to Bismark, 1800–1866*, trans. Daniel Nolan (Princeton, NJ: Princeton University Press, 1996), 441–71.

41. Quoted in Zeeden, *The Legacy of Luther*, 172.

42. Robert Ergang, *Herder and the Foundations of German Nationalism* (New York, 1931), 177–212.

43. Stan M. Landry, *Ecumenism, Memory and German Nationalism, 1817–1917* (Syracuse, NY: Syracuse University Press, 2013), 1–6.

44. Nipperdey, *Germany from Napoleon to Bismarck*, 1.

45. Enno Kraehe, *Metternich's German Policy* (Princeton, NJ: Princeton University Press, 1963), 2:99–110.

46. Nipperdey, *Germany from Napoleon to Bismarck*, 245.

47. Quote from H. W. Koch, *A History of Prussia* (London: Longman, 1978), 209.

48. James J. Sheehan, *German History, 1770–1866* (Oxford: Clarendon Press, 1989), 406–07.

49. Robert Keil and Richard Keil, *Die burschenschaftliche Wartburgfeste von 1817 und 1867* (Jena, 1868), 14.

50. On understandings of freedom at this time, see Leonard Krieger, *The German Idea of Freedom* (Boston: Beacon Hill, 1957), 174ff.

51. Thomas Stamm, *König Preussens grosser Zeit: Friedrich Wilhelm III* (Berlin: Sielder, 1992), 150–80.

52. Howard, *Protestant Theology and the Making of the Modern German University*, 235ff.

53. Martin Redeker, *Schleiermacher: Life and Thought*, trans. John Wallhausser (Philadelphia: Fortress Press, 1973), 189–91.

54. Walter Elliger, ed., *Die evangelische Kirche der Union: Ihre Vorgeschichte und Geschichte* (Witten: Luther-Verlag, 1967), 44–45, 195–96. Prior to this, it should be mentioned, a Protestant union took place in the small duchy of Nassau in August 1817.

55. See Klaus Wappler, "Reformationsjubiläum und Kirchenunion (1817)," in *Die Geschichte der evangelischen Kirche der Union*, ed. J. F. Gerhard and Joachim Rogge (Leipzig: Evangelsiche Verlagsanstalt, 1992), 1:112ff.; and Elliger, *Die evangelische Kirche der Union*, 45f.

56. Hugo Schnell, *Martin Luther und die Reformation auf Münzen und Medaillen* (Munich: Klinkhardt & Biermann, 1983), 75, 231 (image 273); and Elliger, *Die evangelsiche Kirche der Union*, 176.

57. John E. Groh, *Nineteenth-Century German Protestantism: The Church as Social Model* (Washington, DC: University of America Press, 1982), 41–43.

58. Claus Harms, *Ausgewählte Schriften und Predigten*, ed. G. E. Hofmann (Flensburg: Christian Wolff Verlag, 1955), 1:204–22.

59. Rainer Fuhrmann, *Das Reformationsjubiläum 1817: Martin Luther und die Reformation im Urteil der protestantischen Festpredigt* (Bonn: V&V Sofortdruck, 1973), 35.

60. On the Old Lutheran emigration, see Wilhelm Iwan, *Die altlutherische Auswanderung um die Mitte des 19.Jahrhundert* (Ludwigsburg, 1943).

61. Johann Gottlieb Reuter, *Fünf Predigten zu und bei der Secularfeier der Kirchenreformation 1817 gehalten* (Bayreuth, 1817), 23–24.

62. Kurt Nowak, *Schleiermacher: Leben, Werk und Wirkung* (Göttingen: Vandenhoeck & Ruprecht, 2001), 364–65.

63. "Oratio in sollemnibus ecclesiae per Lutherem emendatae saecularibus tertiis in Universitate litterarum Berolinensi," in Schleiermacher, *Kritische Gesamtausgabe*, ed., Hans-Joachim Birkner et al., I. 10 (Berlin: Walter de Gruyter, 1990), 11.

64. August Ludwig Hanstein, *Das Jubeljahr der evangelischen Kirche. Vier vorbereitende Predigten* (Berlin, 1817), 31.

65. Fuhrmann, *Das Reformationsjubiläum 1817*, 54ff.; and Lutz Winckler, *Martin Luther als Bürger und Patriot: Das Reformationsjubiläum von 1817 und der politische Protestantismus des Wartburgfestes* (Lübeck: Matthiesen Verlag, 1969), 23ff.

66. Karl Heinrich L. Pölitz, "Die Änlichkeit des Kampfes um bürgerliche und politische Freiheit in unserm Zeitalter mit dem Kampfe um die religiöse und kirchliche Freiheit im Zeitalter der Reformation," in *Reformations Alamanach für Luthers Verhrer auf das evangelische Jubeljahr 1817*, ed. Friedrich Keyser (Erfurt, 1819), 123.

67. W. M. L. de Wette, "Ueber den sittlichen Geist der Reformation in Beziehung auf unsere Zeit" (1817), in *Reformationsalmanach auf das Jahr 1819* (Erfurt, 1819), 286–87.

68. C. G. F. Goes, *Luthers Kirchenreformation nach ihrer Veranlassung, Eigenthümlichkeit Beschaffenheit und wohlthätigen Wirksamkeit in einigen Kanzelvorträgen am dritten Säkularfeste nebst kurzem Berichte über die hiesige Festfeyerlichkeit* (Erlangen, 1817), 65ff.

69. Hartmut Lehmann, *Luthergedächtnis 1817 bis 2017* (Göttingen: Vandenhoeck & Ruprecht, 2012), 17–34.

70. Fuhrmann, *Das Reformationsjubiläum 1817*, 72.

71. On the awakening movement (*Erweckungsbewegung*) and its influence in the early nineteenth century, see Robert M. Bigler, *The Politics of German Protestantism: The Rise of the Church Elite in Prussia, 1815–1848* (Berkeley: University of California Press, 1972), 128.

72. A nice overview or nineteenth-century commemorations is found in Dorothea Wendebourg, "Die Reformationsjubiläen des 19. Jahrhunderts," *Zeitschrift für Theologie und Kirche* 108 (2011): 270–335.

73. Landry, *Ecumenism, Memory, and German Nationalism*, 90–1.

74. Thomas A. Brady, *The Protestant Reformation in German History*, Occasional Paper no. 22 of the German Historical Institute (Washington, DC: German Historical Institute, 1998), 15. On the large literature from this jubilee, see Hans Dufel, "Das Luther-Jubiläum 1883," *Zeitschrift für Kirchengeschichte* 95 (1984): 1–94.

75. Lehmann, *Luthergedächtnis*, 59.

76. Lehmann, *Luthergedächtnis*, 74ff.

77. Hartmut Lehmann, "Martin Luther as a National Hero," in *Romantic Nationalism in Europe*, ed. J. C. Eade (Canberra: Australian National University, 1983), 197.

78. Heinrich von Treitschke, *Historische und politische Aufsätze* (Leipzig: Verlag von S. Hirzel, 1897), 4:378–80, 384.

79. Treitschke, *Historische und politische Aufsätze*, 4:387.

80. Treitschke, *Historische und politische Aufsätze*, 4:388.

81. Treitschke, *Historische und politische Aufsätze*, 4:390–92.

82. Treitschke, *Historische und politische Aufsätze*, 4:391.

83. Treitschke, *Historische und politische Aufsätze*, 4:393–94.

84. Adolf von Harnack, *Martin Luther in seiner Bedeutung für die Geschichte der Wissenschaft und Bildung* (Giessen, 1911).

85. The *Weimarer Ausgabe*, or "WA," is the unofficial title. The actual title is *D. Martin Luthers Werke: kritische Gesammtausgabe*.

86. *D. Martin Luthers Werke: kritische Gesammtausgabe* (Weimar: Hermann Böhlau, 1883), 1:xv–xvi.

87. From article one of the Society's founding charter. See www.reformationsgeschichte.de/. Cf. Luise Schorn-Schütte, ed., *125 Jahre Verein Reformationsgeschichte* (Heidelberg: Gütersloh, 2008).

2

From Gospel to Law

THE LUTHERAN REFORMATION AND
ITS IMPACT ON LEGAL CULTURE

John Witte Jr.

AS WE REFLECT on the Reformation's 500th anniversary, we would do well to remember that this was not just a theological or religious event, but a legal and political one, too, that had vast and influential implications for the ordering of society and the administration of justice.

On December 10, 1520, Martin Luther burned the canon law books of the Catholic Church. A large group of students and colleagues gathered in Wittenberg for the book burning. Consigned to the flames were Gratian's *Decretum* of 1140 and four thick books of later papal laws. Also cast into the fire were a standard confessional book and several tomes on Catholic sacramental theology. "This might as well go, too," Luther muttered as he threw into the fire the papal bull that threatened his excommunication for heresy. Luther would later write of his canonical bonfire: "I am more pleased with this than any other action in my life."[1]

If there were a single event that signaled Luther's permanent break with Rome, this was the event. Three years before, on October 31, 1517, Luther had posted his 95 Theses. As is well known, there he had attacked the church's crass commercialization of salvation through the sale of indulgences. In several publications and debates in the next year Luther had challenged the biblical integrity of the church's theology of salvation and the sacraments. On October 8–9, 1518, Luther had answered a summons to appear in Augsburg before the Pope's representative, Cardinal Cajetan, but had refused to recant his views. On November 28, 1518, Luther had appealed directly to the Pope, insisting upon his rights, as a professor of theology, to an open hearing of his views at a general church council. On July 4–14, 1519, with no such council forthcoming, Luther had engaged in a sensational public debate at the University of Leipzig with the Catholic theologian Johann Eck over fundamental questions of ecclesiastical authority—a debate that revealed the increasing radicalism of Luther's theological doctrines of justification by faith, the primacy of the Bible, the nature of the church, and the priesthood of all believers.[2]

By then, however, Pope Leo X had issued his bull of excommunication, *Exsurge, Domine,* condemning Luther and his followers:

> Arise, O Lord, and judge your own cause. Remember your re-proaches to those who are filled with foolishness all through the day. Listen to our prayers, for foxes have arisen seeking to destroy the vineyard whose winepress you alone have trod. When you were about to ascend to your Father, you committed the care, rule, and administration of the vineyard, an image of the triumphant church, to Peter, as the head and your vicar and his successors. The wild boar from the forest seeks to destroy it and every wild beast feeds upon it.... Against the Roman Church, lying teachers are rising, introducing ruinous sects, and drawing upon themselves speedy doom. Their tongues are fire, a restless evil, full of deadly poison. They have bitter zeal, contention in their hearts, and boast and lie against the truth.[3]

The bull went on to condemn the heretical teachings of that "wild boar" Martin Luther as "scandalous," "offensive," "seductive," and "repugnant to Catholic truth." The bull had given Luther sixty days after receipt to recant and return to the Catholic fold. December 10, 1520, was the sixtieth day. On that day, Luther had his bonfire, burning his last bridge with Rome.

Luther based his attack on a radical new theology of freedom: freedom of the church from the tyranny of the pope, freedom of the laity from the hegemony of the clergy, freedom of the conscience from the strictures of canon law. "Freedom of the Christian"[4] was the rallying cry of the early Lutheran Reformation. It drove theologians and jurists, clergy and laity, princes and peasants alike to denounce the church's legal strictures and structures with unprecedented alacrity. "One by one, the structures of the church were thrust into the glaring light of the Word of God and forced to show their true colors," Jaroslav Pelikan writes.[5] Few church structures survived this scrutiny in the heady days of the 1520s. The church's canon law books were burned. Church courts were closed. Monasteries were confiscated. Benefices were dissolved. Church properties were seized. Clerical privileges were stripped. Mendicant begging was banned. Mandatory celibacy was suspended. Indulgence trafficking was condemned. Taxes to Rome were outlawed. Ties to the pope were severed. The German people who followed Luther were now to live by the pure light of the Word of God and the simple law of the local community.

Although such attacks built on two centuries of reformist agitation in the West, it was especially Luther's theological teachings that ignited this movement in Germany. Salvation comes through faith in the gospel, Luther taught, not through works of the law. All persons stand directly before God; they are not dependent upon clerics for divine mediation. All believers are priests to their peers; they are not divided into a higher clergy and lower laity. All persons are called by God to serve in vocations; clerics are not the only ones with a Christian calling. The church is a communion of saints, not a corporation of law. The consciences of its members are guided by the Bible, not governed by traditions. The church is called to serve society in love, not to rule it by law. Law is the province of the magistrate, not the prerogative of the cleric. When put in such raw and radical terms, these theological doctrines of justification by faith, the priesthood of believers, law and gospel, and others were highly volatile compounds. When sparked by Luther's pugnacious rhetoric and relentless publications, they set off a whole series of explosive reforms in various parts of central Europe.

In these early years, Luther's attack on the church's canon law and clerical authority sometimes broadened into an attack on human law and human authority. altogether. "Neither pope nor bishop nor any other man has the right to impose a single syllable of law upon a Christian man without his consent," Luther famously wrote in 1520. The Bible contains all the law that is needed for proper Christian living. To subtract from the law of the Bible is blasphemy. To add to the law of the Bible is tyranny. "Wise rulers, side by side with Holy Scripture, [are] law enough." When jurists of the day objected that such radical biblicism was itself a recipe for blasphemy and tyranny, Luther turned on them harshly. "Jurists are bad Christians," he declared repeatedly. "Every jurist is an enemy of Christ." When the jurists persisted in their criticisms, Luther reacted with vulgar anger: "I shit on the law of the pope and of the emperor, and on the law of the jurists as well."[6]

The rapid deconstruction of law, politics, and society that followed upon such shrill rhetoric plunged Germany into an acute crisis in the 1520s and 1530s. Luther had drawn too sharp a contrast between freedom and order within the church. Young Lutheran churches and clerics were treating their new liberty as license for all manner of doctrinal and liturgical experimentation and laxness. Widespread confusion reigned over preaching, prayers, and pastoral duties. Church attendance, tithe payments, and charitable offerings declined abruptly among many who took literally Luther's new teachings of free grace. Many radical social experiments were engineered out of Luther's doctrines of the priesthood of believers and justification by faith.

Moreover, Luther had driven too deep a wedge between the canon law and the civil law. Many subjects traditionally governed by the church's canon law remained without effective legal guidance. The vast church properties that local magistrates had confiscated were disappearing rapidly into private coffers. Drunkenness, usury, and vagabondage reached new heights. Crime, delinquency, and mendicancy soared. Schools, charities, and hospitals closed down. Marriage, divorce, and inheritance became hopelessly confused. Widows, orphans, and the poor were dying in the streets. All these subjects and many more, the Catholic canon law and church institutions had governed in detail for many centuries in Germany. The new Protestant civil law, where it existed at all, was too primitive to address these subjects properly.

In response, the Lutheran reformation of theology and the church quickly broadened into a reformation of law and the state as well. Deconstruction of the canon law for the sake of the gospel gave way to reconstruction of the civil law on the strength of the gospel. Castigation of Catholic clerics as self-serving overlords gave way to cultivation of Protestant magistrates as fathers of the community called to govern on God's behalf. Old rivalries between theologians and jurists gave way to new alliances, especially in the new Lutheran universities.

In the 1530s and thereafter, Lutheran theologians began to pay much closer attention to the legal, political, and social implications of their new teachings. They joined Lutheran jurists to craft ambitious legal reforms of church, state, and society. These legal reforms were defined and defended in hundreds of new writings published by Lutheran theologians and jurists from the 1530s to 1560s. They were refined and routinized in hundreds of new reformation ordinances promulgated by German cities, duchies, and territories that converted to the Lutheran cause.

Critics of the day, and ever since, have criticized this legal turn of the Reformation as a corruption of the original Lutheran message. For some, it was a bitter betrayal of the new freedom and equality that Luther had promised. For others, it was a distortion of Luther's fundamental reforms of theology and church life. For still others, it was a simple reversion to Catholic canonical norms dressed in new theological forms.

Whatever the merits of such criticisms in Luther's day, it was the combination of theological and legal reforms that rendered the Lutheran Reformation so resolute and resilient. The reality was that Luther and the theologians needed the law and the jurists, however much they scorned them initially. It was one thing to deconstruct the framework of medieval Catholic law, politics, and society with a sharp theological sword. It was quite another thing to reconstruct a new Lutheran framework of law, politics, and society with only this theological sword in hand. Luther learned this lesson the hard way in the crisis years of the 1520s and 1530s, and it almost destroyed the early Protestant movement. He quickly came to realize that law was not just a necessary evil but also an essential blessing in this earthly life.

It was thus both natural and necessary for the Lutheran Reformation to move from theology to law. Radical theological reforms had made possible fundamental legal reforms. Fundamental legal reforms, in turn, would make permanent radical theological reforms. The Lutheran Reformation became in its essence both a theological and a legal reform movement. It struck new balances between law and gospel, order and faith, structure and spirit. And it offered new theories and laws of church and state, marriage and education that have become a permanent legacy of the Western tradition.

Luther's Two-Kingdoms Theory

The starting point for this combined theological and legal movement was Luther's complex theory of the two kingdoms. This theory came together in Luther's mind in the later 1520s and 1530s, and became a dominant gene in the genetic code of Lutheran theology and jurisprudence thereafter. God has ordained two kingdoms or realms in which humanity is destined to live, Luther argued, the earthly kingdom and the heavenly kingdom. The earthly kingdom is the realm of creation, of natural and civil life, where a person operates primarily by reason and law. The heavenly kingdom is the realm of redemption, of spiritual and eternal life, where a person operates primarily by faith and love. These two kingdoms embrace parallel heavenly and earthly, spiritual and temporal forms of righteousness and justice, government and order, truth and knowledge. But these two kingdoms ultimately remain distinct. The earthly kingdom is distorted by sin and governed by the law. The heavenly kingdom is renewed by grace and guided by the gospel. A Christian is a citizen of both kingdoms at once and invariably comes under the distinctive government of each. As a heavenly citizen, the Christian remains free in his or her conscience, called to live fully by the light of the word of God alone. But as an earthly citizen, the Christian is bound by law, and is called to obey the natural orders and offices that God has ordained for the governance of this earthly kingdom.[7]

Luther's two-kingdoms theory was a rejection of traditional hierarchical theories of being, society, and authority. For centuries, the Catholic Church had taught that God's creation was hierarchical in structure—a vast chain of being emanating from God and descending through various levels and layers of reality. In this great chain of being, each creature found its place and its purpose, and each human society found its natural order and hierarchy. It was thus simply the nature of things that some persons and institutions were higher on this chain of being and some were lower. It was the nature of things that some were closer and had more ready access to God, and some were farther away and in need of greater mediation in their relationship with God. This chain-of-being theory, which some will recognize in Dante's *Divine Comedy*, was one basis for traditional Catholic arguments for the superiority of the pope to the emperor, of the clergy to the laity, of the canon law to the civil law, of the church to the state.[8]

Luther's two-kingdoms theory turned this traditional ontology on its side. By distinguishing the two kingdoms, Luther highlighted the radical separation between the Creator and the creation, and between God and humanity. For Luther, the fall into sin destroyed the original continuity and communion between the Creator and the creation, the organic tie between the heavenly kingdom and the earthly kingdom. There was no series of emanations of being from God to humanity. There was no stairway of merit from humanity to God. There was no purgatory. There was no heavenly hierarchy. God is present in the heavenly kingdom, and is revealed in the earthly kingdom mainly through "masks." Persons are born into the earthly kingdom, and have access to the heavenly kingdom only through faith.[9]

Luther did not deny the traditional view that the earthly kingdom retained its natural order, despite the fall into sin. There remained, in effect,
a chain of being, an order of creation, that gave each human being and
institution its proper place and purpose in this life. But, for Luther, this
chain of being was horizontal, not hierarchical. Before God, all persons
and all institutions in the earthly kingdom were by nature equal. Luther's
earthly kingdom was a flat regime, a horizontal realm of being, with no
person and no institution obstructed or mediated by any other in relationship to and accountability before God.

Social, Political, and Legal Reforms

Luther's two-kingdoms theory also turned the traditional hierarchical
theory of human society on its side. For many centuries, the church
had taught that the clergy were superior to the laity. The clergy were
special officers of the higher heavenly realm of grace, while the laity
were simply members of the lower earthly realm of nature. As members
of the higher heavenly realm, the clergy had readier access to God and
God's mysteries. They thus mediated the channel of grace between the
laity and God—dispensing God's grace through the sacraments and
preaching, and interceding for God's grace by hearing confessions, receiving charity, and offering prayers on behalf of the laity. In this sense,
the lowliest cleric was superior to the noblest emperor. All the clergy,
from the lowliest parson to the greatest pope, were exempt from earthly
laws, taxes, and other duties, and foreclosed from earthly pursuits such
as marriage and family life.

Luther rejected this hierarchical social theory. Clergy and laity were
fundamentally equal before God and before all others, he argued. Luther's
doctrine of the priesthood of all believers at once "laicized" the clergy and
"clericized" the laity. It treated the traditional "clerical" office of preaching
and teaching as just one other vocation alongside many others that a con-
scientious Christian could properly and freely pursue. He treated all traditional "lay" offices as forms of divine calling and priestly vocation, each
providing unique opportunities for service to one's peers. Preachers and
teachers of the visible church must carry their share of civic duties and pay
their share of civil taxes, just like everyone else. And they may and should
participate in earthly activities such as marriage and family life, just like
everyone else.[10]

Luther expanded on this natural egalitarianism with his robust understanding of the Christian "calling" (*Beruf*) or "vocation" (*vocatio*). Every "good, decent, and useful" occupation in which a Christian conscientiously engages should be treated as a Christian vocation, Luther believed. Each vocation was an equally virtuous and effective calling of God, though none was a pathway to salvation. The carpenter and the prince, the mineworker and the judge, the housewife and the banker—all should accept their Christian responsibility to perform their tasks conscientiously and, so far as possible, in the service of God and others.[11] Public officials, in particular, Luther argued, have a special calling to serve the community. This calling might require them to adopt a Christian social ethic that differs from a Christian personal ethic. A Christian's duty in his direct relationship with God "as a private person, a person for himself alone," is to love his enemy and to suffer injustice and abuse from his neighbor without resistance and without revenge. As a public person, serving in such offices as the military or the judiciary, however, a Christian might well be required to resist his neighbor and to avenge injustice and abuse, even to the point of violence and bloodshed.[12]

Luther did not press his natural egalitarianism to communitarian extremes. He saw no incompatibility between insisting on the equal status of all persons and vocations before God, and accepting the ample disparities in wealth, power, privilege, and respectability among persons and positions in daily life. Some are more blessed, some less so. Some work harder, some play more. Some enjoy goods, some spurn them. Some start with noble inheritances, some start with nothing. Some vocations require more pageantry and property than others. None of these empirical disparities, however, changes the fundamental reality of human equality before God.

Political Reforms

Luther's two-kingdoms theory also turned the traditional hierarchical theory of spiritual and temporal authority on its side. For centuries, the church had taught that the pope is the vicar of Christ, in whom Christ has vested the "plentitude of his power." This power was symbolized in the "two swords" discussed in the Bible (Luke 22:38)—the spiritual and the temporal swords. Christ had handed these two swords to the highest being in the human world—the pope, the vicar of Christ. The pope and his clerical delegates wielded the spiritual sword, in part by establishing canon laws for the governance of all of Christendom. The pope, however, was too holy to wield the temporal sword. He thus delegated this sword to those authorities below the spiritual realm—emperors, kings, dukes, and their civil retinues. These civil magistrates were to promulgate and enforce civil laws in a manner consistent with canon law and other church teachings. Under this two-swords theory, civil law was by its nature inferior to canon law. Civil jurisdiction was subordinate to ecclesiastical jurisdiction. Political authority was subordinate to clerical authority. Medieval popes could rarely make good on these grand claims to universal, preemptory legal authority in Christendom. Indeed, the strongest expressions of the two-swords theory came in the late Middle Ages, when the papacy was losing its power and clutching ever more firmly to a waning ideal. But the two-swords theory remained a staple of traditional political theory in Germany. And a good number of strong German bishops and ecclesiastical princes in Luther's day were still making good on its claims in their local polities.[13]

Luther rejected this hierarchical view of government. For Luther, the earthly kingdom featured three natural forms and forums of government: the domestic, ecclesiastical, and political estates—or, in modern terms, the family, the church, and the state. These three institutions stood equal before God, and were each called directly by God to discharge complementary tasks in the earthly kingdom. The family was called to rear and nurture children, to teach and to discipline them, to cultivate and exemplify love and charity within the home and the broader community. The church was called to preach the word, to administer the sacraments, to discipline their wayward members. The state was called to protect peace, punish crime, promote the common good, and to support the church, family, and other institutions derived from them.

Not only were these three estates equal, rather than hierarchical, in authority, status, and responsibility, Luther argued. Only the state had *legal* authority—the authority of the sword to pass and enforce positive laws for the governance of the earthly kingdom. Contrary to the two-swords theory, Luther emphasized that the church was not a law-making authority. The church had no sword. It had no jurisdiction. It had no business involving itself in the day-to-day administration of law or in the vesting of magistrates in their offices. The church's ministry and mission lay elsewhere. To be sure, each local church needed internal rules of order and discipline to govern its members and officers, and external legal structures to protect its polity and property. But it was up to the local magistrate to pass and enforce these ecclesiastical laws, in consultation and cooperation with the local clergy and theologians. And, to be sure, church officers and theologians had to be vigilant in preaching and teaching the law of God to magistrates and subjects alike, and in pronouncing prophetically against injustice, abuse, and tyranny. But formal legal authority lay with the state, not with the church.[14]

Luther was more concerned with the function than with the form of the state. He had, at first, hoped that the emperor would endorse the Reformation, and accordingly included in his early writings some lofty panegyrics on the imperial authorities of the Holy Roman Empire of his day and of the Christian Roman Empire of a millennium before. When the emperor failed him, Luther turned at various times to the nobility, the peasantry, the city councils, and the princes, and in turn wrote favorably about each of them, and then sometimes unfavorably when they failed him.[15] Such writings must be read in their immediate political context, however, and not used to paint Luther as a theorist of political absolutism, or elitist oligarchy, or constitutional democracy. Luther had no firm or consistent theory of the forms of political office. He did not sort out systematically the relative virtues and vices of monarchy, aristocracy, or democracy. He spent very little time on the thorny constitutional questions of the nature and purpose of executive, legislative, and judicial powers, let alone finer questions of checks and balances, conflict of laws, judicial review, and other such topics that occupied other sixteenth-century Protestant and humanist writers. These were not Luther's primary concern.

Luther was more concerned with the general status and function of the political office—both before God and within the community. On the one hand, Luther believed, the magistrate was God's vice-regent in the earthly kingdom, called to elaborate and enforce God's Word and will, to reflect God's justice and judgment on earthly citizens. The magistracy was, in this sense, a "divine office," a "holy estate," a "Godly calling," within the earthly kingdom. Indeed, the magistrate was a "god" on earth, as Psalm 82:6 put it, to be obeyed as if God himself. "Law and earthly government are a great gift of God to mankind," Luther wrote with ample flourish. "Earthly authority is an image, shadow, and figure of the dominion of Christ." Indeed, "a pious jurist" who served faithfully in the Christian magistrate's retinue is "a prophet, priest, angel, and savior . . . in the earthly kingdom."[16] The magistrate and his retinue not only represented God's authority and majesty, however. They also exercised God's judgment and wrath against human sin. "Princes and magistrates are the bows and arrows of God," Luther wrote, equipped to hunt down God's enemies in the earthly kingdom. The hand of the Christian magistrate, judge, or soldier "that wields the sword and slays is not man's hand, but God's; and it is not man, but God, who hangs, tortures, beheads, slays, and fights. All these are God's works and judgments."[17]

On the other hand, Luther believed, the magistrate was the "father of the community" (*Landesvater, paterpoliticus*). He was to care for his political subjects as if they were his children, and his political subjects were to "honor" him as if he were their parent. This was the essence of the proper authority, *Obrigkeit* or *ordo politicus*, of the political authorities and their subjects that constitute "the state." Like a loving father, the magistrate was to keep the peace and to protect his subjects from threats or violations to their persons, properties, and reputations. He was to deter his subjects from abusing themselves through drunkenness, sumptuousness, prostitution, gambling, and other vices. He was to nurture and sustain his subjects through the community chest, the public almshouse, the state-run hospice. He was to educate them through the public school, the public library, the public lectern. He was to see to their spiritual needs by supporting the ministry of the locally established church, and encouraging their attendance and participation through the laws of Sabbath observance, tithing, and holy days. He was to see to their material needs by reforming inheritance and property laws to ensure more even distribution of the parents' property among all children. He was to set an example of virtue, piety, love, and charity in his own home and private life for his faithful subjects to emulate and to respect. The Christian magistrate was to complement and support the God-given responsibilities of parents and family members for their children and dependents, without intruding on the paternal office. And he was to support the preaching and sacramental life of the local church without trespassing on the ecclesiastical office, let alone that of the invisible church of the heavenly kingdom.[18]

These twin metaphors of the Christian magistrate—as the lofty vice-regent of God and as the loving father of the community—described the basics of Luther's and, later, Lutheran political theory. For Luther, political authority was divine in origin but earthly in operation. It expressed God's harsh judgment against sin but also his tender mercy for sinners. It communicated the law of God but also the lore of the local community. It depended upon the church for prophetic direction, but it took over from the church all jurisdiction—governance of marriage, education, poor relief and other earthly subjects traditionally governed by the Catholic Church's canon law. Either metaphor standing alone could be a recipe for abusive tyranny or officious paternalism; but both metaphors together provided Luther and his followers with the core ingredients of a robust Christian republicanism and budding Christian welfare state.

Legal Reforms

Luther's two-kingdoms theory effectively "flattened" the traditional hierarchical theories of being and order, of clergy and laity, of ecclesiastical and political authority. His earthly kingdom was a horizontal realm with each person, each order, and each official called directly by God to discharge discrete offices and vocations. What kept this earthly kingdom and its activities intact, Luther believed, was the law of God, and its elaboration by earthly authorities and subjects.

Luther defined the law of God as the set of norms ordained by God in the creation, written by God on the hearts of all persons, and rewritten by God on the pages of the Bible. Luther called this variously the "law of nature," "natural law," "divine law," "Godly law," "the law of the heart," "the teachings of conscience," "the inner law," among others—terms and concepts that he did not clearly differentiate either from each other or from traditional formulations.[19] His main point was that God's natural law set at creation continued to operate after the fall into sin, and that it provided the foundation for all positive law and public morality in the earthly kingdom.

The natural law defined the basic obligations that a person owed to God, neighbor, and self. The clearest expression of these obligations, for Luther, was the Ten Commandments, which God inscribed on two tables and gave to Moses on Mount Sinai. The First Table of the Decalogue set out basic obligations to honor the Creator God, to respect God's name, to observe the Sabbath, to avoid idolatry and blasphemy. The Second Table set out basic obligations to respect one's neighbor—-to honor authorities, and not to kill, commit adultery, steal, bear false witness, or covet. Luther believed this to be a universal statement of the natural law binding not only on the Jews of the Old Testament but also on everyone. "The Decalogue is not the law of Moses ... but the Decalogue of the whole world, inscribed and engraved in the minds of all men from the foundation of the world." "[W]hoever knows the Ten Commandments perfectly must know all the

Scriptures, so that, in all affairs and cases, he can advise, help, comfort, judge, and decide both spiritual and temporal matters, and is qualified to sit in judgment upon all doctrines, estates, spirits, laws, and whatever else is in the world." And again: "[A]lthough the Decalogue was given in a particular way and place and ceremony . . . all nations acknowledge that there are sins and iniquities."[20]

Knowledge of this natural law comes not only through revealed scripture, Luther argued, but also through natural reason—one of those "masks" by which the hidden God is partly revealed in the earthly kingdom. Luther built on St. Paul's notion that even the heathens have a "law written in their hearts, their conscience also bearing witness" to a natural knowledge of good and evil (Romans 2:15). Every rational person thus "feels" and "knows" the law of God, even if only obliquely. The basic teaching of the natural law "lives and shines in all human reason, and if people would only pay attention to it, what need would they have of books, teachers, or of law? For they carry with them in the recesses of the heart a living book which would tell them more than enough about what they ought to do, judge, accept, and reject."[21]

But sinful persons do not, of their own accord, readily heed the natural law written on their hearts, and rewritten in the Bible. Thus, God has called upon other persons and authorities in the earthly kingdom to elaborate its basic requirements. All Christians, as priests to their peers, must communicate the natural law of God by word and by deed. Parents must teach it to their children and dependents. Preachers must preach it their congregants and catechumens. And magistrates must elaborate and enforce it through their positive laws and public policies.

The magistrate's elaboration and enforcement of the natural law was particularly important, Luther believed, since only the magistrate held formal legal authority in the earthly kingdom. "Natural law is a practical first principle in the realm of public morality," Luther wrote; "it forbids evil and commands good. Positive law is a decision that takes local conditions into account," and "credibly" elaborates the general principles of the natural law into specific precepts to fit these local conditions. "The basis of natural law is God, who has created this light, but the basis of positive law is the earthly authority," the magistrate, who represents God in this earthly kingdom. The magistrate must promulgate and enforce these positive laws by combining faith, reason, and tradition. He must pray to God earnestly for wisdom and instruction. He must maintain "an untrammeled reason" in judging the needs of his people and the advice of his counselors. He must consider the wisdom of the legal tradition—particularly that of Roman law, which Luther called a form of "heathen wisdom." "The polity and the economy" of the earthly kingdom, Luther wrote, "are subject to reason. Reason has first place. There [one finds] civil laws and civil justice."[22]

But both natural law and positive law had to be applied equitably, Luther insisted. "The strictest law [can do] the greatest wrong," he wrote, citing Cicero. Thus, "equity is necessary" in the application of rules of all sorts, whether in the state or the church, in the household or the classroom. Any ruler, whatever his office, "who does not know how to dissemble does not know how to rule," Luther said pithily. "This is what is meant by [doing] equity (*epiekeia*)." To apply a rule equitably, Luther insisted "is not rashly to relax laws and discipline." It is, rather, to balance firmness and fairness and to recognize circumstances that might mitigate against literal application of the rule or that might raise questions that the rule does not and perhaps should not reach. In such instances, "equity will weigh for or against" strict application of the rule, and a wise ruler will know the juster course. "But the weighing must be of such kind that the law is not undermined, for no undermining of natural law and divine law must be allowed."[23]

Reforms of Marriage and Education

Luther and his followers worked to reform not only church and state but also marriage and the family, one of his three natural estates.[24] Prior to the sixteenth century, marriage was regarded as a sacrament of the church. It was formed by the mutual consent of a fit man and a fit woman in good religious standing. It symbolized the enduring union of Christ and his church, and conferred sanctifying grace upon the couple and their children. The parties could form this union in private, but once properly formed it was an indissoluble bond broken only by the death of one of the parties.

As a sacrament, marriage was subject to the jurisdiction of the medieval church. A complex network of canon laws governed sex, marriage, and family life in detail, from abortion to euthanasia. The church did not regard the family as its most exalted estate, however. Although a sacrament and a sound way of Christian living, marriage (and with it, family life) was not considered to be spiritually edifying. Marriage was a remedy

for sin, not a recipe for righteousness. Marriage was considered subordinate to celibacy. Clerics and monastics were required to forgo marriage as
a condition for ecclesiastical service. Those who could not were not worthy
of the church's holy orders and offices.

Lutheran theologians treated marriage, not as a sacrament of the heavenly kingdom, but as a social estate of the earthly kingdom. Marriage,
they taught, was a natural institution that served the goods of mutual
love and support of husband and wife, mutual procreation and nurture
of children, and mutual protection of both spouses from sexual sin. All
adult persons, preachers and others alike, should pursue the calling of
marriage, for all were in need of the comforts of marital love and of the
protection from sexual sin. Moreover, the marital household served as a
model of authority, charity, and pedagogy in the earthly kingdom and as a
vital instrument for the reform of church, state, and civil society. Parents
served as "bishops" to their children. Siblings served as priests to each
other. The household altogether was a source of evangelical and charitable
impulses in society.

Though divinely created and spiritually edifying, however, marriage
remained a social estate of the earthly kingdom. All parties could partake
of this institution, regardless of their faith or lack of it. Though guided
by biblical norms and clerical counseling, marriage and family life were
subject to the rule of the state, not the church. Civil magistrates were to
set the laws for marriage formation, maintenance, and dissolution; child
custody, care, and control; family property, inheritance, and commerce
and more.

Lutheran magistrates rapidly translated this new Protestant gospel of
marriage into civil law. They passed new civil marriage laws that shifted
marital jurisdiction from the church to the state. They strongly encouraged the marriage of clergy, discouraged celibacy, and prohibited monasticism. They denied the sacramentality of marriage and the religious tests
and spiritual impediments traditionally imposed on prospective marital
couples. They simplified the doctrine of consent to betrothal and marriage, and required the participation of parents, peers, priests, and political officials in the process of marriage formation and dissolution. They
sharply curtailed the number of impediments to marriage. And they introduced absolute divorce on proof of adultery, desertion, and other faults,
with a subsequent right to remarriage at least for the innocent party.

The Lutheran reformers soon extended their reforms to schools, which
Luther called little churches, little states, and little families at once.[25] Prior

to the sixteenth century, schools were dominated by the church. The medieval church had established a refined system of religious education for Germany and beyond. Cathedrals, monasteries, chantries, ecclesiastical guilds, and large parishes offered the principal forms of lower education, governed by general and local canon law rules of the church. Gifted graduates were sent on to church-licensed universities for advanced training in the core faculties of law, theology, and medicine. The vast majority of students, however, were trained for clerical and other forms of service in the church.

The Lutheran Reformation transformed this church-based school system into a new system of public schools that allowed each youngster to prepare for his or her own distinctive Christian calling. In the reformers' view, the magistrate, as "father of the community," was primarily responsible for the schooling of his political "children." Education was to be mandatory for boys and girls alike. It was to be fiscally and physically accessible to all. It was to be marked by both formal classroom instruction and civic education through community libraries, lectures, and other media. The curriculum was to combine biblical and evangelical values with humanistic and vocational training. Students were to be stratified into different classes, according to age and ability, and slowly selected for any number of vocations. The public school was to be, in Philip Melanchthon's famous phrase, the "civic seminary" [26] of the commonwealth designed to combine deep faith and deep learning. As the Reformation unfolded in Germany, the local Protestant magistrate replaced the local Catholic bishop as the chief protector and cultivator of the public school and university. The state's civil law replaced the church's canon law as the chief law governing education. The Bible replaced the scholastic text as the chief handbook of the curriculum. German replaced Latin as the universal tongue of the educated classes in Germany. The general callings of all Christians replaced the special calling of the clergy as the essence of education.

The Cultural and Legal Legacy of the Lutheran Reformation

Nearly half a millennium after it first broke out in the little town of Wittenberg, the Lutheran Reformation still exerts influence on Western theology, law, and culture. It is worth recounting the familiar but fundamental changes to German spiritual life born of the Reformation. The

Lutheran Reformation radically resystematized dogma. It truncated the sacraments. It revamped spiritual symbolism. It vernacularized the Bible and the worship service. It transformed corporate worship and congregational music. It gave new emphasis to the pulpit and the sermon. It expanded catechesis and religious instruction. It truncated clerical privileges and church properties. It dissolved ecclesiastical foundations and endowments. It outlawed pilgrimages and the cult of religious artifacts. It rejected the veneration of non-biblical saints and the cult of the dead. It outlawed the payment of indulgences and mortuaries. It discouraged religious pilgrimages. It reduced the number of holy days. It lightened spiritual rules of diet and dress. It reformed ecclesiastical discipline and church administration, and much more. A leaner, cleaner, more participatory, and more egalitarian church emerged as a consequence.

This theological transformation is one of Germany's enduring legacies to the world. Lutheran and other churches around the world still hold firmly to many of the cardinal theological teachings of the Lutheran Reformation, and the great Lutheran catechisms, confessions, and creeds forged in the Reformation era ring with as much power for many Christians today as they did for Lutherans in the 1520s and '30s. The hymns that Luther crafted still lift the rafters of many modern Protestant worship services. The art and woodcuts that Luther inspired still bring gasps to many modern museum visitors. The Lutheran masterpieces of Johann Sebastian Bach and his sons are, many feel, preludes to the music of heaven. The timeless language and phrases of Luther's German Bible and German Mass capture the imagination of a modern German as much as the magisterial language of the King James Bible and the *Book of Common Prayer* captures the imagination of a modern English speaker.

Much of our modern Western law and politics still bears the unmistakable marks of the Lutheran Reformation. Today in every Western legal system and well beyond, we protect the freedom of conscience, for which Luther risked his life. And we have placed his original understandings of religious freedom, human dignity, liberty, and equality at the cornerstones of our constitutional orders.

Today, in most Western legal systems, marriage is still viewed as both a civil and a spiritual institution, as Luther taught, whose formation and dissolution require special legal procedures. Parents must still consent to the marriages of their minor children. Peers must still attest to the veracity of the marital oath. Pastors or political officials must still confirm the marital union, if not consecrate it. Divorce and annulment still require a special public proceeding before a tribunal, with proof of support for dependent spouses and children.

Today, in most Western legal systems, basic education remains a fundamental right of the citizen to procure and a fundamental duty of the state to provide. Literacy and learning are still considered a prerequisite for individual flourishing and communal participation. Society still places a heavy burden on those who shirk education voluntarily. The state is still the essential monitor of civil education, which task it discharges directly through its own public or common schools, or indirectly through its accreditation and supervision of private schools.

Today, in most Western legal systems, care for the poor and needy remains an essential office of the state and an essential concern of the citizen. The rise of the modern Western welfare state over the past century is in no small measure a new institutional expression of the Lutheran ideal of the magistrate as the father of the community called to care for all his political children. The concurrent rise of the modern philanthropic citizen is, in no small measure, a modern institutional expression of Luther's ideal of the priesthood of all believers, each called to give loving service to neighbors. Sixteenth-century Lutherans and twenty-first-century Westerners seem to share the assumption that the state has a role to play not only in fighting wars, punishing crime, and keeping peace but also in providing education and welfare, fostering charity and morality, facilitating worship and piety. They also seem to share the assumption that law has not only a basic use of coercing citizens to accept a morality of duty but also a higher use of inducing citizens to pursue a morality of aspiration.

Much of our modern Western struggle with law, however, is also part of the legal legacy of the Lutheran Reformation. For example, the Lutheran reformers removed the church as the spiritual ruler of Germany in expression of their founding ideals of religious liberty. But they ultimately anointed the state as the new spiritual ruler of Germany in expression of their new doctrines of Christian republicanism. Ever since, Germany and other Protestant nations have been locked in a bitter legal struggle to come to grips with the legacy of state establishments of religion while also allowing religious freedom for all.

The Lutheran reformers removed the pope who, in their view, impugned the Christian conscience, fleeced the sheep of Christendom, and reduced the German people to quivering obedience for fear of their eternal life. But the reformers ultimately anointed the secular prince as the new vice-regent of God on earth, the *summus episcopus*, with too few constitutional safeguards against his tyrannical excesses and too few intellectual resources to support civil disobedience, let alone political revolt.

The Lutheran reformers removed clerics as mediators between God and the laity, in expression of St. Peter's teaching of the priesthood of all believers. But they ultimately interposed husbands between God and their wives, in expression of St. Paul's teaching of male headship within the home. The Lutheran reformers outlawed monasteries and cloisters. But these reforms also ended the vocations of many single women, placing a new premium on the vocation of marriage. Ever since, Protestant women have been locked in a bitter legal struggle to gain fundamental equality both within the marital household and without—-a struggle that continues in more conservative Protestant communities today.

Luther's legal legacy, therefore, should be neither unduly romanticized nor unduly condemned. Those who champion Luther as the father of liberty, equality, and fraternity might do well to remember his ample penchant for elitism, statism, and chauvinism. Those who see the reformers only as belligerent allies of repression and abuse should recognize that they were also benevolent agents of education and welfare. Prone as he was to dialectical reasoning, and aware as he was of the inherent virtues and vices of human achievements, Luther would likely have reached a comparable assessment.

Such circumspection becomes doubly imperative in drawing connections between sixteenth-century Lutheranism and twentieth-century Nazism. It may be tempting to follow no small number of scholars who have drawn direct and easy lines from Luther to Hitler, from Luther's 1543 sermon *On The Jews and Their Lies* to Hitler's slaughter of the Jews in the ghettoes and the death camps. Such unfathomable tragedies as the Holocaust demand villains to render them a bit more understandable, and so giant a German personality as Luther is a natural and easy target to single out.[27]

But we need remind ourselves of elementary facts and elementary law before drawing this indictment. The elementary facts are that Luther's late-life railings against the Jews were quite in contrast to his earlier solicitude for the Jews, and quite in keeping with a millennium and more of vicious anti-Judaism and anti-Semitism in the Christian tradition. Luther certainly added his ample share of vitriol to this Christian tradition of anti-Semitism, and for that he deserves ample condemnation—doubly so, given that he knew his words would inspire his followers. But Luther's words were not as harsh as those of many other Protestant, Catholic, and Orthodox Christians before and after him who condemned the Jews and called for all manner of savage abuses against them. And Luther did not act on his words in a way that many Christians before him had done, and after him would do in their many campaigns of persecution, ghettoization, ostracism, and plain slaughter of the Jews.

To connect Luther to the horrors of the Holocaust is not only to strain elementary facts but also to strain elementary law. The criminal law of homicide in most Western jurisdictions provides that a defendant can be indicted for homicide only if the victim dies of within a year and a day of that defendant's actions. This rule sometimes produces outrageous decisions at the margins—when victims dies on day 367 or shortly thereafter, or when defendants glory in their escape from liability by the mere accident of chronology. But the point of having this clear rule about causation is for a community to have closure. Nearly four hundred years elapsed between Luther's horrible sermon and the Nazis' horrible actions.

Moreover, an indictment for homicide depends on proof of a clear causal chain between the defendant's culpable action and the victim's ultimate death. The defendant's action must be the cause-in-fact of the victim's death—an action without which the death would not have occurred. The defendant's conduct must also be the proximate cause of the victim's death—close enough in time, space, and foreseeability, without intervening conduct by third parties. It is unquestionable that Luther's late-life railings against the Jews were a link in the chain of causation that ultimately brought on the Holocaust. But it was but one link in a causal chain of many thousands of links, and was far removed in time, space, and foreseeability from the actual horrors of the Holocaust.

I do not pass this judgment lightly. My family suffered massive losses during the Nazi occupation of the Netherlands, and my parents, aunts, and uncles still carry deep scars on their bodies, minds, and souls from the savagery, fear, and deprivation that were visited on them in those long years of occupation. Perhaps the causal period for genocide, unlike that for homicide, should be infinite, not limited to a year and a day. Perhaps long chains of causation should be used to hang in memory, not to exonerate in casuistry, all those Christian hate mongers against the Jews, however distant in time and cause from the actual events of the Holocaust. Perhaps the counsel of emotion is better than the counsel of law to deal with so evil a tragedy. Perhaps so. But for all his rhetorical braggadocio, I think Luther would have been as horrified as any of us to see what the Holocaust had wrought. In the hundred-plus thick volumes of his writings, there is precious little to indicate he would have condoned diabolical savagery of this proportion.

Luther did know political evil in his day, albeit nothing on the scale of the Holocaust. Indeed, it was in response to that evil that he crafted his greatest hymn, "A Mighty Fortress Is Our God." His words in this hymn capture many of the convictions at the core of his dialectical theology: the contrasts between Satan and Christ, body and soul, works and faith, folly and truth, despair and hope, death and life, the mortality of the earthly kingdom and the eternity of the heavenly kingdom. They also capture Luther's abiding faith that God and his Word ultimately remain in charge of both kingdoms, even if the devil and his human minions temporally vie for power in the earthly kingdom. This hymn is perhaps the best response to Luther's own failings and to the failings of countless Protestants after him. So, it will get the last word.

> A mighty Fortress is our God,
> A Bulwark never failing;
> Our Helper he amid the flood
> Of mortal ills prevailing:
> For still our ancient foe
> Doth seek to work us woe;
> His craft and power are great,
> And, armed with cruel hate,
> On earth is not his equal.

> Did we in our own strength confide,
> Our striving would be losing;
> Were not the right man on our side,
> The man of God's own choosing:
> Dost ask who that may be?
> Christ Jesus, it is he;
> Lord Sabaoth his Name,
> From age to age the same,
> And he must win the battle.

> And though this world, with devils filled,
> Should threaten to undo us;
> We will not fear, for God hath willed

His truth to triumph through us:
The prince of darkness grim,
We tremble not for him;
His rage we can endure,
For lo! his doom is sure,
One little word shall fell him.

That word above all earthly powers,
No thanks to them, abideth;
The Spirit and the gifts are ours
Through him who with us sideth:
Let goods and kindred go,
This mortal life also;
The body they may kill:
God's truth abideth still,
His kingdom is for ever.

Notes

1. Jaroslav Pelikan and Hartmut T. Lehmann, eds., *Luther's Works* (hereafter *LW*) (Philadelphia: Fortress Press, 1955–86), 48:186–92.

2. Scott Hendrix, *Luther and the Papacy: Stages in the Reformation Conflict* (Philadelphia: Fortress Press, 1981); Martin Brecht, *Martin Luther*, trans. James L. Schaaf (Philadelphia/Minneapolis: Fortress Press, 1985–93), 78–80.

3. Carl Mirbt, ed., *Quellen zur Geschichte des Papsttums und des römischen Katholizimus*, 2d ed. (Tübingen/Leipzig: Paul Siebeck, 1911), 183–85.

4. See Martin Luther, *Freedom of a Christian* (1520), in *LW* 31:327–77.

5. Jaroslav Pelikan, *Spirit versus Structure: Luther and the Institutions of the Church* (New York: Harper & Row, 1968), 5.

6. *LW* 36:70; *LW* 44:203–04; *WA TR* 3, no. 2809b, no. 2837, no. 3027; *WA* 49:302.

7. John Witte Jr., Law and Protestantism: The Legal Teachings of the Lutheran Reformation (Cambridge, UK: Cambridge University Press, 2002), 87–118.

8. See Arthur Lovejoy, *The Great Chain of Being: A Study of the History of an Idea* (Cambridge, MA: Harvard University Press, 1936). On the legal and ecclesiological implications of this ontology, see Brian Tierney, *Religion, Law, and the Growth of Constitutional Thought: 1150–1650* (Cambridge: Cambridge University Press, 1982), 8ff.

9. *LW* 1:66ff., 52; *LW* 52:57, 79; *WA* 7:73; *LW* 33:295ff.; *WA TR* 1, no. 71; *LW* 54:71; *LW* 26:94–96; *LW* 14:114; *LW* 24:67; *LW* 26:95–96; *WA* 31/1:437; *WA* 40/3:271ff.

10. See detailed sources and discussion in Steven Ozment, *The Reformation in the Cities: The Appeal of Protestantism to Sixteenth-Century Germany and Switzerland* (New Haven, CT: Yale University Press, 1975), 84ff.

11. See detailed sources and discussion in Gustaf Wingren, *The Christian Calling: Luther on Vocation*, trans. Carl C. Rasmussen (Philadelphia: Muhlenberg Press, 1957).

12. *LW* 46:93ff.; *LW* 21:108–15; *LW* 46:93–99.

13. Otto von Gierke, *Political Theories of the Middle Ages*, repr. ed., trans. F. W. Maitland (Cambridge: Cambridge University Press, 1958), 7–21; Ewart Lewis, *Medieval Political Ideas* (New York: Knopf, 1954), 2:506–38.

14. *LW* 45:105ff.; *LW* 36:106ff.

15. See texts in K. Trüdinger, *Luthers Briefe und Gutachten an weltliche Obrigkeit zur Durchfuhrung der Reformation* (Münster: Aschendorff, 1975); J. M. Porter, ed., *Luther—Selected Political Writings* (Philadelphia: Fortress Press, 1974).

16. See Porter, *Luther*, and further texts in *LW* 2:139ff.; *LW* 13:44ff.; *LW* 44:92ff.; *LW* 45:85ff.; *LW* 46:237ff.; *WA* 30/2:554.

17. *LW* 17:171; *LW* 45:113; *LW* 46:95ff.; *WA* 6:267; *WA* 19:626.

18. *LW* 13:44ff.; *LW* 36:106–17; *LW* 45:85–113; *LW* 46:225ff.

19. See the collection of quotations in Hermann W. Beyer, *Luther und das Recht: Gottes Gebot, Naturrecht, Volksgesetz in Luthers Deutung* (Munich: Chr. Kaiser Verlag, 1935); and the detailed analysis in Johannes Heckel, *Lex charitatis: A Juristic Disquisition on Law in the Theology of Martin Luther*, trans. Gottfried Krödel (Grand Rapids, MI: Wm. B. Eerdmans, 2010).

20. *LW* 44:15–114; *WA* 39/1:478, 540; *WA* 18:72; *WA* 30:192.

21. *WA* 17/2:102.

22. *WA TR* 3, no. 3911; *WA* 12:243; *WA* 14:591, 714; *WA* 16:537; *WA* 30/2:557; *WA* 40:305; *WA* 51:211, 241–42; *LW* 45:120–26.

23. *WA TR* 3, no. 4178; *LW* 54:325; *WA TR* 1, no. 315; *LW* 54:43–44; *WA* 14:667ff.; *LW* 46:100.

24. For detailed sources on this topic, see *LP*, 199–256, updated in my *From Sacrament to Contract: Marriage, Religion, and Law in the Western Tradition*, 2nd ed. (Louisville, KY: Westminster John Knox Press, 2012), 113–58.

25. For detailed sources on this topic, see *LP*, 257–92.

26. Robert Stupperich, ed., *Melanchthons Werke in Auswahl* (Gütersloh: C. Bertelsmann, 1951), 3:69.

27. See summary of recent literature in Eric W. Gritsch, *Martin Luther's Anti-Semitism: Against His Better Judgment* (Grand Rapids, MI: Wm. B. Eerdmans, 2012).

3

Redefining the Sacred and the Supernatural

HOW THE PROTESTANT REFORMATION REALLY DID DISENCHANT THE WORLD

Carlos Eire

EVER SINCE MAX Weber proposed that Protestants had caused "the disenchantment of the world"[1] (*Entzauberung der Welt*), this thesis has been the focus of close scrutiny.[2] At issue in this ongoing discussion is the very definition of religion, and how it differs from "magic" (*Zauber*). Also at issue is the question of the role played by Protestantism in the secularization of the West. This chapter has as its central focus that large issue of secularization, not just in reference to Weber's "disenchantment" thesis but also to our present-day understanding of the Protestant Reformation. In particular I will examine in this chapter the concept of "disenchantment" in non-Weberian terms, especially as manifested in some distinguishing characteristics of Protestantism: the redefinition of how "matter" and "spirit" relate to each other, which led to iconoclasm and a new approach to symbols and rituals; and the redefinition of the boundaries between the "natural" and "supernatural" realms, which led to the denial of miracles and mystical ecstasies.

Although we begin with theological and philosophical concepts, this chapter also will consider lived religion and popular piety—that is, the practical, day-to-day changes wrought by the larger shift in thought and belief.

Contemporary Interpretations of
the Protestant Reformation

Secularization.[3] *Confessionalization.*[4] *Social Disciplining.*[5] *Transition to Modernity.*[6] These are the reigning paradigms for understanding the Protestant Reformation in our own day. Whether it is state building, or the emergence of the public sphere, or the triumph of Lent over Carnival, or the revolution of the common man, or any other such entry point into the realm of grand summation, all scholars of the early modern period are stuck with these conceptual formulations—like it or not—that make much more sense to us now than they would have to the very people who are the subject of our studies.

Discerning what differentiates "modern" from "medieval" is an obsession of our times, too.[7] And in this search for boundaries, the concept of secularization looms large, with "medieval" as synonymous with religion, superstition, and mumbo-jumbo and "modern" as the liberation from such nonsense. And in most formulations of the transition from medieval to modern, all changes in religion tend to be seen as wrinkles within some other matrix that is more tangible, as modes of social exchange that flow from deeper material needs. What people *do* rather than what people *believe*: that's the *real* thing, the stuff of history. Religion is an activity: "consecrated behavior," "symbolic behavior," or "social glue."[8] In brief, beliefs, in and of themselves, are never the ultimate or proximate cause of anything.[9]

This is not to say that all such theorizing is necessarily wrong. Not at all. The insight gained through such materialistically inclined perspectives on religion are valuable in and of themselves.[10] But should this be our sole perspective? What if we consider "disenchantment," a concept that takes the innate value of ideas and beliefs very seriously and grants them a causative role, at least in part?

As Max Weber understood matters a century ago, one of the most significant effects of the Protestant Reformation was its reconfiguring of the Western European worldview. Reformation historians have engaged with the legacy of Weber's theorizing for decades,[11] and have disagreed about its value, especially in regard to his concept of "disenchantment." Is there some valuable insight embedded in *Entzauberung*? If one focuses on the German term, and especially the word *Zauber*, which translates as "magic" or "thaumaturgy" in English, it is difficult to conceive of "disenchantment" broadly and easy to think that Protestants were still embedded in a "religio-magical space," just like Catholics, simply because of continuities in ritual. Throw the devil and witchcraft into the mixture, and the similarities seem more intense, simply because Protestants continued to believe in the devil and to persecute witches.[12]

But what if one were to look beyond this troublesome magic/religion dialectic, so central to Weber? Might it be possible to identify some other traits of the Protestant Reformation that reveal it as a genuine rupture in Western history rather than some murky transitional era? Could "disenchantment" have a wider and deeper meaning missed by Weber and his critics that includes magic and superstition, but is not limited by these categories?

What about *desacralization*: a redefinition of the sacred? Not a redrawing of the line between "magic" and "religion" or "superstition" and "religion," as Robert Scribner and many others have seen it but, rather, a fundamental shift in the way in which reality is conceived.[13]

If one turns to the metaphysical concepts championed by Protestants—concepts that were philosophical and theological, but had immense practical ramifications—the Protestant Reformation can be seen as a major cultural shift, and a crucial step in the secularization of the world, as long as the term "secularization" is not understood too narrowly, along lines that confuse it with the current state of church/state relations in the twenty-first-century Western world. Instead, "secularization" should be understood as a process whereby the realm of the sacred was redefined and contained within a more constricted sphere, both privately and publicly. These conceptual shifts just mentioned point more directly to "desacralization" than what we commonly understand as "secularization" in our own day—that is, they manifest a reinterpretation of the *sacred* and its place in human life rather than a redefinition of the magic/religion dialectic or the relation between church and state. These conceptual shifts redefine one of the crucial elements of every civilization: the way in which ontological categories are sorted and reality is conceived.

The fact that these abstract concepts were perceived by Reformation-era Catholics and Protestants as essential markers of the difference between each other is telling.[14] So is the fact that this perceived difference referred to the divine and supernatural, not the demonic and preternatural, or the "religio-magical." As Catholics and Protestants understood it, what divided them was a different understanding of the sacred, not the demonic or magical.

But how, exactly, did this paradigm shift take shape?

First and foremost, the great ontological difference between the physical and spiritual realms upheld by Protestants, especially in the Reformed tradition, drove a wedge between *matter* and *spirit*. Iconoclasm was its initial manifestation, but it extended much further than religious imagery, to other symbols: shrines, relics, the Eucharist, and all rituals. The most extreme version of this reinterpretation of matter and spirit found voice in the Reformed Protestant tradition, and in two of its guiding principles: *Finitum non est capax infiniti* (the finite cannot contain the infinite), and *quantum sensui tribueris tantum spiritui detraxeris* (the physical detracts from the spiritual).

Second, despite the differences among them, Protestants redrew the boundaries between *natural* and *supernatural*, and rejected the commonplace irruptions of the sacred favored in medieval religion. In other words, Protestants largely rejected post-biblical miracles, and especially those practically-oriented supernatural events that historians now classify as *thaumaturgy*. God could work miracles, certainly, and the Bible was full of them, but as Protestants saw it, the age of miracles had passed and God's direct supernatural interventions were a thing of the past, strictly limited to biblical times. What is more, with just a few exceptions among more radical sixteenth-century movements, Protestants denied the possibility of mystical ecstasies, visions, apparitions, revelations, levitations, bilocations, and all other supernatural phenomena associated with intimate encounters between the human and divine.

Relying on the original meaning of the word *secular* (Latin: *saeculum* = "this age" or "earthly time"), one can argue that these changes contributed substantially to the *secularization* of the West by creating societies that were more this-worldly than ever before—societies that rejected the medieval *sub specie aeternitatis* worldview in which human existence and all history had an eternal and supernatural backdrop.[15] In essence, then, this "secularizing" is much more than just a circumscribing of the role of religion in the public sphere. It is a circumscribing of the sacred, and the emergence of a new understanding of reality itself.

These paradigm shifts were much more than a mere change in thinking or in worldview. They also had a profound and immediate impact on the cultural, social, economic, and political structure of Protestant communities—and on Western Europe as a whole.

Matter and Spirit

The Protestant Reformation was a metaphysical and epistemic revolution, a new way of interpreting reality and of approaching the ultimate. To put it in the simplest terms, it redrew the boundaries between heaven and earth, the sacred and the profane.[16]

Ever since the first century, Christians had accepted a binary understanding of the cosmos: God was spirit, and he had created a material world, ontologically related to him, but metaphysically different. Bridging these two essential realms of existence was the role of religion, or, more specifically, of the church and its clergy, and the bridging was effected in myriad ways through rituals and symbols. In sum, the medieval Christian world pulsated with accessibility to the divine, replete as it was with material points of contact with the spiritual realm.[17]

Protestants made matter and spirit much less compatible. The guiding principle of Reformed Protestant metaphysics—and therefore also of their hermeneutic—was the incompatibility of spirit and matter. This principle, in turn, was derived from three assumptions. First, the Reformed Protestant tradition assumed that God was radically transcendent and that the supernatural realm was "wholly other," utterly above and beyond the natural and created order. Ulrich Zwingli argued that the things of earth were "carnal," and that they stood in "enmity against God." He also argued that matter and spirit were as incapable of mixing as fire and water and that "those who trust in any created thing whatsoever are not truly pious."[18] John Calvin was equally adamant: "whatever holds down and confines the senses to the earth is contrary to the covenant of God; in which, inviting us to himself, he permits us to think of nothing but what is spiritual."[19]

Second, Reformed metaphysics proposed that matter is not just incapable of bridging the gap between heaven and earth, but was actually an obstacle. "The more you give to the material," said Zwingli, "the more you take away from the spiritual."[20] John Calvin reasoned similarly: "Whatever holds down and confines the senses to the earth is contrary to the covenant of God; in which, inviting us to Himself, He permits us to think of nothing but what is spiritual."[21]

The Natural and the Supernatural

Redefining the relation between matter and spirit also entailed redrawing the boundaries between the natural and the supernatural. This led Protestants to reject miraculous phenomena and the possibility of merging with God in mystical ecstasy.

In many ways, this second paradigm shift was a desacralization of the world much more intense than that brought about by the Protestant war against idolatry and also more profound than that against those non-Christian practices labeled as "magic" or "superstition." This was the ultimate de-mystification, and a "Copernican revolution" in worldview, even though Weber failed to see it as such.

In the Whiggish view of history, miraculous phenomena and mystical ecstasies are powerful markers of cultural difference, telltale traits of an older, inferior civilization, of the "superstitious" and "magical" culture of the ancient and medieval worlds.[22] Supernatural phenomena are modernity's foil, significant foci for the articulation of the norms of "modernity" itself.[23] And this is not only true of Whiggish history, which sees the Protestant rejection of medieval piety as the first step toward "modernity," but also of postmodern history.[24] Lately, a few historians have emphasized the significance of this redrawing of boundaries.[25]

In their contest for souls, Protestants and Catholics realized very quickly that miracles played a key role in polemics and therefore also in self-definition. Catholics defended the truth of their claims through countless miracles, ancient and contemporary, performed through the agency of sacred sites and objects or by holy men and women. Catholics also argued that the lack of miracles among Protestants proved the falsehood of their teachings beyond a shadow of a doubt. Protestants rejected these claims on several grounds, but especially on these two: that the age of miracles had ceased at the end of the Apostolic age, some time in the first century; and that the miracles claimed by the Catholic Church were either fraudulent or of demonic origin.[26]

Martin Luther was among the first of the Protestant Reformers to reject the possibility of post-biblical miracles, even though he was inclined to emphasize God's absolute power over his creation. Religion was not about miracle seeking, he argued, but about faith and salvation.[27] As he put it, being rescued "from the power of the devil and from eternal death" and being led to "eternal life in heaven . . . far surpasses all outward signs and wonders."[28] Yes, he admitted, the Bible was full of miracle accounts, and especially the Gospels, but Christ and the Apostles had performed these miracles simply to convince unbelievers; miracles, in and of themselves, had no power to arouse faith in those who already believed in Christ. This meant that the miracles recorded in the New Testament had been necessary in their day and age—and only then—to establish Christianity.

> Those visible works are simply signs for the ignorant, unbelieving crowd, and for their sakes that are yet to be attracted; but as for us who know already all we do know, and believe the Gospel, what do we want them for? . . . Wherefore it is no wonder that they have now

ceased since the Gospel has sounded abroad everywhere, and has been preached to those who had not known of God before, whom he had to attract with outward miracles, just as we throw apples and pears to children.[29]

As if this were not enough, Luther added one crowning objection to miraculous claims: the devil could manipulate nature and deceive people. Luther's devil was a prolific and creative artist, capable of thousands of tricks, each a masterpiece of deception. Luther's wonder-working *Tausend-Künstler*[30] could cause people to see or hear the most preposterous things. He could trick hunters into thinking he was a hare, or show up as almost any animal—especially as an ape. Once, Luther found a dog in his bed and flung it out the window, convinced that it was a demon.[31]

Martin Bucer, the Strasbourg reformer, made much of the demonic in his argument against miracles.[32] Arguing against the cult of the saints and the miracles attributed to them, Bucer proposed that it was Satan who worked these "miracles" through his preternatural powers.[33] Bucer's argument would later be picked up and expanded upon by Calvin and also by English Reformers.[34] It is important to stress, however, that this polemically charged Protestant tradition of attributing Catholic miracles to the devil was above all an affirmation of their conviction in the inviolability of natural laws. Nature might be manipulated by Satan, yes, and humans might be easily fooled, but genuine, God-ordained, *supernatural* miracles were restricted to biblical times.

Ulrich Zwingli also argued against miracles, but it would be his French disciple, John Calvin, who would give the Protestant denial of the miraculous its definitive contours. Like Luther before him, Calvin argued that the only function of miracles was to confirm the authority of God's messengers, and that they were restricted to those rare occasions when God had something to reveal. But Calvin also took a metaphysical turn, explicitly stating that the ultimate purpose of all biblical miracles was *not* to alter the fabric of the material natural order, but simply to authenticate revelation.[35] Since Protestants were not revealing anything new, then, it was wrong for Catholics to demand miracles from them. Moreover, Calvin also argued that the countless miracles claimed by the Catholic Church came straight from Hell:

We may also fitly remember that Satan has his miracles, which, though they are deceitful tricks rather than true powers, are such a sort as to mislead the simple-minded and untutored [2 Thes.

2:9–10]. . . . Idolatry has been nourished by wonderful miracles, yet these are not sufficient to sanction the superstition either of magicians or of idolaters.[36]

Satan had no supernatural powers, however; his manipulation of nature was preternatural, a result of his angelic nature, which, while fallen, still granted him an intimate and superhuman knowledge of the laws of nature.[37] This means that scholars in our own day who speak of "magic or "thaumaturgy" without carefully distinguishing between the truly supernatural (the divine) and the merely preternatural (the demonic) fail to take into account a distinction that was immensely significant to those who lived in the Reformation era.

The worldview that Calvin bequeathed to his followers was thus quite naturalistic: only when God decides to break into this world to communicate with humans does he appoint specific instances where the natural, material order is changed.[38] Religion, then, does not seek to change the course of nature, as Catholics claimed but, rather, to understand it as it is: eternally subject to God's will and as always incapable of transmitting any spiritual power in and of itself. To believe otherwise, said Calvin, was to fall into the trap of idolatry.[39]

Although some Protestants continued to believe in natural signs and portents that conveyed messages, such as cloud formations, astronomical and meteorological anomalies, or monstrous births—"wonders" (mirabilia) rather than "miracles" (miraculi)[40]—and even though supernatural miracles eventually worked their way back into Protestant piety in various limited ways during the late seventeenth and eighteenth centuries, Protestantism did much more to disenchant the world through its understanding of miracles than it ever did by its rejection of anything that could be called "magic" or "superstition."

The Mystical Difference

Even more significant, it could be argued, was the disenchantment that Protestants brought to the relationship between human beings and God. Save for a few fringe figures, all Protestants rejected the ultimate goal of medieval Catholic piety and of monasticism in particular: that of mystical union with God.

Purgation, illumination, union—These were the three basic steps in the mystical quest that the Catholic and Eastern Orthodox churches had accepted and elaborated upon since the second century of the Christian era. Becoming ever purer and more God-like, even to the point of experiencing supernatural encounters with him in this life was the goal of monasticism, ostensibly, and the promise held out to every potential saint. This quest and its attending experiences were based precisely on those core metaphysical assumptions that Protestants discarded, especially concerning matter and spirit, the natural and the supernatural, and the human and the divine. In other words, the claims made by Catholic and Orthodox mystics reified their soteriology. Salvation was something to be lived out; theology, belief, and practice were all of one piece. And the most significant manifestation of this mentality was monasticism, a penitential and contemplative way of life discarded by Protestants as useless and without biblical warrant.

The Protestant rejection of monasticism, based as it was on a very different understanding of human nature, is a clear example of massive social change effected by theology: it was not only the largest redistribution of property in Western history before the Bolsheviks came along, but also a social and economic revolution. Suddenly, an entire social class was abolished, along with their sizable assets. In addition, on both the material and conceptual level, a way of life that focused intensely on *other-worldliness* was extinguished. The "disenchanting" or secularizing impact of the extinction of monasticism seems obvious enough, and needs little elaboration. The impact of the rejection of mysticism—the main goal of monasticism—is harder to discern, but no less significant.

Those men and women who reached the pinnacle of holiness were considered living proof of the divinization of matter. They not only conversed with Christ and the Virgin Mary, but had ineffable encounters with the Godhead; they swooned in rapture, went into trances, levitated, bilocated, read minds, prophesied, manifested the wounds of Christ on their bodies, and healed the sick and lame. Once they died, their corpses could emit a wonderful aroma and remain intact.[41]

All this was rejected by Protestants, save, again, for a handful of radicals.[42] Even Martin Luther, who was influenced by the mystics Tauler and Suso, could not abide the ultimate claims made by medieval ecstatics.[43] Luther came to despise all who claimed direct contact with the divine as *Schwärmer*—that is, as unhinged fanatics. John Calvin recoiled in horror at the thought that humans might claim any sort of divinization, for his God was "entirely other" and "as different from flesh as fire is from water."[44] Though he sometimes quoted the twelfth-century mystic Bernard

of Clairvaux, Calvin had no place in his theology for the Catholic tradition
of *unio mystica*, or for its raptures, trances, visions, and miracles.[45] Such
a crossing of boundaries was impossible, argued Calvin, for the human
soul "is not only burdened with vices, but is utterly devoid of all good."[46]

The significance of this radical desacralization can be best appreciated
by contemplating how Catholics responded to it. The sixteenth and seventeenth centuries were a golden age for mysticism, during which the miraculous physical phenomena associated with mystical ecstasy became more
pronounced than ever before among Catholics.[47] And few other Catholic
mystics serve as a better contrasting backdrop than Joseph of Cupertino
(1603–1663) and María de Jesús de Ágreda (1602–1665). Their profiles
with respect to miracles will highlight the "supernatural gulf" separating
Catholics from Protestants. If Protestants sought to curtail or extinguish
mystical encounters, Catholics sought them out ever more eagerly.

Saint Joseph of Cupertino and Venerable Maria de Ágreda

Joseph of Cupertino, beatified in 1753 and canonized in 1767, was a
Franciscan friar from Italy who gained renown in his own day for his
frequent ecstasies and levitations. Friar Joseph was believed to have not
only hovered a few feet off the ground repeatedly, in full view of many witnesses, but also to have risen dozens of feet into the air on many occasions
and to have flown great distances. One time, when he reportedly flew from
one end to the other of the enormous basilica of Saint Francis in Assisi,
his miraculous aerobatics were credited with converting a Lutheran prince
from Saxony into a Catholic.[48]

As outrageous as the miracles of Saint Joseph may seem, they pale in
comparison to those of Sor María de Jesús de Ágreda, a Spanish nun who
was raised to the rank of "Venerable" less than ten years after her death in
1665. Sor Maria pushed miraculous claims to new limits. As if levitating
frequently were not enough, she claimed to have visited America through
mystical trances, and to have preached the gospel to the natives in New
Mexico. Eyewitness reports of her visits to America seemed to confirm this
extreme bilocation as fact, even to the point of convincing the Inquisition
and the king of Spain. Sor María also claimed that she had been visited
by the Virgin Mary repeatedly, and that the Mother of God had dictated
her autobiography to her. This enormous book—over two thousand pages

long—related intimate details about the Virgin Mary's childhood, her life with Joseph and Jesus, and her work with the Apostles after Jesus's death and resurrection.[49] News of her miraculous feats reached King Philip IV, who ended up relying on her as a spiritual adviser through hundreds of intimate letters.[50]

If we examine the details of these claims closely, it becomes apparent that we are dealing with a conception of reality and of divine-human interaction worlds apart from that experienced by Protestants.

When María was fifteen, her whole family left "the world" to enter Catholic religious life. Her father, then in his early fifties, and her two young brothers joined the Franciscan order and moved to Burgos. María, her mother, and her sister established a Franciscan nunnery in their own house through the Order of the Immaculate Conception, and were joined by three nuns from Burgos. Ten years later, when she was only twenty-five, despite many reservations on her part, she was named abbess, a post she would serve for the rest of her life, save for a three-year sabbatical.

Sor Maria began to experience frequent and prolonged ecstasies and levitations in 1620 in the presence of the other nuns, and soon afterwards these trances (*arrobamientos*) were open to the public. During these ecstasies, Maria claimed to visit the New World, where she instructed some primitive nomads in the basic tenets of the Catholic faith. The details of these transatlantic bilocations, most of which ostensibly took place between 1620 and 1623, were made known by Maria to her confessors and also to her sisters in the convent. Though the confessors were sworn to secrecy, the nuns were not, and tales of her adventures in New Spain began to circulate, especially in Franciscan circles. These tales would reach Mexico soon enough, where the Franciscans were very active in mission work.

Franciscan superiors in Mexico began an investigation in 1629, at their mission of San Antonio the Isleta Pueblo on the Río Grande, in central New Mexico. The Franciscan in charge of that mission, Fray Alonso de Benavides, received a delegation of relief missionaries from Mexico on July 22, 1629. The delegation carried a letter from the archbishop of Mexico City, in which he related the claims being made by the nun at Ágreda. Benavides was stunned, for his mission had been receiving requests for baptism from the Jumano tribe since 1620. Although they claimed that they had been instructed to ask for this sacrament by a "Lady in Blue" who repeatedly visited and evangelized them, Benavides had been reluctant to believe them.

Immediately, Benavides sent three missionaries to the Jumano lands, along with the fifty Jumanos who were then encamped at the mission, asking for baptism. The missionaries made inquiries at the tribal lands, baptized the natives, and returned with a full report, detailing the activities of the so-called Lady in Blue.

Benavides would eventually sail back to Spain and interview Sor Maria in person at Ágreda in 1631. His full report, which was sent to his Franciscan superiors and to King Philip IV, eventually drew the attention of the Inquisition. In 1635, the Holy Office opened an investigation, which led to no charges and no conclusions about the bilocation. In 1650, owing to intrigues at the royal court that involved Sor Maria's name in a plot against the king, the Inquisition would reopen the case. Again, Sor Maria was cleared. Fray Antonio Gonzalo de Moral, the examiner (*calificador*) for the case, wrote:

> I recognize in her much virtue deeply rooted in charity, and a great intelligence of the Sacred Scriptures. It appears to me that she has acquired more through continual prayer and interior surrender with God than many accomplish with study and great exterior work.... I say that she is a good Catholic and faithful Christian, well-versed in our holy faith. She embroidered no fiction into her accounts, nor was she deluded by the devil.[51]

In other words, although the Inquisition refrained from affirming that her bilocations had actually happened, it deemed them perfectly possible and pronounced Sor Maria not only above reproach but far ahead in her knowledge of divine realities than most erudite university theologians.

As if claiming hundreds of bilocations across a wide ocean and writing hundreds of letters to the king was not audacious enough, Sor Maria dared to claim an intimate relationship with the Mother of God and to assume the mantle of a heavenly scribe, not much different from that of the four evangelists. Even more audacious, she dared to write a history of salvation that was nearly a million words in length—fourteen times longer than the four canonical gospels combined (roughly 1 million words versus 64,427).

So much for the Protestant principle of *sola scriptura*! That so many details not found in the gospels could be revealed directly to Sor Maria— including the exact number of angels who escorted the Virgin Mary

during every major event in her life and the exact wording of a letter written by the Virgin Mary to Saint Peter in the year A.D. 49—was not just
unthinkable and unnerving for her Protestant contemporaries, but down-
right blasphemous, even demonic.

Among her Catholic superiors in Spain, Sor Maria's claims caused
something of a stir and no small measure of controversy, but eventually
she gained the approval of many influential theologians and churchmen.

Sor Maria began to write her "Divine History of the Mother of God" in
1637, shortly before she was elected abbess. She did so in obedience to the
command of her confessor, with uncommon zeal, writing 400 pages in
the first twenty days. The writing was inseparable from her mystical experiences: the Virgin Mary spoke, and Sor Maria transcribed. Publication
was not the immediate objective. This was a risky venture in a land where
the Inquisition kept a close eye on anyone who might be in league with
the devil or "inventing the sacred," as the Holy Office preferred to call the
malicious business of fraudulent mysticism.

By 1643, when she started her letter-writing relationship with King
Philip IV, Sor Maria had finished the work. It was unlike anything ever
written by any Christian since the first century, either male or female, and
in the very tight monastic circles in which it was read, it caused as much
consternation as excitement.

It is not surprising, then, that in 1645, when she was assigned a new
confessor, she was ordered to destroy the entire manuscript. It is also not
surprising that Sor Maria obeyed, tossing the work into the flames along
with many other writings of hers. One copy survived, however. It had
been sent to King Philip IV, and no one who knew of its existence dared to
ask for its destruction. That copy would remain in the king's hands until
his death, out of everyone's reach, including Sor Maria's.

For ten years after this event, Sor Maria pressed on, living her life as
if she had never written an earth-shaking sacred text, balancing her ec-
static trances with her duties as abbess, and enduring that brief second
encounter with the Inquisition in 1650, which found her guilty of nothing.
After a well-deserved but all too brief sabbatical, during which she sought
to deepen her mystical life, she was re-elected as abbess in 1655 and assigned a new confessor, Andrés de Fuenmayor, who immediately ordered
her to rewrite her biography of the Virgin Mary.

Obedient Sor Maria immediately put quill pen to paper and wrote fe-
verishly for the next five years, in part from memory—simply rewriting
what she had burned—and in part from her constant encounters with the

Virgin Mary, which, according to her, had intensified substantially. On May 6, 1660, she finished writing it.

During the final five years of Sor Maria's life, this monumental second version of the life of the Virgin Mary—all million words of it—began to make the rounds within learned theological circles, Franciscan and non-Franciscan. Five years after her death, in 1670, Sor Maria's otherworldly *magnum opus* was published in Madrid, with the baroque title "The Mystical City of God, Miracle of his Omnipotence, and Mystery of his Grace, Divine History and Life of the Virgin Mother of God, Our Queen and Lady, the Most Holy, Restorer of Eve's Fault and Mediatrix of Grace."[52]

The premise of the book is an affront to Protestant ontology, metaphysics, and theology. Sor Maria declares at the outset that God gave her at first six angels to guide her, and then eight, who purified her and led her into the presence of God. She then beheld the Blessed Virgin, as she is described in the Apocalypse, and was able to see all the stages of her life, from conception to her assumption in heaven. While Sor Maria in no way contradicts the four Gospels, and in fact employs them as the basic structure of much of her narrative, she does claim that the Virgin Mary has revealed many details not contained in them. Many of these details do concern the life of Jesus and the Apostles, but the vast majority of them concern the Virgin Mary herself. Moreover, the main thrust of the narrative is the proclamation of the Virgin Mary's intense and indispensable role in salvation history. In brief, the revelations contained in the 2,800 pages of "The Mystical City of God" could be summed up in one proposition: "The Virgin Mary is co-redemptrix of the human race." Another way of saying it: "No Mary, no salvation."

The book as a whole is riddled with paradoxical claims, and its very structure is determined by the coincidence of opposites and the assumption that crossing the line between the natural and supernatural is eminently possible. This is a new revelation that is not equal to the Gospels but supersedes them; the Virgin Mary is fully human, but substantially different from all other humans, even quasi-divine; the Virgin Mary is not equal to Jesus Christ, but is just as indispensable for salvation; Sor Maria is a sinner and a "vile worm," but she is capable of encountering God and the entire heavenly court and of apprehending the deepest mysteries of existence.

Its focus is historical, but its intent is quasi-apocalyptic: the reason the distant past is being revealed for the first time is that the world is now worse than it was before the Incarnation of Christ, and a new remedy is necessary. "For now the hour has come and the opportune time to let men know the just cause of my anger," says God to Sor Maria, "and they are now justly charged and convinced of their guilt."[53] The remedy proposed by God is not turning to Christ or paying closer attention to the Gospels—as Protestants would expect to hear—but turning to the Virgin Mary and relying more intensely on her intercession. Quoting God the Father directly, Sor Maria writes: "I desire to make known to mortals how much intercession of Her is worth, who brought restoration of life by giving mortal existence to the immortal God."[54]

Sor Maria's message is at once historical and ahistorical. A post-Renaissance woman who obviously had received a good education, and shows ample acquaintance with the Bible, some of the church fathers, some scholastic theology, and a fair amount of early church history, Sor Maria knows that it is essential to set her revelations in historical perspective. But she does so by denying one of the central tenets of the Renaissance and the Protestant Reformation: the privileging of the New Testament and the Apostolic Age. That was a special time, she admits, but so is her day and age. Revelation is not limited to the Bible or the early church. God speaks, and Sor Maria quotes Him:

> I have not revealed these mysteries in the primitive Church because they are so great, that the faithful would have been lost in the contemplation and admiration of them at a time when it was more necessary to establish firmly the law of grace and of the Gospel. Although all mysteries of religion are in perfect harmony with each other, yet human ignorance might have suffered recoil and doubt at their magnitude, when faith in the Incarnation and Redemption and the precepts of the new law of the Gospel were yet in their beginnings. . . . [If] the world was then not yet capable of giving full obedience to the law of grace and full assent to the faith in the Son, much less was it prepared to be introduced into the mysteries of his Mother.[55]

According to Sor Maria, the Virgin Mary's revelations were at once scriptural and a supplement to scripture. Stretching Mary's new revelatory role to the utmost, Sor Maria would also say that if "this sovereign Mistress had written what She understood, we would have many other additions to the sacred Scriptures; and we would be able to draw out of them a perfect understanding of those writings and the deep meanings and mysteries of all those preserved in the Church."[56]

Even more potentially scandalous to Protestants was the claim ostensibly revealed by the Virgin Mary to Sor Maria: that the mother of Jesus had suffered equally in his passion and was therefore co-redemptrix of the human race. As the Virgin Mary herself put it in Sor Maria's "Mystical City of God":

> Knowing the high value which the Lord sets upon the labors, the Passion and Death of my Son, and upon all those who were to imitate and follow Jesus in the way of the Cross, I not only offered to deliver my Son over to Passion and Death, but I asked Him to make me his companion and partaker of all his sorrows, sufferings and torments, which request the Father granted.[57]

The "revelation" that the Virgin Mary had suffered the pain of every blow and wound sustained by Jesus in his passion and crucifixion is the main theme of a very long section of Sor Maria's "Mystical City of God." Switching from the first-person voice of the Virgin Mary to her own, Sor Maria sums up this revelation as follows:

> She prayed that She might be permitted to feel and participate in her virginal body all the pains and the wounds and tortures about to be undergone by Jesus. The petition was granted by the blessed Trinity and the Mother in consequence suffered all the torments of her most holy Son in exact duplication.... For in her most ardent love She would have considered it incomparably more painful to see her divine Son suffer and die without being allowed to share in his torments.... The blessed Mother felt in her own body all the torments of her Son. This was true also of the scourging, which She felt in all the parts of her virginal body, in the same intensity as they were felt by Christ in his body.[58]

Sor Maria underscores the difference between what Catholics and Protestants deem possible in the relation between human and divine realities by revealing new honorific titles for the Virgin Mary that would make every Protestant cringe, such as "Queen of the Universe," or "Sole and universal Heiress of all the gifts of nature ... Mistress and Possessor of them all ... Mistress of angels and men ... Treasurer and

Dispenser of all the goods in heaven and earth,"[59] and also by claiming that the Virgin Mary has revealed that she "shall be seated at the right hand of the Judge, to judge with him all the creatures," and has also been "placed on the royal throne of the Most Holy Trinity, which neither men, nor angels, nor seraphim themselves attain, and will not attain for all eternity."[60]

Although hobbled by controversy within certain Catholic circles, the ultimate success of Sor Maria's "Mystical City of God" makes clear the huge gulf that separated Catholics and Protestants concerning Christianity's miraculous dimension. Although the book was condemned in 1681 by Pope Innocent XI, and by 102 of 132 doctors of theology at the Sorbonne in Paris in 1696, it was declared free of error by the universities of Toulouse and Louvain, as well as by those at Alcalá, Salamanca, and Valladolid; even the supporters of the condemnation eventually shifted their opinion. The publishing history of this singular book is a testament to its overcoming of all official Catholic doubters, for it came to enjoy numerous editions and translations into French, Italian, German, Polish, and Latin throughout the eighteenth and nineteenth centuries, an English translation in the early twentieth century, and a large number of subsequent editions from mid-twentieth century to our own day, each approved with the Catholic seal of approval—*Imprimatur* and *Nihil Obstat*—or even, as is the case with the American four-volume set, the approval of Cardinal Tercisio Bertone, head of the Vatican's Congregation for the Doctrine of the Faith.

Reconstruing Disenchantment

In light of such miraculous phenomena, it is no surprise that a reform-minded Spaniard would complain about his own culture in 1600, as if in prescient affirmation of Weber's disenchantment thesis: "It seems as if one had wished to reduce these kingdoms to a republic of *enchanted* beings, living outside the natural order of things."[61]

Is it possible to imagine a world more "enchanted" than the one inhabited by Saint Joseph of Cupertino and Sor María de Ágreda, or a world more "disenchanted" than the one inhabited by Calvin's followers? Perhaps. But imagining is not the same as examining the hard facts of history. The Protestant rejection of the miraculous and mystical was a significant step toward disenchantment—and "magic" had nothing to do with it.

Protestants did more than simply change beliefs by redefining the relationship of matter to spirit, and the natural to the supernatural, and by
segregating the living and the dead: they reordered their society and their
economy. In the sixteenth century, as in our own, a change in beliefs led
to changes in the world.

Catholics had a way of interweaving metaphysical strands that
Protestants segregated, and of doing so in very concrete ways, not just
through ritual and symbol but also through social, economic, and political
structures. Among Catholics, the world pulsated with the miraculous, or
at least with the expectation of miracles. Among Protestants, what do we
find? What, if anything, fills the void left by the disappearance of miracles
and mystical ecstasies? The "miracle" of conversion, and of the transformation of society. The miraculous became spiritual and moral rather than
thaumaturgic, within the individual and within society as a whole. Rather
than altering the natural world, or filling it with supernatural events, the
Protestant miracle worked invisibly yet powerfully within the natural
world. In this respect, miracles never ceased. But one has to admit that
these miracles were more limited in scope than those of Catholics and
thoroughly indicative of a different understanding of reality.

In *The Protestant Ethic and the Spirit of Capitalism*, Max Weber argued
that Protestants gained an economic edge over Catholics because they developed a "this-worldly asceticism."[62] Weber also argued that Protestantism
hastened "the elimination of magic from the world."[63] Though he did not
focus on miracles per se in order to defend his thesis, perhaps he should
have, for the repercussions of this "this-worldly" turn were profound and
much easier to discern than any turn away from something as peripheral
as "magic."

The Protestant Reformation is a key turning point in Western history
for many reasons, so anyone who singles out one or two or three of the
changes brought about by Protestantism does so at great risk. But way
up on the list, among the most profound changes, we can identify a sea
change best described as *desacralization*, in which we see the earth becoming less charged with the otherworldly and supernatural.

It matters little that the devil was still around for Protestants, fooling
people with his preternatural tricks, wreaking havoc through his witches
and warlocks. Protestants saw the devil as a creature, and as capable
only of manipulating the laws of nature, not of altering them. Of course,
if one thinks of the wonders attributed to him as no different from divinely derived "thaumaturgy" or "magic," or as part of a "religio-magical"

spectrum, it is easy to argue that the Protestant Reformation did not disenchant the world. But if one thinks of the devil as the Protestant reformers did, as a mere creature who can never undo the laws of nature but only
mischievously work with them, then it becomes much more difficult to
mount such an argument.

The Protestant realignment of the natural and supernatural was a full-
scale intellectual revolution with all sorts of immediate, practical consequences. It was also a significant step toward focus on "this world" as the
ultimate reality and, eventually, toward the rise of rationalism and the secularization of the West. To deny or downplay the desacralization effected
by Protestants—or to think of it as mere "disenchantment"—is to short-
change both the past and ourselves. Even worse, it is to enchant ourselves
through an artificially naïve view of the world.[64]

Notes

1. First expressed in Weber's famous essay, "Wissenschaft als Beruf" (Science as
   a Vocation), first published in 1918.
2. Weber borrowed this catchphrase from Friedrich Schiller. See H. H. Gerth and
   C. Wright Mills, "Bureaucracy and Charisma: A Philosophy of History," in R.
   Glassman and W. Swatos, *Charisma, History and Social Structure* (Westport,
   CT: Greenwood Press, 1986), 11–15.
3. Charles Taylor, *A Secular Age* (Cambridge, MA: Belknap Press of Harvard
   University Press, 2007), 26–159.
4. Heinz Schilling, *Konfessionskonflikt und Staatsbildung* (Gütersloh: Mohn, 1981);
   Wolfgang Reinhard, "Zwang zur Konfessionalisierung?" *Zeitschrift für histo-
   rische Forschung* 10 (1983): 257–77; Erika Rummel, *The Confessionalization of
   Humanism in Reformation Germany* (Oxford: Oxford University Press, 2000).
5. R. Po-chia Hsia, ed., *Social Discipline in the Reformation* (New York: Routledge,
   1989); and Philip S. Gorski, *Disciplinary Revolution: Calvinism and the Rise of the
   State in Early Modern Europe* (Chicago: University of Chicago Press, 2003).
6. Wolfgang Reinhard, "Gegenreformation als Modernisierung?" *Archiv für
   Reformationsgeschichte* 68 (1977): 226–52; and Susan R. Boetcher, "Confession
   alization: Reformation, Religion, Absolutism, and Modernity," *History Compass*
   2 (January 2004): 1–10.
7. For example, see Steven Pincus, *1688: The First Modern Revolution* (New Haven,
   CT: Yale University Press, 2009).
8. On consecrated behavior, see Clifford Geertz, "Religion as a Cultural System,"
   in *Anthropological Approaches to the Study of Religion*, ed. Michael Banton
   (New York: Praeger, 1966), 3, 28–29. On symbolic behavior, see Victor Turner,

Dramas, Fields, and Metaphors (Ithaca, NY: Cornell University Press, 1974), 55–56; on social glue, see Emile Durkheim, *The Elementary Forms of the Religious Life* (1912), trans. Karen E. Fields (New York: Free Press, 1995). Also see the critique by John Bossy, "Some Elementary Forms of Durkheim," *Past and Present* 95 (May 1982): 3–18.

9. Among the most extreme examples of this approach one can cite Michael Walzer's *Revolution of the Saints* (Cambridge, MA: Harvard University Press, 1965), which argues that Calvin "was not primarily a theologian" (27) and that Calvinism must be viewed as a political rather than religious phenomenon, a mere "response to disorder and fear" (77).

10. Social scientists such as Victor Turner and Clifford Geertz do not deny the effect that myths, symbols, and rituals have on culture or society, but tend to approach these immaterial factors more as responses than causes. See Geertz, "Religion as a Cultural System," 28; and Victor Turner, *From Ritual to Theatre* (New York: Performing Arts Journal Publications, 1982), 82ff.

11. Weber's "disenchantment" thesis is an essential component of one of the most influential books on early modern religion: Keith Thomas, *Religion and the Decline of Magic* (New York: Oxford University Press, 1971). Unlike Scribner, Thomas does not challenge Weber but, rather, elaborates on his "disenchantment" thesis. Cf. Hartmut Lehmann and Guenther Roth, eds., *Weber's "Protestant Ethic": Origins, Evidence, Contexts* (Cambridge: Cambridge University Press, 1993).

12. R. W. Scribner, "The Reformation, Popular Magic, and "the Disenchantment of the World," *Journal of Interdisciplinary History* 23 (1993): 491.

13. Scribner, "The Reformation, Popular Magic," 475.

14. Louis Richeome, S.J., *Trois discours pour la religion catholique* (Bordeaux, 1597).

15. Charles Taylor has coined the awkward term "social imaginary" to describe this complex relation between conceptual structures and social realities. See *Secular Age*, 146. He has also argued that "modern secularization can be seen from one angle as the rejection of higher times, and the positing of time as purely profane" (196).

16. For a social-scientific take on religion that seems unaware of Protestantism and its take on this basic dialectic, see Mircea Eliade, *The Sacred and the Profane* (New York: Harcourt, Brace, 1959).

17. The most eloquent and succinct summary of this worldview can be found in Peter Brown, *The Cult of the Saints* (Chicago: University of Chicago Press, 1981).

18. "Commentary on the True and False Religion" (1525), in *The Latin Works and the Correspondence of Huldreich Zwingli*, ed. S. M. Jackson (London: G.P. Putnam, 1912–29), 2:92.

19. *Ioannis Calvini opera* [hereafter, *CO*] (Braunschweig: Schwetschke, 1863–1900), 24:387.

20. *Huldreich Zwinglis Sämtliche Werke* [hereafter, *ZW*] (Berlin: Schwetschke, 1905–90), 8:194–95.

21. *CO* 24:387.

22. "Whiggish" historians hail the Protestant Reformation as the beginning of modernity and of the forward march of science, progress, and freedom. See Herbert Butterfield, *The Whig Interpretation of History* (London: Bell, 1931). Butterfield used the terms "Protestant history" and "Whiggish history" interchangeably; see 5–20.

23. An assumption brilliantly questioned by Fabián Alejandro Campagne in "Witchcraft and the Sense-of-the-Impossible in Early Modern Spain," *Harvard Theological Review* 96 (January 2003): 25–62.

24. Anthony Cascardi, *The Subject of Modernity* (New York: Cambridge University Press, 1992); Stanley Jeyaraja Tambiah, *Magic, Science, Religion, and the Scope of Rationality* (Cambridge: Cambridge University Press, 1990).

25. In addition to the work of Fabián Alejandro Campagne, see Andrew Keitt, *Inventing the Sacred* (Leiden: Brill, 2005); Julie Crawford, *Marvelous Protestantism* (Baltimore: Johns Hopkins University Press, 2005); Lorraine Daston, "Marvelous Facts and Miraculous Evidence in Early Modern Europe," in *Questions of Evidence*, ed. James Chandler et al. (Chicago: University of Chicago Press, 1994), 243–74; and Lorraine Daston and Katharine Park, *Wonders and the Order of Nature* (New York: Zone Books, 1998).

26. See D. P. Walker, "The Cessation of Miracles," in *Hermeticism and the Renaissance*, ed. Ingrid Merkel and Allen Debus (Washington, DC: Folger Shakespeare Library, 1988), 110–24.

27. For a detailed analysis of Luther's complex attitude toward the miraculous, see Philip Soergel, *Miracles and the Protestant Imagination* (Oxford: Oxford University Press, 2011), ch. 2.

28. Commentary on the Gospel of Matthew 7:24, in *Luther's Works* (hereafter *LW*), ed. Jaroslav Pelikan and Hartmut T. Lehmann (Philadelphia: Fortress Press, 1955–86), vol. 21.

29. Erlangen edition, xii, 236, quoted by Wilhelm Herrmann, *The Communion of the Christian with God, Described on the Basis of Luther's Statements*, trans. J. Sandys Stanyon, 2nd ed. (New York: Putnam's, 1906), 231.

30. *D. Martin Luthers Werke: Kritische Gesamtausgabe, Tischreden* [Table Talk; hereafter *WAT*] (Weimar, 1912-21), 6:6811.

31. On seeing and hearing, *WAT* 3:3601; on the hare, *WAT* 3:4040; on the ape, *WAT* 3:6814; the dog on bed, *WAT* 3:5358b.

32. "*Martin Butzers an ein christlichen Rath un Gemeyn der statt Weissenburg Summary einer Predig dselbst gehon*" (1523), in Martin Bucer, Opera Omnia, Series 1: *Deutsche Schriften* (Güitersloh: Gerd Mohn, 1960-), vol. 1 (hereafter, *DS*), 1:101.

33. *DS* 1:107–12.

34. Jane Shaw, *Miracles in Enlightenment England* (New Haven, CT: Yale University Press, 2006), 24–26.

35. J. T. McNeill, ed., *Institutes of the Christian Religion* (Philadelphia: Westminster, 1960), 1:5–8.

36. "Prefatory Address," in McNeill, *Institutes*, 16–17.

37. For an exhaustive account of medieval and early modern demonology, see Stuart Clarke, *Thinking with Demons* (Oxford: Clarendon Press, 1997).

38. Commentary on Acts, *CO* 48:104.

39. For a more detailed analysis of Reformed Protestant attitudes toward miracles, see Moshe Sluhovsky, "Calvinist Miracles and the Concept of the Miraculous in Sixteenth-Century Huguenot Thought," *Renaissance and Reformation* 19 (1995): 5–24; and Bernard Vogler, "La Reforme et le Miracle," *Revue d'Histoire de la Spiritualite* 48 (1972): 145–59.

40. On this aspect of Lutheranism, see Philip M. Soergel, *Miracles and the Protestant Imagination: The Evangelical Wonder Book in Reformation Germany* (Oxford: Oxford University Press, 2012).

41. André Vauchez, *Saints, Prophètes et Visionnaires* (Paris: Albin Michel, 1999).

42. Steven Ozment, *Mysticism and Dissent* (New Haven, CT: Yale University Press, 1973).

43. Heiko A. Oberman, "*Simul gemitus et raputs*: Luther and Mysticism," and Steven Ozment, "Homo Viator: Luther and Late Medieval Theology," both in *The Reformation in Medieval Perspective*, ed. Steven Ozment (Chicago: Quadrangle Books, 1971), 219–52.

44. Commentary on John's Gospel, *CO* 47:90.

45. For an ecumenically minded look at mystical influences on Calvin, see Dennis Tamburello, *Union with Christ: John Calvin and the Mysticism of St. Bernard of Clairvaux* (Louisville, KY: Westminster John Knox Press, 1994).

46. McNeill, *Institutes*, II.3.2, 1:292.

47. Montague Summers, *The Physical Phenomena of Mysticism* (New York: Barnes and Noble, 1950); and Herbert Thurston, *The Physical Phenomena of Mysticism* (Chicago: Regnery, 1952).

48. Carlos Eire, "The Good, the Bad, and the Airborne," in *Ideas and Cultural Margins in Early Modern Germany*, ed. Robin Barnes and Elizabeth Plummer (Burlington: Ashgate, 2009), 307–24. See also Angelo Pastrovicchi, *St. Joseph of Copertino*, trans. Francis S. Laing (St. Louis: Herder, 1918).

49. Sor María de Jesús de Ágreda, *La mística ciudad de Dios* (1670), ed. Augustine Esposito (Potomac, MD: Scripta Humanistica, 1990). Abridged English translation as *The Mystical City of God* [hereafter, *MCG*] (Rockford: TAN Books, 1978); this 1978 abridged edition is more readily available in libraries than the four-volume full text (see n. 52).

50. Clark A. Colahan, *The Visions of Sor Maria de Agreda* (Tucson: University of Arizona Press, 1994); Marilyn H. Fedewa, *Maria of Agreda* (Albuquerque: University of

New Mexico Press, 2009); Beatriz Ferrús Antón, *La Monja de Ágreda: historia y leyenda de la dama azul en norteamérica* (Valencia: Universidad de Valencia, Biblioteca Javier Coy, 2008); François-Géraud de Cambolas, *Marie d'Agreda et La Cité Mystique de Dieu* (Nice: France Europe Editions, 2003); and Ana Morte Acín, *Misticismo y conspiración: Sor Maria de Ágreda en el reinado de Felipe IV* (Zaragoza: Institución Fernando el Católico, 2010).

51. Quoted in Fedewa, *Maria of Agreda*, 192–93.
52. English translation by George J. Blatter [Fiscar Marison], facsimile of 1914 edition (Rockford, IL: TAN Books (Rockford, IL, 2006), 4 vols.
53. *MCG*, 23.
54. *MCG*, 24.
55. *MCG*, 24.
56. *MCG*, 134.
57. *MCG*, 432–33.
58. *MCG*, 502, 538.
59. *MCG*, 569.
60. *MCG*, 782, 783.
61. Martin Gonzalez de Cellorigo, *Memorial de la política necesaria* (Valladolid, 1600), trans. J. H. Elliott, in *Spain and its World* (New Haven, CT: Yale University Press, 1989), 262–86.
62. Max Weber, *The Protestant Ethic and the Spirit of Capitalism* (1924), trans. Talcott Parsons (New York: Scribner, 1958), 120.
63. Weber, *Protestant Ethic*, 105.
64. H. C. Erik Midelfort, *Exorcism and Enlightenment: Johann Joseph Gassner and the Demons of Eighteenth-Century Germany* (New Haven, CT: Yale University Press, 2005), 6.

4

Protestantism and the Making of Modern Science

Peter Harrison

HISTORIANS OF SCIENCE tend to be deeply skeptical of overarching stories about the historical relations between science and religion. We might be especially careful about the story we tell, as we anticipate marking this 500th anniversary of the Reformation. The standard position in the profession on this issue is that these past relations are best regarded as "complex" and that there is no single story to be told.[1] Applying this general principle to the question of Protestantism and science, it can be said that any simple story about this relationship is likely to be wrong, and even modest suggestions about patterns of mutual influence need to be hedged with numerous qualifications. Given that this chapter largely will be devoted to setting out such patterns of influence, it is important at the outset to understand some of the reasons historians are dubious about simple stories that assert some straightforward and direct relationship between religion (or some feature of religion such as Protestantism) and science.

The Emergence of "Science" and Versions of Protestantism

The first source of complexity concerns the two entities under discussion. It is tempting to think that *science* is a longstanding practice with roots that go back to the ancient Greeks and Babylonians. But strictly speaking, "science" as we presently understand it really only dates back to the nineteenth century. Over the course of the 1800s, successful attempts were made to unite a range of disparate disciplines under the banner of natural science. It was argued that these sciences were united by a common approach, "the scientific method," and conducted by individuals who shared a distinctive vocation, that of "scientist." These developments gave rise to science as we know it. Before this, the study of nature was conducted within a range of disciplines with diverse methods and objectives. Chief among them was natural philosophy, which in its classic form sought causal explanations for change in the natural world. These explanations had a particular logical shape: although grounded in observations, their conclusions were presented in the form of logical demonstrations. Natural history, by way of contrast, was primarily descriptive rather than explanatory, offering its account of nature by means of detailed empirical description, but leaving aside questions of causation. Its ordering principles tended to be classificatory, rather than causal. Finally, mixed mathematics sought to provide mathematical accounts of various natural and artificial phenomena. Traditionally, mixed mathematics could offer hypothetical models that provided a basis for prediction. However, these models did not uncover causes, and neither were they necessarily thought to map directly onto reality. They often functioned, in other words, as useful fictions, or calculating devices. Crucially, mathematics was the business of the mixed mathematical sciences, and had no place in natural philosophy.

These traditional disciplinary divisions, inherited from the ancient Greeks, underwent significant changes in the seventeenth century, in a protracted process commonly referred to as "the scientific revolution."[2] For the first time, mathematics and natural history were combined with natural philosophy in innovative and creative ways. While it remains true that only in the nineteenth century did these three disciplines recede almost completely into the background, to be replaced by the more unified set of disciplines that constitute "modern science," it is not inappropriate to identify in these innovations the beginnings of the emergence of modern science. For our purposes, the moral of this very brief account of changing understandings of "science" is that there has really never been a unitary thing called "science" that Protestantism could influence upon, and that this is particularly true before the nineteenth century.

Nonetheless we can speak of the *emergence* of modern science, signaled by a decisive move away from the doctrines and methods of Aristotelian natural philosophy, and it is plausible to speak of the role of Protestantism in this process. All that said, in this chapter I will use the terms "science" and "natural philosophy" more or less interchangeably, but it is important to bear in mind that this use of the expression "science" is somewhat loose.

Similar considerations apply to our second category, Protestantism. The Protestant Reformation took quite distinct national forms and gave rise to movements with diverse doctrines, liturgies, and polities. Moreover, the first generation of Protestants was formed within Catholic institutions and drew upon the resources of that tradition. Protestantism began as a Catholic reform movement, and features that we may now think of as distinctively Protestant had significant precedents in medieval Catholicism. Again, then, the message is that it is important not simply to assume that there is some unitary entity "Protestantism" that can be contrasted unproblematically with "Catholicism" (and the Orthodox tradition for that matter), and that was unique in its capacity to influence the study of nature.

Having considered some of the dangers in oversimplifying the nature of the two phenomena that we are seeking to relate to each other, it is worth briefly considering different possible modes of historical relations. When we ask what kinds of historical interactions might obtain between versions of Protestantism and the various disciplines concerned with the study of nature, several options arise.[3] It may be possible to identify some distinctively Protestant *doctrines* or *practices* that were relevant to the content or conduct of the study of nature. In addition to reinforcing the content or methods of science, Protestantism may also have provided some of its *presuppositions*. Similarly, some forms of Protestantism may have fostered distinctive *norms* or *attitudes*—a Protestant ethic, if you will—that were conducive to scientific activity. Less directly, it could be that the Reformation promoted a *questioning of traditional authorities* in a way that opened up possibilities for *new forms of knowledge* or *new institutions* for the pursuit of knowledge. Finally, it might simply have been that Protestantism was *less of a hindrance to science* than Catholicism. In relation to these possible modes of influence, it is also important to understand that some may have resulted from the deliberate intentions of specific Protestant actors, whereas others may have been wholly unintended.[4] This latter point is significant because, in discussing the possible role of Protestantism in the emergence of modern science, our aim is not only to establish whether specific Protestant ideas, practices, or institutions had a direct bearing on the emergence of science but also to consider the more general question: Had the Protestant Reformation not taken place, what might have been different about the way in which modern science developed?

All this suggests that there are good reasons for affirming the complex nature of science–religion relations in the past. But this need not preclude the articulation of certain lines of influence, including all those set out above. Moreover, in early modern Europe, religion was, in a sense, "the only game in town." It would be remarkable if the tumultuous religious upheavals of the sixteenth century, and the subsequent schism between Catholics and Protestants, did not leave an indelible mark on an emerging modern science. So, it is no exaggeration to say that the real question is not *whether* these events influenced the rise of modern science, but *how*.[5]

Religious Reform and the Reform of Learning

The idea that the Protestant Reformation might be linked to innovation in the sciences is by no means new.[6] Already in the seventeenth century, promoters of new approaches to the study of nature viewed their efforts as akin to those of the Protestant reformers, and it was not uncommon for scientific innovators to be identified with key figures of the Reformation. Copernicus and Paracelsus were thus dubbed "the Luther and Calvin" of natural philosophy, while Johannes Kepler was similarly known as the "Luther of astronomy."[7] Observing the remarkable changes in the religious landscape of Europe, and the great revolution in learning that accompanied it, the English philosopher and statesman Francis Bacon (1561–1626) suggested in the early seventeenth century that the reformation of the church provided the model and inspiration for a renovation of knowledge more generally. These sentiments were echoed by numerous seventeenth-century thinkers, who also sought to promote new scientific doctrines and novel approaches to the study of nature.[8] In this way, the Protestant Reformation was invoked to provide social legitimacy to fledgling scientific institutions that were promoting new methods and new doctrines at a time when novelty was generally regarded with suspicion.

In the case of the religious reformers, accusations of unwarranted novelty had been met by the counterclaim that the status quo represented the end product of a long process of corruption. Granting this, "new" doctrines and practices could be represented, not as novelties, but as a return to an original and pure form of religion. The humanist and reformation mottos *ad fontes* (to the sources) and *sola scriptura* (by scripture alone) are clear expressions of this general sentiment. The principle of looking to the past may seem an unpromising foundation upon which to build scientific knowledge, but in fact during the sixteenth and seventeenth centuries it was not uncommon to suggest that "new" scientific theories were, in fact, revivals of some ancient teaching. Copernicanism was thus presented as a recovery of ancient Pythagorean teachings. New atomistic (or "corpuscular") theories of matter were said, with some justification, to have been taught in antiquity by Democritus and the Epicureans. Even Isaac Newton sought to show that his natural philosophy was in agreement with ancient Greek and Egyptian sages.[9] Such appeals to the past would often go further, rehearsing the patristic idea that the ancient Greeks had plagiarized their scientific knowledge from biblical authors such as Moses, Solomon, and Job. Following this logic, seemingly novel scientific theories, most notably Copernicanism and atomism, were argued to have been held by the authors of the Hebrew Bible. It did not necessarily follow that natural philosophy could be directly learned from scripture, since it was widely believed that while Solomon and Job had authored voluminous scientific treatises, these had been lost to posterity. But there was nonetheless a sense among the scientific reformers that they, too, were returning to a pristine scientific tradition known to the biblical authors and able to be dimly discerned in surviving canonical works.

A related feature of the dual reformations of religion and of learning was the impulse to re-Christianize a tradition viewed as suspect on account of its corruption by elements of paganism. The main culprit was identified as Aristotle, whose writings had provided the basis of the arts curriculum in the medieval universities, and whose philosophy was deemed to have contaminated both Christian theology and pious natural philosophy. Luther frequently complained of the domination of the university curriculum by Aristotle, contending that, like the church, the universities, "where only that blind, heathen, teacher Aristotle rules," also stood in need of a "thorough reformation."[10] The reformers' criticisms of the undue influence of Aristotle gave license to those seeking to break the Aristotelian stranglehold on natural philosophy.

In keeping with the Reformation principle of *sola scriptura*, many late Renaissance thinkers held that the only reliable natural philosophy would be grounded in biblical sources.[11] Lambert Daneau, author of *Physica christiana* (*Christian Physics*, 1576) and one of the most influential Calvinist thinkers of his time, sought to use scripture to "reform the works of the philosophers." The best natural philosophy, he declared, came not from the "profane writings of the philosophers," but from "the very Word of God."[12] Other would-be reformers of the sciences rehearsed the same argument. Paracelsian mathematician and cosmologist Robert Fludd (1574–1637) thus insisted that "the subject of true Philosophy is not to be found in Aristotle's works, but in the Book of truth and Wisdom, forasmuch as it is a copy of the revealed Word." Moravian educator Amos Comenius (1592–1670) spoke in a similar vein of "natural philosophy reformed by divine light."[13] This strong tradition of "pious natural philosophy," "mosaic philosophy," or simply "Christian philosophy" represents a significant phase in the emergence of modern science, for while natural philosophers would eventually come to prioritize experience and experiment over written sources, the phenomenon of "Christian philosophy" was important in motivating the quest for new, non-Aristotelian sources for the study of nature. Liberation from the strictures of Aristotelian philosophy was thus a common goal of reformers of both religion and the sciences.

Beyond a general disapproval of the supposedly pernicious influence of Aristotelianism, reformers of natural philosophy focused their attacks on specific features of received Aristotelian teaching that were deemed incompatible with true Christianity: his ignorance of the fallen condition of the world and its inhabitants, his denial that the world had been created, and his teleological conception of the operations of nature. These critiques led to new doctrines and approaches that were vital for the development of modern science.

Fallen Knowledge

The hostility directed toward Aristotle and his medieval followers was not motivated simply by his status as a pagan per se (as the comparatively favorable treatment of Plato attests). It was, rather, that certain of Aristotle's teachings were held to be inconsistent with Christianity, and often in subtle ways had not been fully appreciated by his scholastic appropriators. Two aspects of Aristotelian thought had been "known problems": his doctrine of the eternity of the world and his views regarding the mortality of the soul. These had been uncompromisingly rejected by medieval philosophers, although, arguably, the broader implications of his rejection of the idea of creation had not been fully worked through. But more serious in the eyes of a number of Protestant reformers were other, apparently innocuous, elements of Aristotle's philosophy that had met with qualified acceptance by scholastic philosophers.

One of these concerned Aristotle's confidence in the unaided powers of human reason and his conviction that inherent rationality was the natural condition of human beings. This view was encapsulated in his well-known definition of human beings as "rational animals," which amounted to the conviction that the ability to use reason was an essential distinguishing feature of the species. Allied to this was the uncritical assumption that the senses delivered a relatively accurate picture of the world, and that the workings of nature itself were largely transparent to the human gaze. Accordingly, Aristotelian science was based on commonsense observations about the world, conducted without instruments or experiments. It was this uncritical approach that gave rise to a number of familiar, but erroneous Aristotelian doctrines: a heavy object (the stone) will always fall more quickly than the light one (the feather); terrestrial objects move in straight lines and will eventually come to rest; celestial objects move perpetually in circular paths. Such observations were subsequently worked into generalizations that provided the foundations for logical demonstrations. A feature of genuine Aristotelian science was thus the logical certainty of its conclusions. All this was grounded on the premise that when they function naturally, human reason and the senses deliver an accurate representation of the world as it really is.

What was left out of this picture for a number of Protestant critics of Aristotelian scholasticism was the idea of a human fall from perfection—crucially, a fall that damaged not only human moral capacities but sensory and cognitive abilities as well. To be sure, medieval Christian thinkers had acknowledged the Fall and its significance. But from the perspective of Luther and Calvin, they had failed to take full cognizance of its implications for the conduct and content of the sciences. Luther declared that, "it is impossible that nature could be understood by human reason after the fall of Adam." It was in this context that he went on to express skepticism about the scientific doctrines of "the heathen master" Aristotle, who "taught and still teaches ... that a stone is heavy, that a feather is light, that water is wet, and fire is dry." What was an understandable mistake for Aristotle was less excusable for scholastic philosophers and university masters of arts who, according to Luther, had erroneously accepted the false premise that "natural light or intellect and heathen philosophy are also safe means of discovering truth."[14] John Calvin similarly insisted that as a consequence of the Fall, "the whole soul is vitiated," with the damage encompassing reason, the affections, and the senses. Again, this idea of *total* depravity was contrasted with the views of the "sophists in the Papacy," who held the milder view "that man's soul is vitiated, but only in part."[15] For both Luther and Calvin, the dramatically negative impact of original sin on our capacity to acquire reliable knowledge had been fatally underestimated by both Aristotle and scholastic philosophers.

Neither Luther nor Calvin expended much energy in exploring alternative ways of arriving at a more veridical science of nature. But their analysis left open a range of possibilities. One implication of this more robust version of original sin was that Adam in his innocence would have been possessed of a vastly more extensive and acute knowledge of nature than his fallen progeny. Accordingly, many in the sixteenth and seventeenth centuries held that Adam had enjoyed an encyclopedic knowledge of nature and its operations.[16] A corollary to this view was that the traditions of Adamic science had been known to the biblical patriarchs, and had subsequently found their way into ancient written sources: Jewish, Babylonian, Egyptian, and Greek. This assumption fed into the practices of "Mosaic science" described above.

But even if the traditions of Adamic science had perished in the remote past, the contrasting conditions of Adam in his original and fallen states could nonetheless serve to motivate scientific enquiry in the present. Francis Bacon thus declared in his *Novum Organum* (1621)—a highly influential manifesto for a new, non-Aristotelian science—that "man by the fall fell at the same time from his state of innocency and from his dominion over creation." "Both of these losses," he went on to argue, "can even in this life be in some part repaired; the former by religion and faith, the latter by arts and sciences."[17] Thus, for Bacon, the Fall was not only an occasion for skepticism and despair. Taken together with the biblical injunction to "have dominion" over the Creation, the Fall narrative also provided human beings with a twofold mission: to restore their fallen moral state through religion, and to restore their mastery of the world through the sciences and arts. This mastery was intended both to provide human beings with material necessities in their fallen state and to heal nature from the wounds that it had suffered on account of Adam's transgression. Early supporters of the Royal Society, founded in 1660, commonly spoke in theological terms about the new science recapturing a lost human dominion over nature, and restoring an original state of affairs in which nature had made abundant provision for human welfare.[18]

If the ideas of the Fall and original sin, which had attained a new prominence in elements of reformed thinking, provided a new source of motivation for mastery of nature, they were also to inform some of the methods of the new sciences. Aristotle's commonsense observations were replaced by a regimen of experiments that sought to test nature under a variety of conditions.[19] The new logic of experiment and systematic observation was premised on the idea that reliable knowledge of nature would be hard to come by, both on account of wounded human capacities and on the fact that nature itself was no longer accessible in the way it once had been. Repeated sets of observations, conducted under quite specific conditions, were needed both to interrogate a recalcitrant nature and to compensate for human cognitive failings. At the same time, fallen human senses stood in need of artificial augmentation—most notably with the telescope and microscope—in order to reveal dimensions of the natural world that Adam would have naturally been acquainted with.

The degree of certainty of the knowledge so generated was also diminished. The goal of Aristotelian science had been logically demonstrable knowledge. For experimental natural philosophers, however, such certainty was unattainable, at least in the present life. Knowledge of the world was now attended with a considerable degree of doubt. In his classic *Essay Concerning Human Understanding* (1690), John Locke wrote of the "darkness" that we are presently involved in, and of the impossibility of a science of nature of the kind sought by Aristotle: "as to a perfect science of natural bodies . . . we are, I think, so far from being capable of any such thing, that I conclude it lost labor to seek after it."[20] Locke allowed that we could have an experimental or historical knowledge of nature, but recognized that this fell well short of the lofty criterion of logical certainty demanded by the Aristotelians.

Finally, whereas scientific knowledge had once been thought to be attainable by a few exceptional individuals, now the systematic study of nature would necessarily become corporate and cumulative. Science would henceforth require the combined efforts of many minds, accumulated over the generations. These features of scientific investigation were together known as "experimental natural philosophy," a radical new approach to knowledge that was contrasted with the "speculative" methods of Aristotle.[21] Summing up the connection between the corruption of human nature and the new experimental method, Robert Hooke wrote in his celebrated *Micrographia* (1665) that "every man, both from a deriv'd corruption, innate and born with him, and from his breeding and converse with men, is very subject to slip into all sorts of errors." He continued: "These being the dangers in the process of humane reason, the remedies of them all can only proceed from the real, the mechanical, the experimental philosophy."[22]

The New Vocation

The shift from a natural philosophy concerned with self-mastery to one that aimed at mastery of the world was related to Protestant ideas about the importance of the "active life," and with a new understanding of vocation. The distinction between active and contemplative lives (*vita activa* and *vita contemplativa*) was a longstanding one in the Western tradition. In the Middle Ages, Christian thinkers had largely concurred with the classical consensus that elevated the contemplative life over the active life.[23] For this reason, philosophical activity, including natural philosophy, was largely disengaged from utilitarian concerns. During the Renaissance, this discussion was reopened, initially in the context of political philosophy, with a number of humanist writers arguing for the priority of the active life.[24] Protestant Reformers were also to challenge the idea of the superiority of the contemplative life, albeit for different reasons. Luther insisted that true Christians should avoid emulating cloistered monks, who in his view, crept into corners or retreated to the wilderness. Christians, he urged, should "use" the world: "to build, to buy, to have dealings and hold intercourse with his fellows, to join them in all temporal affairs."[25] John Calvin also argued that in the present world Christians should devote themselves to "utility," "profit," and "advantage," and in consequence contribute to the building up of the commonwealth.[26] Calvin firmly believed that the way to transform and renew society was for Christians to be conscientiously engaged in useful worldly affairs.[27] Once again, readings of the first chapters of Genesis and the reconstruction of Adam's activities in his original state of innocence provided important support for this view. For the Reformers, Adam's labors in the Garden of Eden indicated that practical work was part of God's original plan for the human race. Luther baldly stated that, "Man was created not for leisure, but for work, even in the state of innocence." Calvin agreed, suggesting in his exegesis of Genesis 2:15—"And the Lord God took the man, and put him into the Garden of Eden to dress it and to keep it"—that "men were created to employ themselves in some work, and not to lie down in inactivity and idleness." This advocacy of the active life was contrasted with the counsels of Catholicism and with "present-day monks find in idleness the chief part of their sanctity."[28]

Calvin's teachings about the intrinsic value of work have long provided grist to the mill for those who wish to follow Max Weber in proposing a connection between a Protestant "ethic" and the rise of modern capitalism. Whatever the merits of such arguments, it is not difficult to see how these ideas might also have played a role in a new conception of science that focused on usefulness and active engagement with the natural world.[29] As noted at the outset, throughout the Middle Ages and early modern period, the formal study of nature fell largely within the enterprise of "natural philosophy." As a philosophical enterprise it was concerned to a large extent with the traditional goals of what, for want of a better expression, we might term "spiritual formation."[30] Natural philosophy was not, and did not seek to be, practically useful. It was this feature of the enterprise that earned the derision of scientific reformers such as Francis Bacon, who strenuously argued that the study of nature be redirected away from the traditional goal of contemplation and personal edification toward the practical task of restoring the empire of man over nature. Knowledge, Bacon insisted, is to be sought "not for the quiet of resolution but for a restitution and reinvesting (in great part) of man to the sovereignty and power . . . which he had in his first state of creation."[31] The Baconian program for the study of nature thus entailed a radical reorientation away from the philosophical goals of self-mastery toward a mastery of the natural world that would yield practical benefits.[32]

The elevation of the active life went hand-in-hand with Lutheran and Calvinist notions of the sanctity of earthly vocations. Luther was particularly exercised by the idea that the priesthood represented a religious class that was superior to the laity. "All Christians," he maintained, "are of the spiritual estate, and there is no difference among them except that of office."[33] This doctrine, which subsequently became known as "the priesthood of all believers," received strong support from Calvin and others.[34] The abolition of a strong distinction between priestly and lay estates opened up the possibility of a new kind of religious vocation in which the study of nature could be regarded as a priestly activity. The notion of the scientist-as-priest would become a common motif among seventeenth-century Protestant natural philosophers. Johannes Kepler (1571–1630), for example, had originally studied theology at Tübingen with the intention of becoming a Lutheran minister, but later realized the sanctity of the scientific vocation: "I wished to be a theologian; for a long time I was troubled, but now see how God is also praised through my work in astronomy."[35] Robert Boyle (1627–1691), one of the founders of modern chemistry and a pioneer of experimental methods, spoke in similar terms of the priestly role of scientific investigators. He suggested that the world was the "temple" of God and that this gave warrant to the priestly vocation of investigators of the natural world. He observed that "Philosophers of almost all Religions have been, by the contemplation of the world, mov'd to consider it under the notion of a Temple."[36] The study of nature, he claimed, was "the first act of religion, and equally obliging in all religions." (This was based on the episode of Adam's naming of the beasts in Eden.) Hence, natural philosophy was "philosophical worship of God." True priesthood consisted, not in presiding over religious rituals, but in demonstrating the wonderful designs of nature: "Discovering to others the perfections of God displayed in the creatures is a more acceptable act of religion, than the burning of sacrifices or perfumes upon his altars."[37] The idea that natural philosophy was a religious activity on a par with priestly pursuits was not only important in establishing its social legitimacy. It was also a source of motivation for figures such as Kepler and Boyle, who saw themselves as engaged in a religious mission. This vocational dimension of the new scientific endeavors reinforced the Baconian idea of science as a redemptive enterprise.

The "Two Books" and the Literal Sense

An important feature of the theological justifications of the new sciences that we have been considering up to this point is their reliance on specific biblical warrants. As we have seen, some thinkers attempted to draw new scientific doctrines directly from the pages of scripture. Still more important was the way in which the Bible was used to support a new experimental framework for the sciences, including a new practical orientation and a novel set of critical methods. The biblical figure of Adam, and discussions of his contrasting innocent and fallen states, were of particular importance in the appeal to scripture. One reason for these appeals to biblical authority was, of course, the Protestant principle of *sola scriptura*. But related features of the Protestant approach to scripture were also significant for the new sciences, central among them an emphasis on the literal or historical sense of scripture.[38]

Patristic and medieval exegetes were often given to allegorical readings of scripture. While we sometimes assume that allegory was a process in which words are given a number of different meanings, in fact the logic of allegory was this: in a literal reading of scripture, a word refers to a thing; in an allegorical reading of scripture, things refer to other things. Thus, allegorical reading depended on the assumption that objects in the natural world bear meanings, and that when scripture refers to these objects, we are then invited to contemplate their deeper theological significance. In other words, allegory is not just about written texts; it has implications for our understanding of natural objects. In the thirteenth century, Thomas Aquinas put it this way: "The author of Holy Writ is God, in whose power it is to signify His meaning, not by words only . . . but also by things themselves." Aquinas went on to say that multiple meanings do not lie in the words of scripture, but in the objects that God has invested with these meanings: "The multiplicity of these senses does not produce equivocation or any other kind of multiplicity, seeing that these senses are not multiplied because one word signifies several things, but because the things signified by the words can be themselves types of other things."[39] The idea that nature could be "read" in this way underpinned the medieval commonplace that nature was a "book" that could be read in parallel with the book of scripture.[40] Allegory, in short, was a practice that brought together the reading of the book of nature and the book of scripture. In consequence, a change to the status of allegorical interpretation would necessarily have implications for how nature was conceptualized.

As it turns out, the Protestant reformers were highly critical of allegorical interpretation. Luther maintained that the literal sense was "the highest best and strongest sense" and that the scriptures were to be interpreted "in their simplest meaning." Allegory, he dismissively remarked, was for "weak minds."[41] Calvin also chided those who held that "scripture is fertile and thus bears multiple meanings," insisting that "the true meaning of Scripture is the natural and simple one."[42] While Luther and Calvin were primarily interested in the literal sense as a way of reinforcing biblical authority and the principle of *sola scriptura*, their attacks on allegory necessarily had implications for the way in which nature was understood, for to deny allegory was to deny that the theological significance of natural things lay in their symbolic meanings. Other features of Protestantism made their contribution to the demise of symbolic representation— iconoclasm, condemnation of idolatry, diminution in the number of sacraments, and a shift in the focus of worship from images and rites to words.

Together with the critique of allegory, these developments contributed to the collapse of the symbolic worldview of the Middle Ages, and of what C. S. Lewis memorably described in *The Discarded Image* as "a single, complex, harmonious mental model of the universe."[43]

A cosmos evacuated of symbolic theological meanings left space for alternative ways of ordering the natural world and of reimbuing it with religious significance. One way of doing this, already noted above, was to see the natural world as an object to be redeemed and restored by means of the reestablishment of human dominion. No longer a site for passive contemplation, the world was now the place of a redemptive process through which human mastery would render it useful for the material welfare of its human tenants. Emphasis on the literal sense of scripture reinforced this transition, in the particular case of the Genesis narratives of Creation by focusing attention on the significance of Adam as a literal, historical figure. In allegorical readings, the Garden of Eden had been understood as a symbol of paradise or an allegory of the soul, with the fruits of the garden understood as fruits of the spirit. On this reading, Adam's "cultivation of the garden" could be internalized and understood in terms of spiritual formation. So, too, his dominion over the beasts was interpreted as a mastery of bestial passions that was lost when he fell.[44] The prescriptions of this reading were to do with the moral goal of reestablishing an internal dominion of reason over the passions. With a literal reading of this narrative came a more literal conception of dominion over the natural world. Redressing the losses of the Fall now required the deployment of a science that would seek to return nature to an original acquiescent state in which it had naturally yielded up its bounty for the provision of the material needs of the human race. This was the Baconian project that provided for the plot for a number of seventeenth-century scientific projects.[45]

Natural philosophy would not only discover the practical uses of the creatures and help reestablish a lost dominion over nature, but it would also illustrate in unmatched detail the wisdom and power of God as exemplified in the operations and designs of the natural world. If nature could no longer convey, by symbolic means, a range of theological truths, it could nonetheless provide indirect evidence of certain aspects of God's nature by means of the discoveries of natural science. It is important to understand that the powerful alliance of natural theology and science that is so characteristic of the period from the seventeenth to nineteenth centuries was not, as sometimes assumed, the continuation of a strong medieval tradition. It is, rather, a completely new activity that was developed in order to replace a lost and, in one sense, richer way of reading the-ological meanings from nature. In the thirteenth century, Bonaventure (1221–1274) could claim that "The creature of the world is like a book in which the creative Trinity is reflected, represented, and written." In the seventeenth century, Francis Bacon demurred, insisting that the works of God "show the omnipotency and wisdom of the maker, *but not his image.*"[46] The physico-theology of this period involved a new partnership between theology and science, and one that took over from allegory the role of providing theological readings of nature. This can be seen in the new deployments of the "book of nature" metaphor that now appear, not in the works of theologians and biblical exegetes, but in the writings of natural philosophers and natural historians. Kepler and Galileo thus maintained that mathematics provided the key to interpreting the book of nature; for Robert Boyle, it was physiology that offered a way of reading the creatures.[47]

In sum, the literal approach to scripture promoted by the Protestant reformers was significant for the development of the new science in two main ways. First, it hastened the collapse of the symbolic universe of the Middle Ages, making space for alternative ways of reading and ordering the natural world. Experimental natural philosophy allied with natural theology came to occupy this space. Second, the Genesis narratives of Creation and Fall, now read exclusively in their literal sense, motivated scientific activity which came to be understood as a redemptive process that would both restore nature and extend human dominion over it.

Science, Social Legitimation, and Religious Pluralism

It is worth considering, finally, some of the ways in which, in the after-math of the Protestant Reformation, the natural sciences came to enjoy an increasing prominence and epistemic authority. It is important to un-derstand that at the time of its emergence, modern science was not, as Calvin said of scripture, self-authenticating. On the contrary, the new sciences were often regarded with considerable suspicion or subject to ridicule. The insecure status of experimental science meant that its ad-vocates needed to devote considerable effort to establishing the intellec-tual authority and usefulness of the fledgling enterprise.[48] In this context, the partnership of natural philosophy and natural theology was vital for establishing the religious credentials of the new science, and providing it with much needed social legitimation. One of the reasons that natural science became a mainstream activity in the modern West was that it was given this initial boost by its alignment with projects in natural theology.[49]

Religion, too, was a benefactor of this new partnership, at least at first. The Protestant Reformation had raised in an acute way the problem of religious pluralism. The quandary was how to decide on the true religion, given that the advocates of each religion insist that only one religion is true—their own—and offered arguments in support of their preference.[50] An alternative, of course, was that no religion was true. For this reason the threat of atheism—real or imagined—was a persistent feature of much of the religious literature of the period. In this context, the alliance of natural science and natural theology was proposed as an effective prophylactic against impiety and unbelief, and was seen to provide reliable evidence for the truth of religion in general. The kinds of evidence provided by the new studies of nature, moreover, were said to be far more potent than what Bishop Sprat called "the blind applauses of the ignorant."[51] Indeed, empirically based proofs that looked to design (the teleological or physico-theological arguments) were commonly thought to be superior to the more philosophical and "speculative" proofs (the ontological and cosmological arguments). Science, in short, was seen to offer evidence for the wisdom and power of God in an especially powerful way, and at a time when such support was much needed.

Pious natural philosophers took this even further to argue that their enterprise could also establish the truth of Christianity in particular, and even of specific Christian creeds. As Robert Boyle expressed it, "the New Philosophy may furnish us with some new Weapons for the defence of our ancientest Creed."[52] Elsewhere he argued that the pursuit of "intricate and laborious experiments" better equips one to discover "Solid Arguments for Natural, or Reveal'd, Religion . . . how remote soever those Truths may be from vulgar Apprehensions."[53] Joseph Glanvill, an Anglican clergyman and Fellow of the Royal Society, agreed that the new philosophy helped establish "the Infallible truth of Scripture History, and twists such a cord as is as strong as any thing in Geometry or Nature."[54] Such arguments often rested on a belief that the occurrence of certain events recounted in scripture (such as Noah's flood) were confirmed by the findings of contemporary natural philosophy. Even more specifically, for its Protestant practitioners, natural philosophy was thought to offer resources that would enable a more discriminating choice among competing Christian confessions. This was because natural philosophers were said to be more capable of assessing the relevant testimony and evidence that provided external support for specific beliefs. Robert Boyle thus claimed that experimental natural philosophers "will examine with more Strictness and Skill, than Ordinary Men are able, Miracles, Prophecies, or other Proofs, said to be Supernatural, that are alledg'd to Evince a Reveal'd Religion."[55]

Post-Reformation confessional controversy, then, offered a new context and a new task for natural philosophy. There was now a broad spectrum of religious possibilities, from the extremes of atheism to the unchecked enthusiasm associated with more radical Protestant sects. Somewhere in the middle was a "superstitious" and credulous Catholicism along with a more sober but equally problematic deism. Proponents of natural philosophy argued that their enterprise offered a way of negotiating this spectrum of possibilities and arriving at the right place. Making the case for an irenic Anglicanism, Joseph Glanvill maintained that *"acquaintance* with *nature* assists *RELIGION* against its greatest Enemies, which are Atheism, Sadducism, Superstition, Enthusiasm, and the humor of disputing."[56] The singular virtue of the new natural philosophy was that it offered not only the appropriate expertise for making the relevant judgments, but that it was suitably disinterested. As Boyle put it: "He is fittest to commend divinity, whose profession it is not." The experimental philosopher was best placed to assess the merits of theological claims because he was free of "the usual Temptations to Partiality," unlike the clergyman who might reasonably be accused of being "an Incompetent, as well as Interested [sic], Judge."[57] In the age of "evidences"—itself an outcome of the religious pluralism that followed the Protestant Reformation—the natural sciences thus came to offer a "neutral" epistemic space from which the relative merits of competing "religions" could be evaluated. This transferal of authority to the natural sciences was to have momentous consequences, cementing their epistemic authority and establishing the conditions for their subsequent assumption of the social status once enjoyed by religion.

Conclusion

Philip Pullman's *His Dark Materials* trilogy is built upon the wonderfully imagined conceit of a world that is parallel to ours in many ways, but different in at least one key respect—the Protestant Reformation never happened. This world does have its own science (or "experimental theology," as it is known), but the distinctive features of that science invite reflection on the different paths that scientific development might have followed had the religious upheavals of sixteenth-century Europe not unfolded in the ways they did. Unfortunately, by the close of the third volume, the premise of Pullman's trilogy has collapsed under the weight of the author's intrusive anti-religious prejudices; but the books do serve as a salient reminder that there was nothing inevitable about the emergence of science in the West. Science did not unfold in history according to some inexorable, inner logic, if for no other reason than that the constituents of "science" itself are not a historical constant. Western science may have turned out differently, and even if its content were the same, its position in society and the values that attend it may have been otherwise. Part of the reason it turned out the way it did is a result of contingent religious factors, and among them the Protestant Reformation and its unforeseen aftermath. Certainly, the lines of influence are complex and often indirect or unintended. But my suggestion has been that the methods of modern science, its theoretical content, and its social significance all owe something to Protestantism.

That said, it is worth returning to the Protestant actors who first drew attention to a connection between the reformation of religion and the reformation of the sciences, to sound a final note of caution. Almost from the first, it was a particularly *Protestant* version of history that sought to associate Protestant religion with reason and progress, and Catholicism with superstition, censorial attitudes, and scientific backwardness. This Protestant version of events was a natural partner for a progressivist Enlightenment narrative that promoted a similar view of history. By the end of the nineteenth century, however, this anti-Catholic propaganda had broadened into a general historical critique of the relations between Christianity and science. At this time arose the now familiar "conflict myth" that makes little distinction between forms of religion, and simply asserts that Western history is characterized by an ongoing battle between science and *religion*. Ironically, then, this conflict myth, which in recent decades historians of science have devoted much attention to demolishing, owes not a little to the way in which Protestant apologists first constructed their own history. In a sense, the animus against religion exhibited by some contemporary advocates of scientific enlightenment is simply an extreme version of this "Protestant" position. In a further irony, the original early modern partnership forged between science and Protestant religion has ultimately been corrosive of religious authority in another way. It was pious advocates of the new natural philosophy such as Robert Boyle who, in a context of apparently irresolvable religious disputes, ceded authority to a putatively neutral third party—natural philosophy—to provide the evidentiary basis of a Christianity that came to be understood in terms of propositions that stood in need of scientific support. Science thus came to assume the upper hand over religion, and ever since shows no signs of relinquishing it.

Notes

1. See especially John Hedley Brooke, *Science and Religion: Some Historical Perspectives* (Cambridge: Cambridge University Press, 1992); Geoffrey Cantor, Thomas Dixon, and Stephen Pumfrey, eds., *Science and Religion: New Historical Perspectives* (Cambridge: Cambridge University Press, 2010).

2. Again, the appropriateness of the category has been a subject of discussion among historians. See, e.g., Steven Shapin, *The Scientific Revolution* (Chicago: University of Chicago Press, 1996); and "Thoughts on the Scientific Revolution" of *European Review* 15 (2007): 439–512.

3. For the more general question of ways in which science and religion might be related, see Brooke, *Science and Religion*, 19–33; and Mikael Stenmark, *How to Relate Science and Religion* (Grand Rapids, MI: Eerdmans, 2004).

4. A point that Ernst Troeltsch and, more recently, Brad Gregory have powerfully reminded us. Troeltsch, *Protestantism and Progress: A Historical Study of the Relation of Protestantism to the Modern World* (Eugene, OR: Wipf and Stock, 1999); Brad Gregory, *The Unintended Reformation: How a Religious Revolution Secularized Society* (Cambridge, MA: Harvard University Press, 2012).

5. For general treatments of connections between Protestantism and science, see Robert K. Merton, *Science, Technology and Society in Seventeenth-Century England* (New York: Harper, 1970); John Dillenberger, *Protestant Thought and Natural Science* (Garden City, NY: Doubleday, 1960). Also, for much of what follows I will be drawing on my two monographs that deal with this topic: Peter Harrison, *The Bible, Protestantism and the Rise of Natural Science* (Cambridge: Cambridge University Press, 1998); and Harrison, *The Fall of Man and the Foundations of Science* (Cambridge: Cambridge University Press, 2007).

6. For treatments of parallels between the two kinds of reformation, see Brooke, *Science and Religion*, 82–116; Harrison, *Bible, Protestantism and the Rise of Natural Science*, 64–120.

7. R.B., *The Difference between the auncient Phisicke ... and the Latter Phisicke* (London, 1585), sigs. Cviii.v., Hvii.v. Charles Webster, *From Paracelsus to Newton* (Cambridge: Cambridge University Press, 1982), 4.

8. Francis Bacon, *The Advancement of Learning*, in *The Works of Francis Bacon*, ed. James Spedding, Robert Leslie Ellis, and Douglas Denon Heath (London: Longman, 1857–74), 3:300. See also Thomas Sprat, *History of the Royal Society* (London, 1666), 371; Thomas Culpeper, *Morall Discourses and Essayes* (London, 1655), 63; Samuel Hartlib, Sheffield University Library, Hartlib Papers XLVIII 17, reproduced in Charles Webster, *The Great Instauration: Science, Medicine, and Reform, 1626–1660* (London: Duckworth, 1975), app. 1, 524–28; Noah Biggs, *Mataetechnia Medicinae Praxeos. The Vanity of the Craft of Physick . . . to the Parliament of England* (London, 1651).

9. Nicolaus Copernicus, *On the Revolutions of Heavenly Spheres*, trans. Glen Wallis (Amherst, MA: Prometheus, 1995), 6; J. E. McGuire and R. M Rattansi, "Newton and the Pipes of Pan," *Notes and Records of the Royal Society of London* 21 (1966): 108–43.

10. Martin Luther, *To the Christian Nobility of the German Nation*, in *Three Treatises* (Philadelphia: Fortress Press, 1970), 92. Cf. *Complete Sermons of Martin Luther* ed. John Lemke (Grand Rapids, MI: Baker, 2000), 1:330–31.

11. Ann Blair, "Mosaic Physics and the Search for Pious Natural Philosophy in the Late Renaissance," *Isis* 91 (2000): 32–58.

12. Lambert Daneau, *Physice christiana*, 4th ed. (Geneva, 1602), sig Aiiir, 20.

13. Comenius, *Natural Philosophy reformed by Divine Light* (London, 1651).

14. Martin Luther, "Sermon on Epiphany," in *Sermons*, 1:329, 331, 344; Also, Lectures on Genesis 1–5, in *Luther's Works*, ed. J. Pelikan and H. Lehmann (St Louis: Concordia, 1955–75), 1:142, 166. Cf. Thomas Aquinas on "natural light," *Summa theologiae* 1a2ae. 109, 1. Cf. *Expositio super librum Boethii De Trinitate* 1.1.

15. John Calvin, Commentaries on the Book of Ezekiel Ch. XI:19, 20, in *Calvin's Commentaries* (Grand Rapids, MI: Baker Books, 2003), 11:375. Cf. John Calvin, *Institutes of the Christian Religion*, ed. John McNeill (Philadelphia: Westminster, 1960), 1:271, 355.

16. Harrison, *Bible, Protestantism and the Rise of Natural Science*, 211–23.

17. Francis Bacon, *Novum Organum* II, §52, *Works*, 4:247–48; Cf. *The Great Instauration*, in *Works*, 4:27, 7.

18. Thomas Sprat, *History of the Royal* Society, 62, 438; Joseph Glanvill, *Scepsis Scientifica* (London, 1665), sig. b3v; *Plus Ultra* (London, 1668), 87, 104.

19. Boyle, for example, contrasted the "Vulgar and Superficial Philosophy" of the Aristotelians with the method of "intricate and laborious Experiments." Robert Boyle, *The Christian Virtuoso . . . the First Part* (London, 1690), 49.

20. John Locke, *An Essay Concerning Human Understanding*, Bk. 4, Ch. 3, Sec. 29, ed. Peter H. Nidditch (Oxford: Clarendon, 1975), 560.

21. Peter Anstey, "Experimental versus Speculative Natural Philosophy," in *The Science of Nature in the Seventeenth Century*, ed. Peter Anstey and John Schuster (Dordrecht: Springer, 2005), 215–42; Peter Harrison, "Experimental Religion

and Experimental Science in Early Modern England," *Intellectual History Review* 21 (2011): 413–33.

22. Hooke, *Micrographia* (London, 1665), Preface (unpaginated). The Fall, incidentally, was generally responsible for both "innate" corruption and that owing to "converse with men." The corrupting influences of "converse with men" (which relate to Bacon's idols of the marketplace and of the theatre) were usually regarded as indirect consequences of the Fall. Cf. Boyle, *Some Considerations about the Reconcileableness of Reason and Religion* (London, 1675), 32–33; Boyle, *Some considerations touching the vsefulnesse of experimental naturall philosophy* (London, 1663), 1.

23. See, e.g., Aquinas, *Summa theologiae*, 2a2ae. 182, 2; Augustine, *City of God*, VIII.4, XIX.19; *The Trinity*, I.iii.20–21; VIII.i.2, VIII.vi.20, 25; Sermon 104, *Sermons* IV.81–83. See also Mary Elizabeth Mason, *Active Life and Contemplative Life: A Study of the Concepts from Plato to the Present* (Milwaukee, WI: Marquette University Press, 1961).

24. P. O. Kristeller, "The Active Life and the Contemplative Life in Renaissance Humanism," in *Arbeit, Musse, Meditation*, ed. B. Vickers (Zurich: Fachvereine, 1985), 133–52.

25. Luther, "Sermon for the Third Sunday After Easter," *Sermons*, 7:281.

26. David Little, *Religion, Order, and Law: A Study in Pre-Revolutionary England* (Oxford: Blackwell, 1970), 60.

27. I. Hart, "The Teaching of Luther and about Ordinary Work," *Evangelical Quarterly* 67 (1995): 35–52, 121–35.

28. Calvin, *Institutes*, xiii.10, 2:1264.

29. The implications of this general position for the rise of science in seventeenth-century England were set out by Robert Merton, "Puritanism, Pietism, and Science," *The Sociological Review* 28 (1936): 1–30; and Merton, *Science, Technology and Society in Seventeenth-Century England*. Cf. Dorothy Stimson, "Puritanism and the New Philosophy in 17th century England," *Bulletin of the Institute of the History of Medicine* 3 (1935): 321–24. For representative discussions of the Merton thesis (which still has much to commend it), see Bernard Cohen, ed., *Puritanism and the Rise of Modern Science: the Merton Thesis* (New Brunswick, NJ: Rutgers University Press, 1990); Steven Shapin, "Understanding the Merton Thesis," *Isis* (1988): 594–605.

30. On this theme, see Pierre Hadot, *What Is Ancient Philosophy?* (Cambridge, MA: Harvard University Press, 2002); Remi Brague, *The Wisdom of the World* (Chicago: University of Chicago Press, 2004).

31. Bacon, *Valerius Terminus, Works*, 3:222; cf. Bacon, *Great Instauration, Preface, Works*, 4:21.

32. Stephen Gaukroger, *Francis Bacon and the Transformation of Early-Modern Philosophy* (Cambridge: Cambridge University Press, 2001); Antonio Pérez-Ramos, "Bacon's Legacy," in *The Cambridge Companion to Bacon*, ed. Marku Peltonnen (Cambridge: Cambridge University Press, 1996), 311–34.

33. Luther, *To the Christian Nobility*, in *Three Treatises*, 12.

34. Calvin, *Institutes* I, 502, 2:1473.

35. Johannes Kepler, *Gesammelte Werke* (Munich: C. H. Beck, 1937–45), 13:40. For Kepler's own account, Johannes Kepler, *Selbstzeugnisse*, ed. Franz Hammer, trans. Esther Hammer (StuttgartBad Canstatt: Frommann,1971), 61–65.

36. Boyle, *Vsefulnesse of Experimental Natural Philosophy*, 56. Cf. Joseph Glanvill, *Philosophia Pia* (London, 1671), 138f. For an early account of Boyle's notion of the priest-scientist, see H. Fisch, "The Scientist as Priest: A Note on Robert Boyle's Natural Theology," *Isis* 44 (1953): 252–65.

37. Boyle, *Vsefulnesse of Experimental Natural Philosophy*, 115, 117.

38. For an extended account of the implications of Protestant approaches to scripture for the study of nature, see Harrison, *Bible, Protestantism and the Rise of Natural Science*; Harrison, "The Bible and the Emergence of Modern Science," *Science and Christian Belief* 18 (2006): 115–32; and "The Bible and the Rise of Science: A Rejoinder," *Science and Christian Belief* 21 (2009): 155–62.

39. Thomas Aquinas, *Summa theologiae*, 1a. 1, 10. Cf. Augustine, *De doctrina christiana* I.ii.2.

40. See the essays in Klaas van Berkel and Arjo Vanderjagt, eds., *The Book of Nature in Antiquity and the Middle Ages* (Leuven: Peeters, 2005).

41. Martin Luther, *The Babylonian Captivity of the Church*, in *Three Treatises*, 146, 241; Luther, *Answer to the Hyperchristian Book*, in *Luther's Works*, 39:177. In fact, Luther himself resorted to allegorical interpretation on occasion, but was the only major reformer to do so. For the reformers on the literal sense, see Hans Frei, *The Eclipse of Biblical Narrative* (New Haven, CT: Yale University Press, 1974), 37; and Richard A. Muller and John L. Thompson, eds., *Biblical Interpretation in the Era of the Reformation* (Grand Rapids, MI: Eerdmans, 1996).

42. John Calvin, The Epistle of Paul the Apostle to the Galatians, Philippians, Ephesians, and Colossians, *Calvin's Commentaries*, 21:84f.

43. C. S. Lewis, *The Discarded Image* (Cambridge: Cambridge University Press, 2005), 11.

44. For these allegorical readings, see Joseph E. Duncan, *Milton's Earthly Paradise* (Minneapolis, MN: University of Minnesota Press, 1972), 152–54; Arnold Williams, *The Common Expositor* (Chapel Hill: University of North Carolina Press, 1948), 110. See also Harrison, "Reading the Passions: The Fall, the Passions, and Dominion over Nature," in *The Soft Underbelly of Reason: The Passions in the Seventeenth Century*, ed. Stephen Gaukroger (London: Routledge, 1998), 49–78.

45. In the middle decades of the seventeenth century, there was also a significant eschatological element to these motivations. See Charles Webster, *The Great Instauration*. Cf. Mordechai Feingold, ' "And Knowledge Shall be Increased': Millenarianism and the Advancement of Learning Revisited," *The Seventeenth Century* 28 (2013): 363–93.

46. Bonaventure, *Breviloquium*, II.12; Francis Bacon, *The Advancement of Learning, Works*, 3:350. Cf. Bacon, *Novum organum* I, §89, *Works* 4:88; Robert Boyle, *Some Motives to the Love of God, Works*, 1:264. Italics in original.

47. Kepler, *Mysterium cosmographicum* (1596); Galileo, *Discoveries and Opinions of Galileo*, ed. and trans. Stillman Drake (New York: Anchor, 1957), 337–38; Boyle, *Some Considerations touching the Usefulness of Experimental Natural Philosophy, Works*, 2:20.

48. Peter Harrison, "Religion, the Royal Society, and the Rise of Science," *Theology and Science* 6 (2008): 255–71.

49. Stephen Gaukroger, *The Emergence of a Scientific Culture* (Oxford: Oxford University Press, 2005), 23.

50. For articulations of the question, see Robert Boyle, Boyle Papers, vol. 4, fol. 281; Edward, Lord Herbert of Cherbury, *De Religione Laici*, [1645] ed. and trans. Harold R. Hutcheson (New Haven, CT: Yale University Press, 1944), 87; Samuel Pufendorf, *Nature and Qualification of Religion in Reference to Civil Society*, ed. Simone Zurbuchen, trans. Jodocus Crull (Indianapolis: Liberty Fund, 2002), 11.

51. Sprat, *History of the Royal Society*, 349. See also John Norris, "To Dr. Plot on his Natural History of Staffordshire," lines 27–30; Robert Boyle, *Usefulness of Experimental Natural Philosophy, Works* 2:15.

52. Boyle, *Some Physico-Theological Considerations about the Possibility of the Resurrection* (London, 1675), preface.

53. Boyle, *A free enquiry into the vulgarly receiv'd notion of nature* (London, 1686), 49f.

54. Joseph Glanvill, *Philosophia Pia* (London, 1671), 84.

55. Robert Boyle, *The Christian Virtuoso*, p. 110; Cf. Sprat, *History of the Royal Society*, 358f. For further examples, see Harrison, "Newtonian Science, Miracles, and the Laws of Nature," *Journal of the History of Ideas* 56 (1995): 531–53.

56. Glanvill, *Philosophia Pia*, 16, cf., 85f.

57. Boyle, *Excellency of Theology* (London, 1674), Preface (unpaginated).

5

The Reformation and Higher Education

Karin Maag

IN A LETTER written to young men from Zurich studying at the University of Marburg in 1540, the Swiss reformer Heinrich Bullinger candidly expressed his frustration with the students' ceaseless financial pleas and with the persistent pressure to seek degrees:

> All your letters ask only for more money, but this is impossible— you have 38 gulden a year and no more. You keep thinking up new things, which cost money. Why otherwise are you wanting to compete for a Master's degree? The church of Zurich is satisfied when its students return from their travels well-equipped with knowledge and good morals, even without a degree.[1]

Bullinger's response highlights the complex relationships between the reformers who advocated for higher education within a defined set of parameters, the students who pursued higher education with their own aims in mind, and the educational institutions that sought to provide this education in competition with other centers of learning.

As we approach the commemorations and reflections of 2017, we should consider carefully the interplay between the Reformation and higher education. The Reformation had a significant impact on education, particularly at higher levels, bringing the fragmentation of Western Christendom into the universities and academies of Europe. An assessment of the changes brought about by the Reformation on centers of higher learning leads into an analysis of the effectiveness of these institutions in meeting the expectations of various key players in early modern confessional communities. While the subject areas taught in Protestant centers of learning remained largely similar to those offered in peer Catholic institutions, the increased emphasis on university-level studies for community leaders, particularly pastors, transformed the ethos of these academies and universities and made them into more vocationally oriented institutions. The period covered in this chapter stretches from the early years of the Reformation in Western Europe to the first half of the seventeenth century, allowing for an analysis of the Reformation's impact on higher education in the West for well over a century.

While the early years of religious reform were tumultuous and saw steep enrollment declines for most universities, the institutions of higher education then rebounded in Protestant areas, both in flexibility and in the number of students. Thereafter universities were able to compete quite effectively in most contexts with peer Catholic institutions. Yet the Reformation raised questions for institutions of higher learning that remained unresolved even by the end of our period. Indeed, educational institutions still confront these questions. Beyond imparting knowledge, for instance, how was virtue to be inculcated in students? Should evidence of intellectual preparation as measured through years of academic study and examinations be enough to prepare one for leadership positions, especially in the church? Finally, was the goal of research and scholarship carried out in an academic setting to reinforce the faith and doctrines of a particular confessional group or to push at the boundaries?

In answering these and other questions, scholars have addressed the Reformation's impact on higher education from a wide variety of perspectives. Those coming from within the Protestant traditions have tended to argue for the transformative effect of the Reformation on the world of higher learning, highlighting the reformers' zeal for education and the renewed attention given to scripture in Protestant academies and universities.[2] Studies focusing on the Lutheran world tend to orient their analysis around Philip Melanchthon's educational reforms, stressing the changes in curriculum that emerged from the Reformation, along with the continuities in terms of university structures and pedagogical approach.[3] Scholars working on Protestant higher education in the colonial and revolutionary eras in the United States tend to trace the lineage of universities in the colonial era back to Puritan England, emphasizing the importance of the religious framework, the persistence of the humanist curriculum, and the inculcation of morality.[4] Among the most seminal institutions in this regard was Emmanuel College, Cambridge, which formed a generation of Puritan divines and served as a model for the newly formed colonial centers of higher learning.[5] Finally, in a recent study of the Reformation's impact on Western society and culture, Brad Gregory has posited that the Reformation had a largely detrimental effect on knowledge acquisition and transmission at the university level. He argues that because of the loss of a common foundational belief system following the break-up of Western Christendom, knowledge was eventually secularized and compartmentalized. Furthermore, he suggests that the development of territorial universities upholding a specific confessional viewpoint also led to theological complacency, which significantly weakened the role of faith in the university context.[6]

Rejecting and Rebuilding Higher Education

As the range of perspectives outlined above suggests, there is little firm agreement on the impact of the Reformation on higher education both during the early modern era and in the longer term. A good starting point, therefore, is to consider more closely what happened to institutions of higher learning when the Reformation took hold. In fact, it is fair to say that the early repercussions of the Reformation on preexisting European universities (of which there more than sixty by 1500)[7] produced turmoil. As controversy grew between defenders of traditional Catholicism and supporters of the new Protestant perspectives, professors left, students abandoned their studies, and universities struggled to keep going. A case in point is the University of Basel. Established in 1459-60, the university closed its doors in 1529 when the city formally adopted Protestantism, reopening only in 1532. Throughout the next decade, its enrollment averaged only twenty-nine students a year, compared to around 130 in 1500. Universities in the Holy Roman Empire and in Scandinavia suffered similarly precipitous declines in enrollment or were forced to shut down, sometimes for decades.[8] Enrollment difficulties could be caused by confessional conflict, the Peasants' War, or even a sense among some radical supporters of the Reformation that university-level training was the enemy of purified faith. Protestants skeptical about the value of higher education could point with justification to the important role played by Catholic universities in countering early Protestantism, and to some of

Martin Luther's own statements about the dangers of university studies for people of faith. In his 1520 treatise, *To the Christian Nobility of the German Nation Concerning the Reform of the Christian Estate*, Luther bluntly stated, "I greatly fear that the universities, unless they teach the Holy Scriptures diligently and impress them on the young students, are wide gates to hell."[9] In his 1521 work, *The Misuse of the Mass*, Luther proclaimed, "Since the beginning of the world even the devil himself could not have invented anything more powerful to suppress faith and the gospel than the universities."[10] Although Luther's anti-university polemic was part of his wider campaign to undermine opposition to the Reformation spearheaded by many of the leading Catholic professors and universities, some of his contemporaries could interpret Luther's rejection of these institutions as a broader-based dismissal of the value of higher education in all circumstances. For instance, Andreas Bodenstein von Karlstadt wrote vehemently against the vainglory of higher education in his 1523 tract, *The Meaning of the Term* Gelassen *[surrender] and Where in Holy Scripture It Is Found*:

> What does one seek in the higher schools than to be honored by others? Therefore, one aspires to be a master, another, a doctor and then a doctor of sacred Scripture. They give up goods and chattel for the honor which Christ did not accord his apprentices. Yet they wish to be the ones who teach and maintain Christian faith and to be called masters and doctors, even though they seek doctoral honors with such avarice and greed that they envy and persecute all other equal teaching when they have acquired their honor. They allow no one who does not have the same title to come up and sit with them.[11]

Karlstadt's response to what he perceived as the nefarious influence of status seeking in the universities of his day led him to reject his own university position and titles and adopt the lifestyle of a peasant.[12]

Yet amid this downturn and downgrading of higher education, some religious and political leaders in Protestant areas saw the need to invest in institutions of higher learning. These leaders felt that this task could be done either by transforming older Catholic universities into Protestant ones or by setting up brand-new ones. The University of Wittenberg underwent its own reformation in 1533, followed by two revisions of the university statutes in 1536 and 1546. The universities of Leipzig and Tübingen followed suit in the 1530s and 1540s.[13] For its part, the University of Heidelberg's statutes were overhauled in 1558, two years after the Palatinate adopted the Reformation under Elector Ottheinrich.[14] In the same period, new universities came into being in Lutheran areas. For instance, Philip of Hesse worked with Melanchthon to ensure the establishment of the University of Marburg in 1527, followed by the creation of the University of Königsberg in 1544 and Jena in 1558.[15] These new Protestant territorial universities joined the formerly Catholic universities in offering locally accessible higher education for the future political and religious leaders of Lutheran and Reformed lands.[16]

The Rise of Protestant Academies

In other Protestant areas, particularly ones that adopted Calvinism, new and more flexible institutions of higher studies emerged, known as academies. Pioneered in Strasbourg, in several Swiss cities, including Lausanne and Geneva, and then in Huguenot France and the Reformed German lands, these academies were often hybrids that offered both Latin school education at a "high school" level for younger boys and university-level training for more advanced students. Unlike universities, academies did not grant degrees, but instead provided letters from professors and pastors testifying to students' academic performance and morals.[17] Hence, the first and most visible result of the Reformation's impact on higher education in the sixteenth century was the dramatic growth in the number of institutions providing higher education, particularly in the second half of the sixteenth century.[18] The second outcome was the development of new and more nimble institutions of higher study, not bound to medieval charters and privileges but able to respond more swiftly to the needs of the Protestant churches and government authorities for educated clergy and civil servants. Thus, the Genevan academy within ten years of its inception in 1559 could amend its humanities, Greek, Hebrew, and theology curriculum to include lectures in medicine (temporarily) and civil law (more regularly), depending on the availability of professors to teach these subjects.[19] The statutes of these academies also placed these new institutions carefully under the control of church and state authorities, at least in areas where the government was favorable to the Reformed faith. In Lausanne, for instance, the academy established in 1537 was overseen locally by the pastors of the city and by the bailiff who represented the Bernese government, since Lausanne and the entire Pays de Vaud had come under the

political control of the powerful canton of Berne beginning in 1536. Each
time there was a vacancy in the professoriate, candidates had to be vetted
and approved by the Lausanne pastors, but also by the bailiff, and then by
the political authorities in Berne.[20]

Furthermore, the faculty in these academies did not see themselves
as constituting a guild or corporation separate from the city or territory's
pastors, thus limiting the number of potential clashes between rival factions vying for control of the academy, although the *esprit de corps* uniting
the faculty and the pastors of a given community could at times embroil
the academy in confessional and jurisdictional disputes spearheaded by
the pastors against the government. Again, the example of Lausanne is
instructive. Beginning in 1558, tensions soared between the government
authorities in Berne and the clergy of Lausanne over church discipline
and excommunication. The Lausanne pastors wanted to follow neighboring Geneva's practice, in which the consistory, led by the community's
pastors, vetted parishioners' behavior and controlled access to the Lord's
Supper. The Bernese reserved such powers to government officials. This
jurisdictional dispute drew in the professors of the Lausanne academy,
who resigned one after another in 1558 and 1559 out of solidarity with their
ministerial colleagues, leaving the Bernese authorities to scramble to fill
in the sudden vacancies.[21]

Aside from these major confrontations, the academies proved to be successful providers of higher education at the local level. Like the territorial
universities, the academies became regional magnets for students who
could not afford the time or money to go farther afield, and direct local o-
versight reassured the church and state authorities that their young men's
education was reliable in both its scholarly content and its orthodoxy.[22]

In fact, a closer study of the curriculum of Protestant universities and
academies in the Reformation era shows that their curriculum was in many
ways not very different from the offerings at rival Catholic institutions.[23]
This similarity is hardly surprising if one considers that the Protestant
authorities were as keen as their Catholic counterparts to promote their
excellent education to potential students, and that the top-quality educational approach of the day was shaped by Renaissance humanism. In the
humanities, both Catholic and Protestant centers of higher education concentrated on the study and analysis of classical Roman and Greek texts,
strongly influenced by humanists' call for a return to the sources. The
medieval focus on logic as the heart of study had been replaced already
before the Reformation by a growing emphasis on rhetoric.[24] In Protestant

settings as in Catholic ones, students learned by taking down lectures word for word from their professors, and they practiced their oratorical skills through disputations and declamations.[25] Thus, in many ways the distinguishing feature of early modern Protestant higher education represents a continuity of pedagogical approaches and subject matter when compared with the instruction provided in Catholic peer institutions, particularly in the humanities.

Of course, there were also some distinctives in Lutheran and Reformed curricula. For one, as John Witte notes in this volume, the study of canon law entirely disappeared, to be replaced (if a suitable professor could be found) by civil law. Protestants also added chairs of Hebrew to their academies and universities, making the study of that language a regular feature of the curriculum. In theology, the emphasis first and foremost was on the study and exegesis of scripture, with most institutions having one professor focus on the Old Testament and another on the New Testament. Over time, a professor of church doctrine might be added to the roster. Furthermore, because Protestant churches increasingly expected their future pastors to have gained university-level education, the curriculum of Reformed and Lutheran institutions also reflected the need to prepare clergy for their primary responsibility, namely preaching. The Genevan academy's curriculum, for instance, reserved regular sessions every Saturday afternoon for preaching practice, during which each candidate would preach a sermon on a weekly rotation and have it critiqued by his peers and by individual pastors in turn.[26] By the end of the sixteenth century, bursary students at the University of Basel who had received their masters' degrees preached regularly in the Franciscan church, and all theology students were to preach regularly in German.[27] Adding practical training of this kind made Protestant academies and universities even more attractive to church authorities. Not only did students get some valuable practice in preaching before beginning work in a parish, but churches could also expect an assessment of the student's preaching skills from the pastor or professor who oversaw the training.

Overall, therefore, while the early impact of the fragmentation of Christendom in the early sixteenth century damaged the universities, Protestant churches' and governments' need for well-prepared leaders of the next generation enabled institutions of higher study to rebound. In many areas, non-Catholics were barred from attending Catholic universities, so Protestant authorities had to come up with new strategies to fill the void. In Reformed and Lutheran territories, older universities were transformed, new universities and academies were created, and while the curricula in the humanities in particular followed traditional models, these Protestant institutions did innovate in terms of the academic subjects and practical training considered vital for future pastors.

However, once the first decades of the Reformation had passed, how effective were the Protestant universities and academies in responding to the needs and aspirations of church and state authorities and of the teaching faculty and students themselves? How successful were these Protestant centers of learning in meeting the demands of these at-times competing voices?

Protestant Centers of Learning and Confessional Networks

One way to answer these questions is to consider the successes and struggles faced by Protestant centers of learning in particularly challenging circumstances, such as the Huguenot academies in France. Beginning in the late sixteenth century, eight academies were set up in France and in allied territories to provide higher education to French Protestants close to home. Five of these (Sedan, Saumur, Montauban, Nîmes, and Die) were funded by part of the *deniers du roi*—the king's financial underwriting of the Huguenot church as compensation for its continued payment of the Catholic tithe. The Huguenot church's willingness to earmark a significant portion of the royal largesse for educational purposes signaled that the academies were a highly valued asset for French Protestantism.[28] By the end of the sixteenth century, while the Genevan academy remained an option favored by many young Frenchmen, the Huguenot national church increasingly encouraged its young men to study in their own institutions under the more direct oversight of the French church. Several of these institutions developed strong scholarly reputations, especially the academies of Saumur and Sedan in the north.[29] To ensure adequate supervision and a common approach across institutions, the French Huguenot national synods regularly dealt with the academies in their gatherings. In 1620, the national synod of Alès adopted a set of statutes for all the academies. The statutes provided regulations for student behavior, but also laid out the expected pedagogical and curricular approach of the faculty. For instance, theology professors were to

abstain as much as possible from arcane topics and the vain scholarship of Catholic scholastics. Except where necessary in interpreting passages of Holy Scripture, they will not deal at length with the refutation of heresies which have never surfaced here. Their explanations in dogmatic instruction should be serious and straightforward, following the tone in the writings which God has used in these recent times to rekindle the flame of the Gospel.[30]

This statement highlights some of the anxieties of the French church authorities over the form and content of theological instruction. The synod's declaration also encapsulates some of the major strengths and challenges facing these Protestant centers of learning. On the one hand, the academies could count on the interest of the church in their work—these were not institutions left to find their own way, to sink or swim. On the other hand, the church's interest could translate into pressure regarding pedagogical approaches or curricular content, potentially hampering the faculty's classroom work and scholarship.

By investing time, money, and human resources in the academies, the French Huguenots hoped to ensure their own homegrown supply of educated and trained young men. These students would serve as the leaders of the next generation, especially, but not exclusively, in the church. Once the educational system was set up, it became more feasible for committees examining ministerial candidates to rely on a common set of skills and a similar knowledge base among prospective future pastors. In other words, the Protestant investment in higher education did not simply ensure good schools but was part of a broader plan to standardize and increase the level of preparation for clergy. Vetting committees could reasonably expect that a candidate who had attended one of the Huguenot academies would have adequate preparation in Greek, Hebrew, scriptural exegesis, doctrinal knowledge, and homiletic practice. A student could thus be examined in his proficiency and compared with other candidates who had gone through similar studies.[31] Thus, this standardization of higher education, under the watchful eye of the Huguenot church at the local, provincial, and national levels, allowed for more uniform preparation and a more consistent assessment of candidates' fitness for ministry.

As the network of Protestant academies and universities grew in strength and number in the later sixteenth and early seventeenth centuries, the expectations of church authorities and congregations regarding the educational attainments of their pastors changed as well. While the pre-Reformation model of clerical preparation had largely been one of apprenticeship, in which a neophyte priest learned from a more experienced cleric how to celebrate the liturgy, hear confessions, and take care of a parish, Protestant clergy increasingly were expected to have spent at least a few years in higher education before beginning their ministry. In the Rhineland, for instance, the number of future pastors having attended a university or academy went from 85 percent in 1590 to 90 percent in 1605 and 94 percent in 1619, right before the outbreak of the Thirty Years' War.[32]

This move to an academically trained ministry had a number of significant implications for both the pastorate and higher education. First, the assumption that candidates for ministry would all have a period of academic study under their belt tended to bar young men of more impoverished or less educated backgrounds from seeking a career in the pastorate, although many authorities did try to compensate by offering scholarships to poor but promising students.[33] However, overall, the emphasis on higher education as a prerequisite for ministry did tend to make the pastoral corps more homogenous in terms of their social background and academic preparation.[34] Second, insisting on academic training for future pastors tended to be a key marker of difference between the clergy and their parishioners, especially in rural areas. The emergence of the educated pastor as the intellectual leader of his community could potentially reinforce the attractiveness of higher education for up-and-coming young men, but could also distance the pastor from his congregation.[35] Third, if candidates for ministry were to provide evidence of their studies at academies or universities, it became increasingly important to make sure that such education had taken place in institutions whose confessional outlook and academic reputation were acceptable to the supervising authorities.

One way of ensuring orthodoxy and academic standards was to establish or reform a local center of higher education, but in many cases, churches also wanted their future pastors to study with the leading lights of the day. The end result was that some Protestant authorities, such as the Zurich church, proved surprisingly amenable to sending their own young men on sometimes-prolonged study trips to foreign academies and universities. Young men from Zurich, who later became pastors in the city and countryside, studied at Basel, Heidelberg, Marburg, Geneva, Leiden, and Herborn, among others, thanks to a scholarship program funded by Zurich, even though the city did have its own academy.[36] In other words, when considering the effectiveness and success of Protestant centers of learning, one should not limit oneself to universities and academies set up in the territory under consideration, but understand that these institutions were part of a wider network, albeit one that was sensitive to confessional changes. For instance, controversies between Lutherans and Reformed students at the University of Basel in the 1560s and 1570s led the Zurich educational council to remove its students from this geographically proximate university and send them farther afield, to the more confessionally acceptable Heidelberg University. In turn, when the Palatinate reverted to Lutheranism under Elector Ludwig VI from 1576 to 1583, the number of Reformed students enrolling at the university declined sharply.[37]

This network of Protestant centers of learning was fostered by correspondence: pastors from one city would recommend their traveling students to the pastors and professors of another, and after the end of a period of study, the students would travel home with attestations from their professors about their academic proficiency and behavior. In some cases, the recommendations openly highlighted problems with the students, as in the case of Jean Verneuil, a candidate for ministry sent to the Genevan academy by the church of Bordeaux in 1604. The church informed the Genevan pastors that "[t]he Montauban professors wrote to us that he was dissolute, addicted to his appetites, especially to wine, ill-disciplined, flighty, and a liar as well. Therefore, we have sent him to you, hoping that he will mend his ways in your company." This assessment illuminates several key aspects of the academic network: Verneuil had already spent time in Montauban's academy (for three and a half years, in fact), but now was being given a final chance to change his ways by enrolling in a different institution. Notice that none of the concerns expressed here have to do with the content of his studies but, rather, with his behavior. The letter from Bordeaux went on to require reports from the Genevan Company of Pastors every six months to assess Verneuil's progress. In this instance, both academies and church were committed to keeping each other informed as to his behavior. The final assessment of the Genevan Company of Pastors about Verneuil in 1605 read "reasonably good in terms of his work, poor in terms of his behavior, due to his dissolute life"[38]

Overall, therefore, it seems that the Protestant academies and universities of the early modern period were successful in providing fairly standardized and supervised training to both a local and an international clientele. The creation of a network of confessionally attuned institutions allowed churches the flexibility to have students trained closer to home or farther afield, with the reassurance of letters back and forth to ensure oversight even at a distance. If war or plague broke out, or confessional changes occurred, students could be sent on to another institution that would continue providing academic training in the same vein. Those charged with assessing the preparation of candidates for ministry could increasingly rely on a similar level of education gained by all candidates, and could more readily compare like with like to ensure that the most able candidates were selected for ordination.

Challenges: Funding, Faculty, and Student Diversity

Yet the model of higher education fostered by the Reformation faced some major challenges. Some of these were basic and practical ones tied to lack of resources, whereas other challenges were more principial, targeting the very foundations of Protestant higher education. Among the most basic challenges were the perennial and linked problems of finding sufficient funding and enough able professors to staff the institutions. The funding challenge was particularly acute for new institutions, which could not benefit from any preexisting contributions to higher education at the local level. Fees charged to students were minimal and did not generate enough income to cover institutional costs, chief of which were the salaries of the professors. In some instances, as in Zurich, the church authorities over time could redirect the income that had previously supported the pre-Reformation canons of the Grossmünster, Zurich's cathedral, but this process was slow and subject to reverses if the city government had a more urgent need for these funds.[39] Major financial problems, compounded by a shortage of students owing to the Savoyard blockade in 1586, led to the dismissal of professors and the temporary shutdown of the Genevan a-cademy, in spite of the impassioned protests of the Genevan clergy to the Genevan government.[40] The Genevan pastors seemed aware of the academy's crucial role as the flagship for the Reformed faith, describing it as a "nursery" for future leaders and noting that the Catholics would rejoice to hear that the academy had closed down.[41] In this period at least, the link between the Protestant communities and their centers of higher education was so strong that an injury to one caused grief and harm to the other. Although the academy was able to reopen in 1587, it proved more difficult to attract professors of the same caliber as had been in place before the closure.

The funding problems facing the French Huguenot academies were even more serious. After the king's subsidy stopped being paid in the 1620s and 1630s, the national synod's plan to have each province support the academies through a fifth of their offerings never generated enough income to cover the costs. By 1636, several of the professors at the small academy of Die, in southeastern France, had not been paid in over three years.[42] In the end, even amalgamation and selective closures could not stabilize the situation. Their plight was compounded by the active competition provided by Jesuit institutions and by direct royal action to close the Huguenot academies altogether.[43] The Huguenot academies' dangerous vulnerability lay in their lack of sustained political support. In this sense, even though Protestant territorial academies and universities may well have generated complacent theology by virtue of their official status, they at least had a better chance of survival over the longer term, in that they could count on some measure of political backing and financial underwriting for their operation.

The second major challenge facing Protestant academies and universities was to find, recruit, and retain suitable professors. In some ways, the close links among centers of learning that shared the same confessional outlook, paired with the use of Latin as the international medium of instruction, made recruitment straightforward. However, the same factors that simplified bringing a Scottish professor to teach in Geneva or in a Huguenot academy could equally well induce that same professor to take up a more lucrative or less demanding post in another Reformed academy or university.[44] Mobility seemed to be the watchword for many of these professors, and the academy or university unable to provide the most competitive remuneration package could well lose out to another more ambitious institution. Illustrating this problem of competition, the Genevan academy struggled for years beginning in 1587 to find enough money to pay the renowned Hellenist Isaac Casaubon for his work as professor of Greek. In spite of regular salary increases making him the best-paid professor in the academy by far, Casaubon eventually left Geneva for France and a position in Montpellier in 1596.[45] Given these problems, perhaps the most pragmatic solution was the one adopted by Zurich, which decreed already in 1562 that only citizens of Zurich were eligible to teach in the Zurich academy, known as the Lectorium.[46] This decision avoided salary inflation and promoted loyalty among the men eligible to hold these professorial positions. In a canny move, Zurich then invested the money it saved on salaries in its travel scholarship scheme for students from Zurich to gain added academic experience in other European centers of higher learning. One could argue, however, that Zurich's decision came at a cost—namely, a reduction in the range of viewpoints taught in the Lectorium.

Zurich's decision, however, was exceptional. Other institutions preferred to appoint the best possible professors they could afford, regardless of their place of origin. Indeed, the more important factor for most institutions was to ensure that all the faculty, and in some cases the students as well, upheld the same confessional perspective. In most cases this confessional uniformity was put in place through oaths. At the University of Heidelberg, all the professors had to swear their willingness to uphold the Reformed faith, except from 1576 to 1583, when the Palatinate switched to Lutheranism under Elector Ludwig VI.[47] Confessional changes in a given territory thus usually had repercussions in its center of higher education, since professors upholding the previous confession had to be dismissed and replaced with those willing to support the new order. At the very least, therefore, confessional changes even within Protestantism tended to damage the educational process by causing significant personnel shifts within the professoriate.

The problem was not limited to Heidelberg. Nor did the clashes always emerge between confessional groups but, rather, at times between factions within a given confession. For example, during the first decades of the University of Leiden (founded in 1575), tensions surfaced repeatedly between strong proponents of Calvinism among the pastors and professors at the university and those who wanted to see less confessional rigor and a more open approach. In Leiden, the eventual victory went to the moderates, although the repercussions from the hardline Calvinists' victory at the Synod of Dordt in 1620 led to a temporary purge of the more liberal Arminians and their supporters on the university faculty.[48]

In France, intra-Calvinist debates raged over predestination and universal grace in the 1630s, with Moïse Amyraut, professor at the academy of Saumur, advocating a more liberal understanding of predestination, and Pierre du Moulin, professor at the academy of Sedan, championing the more conservative and orthodox approach. Each man gained support, and the ensuing quarrel, fuelled by polemical writings on each side, went all the way to the national synod meeting in Alençon in 1637. While the synod criticized Amyraut and his supporters for their careless use of certain terms and expressions, his doctrinal stance was not condemned in the end.[49] Yet this scholarly controversy had very real repercussions in the Huguenot church, especially when three students who had attended the academy of Saumur were barred from ministry by the provincial synod of Saint-Maixent in 1643, allegedly because they were thought to have absorbed the controversial theological stance adopted by Amyraut.[50] In this instance, doctrinal divisions exacerbated by academic rivalries proved to be a potent mix. On the one hand, one could argue that the Reformation did in fact have a negative effect on higher education by fostering quarrels and splintering over doctrine, even in institutions that were already vulnerable to criticism from the Catholic majority. On the other hand, it is worth pointing out that Amyraut and his supporters in the academy of Saumur felt sufficiently comfortable to challenge the theological status quo and present a more nuanced understanding of a key Reformed doctrine. In this case at least, professors were pushing at the confessional boundaries, not simply complacently reiterating accepted truths.

While confessional oaths were the norm for professors, especially in theology, pressure on students to uphold a specific confessional perspective was less common. In many instances, government and church authorities could see the advantages of having a more open policy in admitting students of different confessional backgrounds to the university or academy. Even if student fees were minimal to nonexistent, each new student, particularly a wealthy one, represented a significant investment in the local economy.[51] The Genevan academy's experience regarding confessional requirements is particularly instructive. When the academy was established in 1559, students who matriculated had to sign their agreement to an extensive confession of faith, which ran to several pages and explicitly rejected Catholicism, the Lutheran view of the Lord's Supper, and Anabaptism. If students wanted to agree truthfully with the confession, they would have to be reformed.[52] Yet by 1584, less than twenty-five years after the academy opened its doors, the lengthy confession was replaced by a much shorter statement simply declaring that each student would respect and obey the Genevan magistrates and academic authorities. The declaration did include a promise to reject all "papist superstitions" and all manifest heresies, making it highly unlikely that any Catholic student would try to enroll, but the brevity and general nature of the new oath opened the door to non-Reformed Protestants.[53] Geneva itself was no less Reformed in 1584 than it had been in 1559. But the academy was trying to broaden its appeal to a wider range of Protestant students, and had only just begun to invest more heavily in the teaching of civil law. In a bid to attract Lutheran law students in particular, Theodore Beza convinced his colleagues in the Genevan Company of Pastors that a shorter and less comprehensive confession of faith for students would in fact be beneficial for the academy. And yet this change was not an easy one. Some of the Lutheran students who did come to Geneva did not see any need to respect the confessional teachings of their hosts. Notoriously, in 1615 the Genevan pastors complained that some of the German students had been mocking the Genevan Lord's Supper by handing around bread to one another and saying "Here, have some of Calvin's bread!"[54]

Across the board, governing authorities overseeing Protestant academies and universities were struggling with the same issue: How did one ensure the confessional character of the institution would come through clearly and be perpetuated from one generation to the next? Confessional oaths for professors and confessions of faith for students seemed to be one way to keep the faith commitment of the institutions strong. Yet in both cases the desire for consistent confessional allegiances came into conflict with other aims, including recruiting the best possible professors and attracting the broadest possible student body. The commitment to academic excellence and to a broader-based student recruitment involved risks, but in many cases, the authorities seemed willing to take that chance.

Assessing the Impact of the Reformation

Although our focus in this chapter was necessarily limited, what conclusions can be drawn? Overall, the impact of the Reformation on Western higher education in the early modern period was significant. Faced with the urgent need to create or restructure centers of higher education to prepare the next generation of leaders for church and state, government and religious authorities poured resources of time and energy and money into this project. While the first years of transition were difficult ones, the next decades saw the development of an extensive network of academies and universities in both Lutheran and Reformed lands. Linked together by their studies and their confessional commitments, faculty and students created networks of learning that stretched across linguistic and cultural borders.

In emphasizing the importance of a standardized curriculum and assessment process, especially for future pastors, the Protestant universities and academies contributed to the creation of an *esprit de corps* among clergy that often perpetuated itself from father to son in pastoral dynasties. Although church authorities may well have preferred their centers of higher education to reinforce the confessional perspective of the group, sufficient examples of controversy and polemic show that a spirit of academic inquiry had the potential to challenge and blunt strict orthodoxy. In the end, the Reformation's greatest legacy to higher education may, in fact, be the very fragmentation of Christendom decried at the start, since religious division motivated faculty and students to delve into the teachings of their faith in order to defend them. But to do this effectively, a serious and sustained commitment to learning was required.

Notes

1. Quoted in G. R. Zimmermann, *Die Zürcher Kirche von der Reformation bis zum dritten Reformationsjubiläum* (Zurich: S. Höhr, 1878), 75.
2. See, for instance, Leland Ryken, "Reformation and Puritan Ideals of Education," in *Making Higher Education Christian: The History and Mission of Evangelical Colleges in North America*, ed. Joel Carpenter and Kenneth Shipps (St. Paul, MN: Christian University Press, 1987), 38–51.
3. Thomas Albert Howard, *Protestant Theology and the Making of the Modern German University* (Oxford: Oxford University Press, 2006), 60–124.
4. See, for instance, George Marsden, *The Soul of the American University* (Oxford: Oxford University Press, 1994), 33–84; John van Engen, "Christianity and the Universities: the Medieval and Reformation Legacies," in *Making Higher Education Christian: The History and Mission of Evangelical Colleges in North America*, ed. Joel Carpenter and Kenneth Shipps (St. Paul, MN: Christian University Press, 1987), 19–37; and Mark Noll, "The Revolution, the Enlightenment, and Christian Higher Education in the Early Republic," in *Making Higher Education Christian: The History and Mission of Evangelical Colleges in North America*, ed. Joel Carpenter and Kenneth Shipps (St. Paul, MN: Christian University Press, 1987), 56–76.
5. Ryken, "Reformation and Puritan Ideals of Education," 40–43.
6. Brad Gregory, *The Unintended Reformation* (Cambridge, MA: Harvard University Press, 2012), ch. 6, 298–364.
7. Jacques Verger, "Patterns," in *A History of the University in Europe* ed. Hilde de Ridder-Symoens (Cambridge: Cambridge University Press, 1992), 57. Verger comes up with a total of sixty-three to sixty-six universities in operation in 1500—the discrepancy is based on whether institutions in Gerona, Parma, and Lucca really operated as universities at the time.
8. Amy Nelson Burnett, *Teaching the Reformation: Ministers and their Message in Basel, 1529–1629* (Oxford: Oxford University Press, 2006), 22, 78–79.
9. Martin Luther, *To the Christian Nobility of the German Nation Concerning the Reform of the Christian Estate* (1520), in *Luther's Works*, ed. James Atkinson (Philadelphia: Fortress Press, 1966), 44:207.

10. Luther, *The Misuse of the Mass* (1521), in *Luther's Works*, ed. Abdel Ross Wentz (Philadelphia: Muhlenberg Press, 1959), 36:225.

11. Andreas Bodenstein von Karlstadt, *The Meaning of Gelassen and Where in Holy Scripture It Is Found*, in *The Essential Carlstadt*, ed. E. J. Furcha (Waterloo, Canada: Herald Press, 1995), 161–62.

12. Ronald Sider, *Andreas Bodenstein von Karlstadt: the Development of His Thought* (Leiden: Brill, 1974), 176–78. Yet Bill McNeil argues that Karlstadt was not rejecting higher learning per se, but only the self-seeking behavior of some academic colleagues. See McNeil, "Andreas von Karlstadt as a Humanist Theologian," in *Radical Reformation Studies: Essays Presented to James M. Stayer*, ed. Werner Packhull and Geoffrey Dipple (Aldershot: Ashgate, 1999), 117–19.

13. Howard, *Protestant Theology*, 63–67.

14. Karin Maag, *Seminary or University? The Genevan Academy and Reformed Higher Education, 1560–1620* (Aldershot: Scolar Press, 1995), 155–57.

15. Lewis Spitz, "The Impact of the Reformation on the Universities," in *University and Reformation: Lectures from the University of Copenhagen Symposium*, ed. Leif Grane (Leiden: Brill, 1981), 9–31, esp. 20.

16. For more on the impact of university studies particularly on Protestant clergy in the Reformation era, see Bernard Vogler, *Le Clergé protestant rhénan au siècle de la réforme (1555–1619)* (Paris: Editions Ophyris, 1957), 53–68.

17. Maria Rosa di Simone, "Admission," in *A History of the University in Europe*, ed. Hilde de Ridder-Symoens (Cambridge: Cambridge University Press, 1996), 2:291–92.

18. See Willem Frijhoff, "Patterns," in *A History of the University in Europe*, ed. Hilde de Ridder-Symoens (Cambridge: Cambridge University Press, 1996), 2:70–89.

19. For more on the Genevan academy's early developments, see Maag, *Seminary or University*, 23–28.

20. See the detailed study by Karine Crousaz, *L'Académie de Lausanne entre humanisme et réforme (ca. 1537–1560)* (Leiden: Brill, 2012), especially 215–32 on the nomination process for professors.

21. Crousaz, *L'Académie de Lausanne*, 102–19.

22. See Vogler, *Le Clergé protestt rhénan*, esp. 76–78 for more on princes' deep interest in ensuring the orthodoxy and quality of their future pastors' studies.

23. See, for instance, Jean-Paul Pittion's analysis in "Instruire et édifier: les protestants et l'éducation en France sous l'édit de Nantes," in *Les Huguenots éducateurs dans l'espace européen à l'époque moderne*, ed. Geraldine Sheridan and Viviane Prest (Paris: Champion, 2011), 37–38.

24. Van Engen, "Christianity and the University," 24–27.

25. Laurence Brockliss, "Curricula," in *A History of the University in Europe*, ed. Hilde de Ridder-Symoens (Cambridge: Cambridge University Press, 1996), 2:565–67.

26. Karin Maag, "Preaching Practice: Reformed Students' Sermons," in *The Formation of Clerical and Confessional Identities in Early Modern Europe*, ed. Wim Janse and Barbara Pitkin (Leiden: Brill, 2006), 135–36.

27. Burnett, *Teaching the Reformation*, 165–66.

28. Indeed, when the *deniers du roi* trickled away to nothing in the late 1620s and 1630s the Huguenot church was so invested in its academies that it put in place various measures to continue funding the institutions, including having each province collect funds through offerings, a fifth of which would go to support the academies. Karin Maag, "The Huguenot Academies: Preparing for an Uncertain Future," in *Society and Culture in the Huguenot World, 1559–1685*, ed. Raymond Mentzer and Andrew Spicer (Cambridge: Cambridge University Press, 2002), 154–55.

29. Maag, "The Huguenot Academies," 150.

30. Jean Aymon, *Tous les synodes nationaux des églises réformées de France* (The Hague, 1710), 2:203.

31. For an overview of similar issues in the Dutch context, see Willem Frijhoff, "Inspiration, instruction, compétence? Questions autour de la selection des pasteurs réformés aux Pays-Bas, XVIe-XVIIe siècles," *Paedagogica Historica* 30 (1994): 13–38.

32. Vogler, *Le Clergé protestant rhénan*, 57. Vogler suggests further that across the board in Protestant areas about two-thirds of all pastors had pursued studies in a university or academy by the last decades of the sixteenth century (78).

33. The results of the increasing expectation that pastoral candidates would have studied in academies or universities can be seen in Frijhoff, "Inspiration, instruction," 20–31.

34. Vogler, *Le Clergé protestant rhénan*, 78.

35. Van Engen, "Christianity and the Universities," 34.

36. For more on the Zurich travel scholarship system, see Karin Maag, "Financing Education: The Zurich Approach, 1550–1620," in *Reformations Old and New: Essays on the Socio-Economic Impact of Religious Change c. 1470–1630*, ed. Beat Kümin (Aldershot: Ashgate, 1996), 203–16.

37. Vogler, *Le Clergé protestant rhénan*, 60.

38. Matteo Campagnolo, Micheline Louis-Courvoisier, and Gabriella Cahier, eds., *Registres de la compagnie des pasteurs de Genève* (Geneva: Droz, 1989), ix, 239. In the end (and perhaps not surprisingly) Verneuil did not end up in ministry, but instead became an under-librarian at the Bodleian in Oxford.

39. Maag, "Financing Education: the Zurich Approach," 207–08.

40. Maag, *Seminary or University*, 61–64.

41. Maag, *Seminary or University*, 62–63.

42. Maag, "The Huguenot Academies," 155.

43. Maag, "The Huguenot Academies," 155–56.

44. Maag, "Financing Education: the Zurich Approach," 204.

45. Maag, *Seminary or University*, 71–72.
46. Maag, "Financing Education," 207.
47. Maag, *Seminary or University*, 160.
48. J. J. Woltjer, Introduction, in *Leiden University in the Seventeenth Century: An Exchange of Learning*, ed. T. H. Lunsingh Scheurleer and G. H. M. Posthumus Meyjes (Leiden: Brill, 1975), 4–5.
49. François Laplanche, *Orthodoxie et prédication: l'oeuvre d'Amyraut et la querelle de la grâce universelle* (Paris: Presses Universitaires de France, 1965), 158–64.
50. Laplanche, *Orthodoxie et prédication*, 172–74.
51. When the Genevan political authorities were contemplating the shutdown of the academy in 1586, the Genevan pastors pointed out that "for every écu spent, we have profited from 100 écus." Maag, *Seminary or University*, 64.
52. For the full text of the confession of faith (in French), see Sven and Suzanne Stelling-Michaud, *Le Livre du recteur de l'académie de Genève (1559–1878)* (Geneva: Droz, 1959), 1:74–77.
53. Stelling-Michaud, *Le Livre du recteur*, 1:66.
54. Maag, *Seminary or University*, 100–01.

6

The Reformation and Modernity

EXPLAINING THE CAUSAL NEXUS

Brad S. Gregory

HAVING RECENTLY DEVOTED over five hundred pages to examining the relationship between the Reformation era and Western modernity, I can hardly hope to compress its argument into a single chapter.[1]
It might nevertheless facilitate reflection on the Reformation's influence
on the formation and continuing transformations of modernity to present a few major themes from the narrative that I offer in *The Unintended
Reformation* in comparison to two influential, alternative narratives about
the Reformation's relationship to the modern Western world.

Historians should be clear what they are talking about, regardless
of what they are talking about. As with all large-scale narratives about
major historical realities, concepts, and processes, what we understand
by "the Reformation" and "modernity" importantly shapes how we answer
the question about the impact of the first on the second. If, for example,
"the Reformation" means "the Protestant Reformation," which in turn
means "the magisterial Protestant Reformation" (i.e., Lutheranism and
Reformed Protestantism in the sixteenth and early seventeenth centuries),
then our referent is different from instances in which "the Reformation"
means (more narrowly) "the German Reformation" or includes (more
broadly) the Radical Reformation or the Catholic (or Counter-) Reformation
as well. So, too, what we mean by "modernity" affects how we answer the
question—what features we regard as distinctive of it, and whether or not
we view it as an identifiable historical period into which Westerners began
to enter, say, around the time of the Atlantic democratic revolutions of

the late eighteenth century, and out of which in recent decades we have passed into what Daniel Rodgers has called the "age of fracture," a new era of "postmodernity."[2] If we think of modernity, as well as the Middle Ages or the early modern period, as discrete epochs that have come and gone, then the task becomes understanding the relationship between the Reformation and some chosen point between, say, the late eighteenth and late twentieth centuries. Alternatively, we might see "modernity" as still ongoing and thus as a gradually moving target, its salient aspects changing in ways that alter the Reformation's relationship to it over time; the European realities and historical trajectory upon which Ernst Troeltsch commented a century ago on the cusp of the First World War, for example, in *The Meaning of Protestantism for the Origin of the Modern World*, are very different from Western realities and subsequent history a century later, because of all that has transpired in the interim.[3] If we adopt this perspective, we might be more inclined toward something like Zygmunt Bauman's distinction between "solid modernity" and "liquid modernity" as differently relevant to the connections we want to try to see.[4]

Mindful of these considerations, most of this essay will focus on an abbreviated version of two important themes from *The Unintended Reformation*—namely, the unresolved doctrinal disagreements of the Reformation era and their relationship to the protection of individual religious freedom in modern liberal states. It might be useful, however, to compare my own interpretation with two alternative accounts, which I will call the *liberal-progressive narrative* and the *revisionist-confessionalization narrative*. My brief descriptions are not intended to do justice to different versions of and variations on these accounts, but they should help to set my own arguments, which are indebted to both of them, in clearer relief, and perhaps help to facilitate thinking about issues relevant to the relationship between the Reformation and modernity. For the most part the Reformation continues to be conceived as some variation on one of these two narratives, as we will very likely continue to see in the run-up to and recognition of the Reformation's quincentenary.

The passage of time and therefore historical processes impolitely ignore whatever periodization schemes historians devise. Therefore, it seems conducive to greater insight about historical change over time if we regard the processes either set in motion or fundamentally altered by the Reformation as having not yet run their course. The emergence of modern liberal political institutions is historically unintelligible apart from the religio-political conflicts of the Reformation era; in one form or another, they continue to constitute the institutional context within which the inhabitants of North American and European countries hold their beliefs, enact their desires, and live out their lives. We gain greater insight into the character of change over time in general, and into the effects of the Reformation on Western modernity more specifically, if we do not think of the past as a series of more or less discrete stadial epochs that leave earlier ones behind but, rather, as ongoing, complex processes in which the distant past can and does continue to influence the present.

The Liberal-Progressive Narrative

Whether in an avowedly Protestant form that emphasizes the restoration of the gospel or a secular form that belongs to classic sociological modernization theory indebted to the Enlightenment, the Reformation according to the liberal-progressive narrative is conceived as an integral stepping-stone in a (and perhaps *the*) story of human progress and emancipation. Modern Western freedom, autonomy, and the self-determination of individuals in rational, scientific, liberal-democratic states are regarded as the apex not only of Western but also often of world history. Along with the Renaissance, whose humanists recovered ancient philosophical and literary texts and scorned the speculations of scholastic theologians, the Reformation, beginning with and epitomized by Martin Luther's refusal to submit to papal pressure between 1518 and 1521, liberated individuals from thralldom to medieval superstition and the unbiblical traditions of a corrupt and self-serving Roman Church by proclaiming "the freedom of a Christian." The revolutionary idea that individual lay Christians should be the masters of their own religious lives broke Rome's authoritarian stranglehold and laid the foundations not only for modern religious freedom but also for the eventual expansion and political protection of individual rights much more generally.[5] In tandem with the pioneering philological and historical-critical scholarship by Renaissance humanists such as Lorenzo Valla and Erasmus, the Protestant reformers' critical attitude toward the historical and doctrinal claims of the Roman Church established the groundwork for the intellectual achievements of modern history, philosophy, and science in the scientific revolution and Enlightenment. Here, some secular versions of the liberal-progressive narrative indebted to Max Weber view the Protestant Reformation as having contributed to the "disenchantment of the world" by rejecting, in Keith Thomas's phrase,

144 LOOKING BACK

"the magic of the medieval church" and replacing it with a Protestant providentialism more conducive to embracing the uniform natural causality of modern science.[6]

Additional common elements of the liberal-progressive narrative include the Reformation's emphasis on lay Bible reading, which departed from medieval clerical misgivings, if not prohibitions of the same, stimulating lay literacy and leading eventually to modern universal education. The rejection of usury and new respect for lay vocations in the "priesthood of all believers" emancipated economic initiative and, in combination with the application of scientific discoveries in technology, facilitated the emergence of modern capitalism and the material progress associated with industrialization. The taming of the medieval Church's political power ended centuries of divided sovereignty and provided the basis for the eventual, harmonious separation of church and state, with citizens participating in the democratic political life of modern nation-states even as they worshiped God freely (or freely chose not to worship God) according to their consciences.[7] And the evangelical imperative characteristic of the restored gospel, alternately misused or misunderstood by the medieval Church, was appropriated by imperial modern nation-states to spread civilization and progress by way of European colonization throughout the world.

Much more could be said about this narrative, of course, but it is certainly widely recognizable. Despite many qualifications and criticisms in recent decades, some form of it still functions as a procrustean bed of most textbook narratives of Western history between the Middle Ages and the present. Whatever its merits as history, the strong connections it draws between the Reformation and characteristically modern ideas, institutions, and patterns of behavior looked more appealing to many people, I would suggest, before the horrors of the twentieth century that began with the First World War and continued through multiple genocides and the violence of decolonization; disclosures about the atrocities inflicted because of European imperialism; the manifest capacities of technology for destruction and evil, as well as service and good to humanity; developing-world immiseration and the threat of ecological disaster because of globalization and deregulated capitalism; the exercise of individual autonomy in ways that reject all religious belief and reconfigure public ethics and laws in unprecedented ways (e.g., abortion, euthanasia, gay marriage); and so forth.[8] Additionally, numerous aspects of the scholarship presupposed by the liberal-progressive narrative have been seriously called into question,

if not undermined: consider the widespread evidence indicative of lay enthusiasm for the practice of Catholicism in the decades prior to 1517, the
embrace of reform-minded humanism by numerous scholastic theologians and church leaders prior to the Reformation, the extent of late medieval lay Bible reading and number of vernacular printed Bibles except
for in England, the vitality of late medieval intellectual life, the extent to
which scholastic thinkers had already accommodated the prohibition of
usury in the midst of thriving markets in the cities of northern and central Italy, southwestern Germany, and Flanders in the late fifteenth and
early sixteenth centuries, and the extent to which secular authorities were
already exercising control over late medieval church institutions in cities
and territories under their jurisdiction.[9] All of this implies that if there
was a sharp break between the Middle Ages and the Reformation, it assumed a form different in significant ways from the one presented in the
liberal-progressive narrative.

The Revisionist-Confessionalization Narrative

What I am calling for the sake of convenience the revisionist-confessionalization narrative groups together a number of emphases in Reformation
research over the past half-century. Not all of them are found in the scholarship of all the historians who have contributed to and work within the
revisionist-confessionalization paradigm. In contrast to the liberal-progressive narrative, among its major features is an emphasis on *continuities*
between the late Middle Ages and the Reformation, as well as on many
more *discontinuities* than continuities or causal connections between
the Reformation and modernity. Heiko Oberman influentially portrayed
Martin Luther not as the "first modern man" but, rather, as an intensely
apocalyptic medieval Augustinian friar obsessed with damnation and the
devil.[10] The Protestant Reformation is regarded as having grown out of
the vitality and burgeoning self-conscious participation in religious life by
increasing numbers of devout laity and clergy, longstanding late medieval
calls for reform in the Roman Church, and important strands of late medieval mysticism and scholasticism.[11]

Seen from a broader chronological and confessionally comparative perspective, the Protestant Reformation—which in the revisionist-
confessionalization narrative, like the liberal-progressive narrative, overwhelmingly denotes Lutheranism and Reformed Protestantism[12]—in its

most enduring features comprises a parallel to the Catholic Reformation before, and especially after, the Council of Trent. Common goals were being sought by confessional sovereign rulers regardless of their specific commitments, which made the "long Reformation" as a whole part of a broad, centuries-long process of modern state-building that had begun embryonically in the later Middle Ages but intensified significantly in the period of early modern confessionalization.[13] The Reformation's most important continuities with modernity are not ideological or moral but, rather, institutional and behavioral: in Lutheran, Reformed, and Catholic regimes, the Reformation marked a much more determined effort by polit- ical authorities working in tandem with clergy to catechize and discipline their subjects, to render them socially and politically obedient throughout their respective territories. Although the process was far from uniformly successful and met many sorts of resistance and forms of accommoda- tion, by and large it produced Christians that, regardless of confessional affiliation, were better catechized and subjects who were more obedient than their medieval forebears had been.

In contrast to the liberal-progressive narrative, the revisionist- confessionalization narrative regards the Protestant Reformation, like the Catholic Reformation, as fundamentally other and alien. The Protestant Reformation is much closer to medieval Christianity than to modernity in its earnest biblicism, marked providentialism, conspicuous apocalyti- cism, emphasis on confessional uniformity, policing of heterodoxy and dissent, and commitment to Christianity as something that properly should inform public life. The hallmarks of Western liberal modernity— politically protected individual freedom, self-determination, and autonomy within churches and states that are institutionally separated from each other—represent *breaks* with the Reformation rather than its extension or continuation, in what Mark Lilla has called "the Great Separation."[14] The ideological lineage of modern individual autonomy is rooted not in biblical hermeneutics and theologies of salvation but in post-Cartesian moral and political philosophies concerned to set public life since the Enlightenment on rational foundations liberated from reference to scrip- ture, authority, or tradition.[15] Seventeenth-century thinkers such as Locke, Bayle, or Berkeley are transitional figures, but ultimately closer to secular modernity in their commitments than they are to Luther's spiritual anxi- eties (*Anfechtungen*) or Calvin's overwhelming sense of ubiquitous divine providence. Western modernity does not represent a teleological continu- ation or fulfillment of the Protestant Reformation in ideological or moral terms. It is, rather, a rejection of its aspirations to confessional uniformity within a Christian worldview and conception of Christian society, no less than a rejection of the Catholic Reformation's parallel commitments to the same. But the bureaucratizing instillation of political obedience, social discipline, and catechesis across confessional divides throughout the early modern period deeply shaped Western modernity. It constitutes the most consequential, enduring legacy of the Reformation bequeathed to the nineteenth and twentieth centuries, notwithstanding the caesura of the Atlantic Revolutions and Napoleonic era.

It is perhaps not accidental that the revisionist-confessionalization narrative began to emerge in the late 1950s and early 1960s. At some level, European scholars then began to take account of what had happened to the civilization of their continent between 1914 and 1945—and what was still happening to it as once-mighty European empires evanesced, frequently in the face of violent colonial independence movements. The onward-and-upward narrative of Western civilization and progress had not played out as expected. The story's presumptive teleology was seriously called into question, if not subverted, as Max Horkheimer and Theodor Adorno had argued in no uncertain terms in their *Dialectic of Enlightenment* (1947).[16] Europe's horror show and its "bloodlands" made all too apparent that the increased centralization and bureaucratization of modern states could be harnessed for unprecedented violence, depending on how leaders exercised their power.[17] And the most appalling example of all was, of course, Germany, birthplace of the Reformation and for well over a century before the Third Reich widely regarded as the highest exemplar of modern European thought and culture. So, it was perhaps to be expected, even if the connection between contemporary realities and scholarly approaches to Reformation historiography was not necessarily made explicit, that the relationship between the Reformation and modernity would be reconfigured and reassessed. In addition, the astonishingly rapid and unforeseen secularization of Western European countries (including Britain) in the 1960s and '70s, especially after the boomlet in religious practice in multiple countries on both sides of the Atlantic during the long 1950s, suggested contrast rather than continuity with the Protestant Reformation in the ideological roots of modern individualism and the separation of church and state.[18] (It is worth noting that the United States experienced nothing remotely comparable to Europe's trauma in the first half of the twentieth century; nor, outside the academy, has its secularization been nearly as pervasive thus far, although there are recent signs that this might be changing.[19]) In combination with the research mentioned above, which forced reassessments of the character of late medieval Christianity and early modern Catholicism in relationship to the Protestant Reformation, these twentieth-century contextual considerations seem to have played a significant role in the revisionist-confessionalization paradigm becoming the dominant way in which Reformation scholars since the 1980s have viewed their subject. Theology's place in the Reformation has been marginalized as the academy has become increasingly secularized, in both the United States and Europe. And in a virtual reversal of the liberal-progressive narrative, the Reformation is seen to belong, in Peter Laslett's phrase, to an alien "world we have lost," one separated from modernity by a chasm of alterity in ideas, experience, and institutions essentially as deep as that which separates us from the Middle Ages.[20]

A Different Account: Sola Scriptura and the Problem of Authority

In my view, a more explanatorily powerful account of the relationship between the Reformation and modernity than either the progressive-liberal or the revisionist-confessionalization narratives exists, even if it can and should draw on elements from the other narratives. My account does not simply attempt to identify and trace intended continuities and discontinuities of the Reformation, but also *unintended consequences and unforeseen interactions among different domains of human life over long stretches of time.* In order to see how to combine which elements of the other two narratives into fashioning a more compelling account, we must first revisit the foundational rationale of the Protestant Reformation itself and consider what the other two narratively have ignored.

Anyone who knows anything about the Reformation knows that Luther did not intend to establish a "different" church—as if he thought there could be such a thing—but to reform the one and only church there was, the one established by Christ among his apostles. To all indications, for years after his ordination in 1507 and into his early thirties, Luther thought this church was the Roman Catholic Church into which he and all other Christians in Latin Christendom had been baptized. Yet, as Scott Hendrix has shown, when Luther's initially implicit challenge to papal authority through his objections to indulgences in October 1517 was brushed aside, and he was ordered to recant his views, he made his challenge explicit and drew a conclusion shared by certain medieval Christians condemned as heretics: that the Pope was not the Vicar of Christ, but the Antichrist.[21] Because of the liberating, life-giving experience of God's grace occasioned by his immersion in God's word, Luther came to believe by the Leipzig Disputation in the summer of 1519 that scripture alone (*sola scriptura*) was the basis for Christian faith and life, in principle separate from any patristic, conciliar, papal, or canon-legal claims. In his own words: "Even if Augustine and all the Fathers were to see in Peter the Rock of the church," he said, "I will nevertheless oppose them—even as an isolated individual— supported by the authority of Paul and therefore by divine law."[22] Despite the widespread emphasis on God's mercy in late medieval sermons, art, and devotional literature, despite the pastoral counsel and encouragement of his beloved confessor, Johann von Staupitz, Luther's own experience of penitential practices and examination of conscience brought him to the brink of despair.[23] In dramatic contrast, Luther's experience of justification by faith alone convinced him that his understanding of the dialectic of law and gospel was the hermeneutic key to the correct understanding of God's word because of the vivifying liberation of the burdened Christian conscience it offered. Thus, in his *Address to the Christian Nobility of the German Nation* in August 1520, Luther wrote that a Christian should be "courageous and free," and "not let the spirit of freedom (as Paul calls it) be frightened off by the contrived words of the pope, but rather move right through everything and judge what [the Romanists] do and leave undone according to our faithful interpretation of scripture, and compel them to follow the better interpretation and not their own."[24]

All Protestant reformers, who rejected the authority of the Rome, agreed that God's Word sufficed as the single basis of Christian faith and life and accepting its authority freed one from the restrictions of a self-serving and corrupt clerical hierarchy. This conviction not only legitimated the Reformation but also compelled as a duty the repudiation of Rome out of fidelity to God himself. In the German and Swiss cities that were so important in the early Reformation, other anti-Roman reformers concurred with Luther about scripture's foundational importance. For example, in February 1522, when Andreas Bodenstein von Karlstadt was still the dean of the theology faculty in Wittenberg, he stated in a sermon that "all preachers should always state that their doctrine is not their own, but God's.... They can discover nothing out of their own heads. If the Bible is at an end, then their competence is also at an end [*Wan die Biblien aus ist, sso ist ir kunst auch auss*]."[25] The same year in Zurich, Huldrych

Zwingli declared in his treatise on scripture's clarity and certainty that "no such trust should be given to any word like that given to [the Word of God]. For it is certain and may not fail. It is clear, and will not leave us to err in darkness. It teaches itself on its own [*es leert sich selbs*]."[26] In the same vein, Balthasar Hubmaier, who had earned his doctoral degree in theology under Johannes Eck at Ingolstadt, stated in the Second Zurich Disputation in October 1523 that "in all divisive questions and controversies only scripture, canonized and made holy by God himself, should and must be the judge, no one else. . . . For holy scripture alone is the true light and lantern through which all human argument, darkness, and objections are recognized."[27] And to give just one more from among countless similar examples from the early German Reformation, those who composed the Mühlhausen Articles, one of many such lists of grievances articulated during the German Peasants' War, stated in September 1524 that the right standard of justice was given "in the Bible or holy word of God," and asserted that the city's craftsmen and other parishioners who had formulated the articles had "derived their judgments from the Word of God."[28] Referring to the Bible in 1524, Karlstadt put the matter straightforwardly: "The naked truth alone . . . should be your foundation and rock."[29] In his vigorous response to Erasmus's claims about the freedom of the will in Christian life, Luther wrote in 1525 that "Those who deny that the scriptures are supremely clear and evident leave nothing for us except darkness."[30]

The problem evident to anyone who knows even a little about the Reformation is that from its very outset in the early 1520s, the naked truth and clarity of the scriptures proved not only hermeneutically elusive but also doctrinally contentious, and therefore socially divisive and sometimes also politically subversive. Because of the foundational importance of *sola scriptura,* as Mark Noll argues in his contribution to this volume, the most important questions of the Protestant Reformation were asked rhetorically and pastorally by Luther already in 1520: "What then is this Word, or in what manner is it to be used, since there are so many words of God?"[31] Those who rejected Rome answered the question in a range of ways, the vast majority of which went politically unsupported and indeed were actively suppressed, not only by Roman Catholic regimes but also by the new Lutheran and Reformed regimes. And as far as Protestant and Catholic authorities were concerned, for good reason: especially in the wake of the most widespread expression of the early German Reformation, the so-called Peasants' War of 1524–26, political leaders drew the inescapable conclusion that some readings of scripture could be dangerously subversive. They would have to be carefully overseen and policed.

Reformers such as Luther and Philip Melanchthon in Wittenberg, Zwingli in Zurich, and Martin Bucer in Strasbourg agreed that the "freedom of a Christian" did not justify disobedience to secular authorities, for as Paul had written—in what became a widely repeated proof text in such contexts throughout the Reformation era—"whoever resists authority resists what God has appointed" (Rom. 13:2). By the late 1530s, Henry VIII was demonstrating the sufficiency of the royal will for the seizure of the wealth from all of England's nearly 900 religious houses. During 1534–35, an alarming, communitarian and polygamist "New Jerusalem" in Münster led by the prophet-king Jan van Leiden had eliminated whatever doubts about the dangers posed by religious radicalism and dissent might have remained among secular authorities in Europe.[32] The political implications were as serious as they were clear. Lest complacent rulers permit another Peasants' War or Kingdom of Münster, they had to follow Paul and "execute wrath on the wrongdoer" (Rom. 13:5), crushing religiously inspired rebellion in accord with divinely ordained duty. A confessionalizing alliance was thereby created between anti-Roman Christians who supported and cooperated with secular political authorities and those who did not—that is, in a nutshell, the difference between magisterial and radical Protestants. Only a carefully monitored, domesticated Reformation would be permitted to exert a widespread influence. And by and large, that is what happened throughout the Reformation era, which is bookended by England in the 1640s and '50s: another time and place in which the open-ended character of the effects of the Reformation's foundational principle became evident in the absence of effective public control of religion by political authorities.[33]

Why does all of this matter? Because we misunderstand the Protestant Reformation and its relationship to modernity unless we historically reintegrate radical with magisterial Protestants with reference to the foundational principle they shared. By contrast, most Protestant and secular versions of the liberal-progressive narrative, as well as all versions of the revisionist-confessionalization narrative, either marginalize or ignore the radical Reformation. That is, they marginalize or ignore the *large majority of ways* in which Reformation-era Protestants in fact answered the question of what true Christianity was, based on the Reformation's own foundational principle. In some Protestant versions of the liberal-progressive narrative, radical Protestants merit at most a minor reference because "the Reformation"—indeed, perhaps even "Protestantism" as such—is defined theologically, confessionally, or ideologically rather than historically, with reference to interpreters' commitments to some form of Lutheran or Reformed Protestantism. In secular and some different Protestant versions of the liberal-progressive narrative, untied to normative Lutheran or Reformed beliefs, radical Protestants sometimes merit more attention as the harbingers of modern toleration: Sebastian Castellio, Dirck Volckertszoon Coornhert, John Milton, Roger Williams, and others grasped, or at least intuited, the importance of individual freedom of religious belief and practice that would eventually become the basis for the multiplication of modern individual rights as an expansive range of legally defined and politically protected entitlements.[34] But modern freedom of religion and the separation of church and state tend to be viewed as the end of the story, as if history had arrived at its *telos*, rather than also understood as the beginning of a new chapter in the same historical trajectory. The revisionist-confessional narrative tends to pay the least attention to the radical Reformation because, with the exception of some short-lived experiments with "civic Anabaptism" in the early German Reformation, most notoriously with the Kingdom of Münster in 1534–35, no forms of radical Protestantism enjoyed the political support that was a prerequisite for the long-term, demographically widespread processes of confessionalization that are thought to have constituted the most consequential legacy of the Reformation era to Western modernity.

Whether because of Reformed or Lutheran confessional sympathies, sociological theories of modernization, or attachment to the Reformation as confessionalization, the historical fact of *political approval and support for magisterial Protestants*—essential to long-term success in creating demographically widespread Lutheran or Reformed Protestant confessional identities—has for centuries led to the marginalization of most of the ways in which Christians who rejected the Roman Church understood scripture and applied their respective understandings of it to their lives. Lutheran and Reformed Protestantism have been seen as normal and normative, as mainline and mainstream, rather than viewing them as they were: the great exceptions of the Protestant Reformation. Consider only the first two decades of the Reformation in central Europe and the Low Countries. Which Christians who rejected Rome, starting from the principle of *sola scriptura*, sufficiently disagreed with every Lutheran or Reformed Protestant leader to refuse to worship or have fellowship with them? (Note that this is structurally parallel to the disagreement that led to the ecclesial and social rejection of the Roman Church by magisterial Protestants.) An incomplete list would include Karlstadt (before he settled in Zurich in 1530), all the leaders involved in the Peasants' War, the Swiss Brethren, the South German and Austrian Anabaptists who later contributed to the Austerlitz Brethren, Gabrielites, Philipites, and Hutterites, plus the Melchiorites, Münsterites, Batenburgers, Davidites, Mennonites, central German Anabaptists after the Peasants' War, Caspar Schwenckfeld, Sebastian Franck, and Michael Servetus.[35] This does not include the many other anti-Roman Christian reformers, theologians, and communities that also rejected Lutheranism and Reformed Protestantism throughout the remainder of the sixteenth and seventeenth centuries.[36] These various radical Protestants stand apart, of course, from the divisive disagreements within magisterial Protestant traditions—between Philippists and Gnesio-Lutherans in Germany in the decades after Luther's death in 1546, for example, or between Arminians and Reformed Protestants in the Dutch Republic and England in the early seventeenth century.[37]

The Rise of the Modern Liberal State

We cannot accurately construe the relationship of the Reformation to modernity unless we reintegrate the radical Reformation historically with the magisterial Reformation, and in manner that does not privilege the latter. But this is only part of the picture that needs to be brought into sharper focus if we are to explain the ways in which the Reformation not only profoundly influenced but also continues to transform the world in which we live today. In the Reformation era, dissenting religious views were policed and suppressed in confessional regimes; in the modern era, all religious and nonreligious views are tolerated and protected in liberal states, provided their adherents are politically obedient. The transition from one to the other constitutes an institutional aspect of the Reformation's influence on modernity no less important than the unintended and open-ended doctrinal pluralism that becomes clear when we reintegrate the radical Reformation. Indeed, combining the two yields a picture of the Reformation's long-term influence different from either the liberal-progressive or the revisionist-confessional narrative, even as it includes some aspects of both. The institutional aspect of the story was driven, not by the Protestant doctrinal and social diversity that resulted from *sola scriptura* and its adjuncts, but by magisterial Protestant and Catholic confessional regimes in conflict.

Rival Reformation-era Christian protagonists believed that the issues about which they disagreed bore on the possibility of eternal salvation. Hence, they understandably demonstrated their willingness to kill and die for them. This occurred within individual polities, in the judicial executions of unrepentant heretics or religious traitors, which (as far as authorities were concerned) sought to eliminate the danger to souls posed by heretics' deadly errors. From the perspective of executed co-religionists, in stark contrast, such executions created latter-day martyrs whose heroic imitation of Christ extended even through his passion and death.[38] Besides judicial executions, several major civil and international wars of the Reformation era—from the German Peasants' War of the mid-1520s through the Schmalkaldic War, the French Wars of Religion, the Dutch Revolt against Spain, the Thirty Years' War, and the English Revolution—while not motivated exclusively by or concerned solely with religion, cannot be understood apart from their respective protagonists' doctrinal commitments.

The religio-political violence of the Reformation era is lucidly intelligible when seen through the eyes of its respective protagonists. It also proved unsustainable in the long term, destructive to the societies torn apart by it. Different solutions were attempted: conceding to territorial rulers in the Holy Roman Empire their choice of either Lutheranism or Catholicism after 1555; creating a tenuous place for religious minorities, whether English Catholics beginning in Elizabeth's reign, or French Protestants after the Edict of Nantes in 1598 and before its revocation in 1685; or dividing previously united territories, as essentially occurred in the Low Countries by 1585. The creation of a fundamentally new paradigm, though, required the legitimation of Leviathan—as certain pragmatic advocates of compromise began to suggest during the French Wars of Religion, and as Hobbes argued in 1651 amid the tumult of the English Revolution.[39] Confessional conflicts prompted a new rationale for the state: by saving warring Christians from themselves, it would secure for its citizens an apparently otherwise elusive stability. But the place of religion in public life would have to change; indeed, "religion" as something that could be separated from the exercise of power, public social relationships, and economic interactions would have to be invented.

Full-blown religio-political conflict was not exported to the North American British colonies, although post-Reformation Christian pluralism and the suppression of religious dissent certainly were, as men and women learned who ran afoul of authorities in early Puritan Massachusetts. Problems of religious coexistence, rooted in divergent communities that were themselves the social corollary of divergent readings of scripture, remained alive and well in the fledgling United States in the late 1770s and '80s. The enduring significance of difficulties derived from post-Reformation Christian pluralism, among Protestants as well as between Protestants and Catholics, is evident in the notes jotted down in December 1784 by James Madison as the state of Virginia was debating whether to establish and support an official church. Baptists and other dissenters had objected to established Anglicanism in Virginia during the colonial period. Madison's quite remarkable ruminations are as follows:

3. What is Xty [Christianity]? Courts of law to Judge
4. What edition, Hebrew, Septuagint, or vulgate? What copy—what translation?
5. What books canonical, what apocryphal? The papists holding to be the former what protestants the latter, the Lutherans the latter what other protestants & papists the former
6. In What light are they to be viewed, as dictated every letter by inspiration, or the essential parts only? Or the matter in general not the words?
7. What sense the true one, for if some doctrines be essential to Xnty, those who reject these, whatever name they take are no Xn Society?
8. Is it Trinitarianism, arianism, Socinianism? Is it salvation by faith or works also—by free grace, or free will—&c, &c, &c—
9. What clue is to guide Judge thro' this labyrinth? When the question comes before them whether any particular Society is a Xn Society?
10. Ends in what is orthodoxy, what heresy?[40]

We see here, unmistakably, the living continuation of socially divisive and politically contentious doctrinal disagreements rooted in sixteenth-century disputes about the text and meaning of God's Word. They were not only theologically relevant but also politically pressing in the new American nation, a very different context from the confessional regimes of early modern Europe but one no less affected by the Reformation and its long-term, unintended consequences.

We all know what resulted: the birth of the modern liberal state. In certain respects it had already been adumbrated in practice beginning in the Golden Age Dutch Republic, in which commercially minded merchants in the cities of Holland and Zeeland supported Reformed Protestantism as the "public church" but did not make their unusual polity a confessional regime with a state religion.[41] The Dutch deemphasized confessional uniformity in the interests of commerce, with great economic success. And in other ways, the First Amendment of the U.S. Constitution presented no Jeffersonian "wall of separation between church and state" to those states that continued to sanction and support particular churches (until 1818 in Connecticut and 1833 in Massachusetts); much more broadly, David Sehat has argued that a de facto Protestant "moral establishment" remained legally enshrined until well into the twentieth century in the United States and thus demonstrates the American "myth of religious freedom."[42] But eventually, not only in the United States but also in all other Western countries, the outcome has been the state's protection of freedom of religious belief and practice as a solution to the problems posed by religious pluralism. We are all familiar with the basic arrangement: in exchange for political obedience, each individual is permitted to believe (or not to believe) whatever she wishes, to practice (or not practice) whatever religion she prefers, and to express herself with respect to religion in whatever ways she would like. This required a disembedding (and indeed the creation) of religion as something separate and separable from the multiple domains of life with which it had been intertwined in early modern confessional regimes no less than in the Middle Ages. Religion is privatized and religious freedom is made an individual right, with the state alone determining public morality and controlling the public expression of religious practice. The solution to the problem of religious disagreement, intolerance, violence, and coercion, as Western writers and journalists repeatedly invoke today with reference to Islam and *sharia*, is religious toleration and freedom of religion under the secular state and its laws.

Freedom of religion is a means of managing the disruptions that can (and in the Reformation era did) stem from unresolved religious disagreements. Of course, in no respect does it answer questions concerning which, if any, of the rival views might be true—and so it is *not* a solution to *this* problem from the Reformation era. This problem has never gone away. The entire *point* of politically protected religious freedom is to bracket the question of truth claims by permitting individuals to believe whatever they wish. And it is here that the legacy of the Protestant

Reformation as the open-ended range of truth claims pertaining to God's Word has found its latest, and most expansive, development and influence on modernity: in the politically protected individual right to believe literally anything one wishes as a matter of individual preference. Unintended, unwanted, and unresolved conflicts among Christians led to a fundamental reconceptualization of religion in which, as things have turned out thus far, a secularized public sphere has been the price paid for religious and irreligious freedom. But in fact, this preferential arbitrariness—which one paradoxically might argue aligns the Protestant Reformation more closely with postmodernism than with any specific form of confessional Protestantism, liberal Protestantism, or modern philosophical rationalism—was already grasped by Luther in his polemics with Zwingli about the correct understanding of the Eucharist: "Whoever has gone astray in the faith may thereafter believe whatever he wants to, everything is equally valid."[43] Of course, Luther's Catholic critics had said the same thing about him from the earliest years of the Reformation.

Obviously, different Protestant individuals, groups, and traditions have from the early sixteenth century to the present found no less meaning, direction, and fulfillment in their respective beliefs and communities than have the members of other religious traditions. But equally obviously, the hope for the Bible to function as a self-standing authority that "interprets itself" has never been realized at any point between the early 1520s and the present. Karlstadt's "foundation and rock" has proved empirically and historically to be hermeneutical quicksand. Modern liberal states tolerate and protect what early modern confessional regimes sought to suppress and control, but common to both has been the extensive assertion of political authority as a necessary prophylactic against the threat of social anarchy. The liberal-progressive narrative is spot-on, then, in emphasizing the way in which modern and postmodern individual self-determination derives from the Protestant Reformation, albeit in ways directly contrary to the intentions of the Reformation's leading protagonists.

At the same time, the revisionist-confessionalization narrative is correct to emphasize the importance of the behavioral and institutional legacy of the Reformation era, across confessional lines: the regulation of life and policing of behavior with a pervasiveness inconceivable in the most absolutist, monarchical regimes of early modern Europe is the order of the day in the liberal democratic states of the early twenty-first-century Western world. But ours is not a secular age *rather than* a religious age, as some versions of the revisionist-confessionalization narrative or the secular liberal-progressive narrative suggest. Even in putatively secular-ized Western Europe, religion is far from having disappeared, and not only because of the influx of Muslim immigrants. Western societies are, instead, largely secular in their dominant institutions and public cul-tures, which nevertheless comprise individuals who exhibit a wide range of metaphysical and moral beliefs, and embrace a wide variety of priorities and passions, that would have been unimaginable to Christians in the Reformation era.

We can see the modern democratic state, then, with its politically protected guarantees of freedom of religion and irreligion, as not only the product of the Reformation era but also the institutional incubator of what has been called the postmodern condition. By the open-ended ideological pluralism that it permits, it indirectly fosters the *impression* of relativism—the view that all truth claims can only be a matter of in-dividual, subjective, and irrational personal preference, a theater of con-structions and projections. Within legal limits, quite literally anything goes as far as truth claims and practices are concerned—an extension and latter-day manifestation of the full range of views produced by the Reformation unfettered. In the public sphere, not only are all Protestant views derived from the principle of *sola scriptura* and its adjuncts protected but so are any and all religions, religious claims, and post-religious claims that fill a similar niche.

We might not think this important. But the character of public life and civil society over any length of time depends critically on what people be-lieve, what they desire, what they care about, and how they act. For most of American history, a substantially shared yet *unlegislated* consensus about the values and virtues necessary for the flourishing of families, neighborhoods, and communities—about how to live, how to exercise one's freedom, and in what happiness consists—remained common to Protestants and Catholics despite their divisive differences inherited from the Reformation era. The embodied enactment of those values and virtues made viable the sheer emptiness of the founding documents of the United States with respect to religion and morality, supplying content to supple-ment the deliberate vagueness of "life, liberty, and the pursuit of happi-ness." Derived overwhelmingly from Christianity, they made religion, in Tocqueville's famous phrase, "the first of their political institutions" even though it "never intervenes directly in the government of American so-ciety."[44] The increasing heterogeneity of Americans' beliefs, values, and priorities, however, including polar opposition over issues as fundamental as who is a person and what is a marriage, appears to leave only an increasingly legislative, surveillant, and interventionist state as the maintainer of order. For those who might have been in doubt, Edward Snowden provided dramatic evidence of the state's character in 2013: free to believe whatever we want in states whose officials watch over us ever more closely. This is one important and profoundly unintended modern outcome of the Reformation era.

Notes

1. Brad S. Gregory, *The Unintended Reformation: How a Religious Revolution Secularized Society* (Cambridge, MA: Belknap Press of Harvard University Press, 2012).

2. Daniel T. Rodgers, *Age of Fracture* (Cambridge, MA: Belknap Press of Harvard University Press, 2011).

3. Ernst Troeltsch, *Die Bedeutung des Protestantismus für die Entstehung der modernen Welt* (Munich: R. Oldenbourg, 1911). The English translation appeared the following year as *Protestantism and Progress: A Historical Study of the Relation of Protestantism to the Modern World*, trans. W. Montgomery (New York: G. P. Putnam, 1912).

4. Zygmunt Bauman, *Liquid Modernity* (Malden, MA: Blackwell, 2000), and more recently, Bauman, *Does Ethics Have a Chance in a World of Consumers?* (Cambridge, MA: Harvard University Press, 2008).

5. For a sophisticated recent treatment of this theme, see John Witte, Jr., *The Reformation of Rights: Law, Religion, and Human Rights in Early Modern Calvinism* (Cambridge: Cambridge University Press, 2007), and also Witte's chapter in this volume.

6. Keith Thomas, *Religion and the Decline of Magic: Studies in Popular Beliefs in Sixteenth- and Seventeenth-Century England* (New York: Scribner's, 1971), 25.

7. See, e.g., Mark Lilla, *The Stillborn God: Religion, Politics, and the Modern West* (New York: Knopf, 2007).

8. Most of these phenomena are integrated in a global context in Eric Hobsbawm, *The Age of Extremes: A History of the World, 1914–1991* (New York: Vintage, 1995).

9. For a some references in a very extensive historiography, see, for thriving late medieval piety, e.g., Bernd Moeller, "Religious Life in Germany on the Eve of the Reformation," in *Pre-Reformation Germany*, ed. Gerald Strauss (New York: Harper and Row, 1972), 13–42, originally published as "Frömmigkeit in Deutschland um 1500," *Archiv für Reformationsgeschichte* 56 (1965): 3–31; Anne Winston-Allen, *Stories of the Rose: The Making of the Rosary in the Middle Ages* (University Park: Pennsylvania State University Press, 1997); R. N. Swanson, *Religion and Devotion in Europe, c. 1215-c. 1515* (Cambridge: Cambridge

University Press, 1995; Eamon Duffy, *The Stripping of the Altars: Traditional Religion in England, c. 1400-c. 1580*, 2nd ed. (New Haven, CT: Yale University Press, 2005); Caroline Walker Bynum, *Wonderful Blood: Theology and Practice in Late Medieval Northern Germany and Beyond* (Philadelphia: University of Pennsylvania Press, 2007); and John Van Engen, "Multiple Options: The World of the Fifteenth-Century Church," *Church History* 77, no. 2 (2008): 257–84. For reform-minded ecclesiastical leaders and scholars who combined scholasticism and humanism, as well as the vitality of intellectual life on the eve of the Reformation, see Gregory, *Unintended Reformation*, 323–26, and the scholarship cited in 515–517 nn80–92. On lay Bible reading in Germany prior to the Reformation, see, e.g., Andrew Colin Gow, "Challenging the Protestant Paradigm: Bible Reading in Lay and Urban Contexts of the Later Middle Ages," in *Scripture and Pluralism: Reading the Bible in the Religiously Plural Worlds of the Middle Ages and the Renaissance*, ed. Thomas Heffernan and Thomas E. Burman (Leiden: E. J. Brill, 2006), 161–91; and Thomas Kauffmann, "Vorreformatorische Laienbibel und reformatorisches Evangelium," *Zeitschrift für Theologie und Kirche* 101 (2004): 138–74; and for other regions in Europe, see the relevant contributions in *The Cambridge History of the Bible*, vol. 2: *The West from the Fathers to the Reformation*, ed. G. W. H. Lampe (Cambridge: Cambridge University Press, 1969). On the accommodation of late scholastic thinkers to issues pertaining to usury and the pervasiveness of the late medieval market economy, see, e.g., John T. Noonan Jr., *The Scholastic Analysis of Usury* (Cambridge, MA: Harvard University Press, 1957), 100–32; Diana Wood, *Medieval Economic Thought* (Cambridge: Cambridge University Press, 2002), 181–205; *Economy and Nature in the Fourteenth Century: Money, Market Exchange, and the Emergence of Scientific Thought* (Cambridge: Cambridge University Press, 1998), 83–87; and Odd Langholm, *Economics in the Medieval Schools* (Leiden: E. J. Brill, 1992), 51, 318–20, 370, 416, 476–77, 523–27. On the increasing jurisdictional control of ecclesiastical institutions by non-ecclesiastical authorities, see, e.g., Francis Rapp, *Réformes et Réformation à Strasbourg: Eglise et Société dans de Diocèse de Strasbourg (1450–1525)* (Paris: Editions Ophrys, 1974), 410–19; Manfred Schulze, *Fürsten und Reformation: Geistliche Reformpolitik weltlicher Fürsten vor der Reformation* (Tübingen: Mohr, 1991); Ronald K. Rittgers, *The Reformation of the Keys: Confession, Conscience, and Authority in Sixteenth-Century Germany* (Cambridge, MA: Harvard University Press, 2004), 18–21; William Bradford Smith, *Reformation and the German Territorial State: Upper Franconia, 1300–1630* (Rochester, NY: University of Rochester Press, 2008), 17–58; J. Jeffrey Tyler, *Lord of the Sacred City: The Episcopus exclusus in Late Medieval and Early Modern Germany* (Leiden: E. J. Brill, 1999).

10. Heiko A. Oberman, *Luther: Man between God and the Devil*, trans. Eileen Walliser-Schwarzbart (New Haven, CT: Yale University Press, 1989).

11. See the relevant scholarship indicated above in n9, as well as Berndt Hamm, *The Reformation of Faith in the Context of Late Medieval Theology and Piety*, ed. Robert J. Bast (Leiden: E. J. Brill, 2004).

12. For the sake of simplicity, I include the Church of England from Edward VI's reign on, with the obvious exception of the reign of Mary Tudor, as part of the Reformed Protestant tradition; consider the reign of Henry VIII from 1534 as part of the Protestant Reformation even though the king himself was not theologically Protestant in ways crucially important to Lutheranism or Reformed Protestantism; and regard "Anglicanism" as something to which one can refer as a shorthand for the Church of England in a general sense beginning only with the Restoration of 1660.

13. See, e.g., Peter G. Wallace, *The Long European Reformation: Religion, Political Conflict, and the Search for Conformity, 1350–1750* (Houndmills: Palgrave MacMillan, 2004).

14. Lilla, *Stillborn God*, 55.

15. This is a major theme that runs (convincingly or not) through Jonathan Israel's massive works on the Enlightenment: see Israel, *Radical Enlightenment: Philosophy and the Making of Modernity, 1650–1750* (Oxford: Oxford University Press, 2001); Israel, *Enlightenment Contested: Philosophy, Modernity, and the Emancipation of Man, 1670–1752* (Oxford: Clarendon Press, 2006); and Israel, *Democratic Enlightenment: Philosophy, Revolution, and Human Rights, 1750–1790* (Oxford: Oxford University Press, 2011).

16. Max Horkheimer and Theodor A. Adorno, *Dialectic of Enlightenment: Philosophical Fragments* [1947], ed. Gunzelin Schmid Noerr, trans. Edmund Jephcott (Stanford, CA: Stanford University Press, 2007).

17. See Timothy Snyder, *Bloodlands: Europe between Hitler and Stalin* (New York: Basic Books, 2010).

18. See Hugh McLeod, *The Religious Crisis of the 1960s* (Oxford: Oxford University Press, 2007). For Britain in particular, see Callum G. Brown, *The Death of Christian Britain* (London: Routledge, 2001).

19. According to the Pew Research Center's Religion and Public Life Survey from 2013, 16.1 percent of all Americans and one in four Americans aged 18 to 29 claim no religious affiliation. See http://religions.pewforum.org/reports. See also the corroborative data in Robert D. Putnam and David E. Campbell, *American Grace: How Religion Divides and Unites Us* (New York: Simon & Schuster, 2010). On the "transatlantic religious divide," see Thomas Albert Howard, *God and the Atlantic: America, Europe, and the Religious Divide* (Oxford: Oxford University Press, 2011).

20. Peter Laslett, *The World We Have Lost: England before the Industrial Age*, 3rd ed. (New York: Scribner's, 1984).

21. Scott H. Hendrix, *Luther and the Papacy: Stages in a Reformation Conflict* (Philadelphia: Fortress Press, 1981), 22–136.

22. Martin Luther, *Disputatio inter Ioannem Eccium et Martinum Lutherum* [1519], in *D. Martin Luthers Werke. Kritische Gesamtausgabe* (Weimer: Hermann Böhlau, 1883–) [hereafter *WA*], 59:465/1004–1006, quotes in Manfred Schulze, "Martin Luther and the Church Fathers," in *The Reception of the Church Fathers in the West: From the Carolingians to the Maurists*, ed. Irena Backus (Leiden: E. J. Brill, 1997), 2:621 (Schulze's trans.).

23. For the emphasis on divine mercy, see Berndt Hamm, "Normative Centering in the 15th and 16th Centuries: Observations on Religiosity, Theology, and Iconology," in Hamm, *Reformation of Faith*, 1–49, 32–43.

24. Martin Luther, *An den christlichen Adel deutscher Nation von des christlichen Standes Besserung* [1520], in *WA*, 6:412/26–31.

25. Andreas Bodenstein von Karlstadt, *Predig oder homilien uber den propheten Malachiam gnant* [1522], sig. B3v, quoted in Ronald J. Sider, *Andreas Bodenstein von Karlstadt: The Development of His Thought, 1517–1525* (Leiden: E. J. Brill, 1974), 164 (Sider's trans.).

26. Huldrych Zwingli, *Von Clarheit vnnd gewüsse oder vnbetrogliche des worts gottes* [1522], in *Huldreich Zwinglis Sämtliche Werke* [hereafter *ZW*], vol. 1, ed. Emil Egli and Georg Finsler, in *Corpus Reformatorum* [hereafter *CR*] (Leipzig: M. Heinsius, 1905–), 88:382/20–26, quotation at lines 24–26.

27. "Die Akten der zweiten Disputation vom 26.-28. Oktober 1523," in *ZW*, vol. 2, ed. Emil Egli and Georg Finsler, in *CR*, 89:717/9–11, 26–28.

28. "Die Mühlhauser Artikel" [1525], in *Flugschriften der Bauernkriegszeit*, ed. Adolf Laube and Hans Werner Seiffert (Berlin: Akademie-Verlag, 1975), 80/13–14, 3–4.

29. Karlstadt, *Ob man gemach faren, und des ergernüssen der schwachen verschonen soll, in sachen so gottis willen angehn* [1524], in *Karlstadts Schriften aus den Jahren 1523–25*, ed. Erich Hertzsch (Halle: Max Niemeyer Verlag, 1956), 1:75/17–18.

30. Luther, *De servo arbitrio* [1525], in *WA*, 18:656/10–11: "Itaque nihil nisi tenebras nobis reliquas faciunt, qui scripturas negant esse lucidissimas et evidentissimas."

31. Luther, *Tractatus de libertate Christiana* [1520], in *WA*, 7:51/12–13: "Quaeres autem, 'Quod nam est verbum hoc, aut qua arte utendum est eo, cum tam multa sint verba dei?'" Writing for a wider audience, Luther's own German translation of his Latin is significantly different and avoids mention of "so many words of God": "Fragis tu aber 'wilchs ist denn das wort, das solch grosse gnad gibt, Und wie sol ichs gebrauchen?'" Luther, *Von der Freiheit eines Christenmenschen* [1520], in *WA*, 22/23–24.

32. For the number of religious houses in England, see G. W. Bernard, *The Late Medieval English Church: Vitality and Vulnerability before the Break with Rome* (New Haven, CT: Yale University Press, 2012), 165. For a recent overview on the Münster episode, see Ralf Klötzer, "The Melchiorites and Münster," in *A Companion to Anabaptism and Spiritualism, 1521–1700*, ed. John D. Roth and James M. Stayer (Leiden: E. J. Brill, 2007), 217–56; on the immediate reactions

to Münster by both Catholics and magisterial Protestants, see Sigrun Haude, *In the Shadow of "Savage Wolves": Anabaptist Münster and the German Reformation during the 1530s* (Boston: Humanities Press, 2000).

33. For a recent magisterial synthesis, see Austin Woolrych, *Britain in Revolution, 1625–1660* (Oxford: Oxford University Press, 2002); on religious radicalism during the English Revolution, see Christopher Hill, *The World Turned Upside Down: Radical Ideas During the English Revolution* (Harmondsworth: Penguin, 1972); *Radical Religion in the English Revolution*, ed. J. F. McGregor and Barry Reay (London: Oxford University Press, 1984); Nicholas McDowell, *The English Radical Imagination: Culture, Religion, and Revolution, 1630–1660* (Oxford: Clarendon Press, 2003); and Ann Hughes, *Gangraena and the Struggle for the English Revolution* (Oxford: Oxford University Press, 2004).

34. For example, see Perez Zagorin, *How the Idea of Religious Toleration Came to the West* (Princeton, NJ: Princeton University Press, 2003).

35. Werner O. Packull, *Hutterite Beginnings: Communitarian Experiments during the Reformation* (Baltimore, MD: Johns Hopkins University Press, 1995); John S. Oyer, *Lutheran Reformers Against Anabaptists: Luther, Melanchthon and Menius and the Anabaptists of Central Germany* (The Hague: Martinus Nijhoff, 1964); Stephen Boyd, *Pilgram Marpeck: His Life and Social Theology* (Mainz: Verlag Philipp von Zabern, 1992); *A Companion to Anabaptism and Spiritualism, 1521–1700*, ed. John D. Roth and James M. Stayer (Leiden: E. J. Brill, 2007).

36. Up to 1580 or so, by far the most comprehensive work is George Huntston Williams, *The Radical Reformation*, 3rd ed. (Kirksville, MO: Sixteenth Century Studies Publishers, 1992); for the seventeenth century, see Leszek Kołakowski, *Chrétiens sans église: la conscience religieuse et le lien confessional au XVIIe siècle*, trans. Anna Posner (Paris: Gallimard, 1969).

37. For the division between Gnesio-Lutherans and Philippists prior to the Formula of Concord, see Irene Dingel, "The Culture of Conflict in the Controversies Leading to the Formula of Concord (1548–1580)," in *Lutheran Ecclesiastical Culture, 1550–1675*, ed. Robert Kolb (Leiden: E. J. Brill, 2008), 15–64; on conflicts between Calvinists and Arminians in the Dutch Republic and England, see Philip Benedict, *Christ's Churches Purely Reformed: A Social History of Calvinism* (New Haven, CT: Yale University Press, 2002), 305–16.

38. See Brad S. Gregory, *Salvation at Stake: Christian Martyrdom in Early Modern Europe* (Cambridge, MA: Harvard University Press, 1999).

39. Olivier Christin, *La paix de religion: L'autonomisation de la raison politique au XVIe siècle Paris* (Paris: Seuil, 1997); Thomas Hobbes, *Leviathan* [1651], ed. Richard Tuck (Cambridge: Cambridge University Press).

40. James Madison, "Notes on Debate Over Religious Assessment," December 23–24, 1784, in *Jefferson and Madison on Separation of Church and State: Writings on Religion and Secularism*, ed. Lenni Brenner (Fort Lee, NJ: Barricade Books, 2004), 62.

41. See, e.g., *Calvinism and Religious Toleration in the Dutch Golden Age*, ed. R. Po-chia Hsia and H. F. K. van Nierop (Cambridge: Cambridge University Press, 2002).

42. David Sehat, *The Myth of American Religious Freedom* (New York: Oxford University Press, 2011), with reference to the states that continued their support churches at 20, 49. Public provisions for churches and state subsidies for particular religious practices continued in Connecticut until 1818 and Massachusetts until 1833. See Steven D. Smith, *Foreordained Failure: The Quest for a Constitutional Principle of Religious Freedom* (New York: Oxford University Press, 1995), 17–34; Philip Hamburger, *Separation of Church and State* (Cambridge, MA: Harvard University Press, 2002), 213.

43. "Wer des glaubens gefeilet hat, der mag darnach glewben was er wil, gilt eben gleich." Luther, *Sermon Von dem Sacrament des leibs vnd bluts Christi, widder die Schwarmgeister* [1526], in *WA*, 19:484/19–20.

44. Alexis de Tocqueville, *Democracy in America*, ed. J. P. Mayer, trans. George Lawrence (New York: HarperCollins, 2000), 1:2.9, 292.

PART II

The Present

7

Myth and History in Interpreting Protestantism

RECENT HISTORIOGRAPHICAL TRENDS

Matthew Lundin

IT WOULD BE tempting to begin a chapter titled "Myth and History in Interpreting Protestantism" by debunking the myths about the Reformation that earlier generations held dear. Such myths are not difficult to find. The first Protestants contrasted their own recovery of the "pure and clear Word of God" with an anti-Christian Roman Church full of idolatry and lies. Later generations remembered the Reformation as a mighty popular movement inspired by Martin Luther's courageous act of conscience. In the nineteenth century, scholars eager to align Protestant national traditions with progress associated the year 1517 with a whole host of modern goods: freedom of conscience, inwardness, scientific rationality, and spiritual and cultural renewal.[1] More ominously, several German Protestant leaders during the first half of the twentieth century racialized the Protestant Reformation, reading it as a decisive step toward the "dejudification" (*Entjudung*) of Christianity.[2]

I will refrain from criticizing such myths because, in many ways, they need no further debunking. The horrors of the twentieth century have worked to discredit triumphalist narratives of modernization, progress, and national destiny. Since the Second World War, an avalanche of scholarship has swept away assumptions that the Protestant Reformation broke decisively with a medieval past and heralded the dawn of modernity. Historians have challenged traditional assumptions that the Reformation was a natural response to medieval decline, decay, or waning. Highlighting the vibrancy of late medieval Christianity and the complexity of the early Protestant movement, they have problematized any simple equation of the Protestant Reformation with the ideas of Martin Luther. Instead, their attention has shifted to common ways by which Catholic and Protestant princes struggled to forge new confessional cultures and to indoctrinate recalcitrant rural populations.[3]

The body of specialized research on the Reformation is immense. It is not possible in a brief essay to do justice to the scholarship on a single region—let alone all of Europe.[4] But the very heterogeneity of the scholarship is telling. No longer focused primarily on historical theology or church history, research has illuminated the diversity of the Protestant message and the social, cultural, technological, intellectual, and political contexts in which it spread. The label "Reformation era" has largely fallen out of fashion, at least among historians, in favor of the broader "early modern Europe."

And yet, looming over much recent historiography of Protestantism is an implicit question: Is the Reformation still relevant? Have modern Western scholars grossly exaggerated its significance? Clearly, the events that began in 1517 remain important to the hundreds of millions of people worldwide who worship in Protestant churches and who trace their religious inheritance back to the sixteenth century.[5] But compared with the brash, blaring noise of secular modernity, the religious cultures of the early modern period can sometimes appear as so many minor variations on a theme. Is it even possible to draw meaningful connections between the upheavals of the early modern period and the world we inhabit today? As Alexandra Walsham has recently put it, "the equation of Protestantism with processes of modernization which underpins them is no longer as self-evident to our post-Christian society as it was to previous generations." The "tenacious grip [that] ... teleological paradigms hold over the academy is gradually dissolving of its own accord." As a result, early modern Protestantism can slip back into the strange, alien, distant world from which nineteenth-century historians had removed it.[6]

When compared with the vast material transformations generated by capitalism and instrumental science, the difference between early modern Protestants and Catholics can seem minor, indeed. The Protestant world of the sixteenth and seventeenth centuries was no modern, disenchanted sphere of orderly natural law. Rather, it was a mysterious realm full of signs and omens, an arena in which both God and the devil often intervened.[7]

And far from championing freedom of conscience, most early modern Protestants, like their Catholic counterparts, remained committed to a coercive form of Christian civilization, in which rulers duly enforced orthodox belief and suppressed heresy.

But is an alien Reformation an irrelevant Reformation? Ironically, if nineteenth-century scholars believed the Reformation significant because it anticipated modern values, today's scholars often deem it insignificant because it failed to anticipate those very values. While historians no longer believe the Reformation inaugurated modernity, many studies nonetheless retain modern ideals—religious toleration, political liberation, scientific rationalization, egalitarian social relations—as the measure of what was real or important in the sixteenth century. One might say that recent historiography has not historicized the Reformation enough. Only by setting early modern Protestantism *fully* within its original context—a context in which the church was as powerful and visible a reality as the state or the market are today—can one begin to understand its historical significance.

Historicizing the Early Reformation

The most important event in post-World War II Reformation studies was Göttingen church historian Bernd Moeller's call in the 1960s to historicize the Reformation. In Moeller's view, theologians had too long dominated the study of Protestantism. Against the tendency to reduce "the Protestant movement in the sixteenth century to one man," Moeller called for a robust historical investigation "into the *Reformation movement as a whole.*"[8] Many of the questions Moeller asked were simple. Why did Luther's message appeal to so many humanists? How did the Reformation message spread through pamphlets and broadsides? Which groups responded to the Reformation message?

Although Moeller was a church historian, his work resonated with a generation of German and English-language academic historians eager to understand the Reformation not as a theological but, rather, as a political and social event. The resulting "social history of the Reformation" profoundly complicated the notion that the Reformation represented a radical or inevitable rupture in European history.

Fresh explorations of Protestant pamphlets, for instance, revealed that Luther, although the dominant figure in Protestant publishing, was not the only "evangelical" voice in the 1520s and 1530s. Many early Protestant authors proposed visions of spiritual renewal that were decidedly medieval in flavor. In chiliastic and apocalyptic language, some authors proclaimed a new age of the spirit. Others lashed out against the unjust burdens placed on the "common man" by lords both sacred and secular.[9] As the Peasants' War of 1524 and 1525 and the rise of Anabaptism made clear, the principle of "scripture alone" did not lead naturally or inevitably to Luther's insight into justification by faith. Taking cues from Moeller's own work on the popularity of the Protestant Reformation in imperial free cities, historians explored the social, economic, and political appeal the Reformation held for German burghers.[10] To the artisans of Augsburg, for instance, the Reformation promised a restoration of patriarchal order through the domestication of groups—monks, nuns, prostitutes, and female workers—that posed a threat to the "honorable" household.[11]

Meanwhile, research on late medieval piety turned up little evidence that traditional faith was in terminal decline.[12] Given the enthusiasm with which the late medieval laity commissioned artwork in churches, endowed masses, built altars, and purchased devotional literature, the appeal of the Reformation instead became something of a puzzle. In a series of pioneering articles, R. W. Scribner argued that Protestants hastily denounced a ritual culture that had long made Christianity tangible to nonliterate laity. Through the liturgies and "paraliturgies" of the church, argued Scribner, parishioners had marked boundaries, resolved social conflicts, symbolized the social order, and warded off the malevolent work of demons, ghosts, and witches.[13] To many scholars, the more rational and even vibrant late medieval piety appeared, the harder it became to present Protestantism as a natural or inevitable response to the "decadence," "corruption," or "superstition" of the late medieval church.

For many historians, the popularity of Luther's theology could no longer simply be assumed. Although scholars debated just how "wild" the growth of the early Reformation was, they noted that the Reformation was much more than the pious individual's encounter with the vernacular Bible and Pauline soteriology.[14] The "imaginative world of the Reformation" was riotous and carnivalesque.[15] It dealt in apocalyptic imagery and stark contrasts between light and darkness, truth and error. Preachers and pamphleteers argued that the laity had been duped by an arrogant, self-interested, landowning clerical elite— an elite that, in many parts of the Empire, exercised both spiritual and temporal power. Ironically, it was often priests and monks who carried out the most ferocious attacks against the clerical class to which they belonged, affirming the laity's power to defend "pure doctrine." And while the evangelical movement relied on emerging print networks, the new message spread in taverns and village squares, through singing and haranguing, finding visible expression in acts of iconoclasm and desecration.[16]

Despite its theological diversity, the early Reformation created a potentially explosive rhetorical precedent—that of Christians appealing to the pure Word of God, demanding a purification of "idolatrous" doctrine and practice. This gesture, of course, was not entirely new. As Berndt Hamm has noted, the later Middle Ages saw powerful movements to "center" Christian life on simple, clear, and uniform norms.[17] And late medieval laity had often demanded that preachers stick to the "pure word of God." But the 1520s saw an even more radical call to prune everything from the Christian life that did not conform with scriptural norms. Early Reformation pamphlets aimed to expose the church's teaching as so many "human teachings" (*Menschenlehren*), a means by which corrupt churchmen had exploiting a gullible laity. The conversion experience depicted in many early evangelical pamphlets was less a gesture of spiritual contrition than a moment of intellectual illumination—a sudden ability to see the venerated traditions and institutions of Christendom as products of deep, pervasive, and satanic deception.

From the very start, this pattern proved portable. Thanks to printing, "evangelicals" throughout Europe could imagine themselves as participating in God's providential work to restore the gospel. The principle of *sola scriptura* provided leverage against local tradition; it allowed for a radical questioning of the ecclesiastical status quo, forcing even traditionalists to become self-conscious "Catholics." Reformed Protestants (or Calvinists) forged a particularly durable vision of purified worship—of a civic community united in its commitment to the austere Word of God, its conviction of election, its insistence on human depravity, and its rejection of the "abomination of the mass."[18] Centered on the word and the worship of an invisible God, Protestantism thus fostered potent "ideological" communities. The impulse to purify the church—to purge it of all idolatry—worked to destabilize English politics in the seventeenth century. For French Huguenots and English Puritans, religious identities were no longer mediated only through settled customs—kinship, parish boundaries, liturgical traditions—but, rather, through print, doctrine, Bible reading, and hymn singing.[19]

Yet such oppositional movements did not, as modern myths have assumed, champion religious toleration and freedom of conscience. Rather, they strove to create purified Christian commonwealths. Though French Huguenots may have felt a greater affinity with their Swiss co-religionists than their neighbors, they did not set out to "privatize" or "compartmentalize" religion. Even separatist groups such as the Anabaptists broke with Christian establishments not because they sought individual freedom but because they yearned for a purer visible church, for congregations in which nominal Christians would find no refuge.

The Long Reformation

The more historians studied the "wild growth" of the early Reformation, the harder it became to interpret Protestant churches as simple or inevitable extensions of the early evangelical movement. Thus, scholarly attention shifted in the 1970s and 1980s to the long, contested process through which Protestant magistrates worked to curb the disruptive potential of *sola scriptura* and to forge new religious traditions bound together by vernacular liturgies, catechisms and confessions, and a shared memory of founding figures.[20] Literacy, inwardness, sobriety, self-discipline—the traits that nineteenth-century German and Anglo-American historians had proleptically ascribed to 1517—instead appeared as the products of much longer structural transformations.[21]

There can be little question that Protestant authorities embarked on an ambitious pedagogical project. If salvation depended on faith—on one's trust in the promises of a living God—then rulers had a spiritual duty to ensure that their subjects had heard the gospel. Church ordinances, official visitations, consistories, and catechisms became tools through which princes and magistrates worked to instill correct doctrine in the hearts and minds of laity. In the 1970s, Gerald Strauss used visitation records to argue that the Lutheran establishment had struggled in vain to win over a largely nonliterate, rural population, a population that could not afford to send children to school and had little interest in a cerebral religion based on "faith alone."[22] Other historians drew different conclusions from the same material, arguing that the laity did, indeed, acquire a solid understanding of the fundamentals of their faith.[23]

However, in the project of building a confessional culture, Protestants were not alone. Catholic, Lutheran, and Reformed regimes all worked to catechize nonliterate populations, to root out popular superstitions, and to create uniform Christian laws. Relying on sociologist Norbert Elias's theory of the "civilizing process,"[24] several German scholars argued in the 1980s that the formation of Protestant and Catholic confessions was central to the process of European state-building. In this interpretation, the key innovations in early modern Christianity occurred not in the 1520s but, rather, in the second half of the sixteenth century, when Lutheran, Calvinist, and Catholic princes participated in a common process of "confessionalization," working to impose religious discipline on a recalcitrant population. To princes, a common confessional culture seemed a great boon. With it came the internalization of Christian norms—and thus greater compliance from obedient subjects.[25]

There are many questions about the "confessionalization" thesis. As a story about the rise of the modern state, it is no less a modernization theory than were the old teleological narratives of the nineteenth century. And in highlighting commonalities, it risks obscuring the theological and cultural differences that separated early modern Lutherans, Calvinists, and Catholics. After all, the Reformation doctrines of justification by faith and *sola scriptura* entailed a rejection of the church's penitential piety and thus "a radically simplified religious life."[26] Luther reduced the pastorate to its spiritual functions alone: to the tasks of preaching, admonishing, and administering the sacraments. And for Protestants, no priest had the power to mediate grace incrementally to the believer. Sacraments were, rather, signs and reassurances of God's forgiveness, a forgiveness fully received through faith in God's promise. As Luther put it, "grace has no other vessel than the heart.... Vestments, shoes, tonsures, eating, drinking, days, and plays ... are temporal things, and inwardly, in faith, which grants eternal holiness and rests on eternal goods, they are nothing."[27]

However, when viewed against the structural transformations of the *longue durée*, the differences between early modern confessions no longer seem as extreme as they once did. In response to the Protestant Reformation, the Catholic Church also streamlined its hierarchy; it curbed numerous penitential services that the late medieval clergy had performed, emphasizing instead the clergy's core duties in preaching, confessing, and administering the sacraments. Both confessions worked to create a more professionalized clergy and to instill in the laity an intense, orthodox faith.[28] As John Bossy has argued, Western Christianity gradually morphed from a complex of communal practices and rites to a "desocialized" religion of the word. By the eighteenth century, it was customary for both Catholics and Protestants to speak of "religion" as a set of portable doctrinal propositions.[29] From this perspective, it is not difficult to read eighteenth-century Lutheran pietists, Catholic Jansenists, and Anglo-American evangelicals as participants in a common cultural movement.

Not only did these transformations reshape all the confessions; they also predated the Protestant Reformation. Viewed against the *longue durée*, Protestantism appeared to some scholars as merely the latest episode in the church's ongoing work not only to reform itself and to Christianize the laity. It is not difficult to see both early modern Protestants and early modern Catholics as heirs of Gregory VII's efforts to purge the church of worldliness.[30] In many ways, both Protestant and Catholic catechetical efforts continued the work begun at the Fourth Lateran Council in 1215, when the church required yearly confession of all laity. At the same time, thanks to powerful impulses toward laicization, the creation of national, territorial, and civic churches was already under way well before 1517.[31]

This list of deep, mutually reinforcing changes could go on and on. The rise of the conjugal household in the fourteenth and fifteenth centuries, for instance, played a profound role in reshaping all forms of early modern Christianity.[32] Though the Reformation articulated a particularly clear vision of the well-ordered household, there were many similar moves to support the "holy household" in Catholic areas.[33] Late medieval catechisms had often held up the patriarchal household as a defense against sin and disorder.[34] Moreover, this new patriarchal ideology found support in print—in catechisms, in housefather books, in pamphlets and satires. Defined by contract and law, the household became a symbol of order and discipline—one that could be mechanically reproduced. For the early modern state, such patriarchal visions simplified the business of governing, reducing the number of corporate entities with which it had to contend. As one sixteenth-century Catholic lawyer put it, "if the household is well governed, the entire city is well-nigh governed."[35]

For these and other reasons, the Protestant Reformation has come to seem less significant as a religious revolution than as a set of interlocking social, cultural, and political processes, in which religion played a largely functional role. Replacing historical theology with religious anthropology, numerous studies have highlighted the ways in which early modern Protestants developed functional equivalents to Catholic practices that they had rejected. R. W. Scribner, for instance, has suggested that stories of incombustible images of Luther—icons that survived blazing fires— reflected the Protestant demand for wonder-working saints. In recent years, scholars have offered similarly "thick descriptions" of emotions,[36] sacred space,[37] belief in angels,[38] and more. Although early Protestants rejected intercessory prayers on behalf of the dead—and with them, the massive memorial culture of late medieval Europe—belief in ghosts, witches, and the revenant dead persisted.[39] Lutherans developed a complex, baroque funeral culture, replete with memorial altars and funeral sermons that praised the dead for their exemplary lives.[40]

In many recent studies, functional continuities overshadow apparent ruptures. But do such accounts of religion truly capture the dynamics of belief in a confessional age? Ecumenical impulses may have inclined modern scholars to stress similarities rather than differences, to argue that despite all the blustery talk about heresy and the Antichrist, early modern religious foes had far more in common than they realized.[41] But does such an interpretation obscure the faith—the urgent conviction—that produced the Protestant-Catholic divide in the first place?

The Return of Religion

It might seem strange to speak of a "return of religion" in Reformation historiography. The Reformation was, after all, a religious event. However, many scholars have argued that "the social history of the Reformation" has given far too little weight to religious ideas and beliefs. As Hans Hillerbrand has put it, the contextualizing research of the past decades should not obscure the fundamental question: "[D]id there occur in the early sixteenth century dramatic changes in religion and theology that influenced society?"[42] Such questions have been gaining traction in recent years. Several studies have attempted to move beyond depictions of the Reformation as a derivative or minor movement, illuminating instead the distinctive intellectual and spiritual resources that Protestant soteriology made available and the distinctive cultures it spawned.[43]

No scholar has argued more forcefully for the power of religious ideals in the early modern period than Brad Gregory, a fellow contributor to this volume. In his study of early modern martyrdom, Gregory rejects attempts to read Protestant and Catholic beliefs as expressions of deeper material structures. When applied to beliefs in "God, Satan, sin, grace, heaven, and hell," argues Gregory, the methodologies of modern academic disciplines only get in the way, since they foreclose the reality of the very things for which early modern Christians were willing to die. To be sure, notes Gregory, sixteenth-century Christians often sought to prove that the beliefs of other confessions were mere "fictions"; they sought to expose the martyrs of rival Christian groups as false martyrs. But they did so because they believed in the truth of their own theological claims and the blessedness of their own martyrs.[44]

In Gregory's interpretation, martyrdom was not a fringe phenomenon, a product of fanatical belief. Rather, it represented a logical outcome of the most fundamental tenets of early modern Christianity. The problem, argues Gregory, is that modern, post-Enlightenment, ecumenically minded historians do not like martyrdom. Nor do they like the patriarchal conclusions that Protestants drew from the scriptures. As a result, scholars apply a hermeneutics of suspicion to these beliefs, arguing that they were really a product of "deeper" social and cultural anxieties. But, asks Gregory, "is it plausible that men committed to scripture as God's word used it merely to justify social control and to reinforce patriarchal ideology?" If one relativizes religious belief by mapping it onto to a "homogeneous plane of cultural construction," one obscures the clash between "competing absolutisms" that was arguably the most dramatic development of the sixteenth and seventeenth centuries.[45]

Gregory's study of martyrdom is not the only recent attempt to recover the logic behind the fierce religious polemics of the sixteenth century. In her study on the "search for certainty in early modern Europe," for instance, Susan Schreiner explores the belief shared by all early modern confessions that theirs was one true faith. The desire for certainty drove the early Protestant reformers. And in the ensuing polemics, their search for certainty only exacerbated the epistemological and soteriological problems that they sought to solve. Here, Schreiner revives an older tradition of interpretation that reads religious anxieties about certainty as expressions of a cultural crisis generated by the breakdown of the "ontotheological" synthesis of the Middle Ages. The anxious absolutism of sixteenth- and seventeenth-century theologians and martyrs expressed the unease individuals felt in an age of "transition."[46]

Gregory, however, rejects any attempt to read religion as a symptom of something "deeper." In seeking to explain sixteenth-century religious controversies as a product of "anxiety" or "epistemological crisis"—or of power or class conflict—one ceases to understand their urgency for contemporaries. For Gregory, only by following the logic of early modern belief—a logic rooted in a very real and rational desire to live in accordance with God's revealed commands and to avoid sin and damnation—can one understand the causal power of religious ideas in early modern Europe. And only then can one grasp later epistemological crises and outright skepticism generated by early modern Christian pluralism.[47]

Such admonitions offer an important corrective to the reductionist ways in which several historians have read early modern Protestantism. Gerald Strauss, for instance, once argued that urban magistrates were attracted to Lutheran doctrines of original sin because such doctrines confirmed their suspicions about the intractable waywardness of the common man.[48] Entirely missing from Strauss's interpretation, however, was the most pressing problem that original sin posed to sixteenth-century Christians: "How can I be saved?" In this instance, interpreting original sin only as a thinly veiled attempt at social control ignores the search for assurance that lay at the heart of much early modern Protestant experience.

However, is there perhaps a risk of replacing a reductionist materialism with an equally reductionist idealism? Is it possible to separate out religious and secular motives, particularly in a period in which religion pervaded every aspect of life? Certainly one can perceive how persecution and martyrdom followed rationally from contemporary Christian beliefs, as Gregory contends.[49] However, was early modern Christianity lived and experienced with such exemplary clarity and urgency? Should historians reduce their task to understanding the logic of early modern religion in its purest and most dogmatic forms?

One of the greatest challenges facing historians of the Protestant Reformation is to find a historical vocabulary rich enough to avoid both a social reductionism *and* a religious reductionism. There were fervent believers, but there were also countless lukewarm Christians. For some of the faithful, the fires of hell burned close by, indeed. But for other Christians, eternity receded far into the distance. For many, the theological and religious debates that preoccupied theologians were simply part of the background of everyday life, lacking urgency until they interfered with the practical business of buying and selling and raising a family. Not all early modern Christians, after all, lived according to the white-hot logic of the purists, or even approved of it.[50]

In an age in which Christian faith laid claim on practically every area of life, it should come as no surprise that theology and belief had profound social, economic, and cultural implications. When implemented, Protestant doctrines allowed magistrates to dismantle much of the infrastructure of the late medieval church and to reshape communal calendars and liturgies. And yet for this very reason, Protestant ideals reflected the context in which they were forged. To think about theology in the sixteenth century was to think about society, culture, art, economics, the family, and history. For this very reason, theological thinking was also ideological, reflecting the social, cultural, and political values of those who engaged in it. For instance, sixteenth-century Protestants viewed the patriarchal household, not as a contingent product of social and economic forces, but as an institution graciously ordained by God for the worldly and spiritual good of its members. They quite logically searched their Bibles and catechisms for the norms of good household governance. And yet their values and interests as householders shaped their understanding of God's revelation, often in ways that they themselves did not fully understand.

Where Do We Stand Today?

The recent historiography of the Reformation reflects not only the social and cultural changes that have swept through American and European universities since the 1960s but also powerful trends toward globalization. With the decline of Protestant establishments in European and America, scholars have largely succeeded in provincializing the Reformation, in reading it as an exotic event. According to Thomas Brady, "if the fall of [European] confessions brings ... the passing of a particular age of specifically European configurations of Christianity, it may also liberate the particular churches of Europe to find a new kind of history out in the vast global congeries of milieus that has been called 'the next Christendom.' "[51] There are exciting prospects ahead for writing a truly global history of Protestantism, some of which are suggested in this volume by other contributors.

By rejecting the teleological, modernizing assumptions of nineteenth-century historians, the recent historiography has succeeded in making a once-familiar Reformation strange. Take, for instance, the longstanding assumption that the Protestant Reformation "disenchanted the world." According to the traditional story, by insisting on the absolute sovereignty of God, the Protestant Reformation eliminated the sacred spaces, times, and rituals through which medieval religion had channeled divine blessing and power. For R. W. Scribner, however, these changes hardly disenchanted the world. Protestants continued to assume that the boundaries between the natural and the supernatural were porous. They interpreted illness or communal calamities as a sign of God's judgment and believed demons could possess and afflict people, livestock, and crops. In other words, Protestantism did not transform the world into a self-contained nexus of immanent causes.[52]

Yet in problematizing attempts to draw a direct line from the Protestant Reformation to modernity, revisionist accounts such as Scribner's none-theless continue to measure the Protestant Reformation by the standards of the Enlightenment. Scribner's analysis implicitly retains modern "disenchantment" as the yardstick for determining the extent to which it had altered traditional religion. To be sure, his broader point is well taken: Protestantism was not a "modern" faith. Compared with the churn-ing, restless transformations of modernity, the upheavals of the sixteenth century can seem modest, indeed. But does it follow that Protestantism changed little? What is the proper measure of the Reformation's signifi-cance: its distance from modern norms and ideals or its disruptive effects within its original context?

In the past two decades, scholars have begun to develop new synthesiz-ing narratives of the Reformation and its legacies.[53] Seeking to avoid both confessional bias and teleological accounts of the relationship between the Reformation and modernity, these narratives focus less on the con-tent of Protestant doctrine and worship than on the destabilizing effects of religious schism. They highlight the ways in which the Reformation undermined the all-encompassing universalism of Latin Christendom, unintentionally generating the problematic particularism of separate con-fessions of faith, each claiming to be universally valid.

The emerging story goes something like this. For all the medieval church's diversity, Latin Christians in 1500 belonged to a universal *corpus Christianum*. They could imagine their towns and villages as microcosms of a larger Christian and cosmic order. They inhabited a world in which the rites and rituals of the church had, in the words of Thomas Kaufmann, a "self-evident" and "irrefutable omnipresence."[54] By the end of the six-teenth century, by contrast, Europe was divided into rival confessional camps, each branding the other as heretical. In a recent attempt to sketch out a "new history" of the Reformation, Lee Palmer Wandel argues that "it was no longer possible, in 1600, to speak of 'the Christian religion' as a kind of shorthand for the great majority of Europeans.... In a fragmented world, one carried a sense of space, time, matter, and person, and God that bound one essentially to others across the surface of an alien and treach-erous world."[55] By recasting traditional religion as a form of anti-Christian idolatry and by splintering Europe into irreconcilable confessions, the

Reformation introduced a violent, destabilizing self-referentiality into European religious life.

In such accounts, pluralism and secularization were not direct products of the Protestant Reformation. They were, rather, ironic out comes. In his recent *Unintended Reformation*, Brad Gregory argues that the early Protestant reformers hoped to renew Christendom and that they had no intention of dividing Europe into rival Christian communions. Rather, Protestants believed that the Roman Curia, in refusing to reform Christendom, had ceased to represent the church. Or, as Thomas Kaufmann has aptly put it, the Reformation was a "revolt of the Church against the Church."[56] And yet, by appealing to the authority of scripture alone, the Reformation established a destabilizing precedent. Contrary to Luther's expectations, there was no single, self-evident meaning of scripture on which Christians could agree. Instead, the "evangelical" movement spawned several, radically incommensurate visions of Christianity. The problems unleashed by Protestant hermeneutics were resolved not by theological consensus but, rather by princely power.[57]

According to Gregory, these interpretive conundrums brought Christendom to an impasse. Each of the confessions insisted on the need for certainty. Each insisted that it possessed the one true interpretation of the faith. How could one adjudicate among them? Catholics and Protestants used all the scholarly tools at their disposal to debunk each other's interpretation of Christian revelation. Preoccupied with crafting precise doctrinal statements, Catholic and Protestant theologians retreated from the wider field of learning. The rise of confessions created the impression that Christianity was less a "way of life" than a set of propositional truths. Meanwhile, debates over Christian revelation proved socially and politically disruptive, contributing to bloody conflicts between confessional princes and creating new potential for radical opposition and dissent. In this context, rulers and thinkers looked for alternative sources of social cohesion. Beginning in the seventeenth century, they found them in industrious households, consumer pleasures, and religious toleration. However, argues Gregory, these were merely negative principles of integration. They lacked the robust vision of the common good that traditional Christianity had offered and thus were unable to prevent the modern West's long descent into hyperpluralism and moral relativism. Ironically, both sixteenth-century Catholics and Protestants would be appalled at what their righteous religious disputes had wrought.[58]

Such an interpretation of the Reformation has the advantage of simultaneously rooting the Reformation in the medieval world and yet explaining how attempts to reform Christendom nonetheless represented a decisive break. However, is "schism alone" Protestantism's only defining religious legacy? Were its most important consequences negative and unintended? Is there anything internal to the history of Protestantism—its distinctive theological and cultural patterns—that belongs in a grand narrative of the Reformation? Are most of the modern West's problems a product "scripture alone" alone and its ironic consequences? The Reformation, after all, was far from the first disruptive force in Christian history. Well before the sixteenth century, the church faced deep structural and hermeneutical problems that it dealt with through schism, conciliarism, the persecution of religious dissidents, and the construction of a complex ecclesiastical bureaucracy. To minimize these prior problems risks turning a challenge faced by every culture—namely, how to generate consensus about core values—into a singular, watershed problem created in the 1520s.

Perhaps a more sympathetic way to read the Reformation is as an attempt to translate Christianity into new cultural contexts, to respond to the dramatic ways in which social, economic, political, and technological change were already roiling the Christian order. In distinctive ways, Protestants responded to the new challenges and opportunities created by printing, a fledgling householder economy, laïcizing magistrates, a demographic rebound from the Black Death, and European expansion. New networks of communication, for instance, opened up the possibility of appealing to lay readers and a nascent reading public. Although the effects of print should not be exaggerated, it was already beginning to mediate the Christian faith in new ways before 1517, leading many scholars to refer to the Reformation as the first "mass media" event in the West. Indeed, one might marvel at the ability of Protestant communities over the past five hundred years to sustain a modicum of consensus despite the lack of a magisterium.[59]

Few contemporary observers, whether Catholic or Protestant, doubted that the Protestant Reformation was a significant event. The writings of Cologne lawyer and rentier Hermann Weinsberg (1518–1597), one of the more unusual sixteenth-century diarists, provide insights into just how disruptive contemporaries could perceive the Reformation to be. An Erasmian Catholic, Weinsberg contented himself with the "good old customs" of his parish. For this reason, however, he found himself profoundly disturbed by the "great schism." Reports of iconoclasm in the neighboring Netherlands prompted him to safeguard a family altarpiece by taking it from the parish church and bringing it to his home. Skeptical about the certainty that both Catholics and Protestants claimed to possess, he refrained from passing judgment on contemporary events. Many entries in his diary ended simply: "God only knows." Frustrated by the "vanity" of polemical literature, Weinsberg struggled to set the record straight in his secret diary, reconciling Catholic and Protestant histories or the contradictory reports of news sheets and pamphlets. For Weinsberg, the religious pluralism in the empire had already worked to relativize traditional religion: he fretted that the "Catholic religion will not last long here in Cologne."[60]

Although a committed Catholic, Weinsberg was also a "middling" burgher, and as such he sympathized with many Protestant complaints against the clergy. In his view, the religious life ought to take place within a domestic, patriarchal framework. The household was the foundation of the social order; the world was God's house, and Adam its original housefather. Against the traditional denigration of marriage and industry, Weinsberg set out a distinctively Catholic vision of the "holy household," arguing that the household participated in God's sanctity and that his family members and heirs could pray for his departed soul and preserve his memory as well as any priest could.[61]

Sources such as Weinsberg's offer an opportunity to put 1517—and by extension, 2017—in a much broader perspective and thereby to glimpse the Reformation's complex and contested effects. The Protestant Reformation, after all, was one of many transformations in Christendom between 1400 and 1800. In the Holy Roman Empire, both Protestant and Catholic burghers participated in the reorganization of social and economic life around the conjugal household. Both participated in a dramatically expanding culture of print, rumor, and polemics. Both had access to a wide range of vernacular religious and historical literature. And, if Weinsberg's quirky theological reflections are any indication, both Protestant and Catholic burghers worked in different ways to "translate" traditional Christianity into a changing cultural and economic environment.

In the years ahead, historians have a chance to move beyond the yes-or-no logic that has so often dominated the historiography: "Was the Reformation medieval or modern?" "Was it a success or failure?" "Was it a liberating force or the source of all that ails the modern world?" By widening the lens, so to speak—that is, by exposing the broader world of late medieval and early modern Christianity of which the Reformation

was one part—recent scholarship arguably offers something more significant: it reveals the new cultural and religious resources that Protestantism
opened up and the new dynamics it set in motion.

If we judge the Reformation by the standards of liberal politics, modern
science, or global capitalism, it will likely appear a curious and perhaps
even retrograde movement. However, if we read the Reformation *within*
its original context—within a world in which the "ubiquity" of the church
was taken for granted—the Reformation's attempt to redefine religion
appears radical, indeed. Although early modern Protestants rarely challenged the fundamental project of Christian civilization, they nonetheless
revived in an acute form older Augustinian questions about the relationship between the City of God and the City of Man. However established
Protestantism became, it nonetheless assumed a theoretical disjunction
between faith's outward, material manifestations and its true, invisible
reality. Indeed, much of the drama of the post-1517 world lies in the tension between these ideas and the particular contexts in which they took
root. Perhaps the very persistence of Reformation myths pays tribute to
Protestantism's emphasis on the Word—its power to generate communities grounded in a rereading of the world.

Notes

1. For overviews of Reformation myths, see R. W. Scribner, *The German
   Reformation*, Studies in European History (London: Macmillan, 1986), 1–5;
   and Peter Opitz, ed., *The Myth of the Reformation*, Refo500 Academic Studies
   9 (Göttingen: Vandenhoeck & Ruprecht, 2013). Some scholars have questioned whether the very notion of the Reformation is a product of Protestant
   myth making. See, for instance, Constantin Fasolt, "Hegel's Ghost: Europe, the
   Reformation, and the Middle Ages," *Viator* 39 (2008): 345–86.
2. Susannah Heschel, *The Aryan Jesus: Christian Theologians and the Bible in Nazi
   Germany* (Princeton, NJ: Princeton University Press, 2010).
3. For recent overviews of the literature, see C. Scott Dixon, *Contesting the Reformation* (Malden, MA: Wiley-Blackwell, 2012); David M. Whitford, ed., *Reformation
   and Early Modern Europe: A Guide to Research*, Sixteenth Century Essays &
   Studies 79 (Kirksville, MO: Truman State University Press, 2008); Tom Scott,
   "The Reformation between Deconstruction and Reconstruction: Reflections
   on Recent Writings on the German Reformation," *German History* 26, no. 3
   (2008): 406–22. The recent 100th volume of the *Archive for Reformation* (2009)
   contains a wealth of articles on the historiography of the Reformation since the
   Second World War.

4. R. W. Scribner, Roy Porter, and Mikuláš Teich, eds., *The Reformation in National Context* (Cambridge: Cambridge University Press, 1994).

5. Mark A. Noll, *Protestantism: A Very Short Introduction* (Oxford: Oxford University Press, 2011).

6. Alexandra Walsham, "The Reformation and 'The Disenchantment of the World' Reassessed,"' *The Historical Journal* 51 (2008): 528. Somewhat ironically, Walsham relies here on an image of steady decay no less predetermined than the old teleological visions of progress.

7. Robert W. Scribner, "The Reformation, 'Popular Magic,' and the Disenchantment of the World," *Journal of Interdisciplinary History* 23 (1993): 475–94; R. W. Scribner, "Reformation and Desacralisation: From Sacramental World to Moralised Universe," in *Problems in the Historical Anthropology of Early Modern Europe*, ed. R. Po-Chia Hsia and R. W. Scribner (Wiesbaden: Harrassowitz Verlag, 1997), 75–92; Walsham, "Reformation and 'The Disenchantment of the World."'

8. Bernd Moeller, "Problems of Reformation Research," in *Imperial Cities and the Reformation: Three Essays*, ed. and trans. H. C. Erik Midelfort and Mark U. Edwards (Philadelphia: Fortress Press, 1972), 11, 15. Moeller's original essay appeared as "Probleme der Reformationsgeschichtsforschung," *Zeitschrift für Kirchengeschichte* 76 (1965): 246–57.

9. The literature on early Protestant pamphlets is far too vast to cite. For accounts of the rhetoric of early pamphlets, see Peter Matheson, *The Imaginative World of the Reformation* (Minneapolis, MN: Fortress Press, 2001); Steven Ozment, *Protestants: The Birth of a Revolution* (New York: Doubleday, 1991). For lay perspectives in pamphlets, see Paul A. Russell, *Lay Theology in the Reformation: Popular Pamphleteers in Southwest Germany, 1521–1525* (Cambridge: Cambridge University Press, 2002); and Miriam Usher Chrisman, *Conflicting Visions of Reform: German Lay Propaganda Pamphlets, 1519–1530* (Atlantic Highlands, NJ: Humanities Press, 1995). For a celebrated analysis of popular woodcuts and images, see Robert Scribner, *For the Sake of Simple Folk: Popular Propaganda for the German Reformation* (Oxford: Oxford University Press, 1987).

10. "Problems of Reformation Research," 41–155; Moeller's essay was originally published as *Reichsstadt und Reformation*, Schriften des Vereins für Reformationsgeschichte 180 (Gütersloh: Gerd Mohn, 1962). A classic example of such the urban history of the Reformation is Thomas A. Brady, *Ruling Class, Regime and Reformation at Strasbourg, 1520–1555*, vol. 22: Studies in Medieval and Reformation Thought (Leiden: Brill, 1978). For an argument that the Reformation held deep cultural and religious appeal for German burghers, see Steven Ozment, *The Reformation in the Cities: The Appeal of Protestantism in Sixteenth-Century Germany* (New Haven, CT: Yale University Press, 1975).

11. Lyndal Roper, *The Holy Household: Women and Morals in Reformation Augsburg* (Oxford: Oxford University Press, 1989).

12. For a summary of this reassessment of late medieval religion, see Euan Cameron, *The European Reformation*, 2nd ed. (Oxford: Oxford University Press, 2012), 11–25.

13. See the essays collected in R. W. Scribner, *Religion and Culture in Germany (1400–1800)*, ed. Lyndal Roper (Leiden: Brill, 2001). Whereas Scribner, who used the methods of cultural anthropology, presented late medieval rural religion as structurally and functionally similar to other peasant religions, other scholars insisted on its profoundly Catholic nature. See, for instance, Eamon Duffy, *The Stripping of the Altars: Traditional Religion in England 1400–1580* (New Haven, CT: Yale University Press, 1992); John Bossy, *Christianity in the West, 1400–1700* (Oxford: Oxford University Press, 1985).

14. See Susan Karant-Nunn, "What Was Preached in German Cities in the Early Years of the Reformation?" in *The Process of Change in Early Modern Europe: Essays in Honor of Miriam Usher Chrisman*, ed. Philip N. Bebb and Sherrin Marshall (Athens: Ohio University Press, 1988), 81–96; Susan Karant-Nunn, "Preaching the Word in Early Modern Germany," in *Preachers and People in the Reformations and Early Modern Periods*, ed. Larissa Taylor (Leiden: Brill, 2001), 193–200. Bernd Moeller challenged the notion that the early Reformation was characterized by anarchic diversity. "Was wurde in der Frühzeit der Reformation in den deutschen Städten gepredigt?" *Archiv für Reformationsgeschichte* 74 (1984): 176–93.

15. Matheson, *The Imaginative World of the Reformation*; Robert Scribner, "The Reformation, Carnival, and the World Turned Upside-Down: Oral Culture and Diffusion," in *Popular Culture and Popular Movements in Reformation Germany* (London: Hambledon Press, 1987), 71–101.

16. See R. W. Scribner, "Oral Culture and the Diffusion of Reformation Ideas," in *Popular Culture and Popular Movements in Reformation Germany* (London: Hambledon Press, 1987), 49–69; Andrew Pettegree, *Reformation and the Culture of Persuasion* (Cambridge: Cambridge University Press, 2005), 237. Several vivid accounts of Protestant rituals of desacralization are found in Joseph Koerner's magisterial account of iconoclasm, *The Reformation of the Image* (Chicago: University of Chicago Press, 2004). For the role of singing, see Rebecca Wagner Oettinger, *Music as Propaganda in the German Reformation* (Aldershot: Ashgate, 2001); Christopher Boyd Brown, *Singing the Gospel: Lutheran Hymns and the Success of the Reformation* (Cambridge, MA: Harvard University Press, 2005).

17. Berndt Hamm, *The Reformation of Faith in the Context of Late Medieval Piety* (Leiden: Brill, 2004), 1–49; Berndt Hamm, *Bürgertum und Glaube: Konturen der städtischen Reformation* (Göttingen: Vandenhoeck & Ruprecht, 1996), 73–76.

18. Philip Benedict, *Christ's Churches Purely Reformed: A Social History of Calvinism* (New Haven, CT: Yale University Press, 2002).

19. Donald R. Kelley, *The Beginning of Ideology: Consciousness and Society in the French Reformation* (Cambridge: Cambridge University Press, 1983).

20. Joachim Eibach and Marcus Sandel, eds., *Protestantische Identität und Errinerung: Von der Reformation bis zur Bürgerrechtsbewegung in der DDR. Formen der Errinerung* (Göttingen: Vandenhoeck & Ruprecht, 2003).

21. For a concise overview of work on the "long Reformation," see Thomas A. Brady, "From Revolution to the Long Reformation: Writings in English on the German Reformation, 1970–2005," *Archive für Reformationsgeschichte* 100 (2009): 48–64. Several recent surveys of the Reformation era reflect the idea that the Reformation was a "process" spanning several centuries. See, for instance, James D. Tracy, *Europe's Reformations, 1450–1650* (Lanham, MD: Rowman & Littlefield, 1999); Peter G. Wallace, *The Long European Reformation: Religion, Political Conflict, and the Search for Conformity, 1350–1750* (New York: Palgrave Macmillan, 2004).

22. Gerald Strauss, *Luther's House of Learning: Indoctrination of the Young in the German Reformation* (Baltimore, MD: Johns Hopkins University Press, 1978).

23. See, for instance, James Kittelson, "Successes and Failures in the German Reformation: The Report from Strasbourg," *Archiv für Reformationsgeschichte* 73 (1982): 153–175. Judging the "success" of Reformation according to its ability to transform *entire* populations is arguably a poor measure of its legacies. In the words of Steven Ozment, "historians today have a predilection for evaluating the Reformation's success primarily by focusing on individuals and groups whose exposure to it was brief, intermittent, or only confrontational. In doing so, they stack the deck in advance to find an ugly Protestantism and a failed Reformation." Ozment, *Protestants*, 42.

24. Norbert Elias, *The Civilizing Process*, trans. Edmund Jephcott (Oxford: Wiley-Blackwell, 1994).

25. For concise summaries of the topic, see Ute Lotz-Heumann, "Confessionalization: A Guide to Research," in *Reformation and Early Modern Europe: A Guide to Research*, ed. David Whitford (Kirksville, MO: Truman State University Press, 2008); Heinz Schilling, "Confessional Europe: Late Middle Ages, Renaissance, and Reformation," in *Handbook of European History: Late Middle Ages, Renaissance, and Reformation*, ed. Thomas A. Brady, Heiko A. Oberman, and James D. Tracy (Leiden: Brill, 1995), 1:641–75. For a recent collection of essays, see John M. Headley, Hans J. Hillerbrand, and Anthony Papalas, eds., *Confessionalization in Europe, 1555–1700: Essays in Memory of Bodo Nischan* (Aldershot: Ashgate, 2004). The literature on confessionalization has begun to have an influence beyond the historical profession. For instance, the philosopher Charles Taylor relied extensively on the confessionalization thesis in his ambitious account of secularization. See his *A Secular Age* (Cambridge, MA: Belknap Press of Harvard University Press, 2007).

26. Ozment, *Protestants*, 216.
27. Martin Luther, *Martin Luther's Basic Theological Writings*, ed. Timothy F. Lull (Minneapolis: Fortress Press, 1989), 82–83, 84, 92.
28. Luise Schorn-Schütte, *Evangelische Geistlichkeit der Frühneuzeit: Deren Anteil an der Entfaltung frühmoderner Staatlichkeit und Gesellschaft dargestellt am Beispiel des Fürstentums Braunschweig-Wolfenbüttel, der Landgrafschaft Hessen-Kassel und der Stadt Braunschweig* (Gütersloh: Gütersloher Verlagshaus, 1996); R. W. Scribner, "Pastoral Care and the Reformation in Germany," in *Religion and Culture in Germany (1400–1800)*, ed. Lyndal Roper (Leiden: Brill, 2001), 172–94. The relationship between the clergy and laity in early modern Europe remains an area of vibrant, ongoing debate. See C. Scott Dixon and Luise Schorn-Schütte, eds., *The Protestant Clergy of Early Modern Europe* (London: Palgrave, 2003); Wim Janse and Barbara Pitkin, eds., *The Formation of Clerical and Confessional Identities in Early Modern Europe*, vol. 85: Dutch Review of Church History (Leiden: Brill, 2005); Amy Nelson Burnett, *Teaching the Reformation: Ministers and the Message in Basel* (Oxford: Oxford University Press, 2006).
29. Bossy, *Christianity in the West*, 98–99.
30. For a particularly stark statement of this argument, see Fasolt, "Hegel's Ghost."
31. Steven Ozment, *The Age of Reform, 1250–1550: An Intellectual and Religious History of Late Medieval and Reformation Europe* (New Haven, CT: Yale University Press, 1980).
32. Heidi Wunder, *He Is the Sun, She Is the Moon: Women in Early Modern Germany*, trans. Thomas Dunlap (Cambridge, MA: Harvard University Press, 1998).
33. For an example of one such effort, see Matthew Lundin, *Paper Memory: A Sixteenth-Century Townsman Writes His World* (Cambridge, MA: Harvard University Press, 2012), 130–60.
34. Robert James Bast, *Honor Your Fathers: Catechisms and the Emergence of a Patriarchal Ideology in Germany, 1400–1600*, Studies in Medieval and Reformation Thought 63 (Leiden: Brill, 1997).
35. Lundin, *Paper Memory*, 95.
36. Susan Karant-Nunn, *The Reformation of Feeling: Shaping the Religious Emotions in Early Modern Europe* (Oxford: Oxford University Press, 2010).
37. Will Coster and Andrew Spicer, eds., *Sacred Space in Early Modern Europe* (Cambridge: Cambridge University Press, 2005); Andrew Spicer, ed., *Lutheran Churches in Early Modern Europe* (Burlington, VT: Ashgate, 2012).
38. Peter Marshall and Alexandra Walsham, eds., *Angels in the Early Modern World* (Cambridge: Cambridge University Press, 2006).
39. Bruce Gordon and Peter Marshall, eds., *The Place of the Dead: Death and Remembrance in Late Medieval and Early Modern Europe* (Cambridge: Cambridge University Press, 2000); and Peter Marshall, *Beliefs and the Dead in Reformation England* (Oxford: Oxford University Press, 2002).

188　　THE PRESENT

40. Susan Karant-Nunn, *The Reformation of Ritual: An Interpretation of Early Modern Germany* (London: Routledge, 1997); and Craig Koslofsky, *The Reformation of the Dead: Death and Ritual in Early Modern Germany, 1450–1700* (New York: St. Martin's Press, 2000).

41. See, for instance, Derek A. Wilson and Felipe Fernandez-Armesto, *Reformations: A Radical Interpretation of Christianity and the World, 1500–2000* (New York: Scribner, 1996).

42. Hans J. Hillerbrand, *The Division of Christendom: Christianity in the Sixteenth Century* (Louisville, KY: Westminster John Knox, 2007), 551.

43. Ronald K. Rittgers, *The Reformation of Suffering: Pastoral Theology and Lay Piety in Late Medieval and Early Modern Germany*, Oxford Studies in Historical Theology (Oxford: Oxford University Press, 2012); and Alec Ryrie, *Being Protestant in Reformation England* (Oxford: Oxford University Press, 2013).

44. Brad S. Gregory, *Salvation at Stake: Christian Martyrdom in Early Modern Europe* (Cambridge, MA: Harvard University Press, 1999), 1–15.

45. Gregory, *Salvation at Stake*, 12.

46. Susan E. Schreiner, *Are You Alone Wise?: The Search for Certainty in the Early Modern Era* (Oxford: Oxford University Press, 2011), 7–15.

47. Gregory, *Salvation at Stake*, 12.

48. Gerald Strauss, "Protestant Dogma and City Government: The Case of Nuremberg," *Past and Present* (1967): 38–58. For a critique of Strauss's argument, see Ronald K. Rittgers, *The Reformation of the Keys: Confession, Conscience, and Authority in Sixteenth-Century Germany* (Cambridge, MA: Harvard University Press, 2004), 95.

49. According to Gregory, the martyr's willingness to die for faith was what the early modern confessions "ideally produced." Gregory, *Salvation at Stake*, 8.

50. For accounts of "pragmatic toleration" in early modern Europe, see Benjamin J. Kaplan, *Divided by Faith: Religious Conflict and the Practice of Toleration in Early Modern Europe* (Cambridge, MA: Belknap Press of Harvard University Press, 2007); C. Scott Dixon, Dagmar Friest, and Mark Greengrass, eds., *Living with Religious Diversity in Early-Modern Europe*, St. Andrews Studies in Reformation History (Aldershot: Ashgate, 2009).

51. Thomas A. Brady, *German Histories in the Age of Reformations, 1400–1650* (Cambridge: Cambridge University Press, 2009), 420.

52. Scribner, "Reformation and Desacralisation"; and Scribner, "Reformation, 'Popular Magic.'"

53. Brady, *German Histories*; Diarmaid MacCulloch, *The Reformation: A History* (New York: Viking, 2003); Brad Gregory, *The Unintended Reformation: How a Religious Revolution Secularized Society* (Cambridge, MA: Belknap Press of Harvard University Press, 2012); Thomas Kaufmann, *Geschichte der Reformation* (Frankfurt am Main: Verlag der Weltreligionen, 2009); Hillerbrand, *The Division of Christendom*; Lee Palmer Wandel, *The Reformation: Towards a New*

History (Cambridge: Cambridge University Press, 2011); and Schreiner, *Are You Alone Wise?*

54. Thomas Kaufmann insists that the Reformation is comprehensible "only from the background of the absolute omnipresence of the church." Kaufmann, *Geschichte der Reformation*, 15.

55. Wandel, *Reformation*, 263–64.

56. Kaufmann, *Geschichte der Reformation*, 17.

57. Gregory, *Unintended Reformation*, see esp. ch. 2.

58. Gregory, *Unintended Reformation*, 368–69.

59. On this point, see Mark Noll's chapter in this volume.

60. Lundin, *Paper Memory*, ch. 8.

61. Lundin, *Paper Memory*, ch. 5.

8

Commemorating the Reformation in "Post-Christian" Europe?

Herman J. Selderhuis

THE DEBATE OVER the meaning of Reformation jubilees or commemorations is an old one. As seen already in this volume, such celebrations can be put to different uses and interpreted in a range of ways. For example, at an early marking of the occasion in 1617, Friedrich V (1596–1632), elector of the Palatinate and an enterprising Calvinist, was perhaps the first to propose the celebration of the 100th anniversary of the Reformation. He wanted to observe it as a single, common celebration for Lutherans and Calvinists. But his plan was criticized by Lutheran statesmen and theologians, who accused him of making this proposal for improper reasons.[1] Some suspected that his motive was political—namely, to show that the Reformed or Calvinist Christians in the Palatinate *did* belong to Luther and his tradition, and that therefore they were entitled to full legal recognition in the Holy Roman Empire under the umbrella of the Peace of Augsburg (1555). In his defense, Friedrich claimed that he was proposing the commemoration, first and foremost, simply to thank God for what he had accomplished through Martin Luther's rediscovery of the gospel. The subordinate political reason was tied to the theological one, demonstrating to the Church of Rome and the Catholic emperor that Protestants possessed, despite their internal disputes, a firm unity. As things turned out, Friedrich was not able to convince his fellow Protestants, and so in 1617 Calvinists and Lutherans held commemoration events apart from one another.

As this episode illustrates and as chapter 1 in this volume shows, questions about why, how, and with whom to commemorate the Reformation have been around for a long time. For different reasons they remain highly relevant, even more so since conditions in Europe and the world have changed massively since Friedrich V's first proposal. Indeed, in the last fifty years, the position of Christianity in Europe has changed more dramatically than in the almost 450 years between 1517 and the middle decades of the twentieth century. In spite of these changes many people, especially among Protestants, take as self-evident that the 500th anniversary of Luther's 95 Theses will be celebrated, some way, somehow. Events have long been in the works for this purpose across Europe.[2] But fundamental questions about to *how* to do this, and even more *why* to do so, are seldom posed, let alone answered adequately. In this chapter, I attempt to pose these questions and sketch some tentative answers as someone who for many years has been tasked with planning appropriate commemorations in 2017.

Why Commemorate the Reformation?

Before the question of *how* to commemorate the Reformation in Europe comes the question of *why* the 500th anniversary of the Reformation should be commemorated at all. Amid the flurry of activities connected to this jubilee, that fundamental question deserves priority. Of course, if you are a German, you might want to recognize a national figure who helped shape your language and was deeply influential in your country's history. But what does such a Reformation jubilee mean for someone living in Madrid or Palermo—much less Istanbul or Moscow, and perhaps even much less in Beijing or Kampala?

We also must pause to reflect on the choice of words: *commemoration* must be explained. The word *celebration* is too positive to be helpful in settings that strive to be neutral, to remain above religious or other forms of partisanship. Yet *commemoration* can indicate, misleadingly, that we are dealing with something purely historical, a relic that is no longer relevant. Still, *commemoration* is preferable since the term carries less of an ideological connotation, even if we insist that we are not dealing with a dead past.

Since question of "why commemorate?" deserves an elaborate philosophical analysis that is certainly beyond the scope of this chapter, the following might be considered thumbnail sketches of motives for commemorations in general, and for the specific commemoration of the Reformation in 2017.

a. *Historical motivation.* Historical interest in who did what, why, and where can be a motive. This motive can engage scholars and others interested in history, as it did for the heightened focus in Luther research on the 400th anniversary of his birth in 1883, as has been shown in chapter 1, and for John Calvin's comparable birthday anniversary in 1909. The present-day identity of Europe has been shaped fundamentally by the religious developments set in motion by Martin Luther, so the search for the causes, origins, and consequences of this movement deserve validation.

b. *Theological motivation:* Under the "theological" can be included a variety of motives. These might be ecumenical in the sense that remembering 1517 in 2017 can help restore the unity of the Western church that was over the *causa Lutheri.* This opportunity seems especially pertinent after the ecumenical breakthroughs in the wake of the Second Vatican Council, which recently celebrated its fiftieth anniversary. The theological motive can, however, also be the opposite. The Reformation jubilee might be seen as an occasion to show how wrong the Reformers were and how lamentable their long-term influence has been. Or, in a different judgment, it might be used to justify Luther's actions, to revitalize the polemical features of his theology, to demonstrate the rightness of certain Protestant confessional positions, and replay traditional Protestant habits by pointing out the deficiencies and falsehoods of Roman Catholicism.

c. *Economic motivation:* Commemorations quite often have an economic dimension, as was the case in the former East Germany for several earlier commemorations of Luther's life. In other words, jubilees can be big business for publishers, travel agents, cities, and museums that see a chance to boost the number of visitors and customers. And let's not forget the university administrators who send their professors as writers and presenters to gather grant funding and to put their institutions in the spotlight, garnering attention and perhaps increased enrollment.

d. *Political motivation:* Today there might be political reasons for marking the Reformation, just as much as in the sixteenth century. Fortunately, we are decades away from the situation in which the Luther jubilee in 1983 (the 500th anniversary of Luther's birth) was used by the German Democratic Republic to promote socialism—even as this instrumentalizing of the occasion had many critics in the church. But the jubilee in 2017 is not without its own political aspects. It allows historically Protestant countries to promote their national inheritance. It promises to allow Protestant minorities in other countries to call attention to their identities. In Germany, at a regional level, it allows the federal states to showcase their particular histories and cultures. At the same time, many want to focus on the Reformation as a pan-European, liberating event that, properly commemorated, can help strengthen the idea of a unified Europe. Still others want to blame Luther for introducing so much divisiveness and conflict into Europe's past.

None of these motives is completely new. They have all appeared in some form or another ever since special—or, should we maybe say holy?—places, persons, and dates have been commemorated. Although motivations may vary, one answer to the question of why commemorate the Reformation seems quite clear. The Reformation was one of the most influential events in the history of the world generally and of the Christian church in particular. Without it, the present global society would look completely different. If we want to understand the world and the church today, and if we want to behave responsibly toward the world and the church, we need to know about the Reformation, its broader context, its actors, its message, and the reactions to it. A commemoration judiciously planned and executed can stimulate and improve such an understanding. In order to reach this understanding, all of the motives mentioned possess a claim to legitimacy. But a commemoration will be fruitful only if the higher-minded motives are combined in productive ways and without being dominated by narrowly partisan or pecuniary agendas.

How to Commemorate: Options and Complications

A number of options present themselves in response to the question of *how* to commemorate the 500th anniversary of the Reformation. These options are related to the various motivations and each presents complications. The historical option, for example, can approach the Reformation with an unbalanced focus on the person Martin Luther, but that approach leaves him as a figure from the distant past with little or no connection to the present.[3] Luther in this account might then show up as the monk who rocked the church, irritated pope and emperor, got married, drank beer, preached, gained too much weight, and died. This Luther might be interesting, even entertaining, but as only a curiosity from yesterday, with no relevance for today or tomorrow.

In the theological approach, Luther might be instrumentalized as an apostle of freedom, a rebel against Rome, the father of modern tolerance, the inventor of grace, or other such idealizing titles. Yet all such images, if accepted uncritically and without greater nuance, create more problems than they resolve.

In the economic option, where Luther and the Reformation are "sold," cities and regions expect millions of visitors to open their wallets. Tourists will come to the places where Luther lived—where he stayed for at least one night, or the places he had presumably intended to visit—what some have called "almost Luther" cities. The irony here is that publishers, brewers, and producers of "Refo relics" hope to reap in 2017 the same sort of profits as Albrecht von Mainz expected went he started Johannes Tetzel on an indulgences tour in 1517!

Since such marketing ventures are already well under way, soberminded scholars should not have the illusion that they can do much about it. But they can provide alternatives, even capitalizing on the more questionable approaches to strengthen the more responsible commemorations. Still, everyone—academics, commemorators, and celebrators alike—needs awareness that the complications of the Reformation should not be ignored but dealt with openly. To begin with the most obvious: Martin Luther is both a fascinating personality and a problematic one. Those who take 2017 more as a moment of celebration than commemoration should be cognizant of the excruciatingly harsh attacks that Luther leveled at Jews, Catholics, Anabaptists, Muslims, and at anyone else with whom he disagreed—and there were many! Of course, this was true not only of Luther.

But Luther is purported to be the (re)discoverer of the gospel, of the authority of the Word, and of the power of grace. How, then, can he have said so many offensive, indeed, abusive things? Many Protestants wish the ugly side of Luther would simply vanish from history. But it will not. The problem, of course, goes well beyond Luther. Luther and the Reformation as a whole have many regrettable aspects. Whether the topic is Luther and the Jews, Calvin and Servetus, or *cuius regio, eius religio*, evidence does not support the notion that the "Era of the Reformation" led to the "Age of Toleration." Any attempt to present the Reformation as the initiator of tolerance and equal rights in order to claim its importance and current relevance is doomed to fail. The facts require much greater nuance.

Furthermore, a focus on Luther as an evangelist of freedom must make clear that his great concern remained freedom from sin and guilt, not freedom in a political sense as we would understand this today. That view of Luther is really a child of modernity, not of the sixteenth century. If it were up to Luther, for example, the Netherlands would still be occupied by Spain, and Dutch Protestantism most likely would have been eradicated by the Inquisition long ago. Luther opposed any resistance to political authorities. Luckily for the Dutch, their prince, William of Orange, though raised as a Lutheran, turned Catholic and then went back to Protestantism and did not strictly keep to the "obedience to authority" (*Obrigkeitsgehorsamkeit*) that Luther defended. It is a common historical judgment that elsewhere in Europe this posture led to unintended yet disastrous consequences, as later times revealed. Instead, William chose Calvinism with its "right to revolt," a theory *in nuce* developed by John Calvin.[4]

Problems created by Luther also beset the realm of theology. To mention just one well-known example: his attitude in the debate about the Lord´s Supper in Marburg in 1529, when he not only held off any attempt to find peace with Zwingli and other Swiss reformers, but also was ready to accept, as a logical consequence of his position, conclusions on the person of Christ that many of his fellow reformers regarded as irrational. Many other examples of his intransigence could be adduced. In short, Luther presents too much controversy and belligerence to qualify him for placement on a pedestal in 2017 as hero or saint.[5]

Looking at the larger picture, it is imperative to remember the obvious fact that the Reformation entailed a split in the church. It contributed to religious wars that brought personal tragedy into the lives men and women in the sixteenth century and afterwards. A convinced Protestant today might still be able to declare with approval: "Where would we be without the Reformation?" Yet for others, that question might prompt a very different answer. Some might even say that the world would have been much better off without the Reformation. Even Protestants who affirm the value of the Reformation should take full account of those dissenting from doing so in 2017.

Myopia is an additional complication. Luther started the whole thing, or as Calvin put it: "The Gospel started in Wittenberg."[6] Yet the focus of 2017, again, should not be just on one man but also on those who supported and opposed him, on the Reformation as a whole in all its vexing complexity. Excessive focus on Luther could seriously undermine commemorative events; just a few quotations from Luther on Jews, women, and Turks could tag him as an intolerant fundamentalist with no message for the present. Even more, it is a mistake to look at the Reformation from a generically Protestant perspective. A better path to more a satisfying commemoration can be opened by speaking of the plural "Reformations," as has become custom in Reformation research today.[7]

For commemorations in 2017 to avoid such problems, it must be constantly kept in mind that Luther worked in a world where much was changing. For example, it is clear that his actions stimulated other varieties of reform, such as the Catholic reformation—what used to be called the "Counter Reformation"—and the Anabaptist movement, or the "Radical Reformation." What is more, the notion of "sixteenth-century reformations" can also be applied to other areas of human endeavor. As demonstrated by other chapters in this book, the sixteenth century witnessed not only major shifts in church, theology, and spirituality, but also in science, culture, law, politics, cartography, medicine, and more. The great variety of related national and regional developments must also be considered when commemorating the Reformation in "Post-Christian Europe." If such complexities are kept in mind, much can be learned in 2017.

Post-Christian Europe: Facts and Concepts

Perhaps an even bigger challenge than the problematic aspects of Luther's career or general developments in the sixteenth century is the question of how to commemorate the Reformation in a *post-Christian Europe*.[8] Much literature has been published lately trying to define what "post-Christian" means, even whether or not it is the best term to characterize the situation in Europe today.[9] This chapter is not the place to analyze the overall role of faith in Western Europe, although many indisputable facts do indicate that Europe is a substantially secularized continent, especially when compared to other parts of the globe. Churchgoing, church membership, and numbers of those who profess belief in a personal God are all declining.

This reality, too, deserves full consideration when approaching the commemorations of 2017.

Still, it is possible to wonder if "post-Christian" is an entirely accurate
way of characterizing contemporary Europe. Some research suggests that
Europe is not as secularized or post-Christian as it might seem. For example, about half of all Europeans tell survey researchers that they pray
or meditate at least once a week. Three out of four Europeans say they
are "religious persons." The number of outright atheists is relatively low.
In countries like Italy and Greece, the Christian faith is alive and visible
every day of the week. In Eastern Europe, churches are being built, people
in some areas are returning to church, a growing number of children and
adults come to be baptized—and these developments are taking place in
the wake of fundamental political changes in these countries, maybe even
as a result of these changes. The fall of the Berlin Wall (1989) as a symbolic end of the artificial divide between "East" and "West" Europe demonstrated the power of the church and its believers. As has been widely
documented, the Monday evening church prayer meetings that began
in Leipzig in September 1987 sparked a chain of events that eventually
brought down the wall—and that, in a socialist country where the influence of the church had been massively degraded. It is also noteworthy,
although Luther might not have been too happy about such a development, that Pope Francis today enjoys great popularity and regular, positive
notice in European newspapers, magazines, and online. In sum, it might
be premature to speak of a "post-Christian era" in Europe today.[10]

Yet one cannot deny that the religious situation in Europe now
is fundamentally different from that of the sixteenth century, even
from fifty years ago. Public life is certainly less visibly shaped by the
Christian tradition—a fact best illustrated by empty pews on Sunday,
by the growth in the number of mosques in recent years, and by the
ongoing conversion of church buildings into bookstores, apartments,
and for other nonreligious purposes. As Europe has moved from a post-
Westphalian, multi-confessional society to a multi-religious/secular
one, it has witnessed a parallel transition from a public to a private form
of Christianity. What is more, Christian profession has mostly become
a local, voluntary, "optional" designation of one's identity. It is less often
the case that individuals are simply born and baptized into a particular
confession (Lutheran, Anglican, Calvinist, etc.), but instead living as "a
Christian" results from a conscious choice. The fading of church membership as simply a traditional inheritance entails a different awareness

of what it means to be a Christian. Those who identify as believers often have a keener sense that "I am a believer at the workplace" or "I am a Christian in my town," as opposed to, say, "I am a member of the Church of England." The notion of "believing without belonging"—to use the phrase of the sociologist Grace Davie—speaks to a situation where ecclesiastical mobility prevails in parallel with the way people switch jobs or move houses.[11] This way of thinking about religious i-dentity in terms of flexible relations rather than in defined obligations marks a major change from the age of Luther, and for what prevailed during many centuries after his passing.

In large parts of Europe, those who do believe often express ambiguity about church structures and hierarchies, especially in cases where flagrant abuses of office have occurred. The positive image of Pope Francis cannot obscure the incredible damage the priest sexual scandal has done to the Roman Catholic Church. For many of the Protestant churches, a similar image problem attends their interminable bickering over positions on marriage and sexuality. Those churches also receive ridicule for tolerat-ing theologians who deny essential doctrines of the Christian faith. Both church members and nonmembers are regularly troubled by a sense that Europe's historical religious institutions have drifted from their primary responsibilities and have entangled themselves excessively in "worldly" affairs. But perhaps precisely at this point the contemporary situation re-sembles that of the sixteenth century. Luther was moved to protest by what he saw as a theology and a church adrift from its foundation and primary message. As in contemporary Europe, during the Reformation the laity often experienced the church as a distant, bureaucratic entity obsessed with power and money, its clergy disconnected and ethically lax. Parallels on this score between the early sixteenth century and the early twenty-first deserve attention in 2017 and beyond.

There are still other features of European life today that suggest simi-larities with the sixteenth century. Economic instability, a distrust of poli-tics and politicians, the disorientation of many young people, and a host of marital and family issues are just a few of the items that beg comparison. In addition, at the same time that much of Europe seems to be moving in a post-Christian direction, a growing interest in religion and "spirituality" can also be seen.[12] In light of the fact that the visibility of institutional Christianity in Europe has declined, even as many consider themselves believing Christians or religious at least in some sense, perhaps the term "secularized" may be more fitting than "post-Christian."[13]

But a secularized Europe, again, is strangely also a religious Europe, with the emphasis on "religious," not "Christian." Dietrich Bonhoeffer may have offered an especially prescient forecast when he predicted that Christianity would decline and religion would return.[14] It has done so, if in fact religion, understood in its most general sense, ever departed in the first place. Religion, particularly as concerns the growing Muslim presence in Europe, plays a larger role in politics and society than it has formerly. Thus, it is now most intriguing, and maybe even imperative, to be thinking about the 500th anniversary of the Reformation at a time when faculties of theology at state universities are relabeled as departments of religious studies and when Western Europe's traditional two confessions (Catholic and Protestant) have become a new situation with two religions (Christianity and Islam). Commemorating five hundred years of the Reformation in a so-called post-Christian Europe, at once secularized and religious, residually Christian and newly Islamic, does make sense. But it does so only if we honestly seek to understand what the Reformation, at its core, was really about.

Ad fontes: *What Was the Reformation About?*

In 2011, great expectations accompanied the former Pope Benedict XVI when he visited his homeland, Germany. Perhaps with an eye on the near approach of 2017, he carefully avoided Wittenberg and the Wartburg, sites forever associated with the dawn of Protestantism, but chose instead to visit Erfurt, where Luther lived while he was still a Catholic monk and a city that has a history of ecumenical engagement. Many anticipated that the pope would say kind words about Luther and then make some kind of conciliatory overture. But this did not happen, and they found themselves afterwards in confusion and disappointment, since the pope instead spoke, not about the church divisions that Luther's life had sparked, but about the gospel message that Luther had tried so hard to proclaim.[15] That message, according to the pope, was the central theological question about the relation between the righteous God and sinful humanity. In Benedict's speech he urged that this question should be taken up again today. Instead of lifting the ban on Luther or making an ecumenical gesture, the pope had the chutzpah to remind German Protestants about the gospel that Luther proclaimed.

But, really, do Protestants need the pope to tell them what the Reformation was all about? Perhaps, since most Protestants no longer view the pope as the Antichrist, this idea that once would have seemed impossible may actually be true. In fact, not a few Protestants today perceive the recent popes as the last redoubt of genuine Christian witness; for them, as hard as it would have been for Luther to imagine, Rome has become the last bastion of a visible and assertive Christianity. Historians and historical theologians might have a clear idea of Luther's central message, but for the wider Protestant—or vestigially Protestant—world, he has been too often reduced to a comic figure, a beer-drinking monk with a simplistic message: "Be merry and get married, for free grace will let you." The commemorations of 2017, therefore, provide the opportunity to ask what would happen if Protestants, not to speak of Europeans in general, would turn to what Luther actually desired and preached, and for which he lived and died. That prospect essentially, was what Pope Benedict offered to Protestants at Erfurt in 2011.

In recent decades, Reformation research has profited immensely from the influx of social historians into the field. For a very long time, Reformation research was dominated by church historians, who focused more on ecclesiastical matters and theology than on historical contexts. Because of that concentration, these scholars often did not pay sufficient to connections between religious matters and the broader worlds of politics, society, and culture. Social historians taught such narrowly focused scholars that historical contexts were in fact very important, and that a description of institutions could not be complete without a description of the people and social forces afoot within these institutions. It was at first difficult for church historians to accept this message, but eventually they did, and this has brought about a needed correction of emphasis.

Yet one problematic result of this healthy correction was that the theological center in the Reformation often gets lost from view. Scholars with great skills in history, demographics, ethnography, and class and gender analysis have transformed our academic understanding of the sixteenth century, but often they show little interest in questions of biblical interpretation and theology that both reformers and their critics treated as primary. In excellent efforts to contextualize the theology of the sixteenth century, sometimes theology gets eclipsed.

Therefore, we should remind ourselves in 2017 that Luther's primary goal was not a reformation of society, nor a revolution in natural sciences, nor a restructuring of political and social life in Europe, nor a re-evaluation of marriage, family, and education. As much as it is legitimate to study these changes, sober scholarship knows that these

were not Luther's main concerns. His goal was not even in the first instance a reformation of the church. Certainly, he was concerned about
the state of the clergy and the abuse of power in the church. But his
main concern, and for him a profoundly existential concern, was the relation between God and human beings—more specifically, the relation
between God in his holiness and human beings in their sinfulness, or
what theologians call the doctrine of justification. When in 1545 Luther
penned a foreword to the first edition of his collected works, he wrote
that it was as if the gate of paradise was opened to him when he discovered what justification by faith really meant. That insight was the
essential ingredient of the Reformation.[16] It is noteworthy that this observation came in the next to last year of his life (he died in 1546), after
he had witnessed many positive and many negative results from the
Reformation movements that he had sparked. By recalling that it was as
if the gate of heaven opened to him, he did not mean that all of a sudden
he saw that Europe needed a new political system, or that monks and
nuns should get married, or that human beings needed freedom for
self-development. Instead, he was claiming to understand a central
theme of the Bible in a new light, which was that men and women
could be saved from God's judgment and eternal death by the free and
unmerited grace of God in Jesus Christ. Although this teaching im-
plicates matters of great depth and breadth, Luther's understanding of
Reformation was as simple as that. This was the new insight that he
enthusiastically wanted to circulate.

The momentous debate that Luther carried on with Erasmus in 1525
underscores that the question of justification by faith was for Luther the
fundamental issue; on this point Erasmus had attacked him. On the last
page of his long reply to Erasmus's book on free will, Luther made his central concern glaringly clear:

> Therefore then I give you great praise and proclaim it that among
> all you are really the only one who got into what in fact is the true
> issue at stake here, which is, the heart of the matter and that you
> have not wearied me with those irrelevant issues about popery,
> purgatory, indulgences, and other trifles—for that's what they are
> more than real issues—with which so far nearly all have troubled
> me and in vain I must say. It's you, and only you who has seen what
> was the point on which everything turns, and so you attacked the
> main issue; and I want to thank you heartily for that.[17]

The "point on which everything turns," as Luther called it, was the theme of his discussion with Erasmus. That, then again, concentrated on how sinful humans can come to terms with a righteous and holy God. In turn, that message was tied to questions of personal and institutional guilt, public justice, forgiveness, reconciliation, and righteousness—and more.

These issues remain relevant today. In fact, it is remarkable how many current novels, plays, and movies are obsessed with the notion of "guilt"— even as "guilt" has receded as a central theme in sermons, catechesis, and in Christian education. In Luther´s Reformation, confronting guilt was essential. It would, therefore, be entirely fitting if commemoration in 2017 focused on questions of guilt and sinfulness again. Such commemoration would reflect not only the basic Christian message but also one of the most basic concerns of a secularized society. One sees this clear in our ecological crisis, which Pope Francis addressed in his 2015 encyclical *Laudate si*. Our earth might well be ceasing to hold up under the sins of an avaricious society of consumers and waste producers. Theological resources from the Reformation, and from Luther in particular, might well offer us means to deliberate wisely about this issue.

But once we view Luther's theology as the central factor in the Reformation, we must return to the question of *how* to commemorate the 500th anniversary.

Of first importance is to recover Luther the preacher, the pastor, the professor, and the believer. Political, social, and cultural movements related to the Reformation, again, remain important, but these movements ought to be considered in relation to his theology. The 500th year since the Reformation is not marked five centuries after 1529, when at the Diet of Speyer statesmen first coined the term "Protestant," nor does it mark 1525, when Luther, the former monk, married a former nun, Katharina von Bora. In 2017, we are commemorating five hundred years since 1517, when a professor at new university (Wittenberg was only founded in 1502) on a town on the outskirts of European civilization published a number of theological theses that dealt with the relation between a righteous God and sinful humanity.

But, of course, if we only focus on this event and focus solely on Luther, we miss the breadth and international character of Protestantism, and thereby underestimate the impact of Luther's theological rediscovery. The message of justification by faith alone soon enlisted influential figures such as Philip Melanchthon, Martin Bucer, and John Calvin, who worked out concepts of personal holiness and church reform from the basis of justification by faith. That message also helped these theologians and others fashion a Christian worldview on education, politics, social life and culture. These things, too, are relevant in a commemoration of the Reformation in 2017.

Luther's central theological concern also relates directly to the many upheavals of sixteenth-century Europe—to a plurality of "reformations." Protestant Reformers, Anabaptists, and reform-minded Catholics alike agreed in their conviction that Europe, because it was not sufficiently Christian, required a deeper, truer Christianization. Naturally they varied in their conceptions of how to realize this goal, but they agreed that reform was necessary. Furthermore, they were agreed that such reform began with theology. Whether Europe today is Christian, post-Christian, pre-Christian, or something else, commemoration of 2017 can only be fruitful if European churches unite, not in vague paeans to unity, but in a spirit that desires to understand correctly the theological emphases of the sixteenth century and their present-day implications.

The Sixteenth Century and Today: A Complicated Relevance

Permit me to conclude on a note of "prophecy": in the coming decades, religious and theological issues will become more pronounced and important. Given this possibility, it is fitting to observe some parallels between Europe in the early sixteenth century and Europe in the early twenty-first century. The first similarity might be characterized by the German word *Orientierungslosigkeit*, which we might render in English as "the loss or absence of orientation." In this condition, basic certainties are either lost or questioned and many, mainly young people, are adrift from normative points of reference—what we call "values" today and which were called "virtues" in the past. Second, religious tolerance concerns us now, as it did in the sixteenth century. Although at that time it was tolerance between Catholics and Protestants (or among Protestants) that was most needed, now it is tolerance as a basic framework for pluralistic, multi-religious societies; such tolerance is vital for society and politics to function. Third, a media revolution took place in both eras, with its possibilities, challenges, and dangers. The spread of the printing press, combined with the increased abilities of people to buy and read books, was quite similar to recent developments in digital data and social media. Both revolutions should make us think about the responsible use of the media that we possess. Fourth, in economic terms, we face a range of issues from corruption and greed at the top of organizations to a growth of debts and poverty. Just think of the situation in Greece today or of Europe's immigration crisis. Then and now, society was constructed so that many could strive but only a few succeed. (A relevant difference between then and now is that once where saints were celebrated for the merit that they had gained to enter heaven, we now regard as blessed the soccer players, movie stars, and CEOs who earn enough to live in heaven on earth!) Fifth, church-state relations are becoming increasingly fraught in Europe. The issue is related to changes in society and in the decline of churches' institutional power. Yet questions about the state's responsibilities for the church, the independence of the church, and the church's opinions about politics and law grew in importance because of the Reformation. Thinking about the long arc of church-state relations since the sixteenth century might help us better understand these relations today. Sixth, while we recognize that people in the sixteenth century were preoccupied with sin and salvation, it is true that people are also concerned about these today, but in a different sense and setting. Although "sin" is no longer connected to death, let alone eternal death, sin and guilt are the major problems for which people seek help from psychiatrists and therapists. Related is the quest for spirituality and spiritual stability. In recent decades, tour operators and former monasteries have discovered "spiritual tourism," a market niche addressing their visitors' needs to escape workplace stress or psychological turmoil. Now as then, the church in its preaching does not seem to meet people with the answers they seek, but many still look to the church as a way of finding space to seek inner stability. Sometimes, though, it seems as if the physical space of the church, more than its message, is what touches people.

Neither Luther, Calvin, nor any other reformer viewed Europe as a vibrantly Christian place. They did recognize that Europeans were almost all baptized, but also concluded that only a small minority of them actually lived up to their baptism. They complained about Europeans as not being Christian in any genuine sense. Calvin spoke of "Europa afflicta"[18] and in his lifetime came to the conclusion that Christianity worldwide—not just in Europe—was on the brink of collapse.[19]

He might conclude the same today. But it merits asking if Europe's church is as post-Christian as Europe's society. In the centuries since the Enlightenment and its aftermath, fundamental changes have come about in the way that the major Protestant churches view the Bible and the gospel. Have these changes been so fundamental that the gap between the Protestant churches today and the theology of the six-teenth century is unbridgeable? The answer might be mixed. To men-tion only Luther, his vision of the church continues to sound a clarion call: "Churches are there for no other function than that the Lord Jesus speaks to us through his Holy Word and that we in turn speak to Him through prayer and hymns."[20] In a formal sense, this function persists. But one might be forgiven for asking if the substance of what takes place in present-day Protestant church buildings is close enough for Luther to understand.

When the last bus has departed Wittenberg on the day after October 31, 2017, what will have entered the hearts and minds of those who in 2017 have visited the sites, purchased the memorabilia, read the books, joined the tours, or otherwise paused in some sense to observe the 500th anniversary of the Reformation? The answer certainly depends on the motivation. If we stay close to Luther's chief concern, the answer will be clear. A proper commemoration requires reflection on the meaning of jus-tification by faith. If Europe is post-Christian already, or if it is about to become post-Christian, then the commemoration of the Reformation at five hundred years may be quite salutary for Europe. For this observance may show Europe aspects of where it came from—and where it might want to go. And this is a task for historical scholarship to show. But beyond the history of the Reformation and its influence, what of its theological, existential core—human beings' proper relation to God? This question, too, begs to be loudly asked and discussed in 2017.

Notes

1. Herman Selderhuis, *"Wem gehört die Reformation? Das Reformationsjubiläum 1617 im Streit zwischen Lutheranern und Reformierten,"* in *Calvinismus in den Auseinandersetzungen des frühen konfessionellen Zeitalters*, ed. Herman J. Selderhuis, Martin Leiner, and Volker Leppin (Göttingen: Vandenhoeck and Ruprecht, 2013), 66–78.

2. For an overview of projects in process for the commemoration, see: www.luther2017.de and www.refo500.com.

3. For an overview of the way Luther has so far been presented in commemora-tions of the Reformation, see the collection of articles by Hartmut Lehmann, *Luthergedächtnis 1817 bis 2017* (Göttingen: Vandenhoeck & Ruprecht, 2012).

4. On this point, see John Witte Jr., *The Reformation of Rights: Law, Religion, and Human Rights in Early Modern Calvinism* (Cambridge: Cambridge University Press, 2007).

5. For such presentations, see Robert Kolb, *Martin Luther as Prophet, Teacher and Hero. Images of the Reformer, 1520-1620* (Grand Rapids, MI: Baker Academic, 1999).

6. A.L. Herminjard, *Correspondance des Réformateurs dans les pays de langue française* (Nieuwkoop: De Graaf, 1896), ix, 223.

7. Thomas A. Brady, *German Histories in the Age of the Reformations, 1400-1650* (Cambridge: Cambridge University Press, 2009); Carter Lindberg, *The European Reformations*, 2nd ed. (Chichester: Wiley-Blackwell, 2010); Scott H. Hendrix, *Recultivating the Vineyard. The Reformation Agendas of Christianization* (Louisville, KY: Westminster/John Knox Press, 2004).

8. I will not take up the question of whether the Reformation was a prime cause of the movements that led to a post-Christian Europe. As indicated by Brad Gregory's contribution to this book, opinions and arguments on this question are many, multifaceted, and not seldom mutually exclusive.

9. See, inter alia, Hartmut Lehmann, *Das Christentum im 20. Jahrhundert: Fragen, Probleme, Perspektiven*. Kirchengeschichte in Einzeldarstellungen IV/9 (Leipzig: Evangelische Verlagsanstalt, 2012); Hugh McLeod and Werner Ustorf, eds., *The Decline of Christendom in Western Europe 1750-2000* (Cambridge: Cambridge University Press, 2007); and Hugh Mcleod, *The Religious Crisis of the 1960s* (Oxford: Oxford University Press, 2007), and the literature mentioned therein.

10. Hugh McLeod, "The Crisis of Christianity in the West: Entering a Post-Christian Era?" in *The Cambridge History of Christianity*, vol. 9: *World Christianities c.1914-c.2000* (Cambridge: Cambridge University Press 2006), 347.

11. See Grace Davie, *Religion in Britain since 1945: Believing without Belonging* (Oxford: Blackwell, 1994).

12. Friedrich Wilhelm Graf, *Die Wiederkehr der Götter. Religion in der modernen Kultur* (Munich: C. H. Beck, 2004); and Martin Riesebrocht, *Die Rückkehr der Religionen* (Munich: C. H. Beck, 2000).

13. For the discussion on secularization and de-Christianization, see Matthias Pohlig et al., eds., *Säkularisierungen in der Frühen Neuzeit. Methodische Probleme und empirische Fallstudien*. Zeitschrift für Historische Forschung: Beiheft 41 (Berlin: Duncker & Humblot, 2008), 9–109.

14. See Jeffrey Pugh, *Religionless Christianity: Dietrich Bonhoeffer in Troubled Times* (London: T & T Clark, 2008).

15. The headline of the prominent *Süddeutsche Zeitung* the day after (September 24, 2011) was: "Benedikt XIV macht Hoffnungen der Protestanten zunichte" [Benedict XIV disappoints the hopes of Protestants].

16. "Hic me prorsus renatum esse sensi, et apertis portis in ipsam Paradisum intrasse." Martin Luther, *Luther's Werke. Kritische Ausgabe* (Weimar: H. Böhlau1883–) [hereafter, *WA*], 54:186.

17. *WA* 18:786.

18. "*afflicta est Europa*," *Ioannis Calvini Opera Quae Supersunt Omnia, Ediderunt Guilielmus*. Baum, Eduardus Cunitz, Eduardus Reuss, eds. Vol. 1–59 (Brunsvigae: Berolinae 1863–1900) [hereafter, *CO*], 36:202.

19. "*videmus statum religionis in toto orbe christiano fere collapsum*," *CO*, 36:178.

20. Torgau, Oktober 1544, *WA* 51:333.

9

What Hath Wittenberg to Do with Lagos?

SIXTEENTH-CENTURY PROTESTANTISM AND GLOBAL SOUTH CHRISTIANITY

Philip Jenkins

WRITING HISTORY DEPENDS on how exactly we divide up the periods we are studying. For Western Christians, the Reformation commonly marks the key dividing point: the story of the faith is usually told B.R. and A.R. But other periodizations and markers are also possible. We might for instance divide that story according to the shifting location of the church's geographical and cultural centers. For over a millennium, Christianity was a global, or at least transcontinental, faith before becoming identified with Europe (and the Euro-American world) in the late Middle Ages. In modern times, largely in the past half-century, it is again resuming that global dimension, with enormous expansion in Africa, Asia, and Latin America. A faith founded in Africa and Asia has decided, seemingly, to return home. By 2050, the largest concentration of the world's Christians will be found on the African continent, where they should represent a population of around a billion. By that time, the number of Christians who will be non-Latino whites should be around 20 percent of the global total. We are thus living through a historic era of transition and transformation, even of revolution, of no less significance than the Reformation.[1]

It is scarcely possible, of course, to draw any straight comparison between the two eras, the Reformation and modern globalization, as we are dealing with such different kinds of phenomena. Yet having said this, there are parallels that help us understand both eras.[2]

Night and Day?

The differences between the two eras are obvious enough. The Reformation was driven by new theological and intellectual insights, and often grew out of universities and academic institutions. Modern globalization is a social, demographic, and cultural phenomenon, which certainly demands theological reflection, but those ideas do not represent the driving force. Nor have academic institutions played any great role in the process.

Another key contrast is in the role of the state. What made the Reformation possible was not so much a sudden upsurge of dissidence or heresy, for these had been common enough throughout medieval history, but, rather, the rise of kingdoms and states prepared to break with the Catholic Church in their support of the new movement(s). It was thus a political development at least as much as a religious change. Global Christian growth in recent decades simply has not been driven by state activism.

The Reformation also was a European event, in which participants of all factions shared broadly similar cultural backgrounds and assumptions. In contrast, so much of the ferment in the contemporary world concerns the adaptation of the Christian faith to the many and various cultures in which it grows around the globe—issues that go far beyond the simple translation of texts.

In fact, the closest early modern analogy that we find to the present-day global church is not with the Protestant world at all but, rather, in the Catholic Reformation. Between 1550 and 1650, the Catholic Church led the great drive toward global mission. Pope Paul V presided over a church deeply concerned with its expansion into Latin America, Africa, the Philippines, China, and Japan, with all the now-familiar dilemmas of cultural confrontation and assimilation. The greatest axis of global mission was the Spanish empire's maritime route between Manila and Acapulco. Catholic polemicists vaunted such globalization of their faith, pointing out the embarrassing contrast to the paltry European spread of the Protestant churches.[3]

Scripture Alone

Differences acknowledged, parallels between the two eras are striking, not the least in attitudes toward the authority of scripture. If there was a single core theme in the various Protestant movements of the sixteenth century, it was the emphasis on the authority of scripture as the absolute and sole source of authority within religion, on *sola scriptura.*

Today, a conservative and literal biblical emphasis often divides Global South churches from their European or North American counterparts. African and Asian Christians are much more likely to show respect for the authority of scripture, especially in matters of morality; a willingness to accept the Bible as an inspired text and a tendency to literalism; a special interest in supernatural elements of scripture, such as miracles, visions, and healings; a belief in the continuing power of prophecy; and a veneration for the Old Testament, which is considered as authoritative as the New Testament. Biblical traditionalism and literalism are still more marked in the independent churches and in denominations rooted in the Pentecostal tradition, but similar currents are found among Anglicans and Roman Catholics. In recent years, northern and southern churches have clashed over issues of sexual morality and identity, as well as the theme of gay ordination. As these controversies have developed, they have increasingly focused on the authority of scripture.

We can find many reasons for the scriptural conservatism of Global South churches, and many find parallels in the Reformation era, whose mixed legacies were inherited here in different measures. To take one point, modern readers in Africa (say) are able to relate to the Bible's social and economic arrangements just as closely as were early modern Europeans, but as modern Westerners are not. They could understand the agricultural and pastoral values described in those pages, not to mention such other familiar ideas as the value of family and the code of honor that shaped social relations. If the Bible seems to speak to you so directly in terms of the world it portrays, then you are more likely to accept its spiritual and moral messages.[4]

A far more significant parallel, though, is the manner in which the Bible has entered popular consciousness. In both worlds—Germany in 1520, Nigeria or Uganda today—the Bible reached mass popular consciousness as part of a wider transformation of attitudes toward the word, to writing, and to literacy. As in the sixteenth century, cultural transformation has profoundly affected attitudes toward religious authority. While the Bible had existed previously on shelves of elite readers, it suddenly has exploded into the lives of the poor.

A *Media Revolution*

Coming shortly after Guttenberg, the Reformation entailed a media revolution. The Reformation challenged the idea that authority should be mediated through institutions or hierarchies, and denied the value of tradition. Instead, it offered radical new notions of the supremacy of written texts, interpreted by the individual conscience. In consequence, scriptural authority gained absolute hegemony in religious discourse.[5]

In no respect were the reformers more radical than in the dominant forms of media used to teach and discuss religious truths, with all that shift implies for cultural sensibilities. Traditional societies had taught their truths through visual imagery, such as stained glass and sculpture, through music, and above all, through drama and ritual action, which often involved a large amount of communal participation. Protestants focused on the word, in the form of books and tracts, hymns and sermons.

The new religious model was made possible only by the rise of printing, which we think of most directly in terms of books and Bibles. Equally significant, though, were pamphlets, handbills, songbooks, chapbooks, and especially cartoons, which were a major vehicle for distributing the Reformation message throughout Germany and northern Europe. Although books had, of course, existed throughout the European Middle Ages, only now did they become widely accessible to lower social orders. In creating the modern world, printing was as significant as the new mechanisms of central state power made possible by artillery. Thomas Carlyle famously listed "the three great elements of modern civilization, Gunpowder, Printing, and the Protestant religion."[6]

In much of modern Africa especially, the Word arrived in the same package as the revolutionary idea of the written word, and it takes a real act of imagination to recall the power and the authority of the written text. In some areas, the word *reader* might be synonymous with *Christian*.

Here it is instructive to look at Yvonne Vera's novel *Nehanda*, which presents a fictionalized but credible account of an African's first encounter with a white Christian cleric. The scene is set in the opening years of the twentieth century, in what is today Zimbabwe. Seeing the missionary reading a Bible, the African, Kaguvi, asks him: "What will happen when these leaves turn to dust?" The European explains, "There are many copies of this book, and more can be produced. This book can never die." Kaguvi is puzzled, all the more so when the clergyman asserts that he only worships one God. But is not the immortal book a god? As the story continues, "Kaguvi is fascinated. The priest's god can break into many pieces. But he also feels pity for a god who has to manifest himself in this humble manner. He does not understand why a god would hide behind the marks on a page. 'He is inside your book, but he is also in many books. . . . Your god is strange indeed.'" In some mysterious way, the book is associated with the power of divinity.[7]

The Bible is still a relatively new book in most of the Global South, where Christian communities are in the initial phases of a love affair with the scripture, before the texts and stories become dulled by familiarity.

In speaking of novelty, especially of the printed word, I am not ignoring the far older Christian origins in such nations, especially China, but thinking, rather, of the modern phase of growth. In this sense, Christianity in its present form represents a new force even in Latin American lands such as Brazil, a land with Christian roots dating back five centuries. Yet the more biblically centered versions of the faith, whether Catholic or evangelical, represent a much newer arrival, as does the whole attendant culture of Bible study and popular Bible reading. The Bible did not occupy anything like its central role in the belief or worship of the vast majority of Christians until the second half of the twentieth century. Only in the 1960s did Bible reading acquire its exalted status among Latin America's lay Catholics, while the massive growth of Protestant and Pentecostal communities begins in the same era. Today, though, Latin American nations—above all, Brazil—are among the world's greatest producers and consumers of Bibles.

A New World

In most settings, the Bible did not arrive as one book among many, but came together with certain revolutionary assumptions about the nature of reading and the means of communicating information. Here again we see varied consequences of the Reformation played out in the Global South churches. Understanding the means by which the Bible is understood and communicated allows us to appreciate the special weight of authority that the text bears there.

The new Christianity advanced alongside literacy, in societies in which orality had been the traditional form of communication and knowledge transmission. As in the Reformation era, the shift from orality to literacy gives an enormous symbolic power to the written text, to the Book, which in many cases might be the only actual book in a given household. In much of modern Africa, even many pastors might not own any books except a Bible—and that, not an elaborate study edition.

Even when people began to read, they were not immediately at ease with books or texts. Not for generations would books and magazines be things that one picks up casually in an idle moment. To understand the attitudes of the newly literate, we can look at the global impact of John Bunyan's seventeenth-century text *The Pilgrim's Progress*, which has enjoyed phenomenal success in Christian Africa. According to South African scholar Isabel Hofmeyr, part of Bunyan's appeal was that he himself grew out of a plebeian culture that, in terms of the status of literacy, resembled much of twentieth-century Africa: in this sense, like was speaking to like. Bunyan himself was literate, but he came from a society still rooted in oral culture, with an ambiguous attitude toward the written text. Though documents carry immense weight, they are mysterious things, glimpsed in visions or bestowed by angelic visitors. In *The Pilgrim's Progress*, documents appear as flying scrolls or cryptic engravings on a throne. Texts "are held in awe, but not entirely trusted," so that their authenticity must be confirmed by a mystical visitation, by a dream or vision.[8]

In such a semi- or new literate world, the power to read can itself be seen as a miraculous phenomenon. Bunyan was a distinguished leader, but we see similar attitudes to texts in the countless would-be prophets and messiahs of the sixteenth and seventeenth centuries, Anabaptists and others. These accounts resonate strongly in the emerging non-European churches of the past century. Some modern African prophets report receiving the gift of literacy through heavenly intervention, or they transmit their revelations through special scripts revealed to them through divine inspiration. The Xhosa prophet Ntsikana "discovered hymns fully formed on the hem of his cloak." Another South African prophet, Isaiah Shembe, reported, "No, I have not been taught to read and write, but I am able to read the Bible a little, and that came to me by revelation and not by learning. It came to me by miracle. . . . God sent Shembe, a child, so that he may speak like the wise and educated."[9]

A *Familiar Gospel*

In whatever form, reading today means reading in the vernacular, and in that respect the contemporary experience powerfully recalls the Reformation. A translated text presents the inspired Word of God in vernacular speech, at once domesticating the divine and elevating the language that becomes its vessel. The Bible's impact could be seductive, even harrowing. Martin Luther famously wrote that "The Bible is alive—it has hands and grabs hold of me, it has feet and runs after me," and countless readers of his German translations reported similarly unnerving encounters with the text. After the early English Protestant John Rogers was captured by church authorities, a bishop lectured him about the foolishness of putting vernacular texts into unlearned hands. After all, he said, this Bible is just dead words, unless and until it is interpreted by qualified experts. No, cried Rogers, the scripture is alive! It burns.

For over four centuries, European and North American Protestants have recognized the paramount need to translate the scriptures into local vernaculars, as the foundation for Christian growth in those societies. As Kwame Bediako observes, the history of African missionary Christianity is the history of Bible translation. Today, at least one book of the Bible is available for approximately 650 of Africa's 2,000 languages, and 150 languages have complete Bibles. A translated Bible defies conventional images of missionary imperialism. Once the Bible is in a vernacular, it becomes the property of that people. It becomes a Yoruba Bible, a Chinese Bible, a Zulu Bible; and the people in question have as much claim to it as does the nation that first brought it.[10]

The sheer scale on which these translations are circulated is mindboggling. In a typical year, the United Bible Societies distribute some 25 million Bibles, the largest recipients being China and Brazil, and those figures refer only to complete Bibles, not counting New Testaments, portions of scripture, or selected readings. In India, some 30 million selections and "portions" were circulated, over and above the complete scriptures. All told, in just one year, the societies distributed 390 million versions of the scriptures, complete or partial. Once the Bible is made available in cheap editions and circulated widely, it has the potential to initiate social revolution.

In vernacular translation, the Bible offers a direct link between the specific nation or community and the kingdom of heaven. Cardinal Newman once remarked that all ages are equidistant from eternity—but so are all places, Rome and the distant cliffs of Ireland in the Middle Ages, Los Angeles and Lagos today. The use of vernacular scriptures means that all Christian communities are equidistant from Jerusalem.

Spreading the Gospel

As in the Reformation era, formal books were only one means of disseminating religious ideas, and much of the movement's success depended on finding alternative vehicles. I have already mentioned the use of cartoons, prints, and chapbooks. In the contemporary world, we might look at the incredible success of evangelical or charismatic video production, which stands at the forefront of evangelism in modern Africa.

In the past twenty years, Nigeria especially has produced literally thousands of such films, part of the astonishing cinema boom that has become known as "Nollywood." This now constitutes the world's third-largest film industry, after Hollywood and the Indian Bollywood. Some three hundred Nigerian producers churn out around two thousand films each year, serving a huge domestic market, with almost 150 million people. Most of these films are passionately charismatic, teaching lessons of healing and deliverance, spiritual warfare and exorcism. The films go straight to DVD and sell cheaply. The biggest hits can easily sell hundreds of thousands of copies in Nigeria alone, not to mention circulating among the Nigerian diaspora in North America and Western Europe. As videos are freely passed on from hand to hand, the actual viewership is impossible to know.[11]

Explicitly Christian videos make up a large part of the output, which is not surprising when we realize that perhaps 45 percent of Nigerians follow this faith. Made largely in a mixture of Yoruba and English, Nigerian Christian videos enjoy a continent-wide distribution through satellite networks and cable channels. These films have also helped spawn imitators in other countries, in Ghana, and now Kenya, and many have been subtitled for use in French-speaking Africa. So influential have they been that Nigerian Muslims are now producing their own Islamic counterparts in an attempt to play catch-up.

In other ways, too, churches today have exploited new media quite as fully as the Protestant reformers did in their day. Apart from DVDs, satellite television has allowed churches to spread their influence across Europe and Africa, to permit emerging denominations to claim a presence in twenty or thirty nations at once.

Singing Truth

Echoing the Reformation era, hymnody has had a huge impact on churches of the Global South. Certainly since Luther's time, Protestants have not so much been people of the Book but, rather, of the Bible-and-hymnbook, and the two volumes complement each other splendidly. As you sing, so you believe, and so you pray—and so you learn much of your theology. As Christian churches grow around the world, then, it is not surprising to find an astonishing efflorescence of hymn composition. We must avoid the loose term "hymn writing," as many of the creators are primarily oral artists and only gradually do their works find their way into written form. However they are made, though, the sheer abundance and quality of those hymns is overwhelming, whether in Yoruba or Swahili, Tamil or Zulu. Arguably, we live today in the golden age of Christian hymn making.

Trying to understand emerging Christian cultures without some knowledge of those compositions is like trying to tell the German religious story without referring to "Ein feste Burg ist unser Gott," or the Anglo-American experience without "Amazing Grace." And as in the European world, modern hymns do not stand solely on the artistic merits of their words and music. To hear great hymns is to be drawn into a familiar story, which in its way forms part of an epic mythology. "Ein feste Burg" appealed so much because it reflected the worldly realities of a Europe under siege from the Muslim Ottoman Empire that lay perilously close at hand, and which at any time might breach the material defenses of the Christian continent.

The newer Christian world, too, has its legendary hymns, but few as potent as the "Tukutendereza Yesu," the mighty Luganda song that has since the 1930s become the anthem of evangelical faith across East Africa, especially for the pious *Balokole*—the Saved. The hymn grew out of a revival that emerged in Uganda and Rwanda and subsequently transformed churches in Kenya and farther afield. It is the music heard at the region's frequent revival meetings and crusades, as the words mark the believer's acceptance of Christ. These days, the hymn is a staple of Kenya's booming Christian music industry, and features in up-tempo gospel videos. Across modern East Africa, the "Tukutendereza" is as hard to avoid as "Ein feste Burg" was in early Protestant Germany.

The lyrics of "Tukutendereza" seem conventional enough as an expression of evangelical faith: "Tukutendereza Yesu / Yesu Omwana gw'endiga / Omusaigwo gunaziza / Nkwebaza, Omulokozi" (We praise you Jesus /

Jesus Lamb of God / Your blood cleanses me / I praise you, Savior). But we have to remember the setting, in a society where animal sacrifice still remains commonplace, and where people have a deep appreciation for the value of the blood that is the life. In such a setting, concepts of atonement and sacrifice have an intuitive power that they lack in the modern West. Is it any wonder that evangelical faith, with its central notion of being saved in the blood, has exercised such appeal across modern Africa?[12]

In turn, total dedication to the blood of Christ forbids believers from being drawn into militias or secret societies that enforce loyalty by paths based on blood and sacrifice. Those who sing the "Tukutendereza" accept only one sacrifice—that of Christ alone—and that faith has repeatedly caused them to suffer violence at the hands of brutal oppressors, including the Mau Mau guerrillas of the 1950s, the Idi Amin regime of the 1970s, or the more recent Lord's Resistance Army. Each such episode has enriched the ever-growing narrative associations surrounding the "Tukutendereza," as stories tell how martyrs went to their deaths singing the hymn, or how hearing it softened the hearts of persecutors. These accumulated memories add immeasurably to the hymn's impact.

The Storm of Images

However the faith spread, in both eras it soon gained a grassroots following, and these believers adopted a radically different sensibility about the proper manifestations of religion. In the Reformation era, the enemy was identified in terms of the old world of popular Christianity, with all its shrines and saints, relics and holy wells, its pilgrimages and processions, and its thorough accommodation with the seasons and the ritual year.

As the sixteenth century progressed, Protestant reform often manifested itself in iconoclasm—in the removal or destruction of images. Clashes over the cult of the Virgin marked perhaps the starkest dividing line between old and new religious forms. Conflict was so intense because so much social life was rooted in religious congregations or guilds that claimed the blessing of some particular saint. To smash the images was to rend the community, and yet this became a religious imperative.[13]

In the Netherlands, for example, monuments in every town recall that country's great war of independence, the Dutch Revolt: Europe's greatest cultural and political transformation between the Renaissance and the French Revolution. Although the war against Spanish Catholic rule lasted for decades, the bloodiest and most crucial period followed the mighty popular upsurge of 1566, when the Dutch people rose en masse against oppression. Besides targeting royal symbols, the Protestant movement was directed against Catholic material symbols—against stained-glass windows, statues of the Virgin and saints, holy medals and tokens. One Calvinist lord sat happily on a desecrated church altar, feeding plundered Hosts to his parrot. This was the *Beeldenstorm*, the Storm of Images, and it marked a religious declaration of independence against ideas rooted in the oldest human cultures: it reflected a whole new religious consciousness. Going further than Luther had ever done, Calvinists proclaimed a stark new vision of Christianity, rejecting any suggestions that divinity might take a material form other than Jesus Christ himself.[14]

Even more perhaps than the events of 1517, the tumult of 1566 is arguably *the* crucial moment of the European Reformation, and it set the agendas that reformers would pursue for over a century. In the English-speaking world, the heirs of 1566 were the Puritans—the radicals who dreamed of an austere New England. When Puritans seized power in England itself in the 1640s, their agents toured the country, smashing statues and windows in every parish church they could find.

Depending on local circumstances, such clashes resonate mightily with modern Global South churches. In Africa or Asia, new churches emerge against a background that was non-Christian, and often pagan or animist. Despite some accommodations, the faith advances by declaring its resolute opposition to the symbols of that older worldview, which so thoroughly penetrated every aspect of daily life. In 1913, for instance, William Wadé Harris began his hugely successful evangelistic crusade in West Africa by burning the sacred images of the old faith, the fetishes. When he survived unscathed, the power of the new faith was triumphantly displayed, just as thoroughly as it had been by the deeds of sixteenth-century iconoclasts. Modern African churches pledge themselves to fight the old shrines and idols quite as enthusiastically as Egyptian monks did back in the fourth and fifth centuries.[15]

Holy Wars

In other parts of the world, though, the old religious order to be challenged is itself Christian, just as it had been in the days of Luther or Calvin. Since the 1970s, Protestant and Pentecostal numbers have burgeoned in what has always been the solidly Catholic stronghold of Latin America. They might make up roughly a quarter of Brazil's people today, 30 percent of Chile's, at least a third in Guatemala. Brazil by mid-century could conceivably have a Protestant majority.

A religious revolution of this scale could not occur without conflicts that spill over into the political realm. Usually, Protestants and Catholics fight with words, contending in the mass media, or in elections and parliamentary debates. In some countries, though, the fights have become all too literal, to the point of armed struggle, night-riding, and ethnic cleansing. And the motives driving the combatants look very familiar to anyone who knows the story of France or Germany during the Reformation era.

However strongly modern people feel about theological debates, they are not likely to pursue their grievances through armed violence. But in pre-modern societies, religion can become thoroughly institutionalized in the life of the community. Religious practice defines the cycle of the year, the boundaries of the community, the shape of popular loyalties. Often, it becomes localized, with devotion to this particular saint, to that church or shrine, even to this particular version of the Virgin Mary. The authority of faith is rooted in community and tradition, ritual and place.

But a radical new concept of the faith, which grounds authority in the written word and which spurns those local traditions as pagan excrescences, can have a violent impact. In the 1990s, for instance, the founder of Brazil's wildly successful Universal Church of the Kingdom of God earned national notoriety by a televised broadcast in which he punched a figure of Our Lady of Aparecida, whom he denounced as a "dumb idol." People who might not understand church doctrines become sensitive indeed to attempts to take away their shrine or their Virgin. In extreme cases, local riots and purges can grow into wider uprisings, even dangerous religious rebellions. That was the story of grassroots religious violence in sixteenth-century Europe, and something very like it is in progress today in rural areas of Latin America.[16]

Although *evangélicos* have made their greatest advances in the megacities, the new faith has also had a special impact on traditionally marginalized Indian communities, in Mayan regions of Central America, and in Andean countries like Peru and Bolivia. For centuries, these communities accepted Catholicism as the official religion, but with a strong dose of native tradition. Membership in the community depended on participating in communal rituals focused on the church.

But then the Protestants came, proclaiming their membership in a new universal community, the New Jerusalem. They denounced the old beliefs as superstition, particularly the Indian customs that survived easily within the Catholic framework. Moreover, they condemned the alcohol use that usually marks popular fiestas. In effect, they refused to pay the Catholic "cultural tax." In Guatemala, extreme evangelicals have tried to enforce popular morality through vigilante campaigns. Catholic village authorities in turn strike back against those who tear the community apart by refusing to join in processions and devotions. They pressure evangelicals by cutting off water and utilities, and driving their children from the schools. Some battles follow a cycle very familiar from Reformation Europe. Protestants mock a procession in which faithful Catholics carry a figure of the Virgin, Catholics burn the local Protestant chapel, and the violence continues with night-time raids and expulsions.

Although such unrest has surfaced in several countries, it has been most marked in the Chiapas region of Mexico, where inter-faith tensions since 1994 have left hundreds dead and thousands more expelled from their homes. Although Zapatista guerrillas are sometimes portrayed as anti-colonialist champions, the Chiapas affair must be understood in terms of social tensions between Protestants and Catholics. At the heart of the war is the struggle within the faith between traditional and textual sources of authority.

Explaining Change

I have been describing the strictly religious aspects of the two eras, but they also offer certain parallels in terms of their social context, and the reasons underlying their growth.

If I might offer a digression here, let me briefly describe the Reformation as it affected one country very rarely discussed in this context—namely my own homeland of Wales. Protestant ideas appeared on the country's margins fairly early, and the reign of "the Bloody Mary" produced a handful of martyrs. In 1588, a bishop translated the whole Bible into Welsh, in what is commonly recalled as a decisive event in the language's history. Literally, it saved the language by standardizing it, and prevented it from degenerating into a patois. In the 1630s, Anglican parson Rhys Prichard began rural evangelism by composing popular verses to spread Protestant views.[17]

Generally, though, from 1560 through 1650, the new faith remained strictly on the margins, at least if we define faith as convinced and well-informed Protestant sentiment. It was largely confined to those southern commercial towns in contact with the metropolis of Bristol—communities like Carmarthen, Cardiff, and Haverfordwest. These towns were the critical bridgeheads for Protestant expansion in the civil war years. North Wales, though, remained virtually untouched until the Methodist revival of the 1740s, largely because of its lack of towns or serious commercial activity. In large tracts of rural southwest Wales, a famous Anglican jeremiad in 1721 describes a ritual life that would have been wholly familiar in Chaucer's day, with a similar roster of saints, pilgrimages, and holy wells. Not until the end of the eighteenth century did the country as a whole experience the mass conversions that made it the nonconformist/Puritan bastion of later legend.

The Welsh story recapitulates in miniature so many of the themes that I have identified so far, especially in terms of the use of the vernacular and popular evangelism. But it also raises other key points about the Reformation story, including the incredibly slow pace of change in much of Europe. This point is often lost on non-Europeans, who find it hard to imagine the tiny distances that separate Europe's leading cities and cultural centers—or at least, tiny by U.S. standards. In Wales, a movement that began under Henry VIII took some 250 years—eight generations—to complete its conquest of a country somewhat smaller than the state of New Jersey. The Welsh might have been extraordinarily stubborn, but plenty of other regions within Protestant states demonstrate similar histories; again, the Great Awakenings of the eighteenth century look like new phases of a continuing Reformation movement spread over several centuries.

In contrast, the modern global expansion of Christianity has been astonishingly rapid. Just to take one example, in 1900, the lands that would become Nigeria had a population that was roughly 28 percent Muslim and 1 percent Christian, the remaining people being animist or pagan. By 1970, Nigeria's population was 45 percent Muslim, and 45 percent Christian. During the twentieth century, half of Africa's population made a transition from animism to either Islam or Christianity, with Christian converts outnumbering Muslims four to one. In Latin America, the Protestant expansion was still new and startling as late as 1970.

The accelerated pace of religious change is not surprising, given much greater ease of travel and migration, and new forms of media and communication. But that pace marks a critical difference in the impact of new forms of religion, with less time for society to "digest" and accommodate innovation, and greater opportunities for old and new forms to coexist, however uncomfortably.

Urban Evangelism

The Welsh experience also reminds us of the Reformation's economic context. Even if a particular nation-state accepted and established Protestantism, that religious model could only advance as far as networks of towns and trade allowed. There certainly could be exceptions to that rule—for instance, where local aristocrats devoted themselves wholeheartedly to evangelizing rural areas under their absolute control—but generally, any map of Protestant growth correlates very well with the urban framework. The Reformation flourished in cities and towns, and spread through merchants and migration. Nor was that pattern anything new in European history; at least from the eleventh century, church authorities and Inquisitors knew that the towns were the most fertile centers of proto-Protestant activity, by which I mean groups who aspired to read the Bible in the vernacular, while preaching anti-clerical and anti-sacramental views. The more successful and flourishing the towns, the more abundant and persistent the heresies. The medieval maxim held that "Town air makes free." Perhaps it also encouraged religious dissent.

Many of the European cities and provincial towns that were pivotal to Protestant growth were tiny indeed by modern standards, in an age when ten or twenty thousand people marked a thriving metropolis. Those urban centers are, of course, dwarfed by modern megacities, but we still observe a clear linkage between faith and urbanization.

We live today in the greatest era of urbanization in human history, and that trend should continue unabated over the next three decades, especially in Africa. This fact has huge religious consequences. However widely they vary in other ways, the newer churches of the Global South are growing in response to similar economic circumstances. As predominantly rural societies have become more urban over the last forty years, millions of migrants are attracted to ever-larger urban complexes, which utterly lack the resources or infrastructure to meet the needs of these new arrivals. Sometimes people travel to cities within the same nation, but often they find themselves in different countries and cultures, suffering a still greater sense of estrangement.

In such settings, the most devoted and fundamentalist-oriented religious communities emerge to provide functional alternative arrangements for health, welfare, and education. This sort of alternative social system has been a potent factor in winning mass support for the most committed religious groups, and it is likely to become more important as the gap between popular needs and the official capacities to fill them becomes ever wider.

In Latin America especially, the move to the cities over the last half-century has liberated ordinary people from traditional religious structures. No longer were they restricted to the churches that landowners would permit on their estates, which in virtually every case were Catholic. Yet while liberating themselves, people were also seeking social structures not so very different from what they had previously known when they had lived in small villages or on landed estates; there were features of village life that they missed badly. One theory holds that the new Latin American churches provide the uprooted with the kind of familiar structure to which they were accustomed. In Africa, too, the independent churches find their firmest support in the swollen cities, among migrants and the dispossessed. On both continents, the pastors of the new churches exercise a paternalistic role reminiscent of familiar figures from rural society, of landlords in Latin America, of tribal authorities in Africa. The congregations replace the family networks that prevailed in the older villages.

In such circumstances, the urban/rural religious split becomes a yawning gulf. Today, the typical Brazilian Catholic is elderly, rural, white, and male; the typical Protestant is young, urban, dark, and female.

Beyond the practical needs of life, new urban dwellers look to the churches for fellowship and friendship, for social networks, and also for forms of entertainment and recreation, which often take religious forms. One characteristic of Global South religious life is the culture of spectacle, manifested in vast religious revival or miracle crusade. These sensational gatherings can draw together literally millions at a time, with healing commonly the most alluring prize on offer. We see this, for instance, in a city like Lagos, a classic example of speedy urbanization. In 1950, Lagos was a ramshackle port community with around a quarter of a million people. The official population in 1990 was 1.3 million, but the surrounding metropolitan region had then grown to 10 million people, and today it approaches 20 million. Although Lagos is divided between Christians and Muslims, the city has played host to some of the largest evangelical gatherings in world history, with the biggest revivals—such as the ones organized by the Redeemed Christian Church of God—claiming attendance running into the millions.

Making a New World, a Secular World?

Few scholars would deny that the sixteenth-century Reformation, broadly defined, was a major component of emerging modernity. It influenced the creation of the modern nation-state and modern notions of political authority, as other contributors to this volume have suggested. Regardless of the intentions of particular kings or churches, the movement laid a foundation for mass education and literacy, with all the self-confidence these things created, and ultimately informed Western concepts of individualism. Rudyard Kipling summed this view up well in his poem, "The Dawn Wind:"

So when the world is asleep, and there seems no hope of her waking
Out of some long, bad dream that makes her mutter and moan,
Suddenly, all men arise to the noise of fetters breaking,
And every one smiles at his neighbor and tells him his soul is his own![18]

Some argue that these same impulses were the essential prerequisites for the Western economic order, with its values of thrift, industry, and individual enterprise.

Might we foresee any parallels with our own era in the Global South? I have stressed similarities between Global South churches and early Protestants, and the strong Pentecostal/charismatic current in these modern bodies particularly leads us to see resemblances with the Radical Reformation. However authoritarian some might be in terms of overall leadership, their dominant ethos is highly democratic, participatory, and nonhierarchical (and, critically, opposed to any kind of racial hegemony). Beyond opening their doors to all comers, these churches also give opportunities to all ministries, including preaching.

Not surprisingly, then, a sizable literature points to the liberating effects of the new churches, which serve as training grounds for democratic participation.[19] Contemporary observers comment on the self-confidence and leadership experience that ordinary people, even of the lowest classes and disfranchised races, acquire in these congregations. Here, they are encouraged to speak out publicly, to organize autonomously for the good of the community. In the words of the sociologist David Martin, they acquire "tongues of fire" that will certainly be heard equally in the public political realm. This trend, too, contributes to the creation of a wider civil society. [20]

That liberating effect applies particularly to women, who constitute such a critical component of the rising churches. The sixteenth-century reformers had tried to spiritualize the household, and those efforts resonate today as newer churches elevate domestic values, with a transformative and often positive effect on gender relationships. In Latin America or Africa, membership in a new Pentecostal church means a significant improvement in the lives of poor women, since this is where they are more likely to meet men who do not squander family resources on drinking, gambling, prostitutes, and even second households. Christianity is far more than an opium of the disinherited masses: it provides a very practical setting in which they can improve their daily lives. Elizabeth Brusco has memorably christened this domestic revolution the "Reformation of machismo."[21]

In worldly terms, this might yet be the most influential and lasting aspect of the religious transformation.

Finally, and though some will dispute this, in the long term the Reformation itself set the stage for Enlightenment and secularization. Calvinist ideas that to us seem intolerably theocratic dominated not just the Netherlands but also New England, Switzerland, and Scotland, and were struggling for ascendancy in the whole British Isles. Religious zeal often expressed itself through witchcraft persecutions.

But that same Calvinist geography ought to give a believer pause, because that is also a map of the major centers of Enlightenment thought in the later eighteenth century, the safe havens where thinkers from more restrictive lands could go to explore daring ideas. In later years, the old Calvinist societies also became bastions of secularism. New England's Calvinism, as is well documented, gave way to Unitarian and Universalist creeds, and in some cases to searching skepticism. The Netherlands' ancient churches today are commonly secularized as museums or community centers—places where God once was, but remains no longer.

Several reasons suggest themselves for this odd and ironic transition, for how the world turned itself upside down. In condemning images, the reformers were cutting faith loose from its assumed connections with the old social structures, the old world of social hierarchy, and the cycles of the rural year. God was too absolute to need any such reinforcement, and his followers had an equally unlimited confidence in their own immediate relationship to him. They had equal certainty in their own salvation, which came through reason, the mind, and a world of knowledge founded in scripture. At first, access to these scriptures was available only to learned and literate clerical elites, but the logic of the new faith demanded that equal access be given to every man—and eventually, to every woman. This meant a deep devotion to spreading universal literacy and, through new forms of technology, to easily available printed books.

The problem is, of course, that training people to think and read for themselves doesn't prevent them from drawing their own conclusions, and boldly going where earlier generations might have dared not tread. If you have absolute assurance of salvation, and you despise the inferior standards of the secular world, why should you not freely explore the implications of your continuing interior revolution of the mind and spirit? After all, the old images and idols were no longer there to prevent you. Such intellectual individualism is arguably a likely, if not inevitable, outcome. So, too, is secularization.

I have been describing the world of the seventeenth and eighteenth centuries: might similar trends emerge in the twenty-first? David Martin, especially, links Pentecostalism to ultimate secularization, making it thus another stage in the process begun by the Reformation. I do not venture to prophesy the future in this way, but I do point out some striking parallels.

Of course, no reasonable scholar expects that the relationship of politics and religion in coming decades will precisely reproduce that which developed in the European world of four or five centuries ago. Nonetheless, that past experience is the best model that we have to go by presently, and an instructive guide.

Notes

1. Philip Jenkins, *The Next Christendom*, 3rd ed. (New York: Oxford University Press, 2011). See also Klaus Koschorke, Frieder Ludwig, and Marian Delgado, eds., *History of Christianity in Asia, Africa, and Latin America, 1450–1990* (Grand Rapids, MI.: Eerdmans, 2007); Lamin O. Sanneh, *Disciples of All Nations* (New York: Oxford University Press, 2007); Martin E. Marty, *The Christian World* (New York: Modern Library, 2008); Robert Bruce Mullin, *A Short World History of Christianity* (Louisville, KY: Westminster John Knox, 2008).
2. For analogies between past and present movements, see for instance Allan H. Anderson, *African Reformation* (Trenton, NJ: Africa World Press, 2001); and Eric Patterson, *Latin America's Neo-Reformation* (New York: Routledge, 2005).

3. See Sanneh, *Disciples of All Nations*; Koschorke, Ludwig, and Delgado, *History of Christianity in Asia, Africa, and Latin America*; and Dana L. Robert, *Christian Mission* (New York: Wiley-Blackwell, 2009).

4. I have drawn throughout on Philip Jenkins, *The New Faces of Christianity* (New York: Oxford University Press, 2006).

5. Diarmaid MacCulloch, *The Reformation* (New York: Viking, 2004); and MacCulloch, *Christianity: The First Three Thousand Years* (New York: Viking, 2010).

6. Thomas Carlyle, *Critical and Miscellaneous Essays* (New York: D. Appleton, 1864), 16.

7. Yvonne Vera, *Nehanda* (Bedminster, NJ: Baobab Books, 1993), 104–05.

8. Isabel Hofmeyr, *The Portable Bunyan* (Princeton, NJ: Princeton University Press, 2003); Hofmeyr, "African Christian Interpretations of *The Pilgrim's Progress*," *Journal of Religion in Africa* 32, no. 4 (2002): 440–56, 445.

9. Shembe is quoted in Jonathan Draper, "The Bible as Poison Onion, Icon and Oracle," *Journal of Theology for Southern Africa* 112 (2002): 39–56.

10. Kwame Bediako, "Epilogue," in Ype Schaaf, *On Their Way Rejoicing* (Carlisle, UK: Paternoster Press, 1994). Lamin O. Sanneh, *Translating the Message* (Maryknoll, NY: Orbis, 1989). Phillip C. Stine and Ernst R. Wendland, eds., *Bridging the Gap* (New York: American Bible Society, 1990). Statistics for Bible translation and distribution are from the website of the United Bible Societies at www.unitedbiblesocieties.org/sample-page/bible-translation/.

11. Philip Jenkins, "Nigeria's Christian Videos," *Christian Century*, November 4, 2008, 45.

12. Philip Jenkins, "Tukutendereza Yesu," *Christian Century*, January 25, 2011, 45.

13. Carlos Eire, *War against the Idols: the Reformation of Worship from Erasmus to Calvin* (New York: Cambridge University Press, 1986).

14. Philip Jenkins, "Storm of Images," *RealClearReligion*, August 2012, www.real-clearreligion.org/articles/2012/08/06/when_calvin_and_qutb_went_smashing.html.

15. Philip Jenkins, "Church of William Harris," *Christian Century*, April 17, 2013, 45.

16. See my lengthier discussion of this in Jenkins, *The Next Christendom*.

17. This account of Welsh matters is drawn from Philip Jenkins, *A History of Modern Wales 1536-1990* (London: Longmans 1992).

18. Rudyard Kipling, "The Dawn Wind," www.bartleby.com/364/400.html.

19. On this point, see Robert Woodberry, "The Missionary Roots of Liberal Democracy," *American Political Science Review* 106 (May 2012): 244–74.

20. David Martin, *Tongues of Fire* (Oxford: Blackwell, 1990).

21. Elizabeth E. Brusco, *The Reformation of Machismo* (Austin: University of Texas Press, 1995).

10

Protestantism Comes East

THE CASE OF KOREA

Sung-Deuk Oak

MY FELLOW CONTRIBUTOR to this volume, Philip Jenkins, has asked
what Wittenberg has to do with Lagos. In that vein, I would ask what
Wittenberg or Geneva, or the movements those European cities represent,
have to do with Korea; and I conclude that there are important parallels
between events in sixteenth-century Europe and those during the last century or so of Christian experience in Korea. As scholars and churches
consider what it means to commemorate the Reformation, it is important
to think through Christianity's comparative vigor in parts of the world
where, at the start of the sixteenth century, it was minimal or nonexistent. Korean experience offers a particularly interesting example of this
because, unlike its neighbors Japan and China, once the Christian faith
took root, it soon expanded into a major public presence. Whereas post-
Reformation Christianity has enjoyed a continuous history in China since
the late sixteenth century, and in Japan since the mid-nineteenth century, communities of Christian believers in those two countries, whether
Catholic, Protestant, or Orthodox, have never occupied as much ground
near the cultural center of their respective countries as has Christianity in
Korea since the early twentieth century.

The initial spread of Christianity in Asia dates from the time of the
apostles—the apostle Thomas is believed to have brought the faith to
India, for instance—while so-called Nestorian Christians were active in
China as early as the seventh century. There is evidence of a Christian presence in Asia at points throughout the Middle Ages, but a more enduring

presence came later. In the late fifteenth and early sixteenth centuries, Roman Catholics, particularly Jesuits, launched missions in Asia. The Spanish Jesuit Francis Xavier and his colleagues worked in Japan, while the Italian Matteo Ricci, who ignited controversy through his willingness to embrace some elements of local culture, began building the church in China. In 1784, Yi Seung-Hun, a Korean Confucian scholar who had studied Chinese Jesuit literature was baptized in Beijing, returned to his native land and began making converts, though he was killed in 1801 during a state persecution of Catholics. It was not until nearly a century later that a Protestant medical missionary, in 1884, opened the way for the expansive surge of Christianity in modern Korea. These churches grew rapidly with indigenous leadership.

In the early decades of the twenty-first century, the Korean church has offered a history of growth, church building, and missions, but also shown some evidence of stagnation and even prospects of decline. The statistical measures in this chapter take stock of this trajectory of Korean churches and also evaluate their relationship to the controversies surrounding the Reformation. The numbers and tables given here illustrate how Christianity has grown in Korea, how its growth has wrought cultural change, and what sorts of challenges it faces now in the twenty-first century.

To consider this Korean history in light of the Reformation does, however, present complications. The first such complexity requires recognition that active Protestantism arose in Korea not, as in Europe, as efforts to renew the well-established traditions of Western Latin Christendom but, rather, in a setting in which Christianity had been at best negligible, trickling into Korea from a few Catholic sources in China. A second complexity is the fact that modern Korean church history involves several quite distinct phases that cannot be mapped directly onto the sequence of Western Protestant history. These complications do not render Korean history irrelevant in regard to worldwide Protestant history but, rather, require care to identify genuine points of Korean-Western parallel, as well as points of stark difference.

As the narrative that follows demonstrates, modern Korean Christianity began with a strong, but limited record of evangelism, education, and cultural influence. In two particular instances, this early history looks similar to the early history of European Protestantism. First, the Bible translated into the vernacular was the engine that drove conversions, preaching, church organization, and especially lay involvement. Second, fairly rapid indigenization meant that Koreans quickly came to the fore as church leaders, very much as the key leadership in Europe's emerging

Protestant regions came out of those regions to replace the leadership of distant Catholic bishops or the pope.

Yet, the early Korean experience also differs sharply from early European Protestantism in regard to leadership. As soon as European leaders like Martin Luther, Ulrich Zwingli, John Calvin, and Thomas Cranmer moved toward theological reform, they were immediately caught up in the political domain, achieving a full Christian reformation of political life. Even though the process of turning Catholic regions into Protestant regions moved at different paces—swiftly for Luther in electoral Saxony and Zwingli in Zurich, more slowly for Calvin in Geneva and Protestants in England—the end result was the same: what historians have called "confessional Protestant states." In these confessional regimes, the Protestant religion became not only the religion of the people but also the law of the land.

Korea offers a contrast in this regard. The emerging Protestant churches in Korea did display much inner strength, but they did not orchestrate a wholesale reformation of the tributary system with China or the local Korean monarchy, or the colonial Japanese regime. Thus, in the early stages of Korean Protestant history, nothing existed that was comparable to the confessionalization of the European model.

Nonetheless, in the second phase of modern Korean church history, something at least vaguely resembling confessionalization did take place. In the years after World War II and the Korean War, when the church growth blossomed in South Korea, there was significant influence from the Christian churches, now including a substantial Catholic presence, on the nation as a whole. In very recent years, a third phase of historical development, during which church growth has come to an almost complete halt for Protestants, some of that broader institutional, cultural, and educational influence has nevertheless continued. This "semi-confessional" influence might be regarded as, in some ways, similar to the broad cultural influence that European Protestantism had exercised from its Reformation beginnings.

It is possible to view another parallel during that second phase of modern Korean church history. As a number of historians have pointed out, the broad "Protestantization" of European people did not take place immediately on the heels of the early Reformation. Instead, it involved developments that came considerably later, when more of the laity could read, when educational levels had risen, when economic opportunities began to spread, and when large-scale social changes were inspiring more self-direction among people who had been accustomed to take their directions from on high. Whether through the Puritan movements in England or Pietist movements on the continent, the seventeenth century probably witnessed a sharper rise in local religious practice among lay Protestants than had occurred during the sixteenth century. If so, that parallels what happened in Korea: there was a sturdy but small beginning period followed by a second, later period of unusually rapid church growth.[1]

The final part of this chapter notes yet another parallel between Korea and sixteenth-century Protestantism—but with a twist. In the Korean case, doctrinal uncertainty between advocates of Minjung theology (defined in endnote 9) and their opponents; a few spectacular cases of immoral behavior among church leaders; and a general sense of religious malaise provide parallels to what early Protestants had complained about in Roman Catholicism. The twist here is that, in the Korean churches, the Protestants were protesting against other Protestants and calling them to reform.

Three principal foci will guide our steps in this chapter. The first is historiography. The story of Korean Protestantism has been told primarily in two ways: from a *missionary perspective* and from a *nationalist perspective*. I propose an alternative, correcting the weaknesses in these two perspectives. The second and chief focus is the transformation of Korean society by the introduction of Protestantism, and its further transformation through indigenous development at the turn of the twentieth century. In explaining the rapid growth of Korean Protestantism in the first three decades, we require brief introductions to some important Koreans who enabled that growth. Finally, the third focus in this chapter addresses questions of "reformation" directly, by which I mean the necessity of reforming contemporary Protestantism in South Korea to rescue it from stagnation and decline. Here, the chapter pivots from historical argument to a contemporary analysis of the flattening of Korean Protestant church growth from about 1995 to the present.[2] This abbreviated sketch—of a quickly growing and dynamic church that now is declining into an institution in need of reform—may recall the Protestant mantra, *Ecclesia semper reformanda est.*

Competing Historical Perspectives: Missionary and Nationalist Lenses

In 1984, Korean Protestantism celebrated its first centennial, marking the arrival of the first resident missionary, Dr. Horace N. Allen (1858–1932) in September of that year. (It should be noted that Protestants in Korea use *Kidog-gyo*, meaning "Christ-Church," or *Yesu-gyo*, meaning "Jesus-Church," for "Protestantism"; while the Roman Catholic Church is identified as *Ch'ŏnju-gyo*, or "Lord of Heaven Church." No denomination in Korea uses "Protestantism," or *Kaesin-gyo*, in its name.) The 100th anniversary lauded the astonishing growth of Christianity from a handful of members in the first Presbyterian and Methodist churches in 1887 to about 7 million adherents in 1984. The landing of Horace G. Underwood (1859–1916) and Henry G. Appenzeller (1858–1902), the first Presbyterian and Methodist clerical missionaries, respectively, at Incheon on Easter Sunday in 1885 was likewise commemorated with the installation of a "Monument of the 100th Anniversary of Christianity in Korea." Despite these celebratory observances, church leaders had produced little rigorous, detailed history attending to the circumstances of Korea's past.[3] Instead, they largely adopted the missionary perspective, taking on the idiom of commemoration from 1934, when the Presbyterian (PCUSA) and Methodist missions celebrated their 50th anniversary. Then counting more than 250,000 Korean adherents—a tenfold increase in three decades—the dominant spirit of their jubilee was missionary triumphalism.[4]

Two statistics help us understand such an American missionary-centered view of this early history of Protestantism in Korea. Americans occupied about 70 percent of the Protestant missionary corps up to 1910.[5] Their colleagues in the mission field, British Anglicans, served for a short term, so Americans dominated the missions to Korea. Since Korea was regarded as a small and insignificant country compared to its neighbors China and Japan, only several denominations sent missionaries. Yet this fact facilitated ecumenical cooperation among the missions and churches in Korea.

In 1908, the American mission societies counted 104,804 (94%) among 111,379 Korean adherents, whereas the British societies had only 6,575 (6%). Within those groups, the Presbyterians had about 77 percent of the Korean adherents and the Methodists had 20 percent, for a total of 97 percent. Two American Presbyterian missions had about 74 percent of all Korean Protestant Christians (PCUSA 73,844, at 66.3%; and PCUS 8,410, at 7.6%).[6] Thus, Protestant churches had far more adherents than the Roman Catholic Church and have kept that numerical lead up to today.

In a 2004 address in Seoul, my fellow contributor Mark A. Noll looked at the historical influence of American evangelicalism on Korean Protestantism and asked, "What can Korean believers learn from American

evangelical history?" His preliminary survey found seven historical similarities: indigenization, anti-imperialism, Bible Christianity, modernization, the impact of wars, the prominence of revival, and missionary zeal.[7]
All these similarities, however, did not result from some simple transpacific transmission of American Protestantism to the Korean peninsula.
Chinese and Japanese Protestantism, along with earlier Korean religious
currents, contributed their influences as well.

In 1984, a few historians challenged the American missionary-centered
perspective. They emphasized the influence of Roman Catholicism, and
stressed lay acceptance of the Riccian Catholic literature from Beijing
and the organization of the first church in Seoul without missionary
help in 1784. These scholars emphasized Koreans' initiative and agency
in accepting Protestantism, and suggested some different starting points
for the timeline. First, in this narrative, came four young Korean men,
who in 1879 read Chinese scriptures and tracts and were taught by John
Ross (1841–1915), and who were baptized by John McIntyre of the Free
Presbyterian Church of Scotland in Manchuria. Second, in 1882, the first
Korean gospels were published and circulated in the border towns on both
sides of the Yalu River. Third, in 1884, Sŏ Sangnyun (1848–1926) began
to hold regular Sunday services with his brother Sŏ Kyŏngjo and a small
band of believers in his hometown Sorae, Hwanghae province, which
became "the cradle of Korean Protestantism." Sŏ Sangnyun was baptized
by John Ross in 1882, and sent to Seoul as a colporteur of the British
and Foreign Bible Society in 1883. He became one of the first helpers of
American missionaries in Seoul and Pusan in the 1890s.

Among the earliest historical evidences of Korean Protestantism were
the results of John Ross's work in Manchuria. Some young Korean merchants in Ŭiju decided to become Christians after reading Chinese scriptures and tracts. They published the whole Korean New Testament in 1887.
The group distributed the scriptures secretly among Koreans and began
holding regular worship services in their hometowns *before* American missionaries came to Korea. In January of that year, three Koreans in Sorae
went to Seoul to meet American missionaries. At that time, they were
examined and baptized by Horace G. Underwood, after confessing that
"though my king cut off my head for obeying my God, I will be alright."[8]

With this characterization, Korean nationalist historians have argued
that Koreans actively accepted Protestantism; participated in the establishment of nationwide self-supporting, self-propagating, and self-governing
churches; and invented indigenous Korean Protestantism by engaging

in the national agendas of modernization and independence, on one hand, and by introducing theological and liturgical innovations, on the other hand.

Without slighting the American missionaries' decisive contribution to the development of Korean Protestantism, we can, however, give much credit to those Korean workers for that process. Figure 10.1 shows that in 1910, missionaries in Korea occupied 5.5 percent of all the missionary forces in China, Japan, and Korea combined, whereas total Korean workers occupied more than 12 percent and Korean contributions were more than 22 percent. These statistics indicate that a good part of the impressive achievement of making 20,253 communicants in a single year of 1909 (45.4% of three nations)—when Korea had more Protestant Christians than Japan—came from the voluntary devotion and sacrificial commitment of Koreans themselves.

In the past six decades, many Korean church historians and theologians have constructed a nationalist interpretation of the history of Protestantism in Korea to overcome the Japanese colonial legacy and to contribute to nation-building projects. Liberals and Minjung theologians criticized earlier North American missionaries' fundamentalist exclusivism and spiritual imperialism, and instead attempted to make indigenous and contextual Korean theologies.[9] They minimized the Western missionary legacy; in contrast, theological conservatives have affirmed the founding missionaries' commitment to orthodoxy. Despite their differences, both camps have produced an image of strongly conservative North American missionaries and Korean converts who heroically defeated Korean heathenism, and then fought against Japanese Shinto shrine worship.

A Tripartite Perspective

I would like to challenge the foregoing image of early Korean Protestantism and present instead some more diverse aspects of its indigenization, in an effort to find a way between these two extremes. More fully, we need a comparative perspective, considering Korean, East Asian, and global contexts and developments, so as to gain a more comprehensive history of Korean Protestantism. This perspective, in turn, reveals some important ways in which Korean history has followed the patterns of Western Protestant history.

The emergence recently of studies in world Christianity or global Christianity has improved the overall historiography of Christianity. To

	Japan	Korea	China	(%): Percentage of three nations Total
Ordained missionaries	305 (23.1)	97 (7.3)	920 (69.6)	1,322 (100)
Physician missionaries male + female	10 + 1	24 + 12 (8.4) + (9.4)	251 + 114	285 + 127
Unmarried woman missionaries	353	71 (4.7)	1,093	1,517
Total foreign missionaries	1,029 (18.6)	307 (5.5)	4,197 (75.9)	5,533
Ordained natives	474	34 (3.3)	513	1,021
Unordained native workers	1,664	1,887 (12.5)	11,595	15146
Total native workers	2,138	1,981 (12.2)	12,108	16,227
Church organizations	612	462 (14.9)	2,027	3,101
Communicants added last year	8,639	20,053 (45.4)	15,521	44,213
Total communicants	67,024	57,414 (19.0)	177,774	302,212
Baptized members	82,196	89,609 (23.2)	214,642	386,447
Total adherents all ages	97,117 (13.0)	178,686 (24.0)	470,184 (63.0)	745,987
Sunday schools	1,389	1,291 (28.4)	1,859	4,539
Total Sunday school membership	87,283	110,865 (42.1)	65,482	263,640
Total native contribution ($)	171,694	109,460 (22.1)	213,259	494,413

FIGURE 10.1 Statistics of the Christian Missions and Churches in East Asia, 1910.*

*The Student Volunteer Movement, World Atlas of Christian Missions (New York: SVM, 1911), 83.

understand the history of Korean Protestantism, we must adopt this global perspective and consider the interactions among world Christianity, East Asian Christianity, and Korean Christianity. Doing so will help overcome the limitations of Korean church history as viewed from either the missionary or the nationalist perspectives.

Under this global scheme, the early encounters between Protestantism and Korean religious cultures are considered a form of cultural exchange, one that cannot be reduced to mere Western imperialism. As Andrew Walls has reminded us, we need to balance what he calls the "pilgrim principle" with the "indigenizing principle."[10] Put differently, this new paradigm in the historiography of world Christianity calls for a creative combination of the principles of Christian universality (vertical transcendence) and those of enculturation (horizontal adaptation). This paradigm also throws considerable light on parallels existing between Korean Christian development and sixteenth-century Reformation. Borrowing from Walls's analysis again, we see that plural centers of world Christianity have emerged in a hundred places, learning from each other and yielding many riches.[11]

Exploring the localization of Christianity in Korea requires noting three key developments. First, the transpacific transmission of North American Christianity resembles in some ways the sharing of the renewed Gospel message that characterized the early Reformation; while that earlier history lacked the cross-cultural dimension, it involved the movement of ideas, protests, and books. Second, the interactions between naturalized Chinese Protestant mission theories, methods, and literature and the emerging Korean Protestantism highlights the forces of indigenization; although the details are different, that speedy indigenization of Korean Protestant Christianity closely resembles also what happened in European settings, when local Protestant leadership began to shape the Protestant churches according to local cultural patterns. Third, the synthesis of Anglo-American–Sino Christianity with congenial elements of Korean religion shares something with early Protestantism, in that early Korean Protestants also embraced empirical science, political experimentation, and emerging capitalism.

This set of geographical and cultural convergences produced a singular Korean Protestantism by the turn of the twentieth century. An indigenous identity contributed, in turn, to a rapid spread of Protestant Christianity as a new national religion. As with the European Reformation, the agency of Korean Christians in this process should be emphasized.[12]

The First Three Decades, 1884–1913

Protestant churches in Korea grew rapidly after the Sino-Japanese War (1894–95) and then explosively after the Russo-Japanese War (1904–05). The Tonghak Uprisings (1894–95) and the Sino-Japanese War hit the western provinces of Korea, preparing the soil for the seeds of Christianity to grow among the poor, sick, and abused. The Japanese victory shattered a centuries-old Sino-centrism and its tributary system between Qing China and Chosŏn Korea. The Korean people saw that the traditional Chinese gods were powerless before this "Westernized" or "civilized" Japan.[13] A great famine and epidemics of cholera and smallpox plagued the middle part of the Korean peninsula from 1899 to 1903, as well as during the Russo-Japanese War. American and British Protestant missionaries had feared that a Russian victory could make Korea a country of Russian Orthodoxy. So, supported by their own governments' foreign policies, Anglo-Saxon missionaries in Korea welcomed Japan's colonization of Korea, believing that would guarantee the future of Korean Protestantism. Japan's victory over Russia further promoted Japanese pan-Asianism and encouraged the Shinto religion in Korea

Many missionary scholars have suggested various factors to explain the "miraculous success" of Protestantism in Korea. Up until 1910, missionaries stressed the unique political and religious contexts that facilitated the introduction of Protestantism to Korea more easily than to China and Japan. Then, in the late 1920s, academic studies in the United States presented sociological and anthropological interpretations, competing with the missiological views. These contrasting perspectives were revived by Korean scholars in the 1960s.[14] In view of all this, I prioritize three major transformations that account for the growth of Korean Protestantism up to 1910—namely (1) political "Christian nationalism," (2) socioeconomic "Christian civilization," and (3) indigenous "Korean Christianity."

Political Transformation: Christian Nationalism

As was the case in Europe during the sixteenth century, Protestantism in Korea contributed to modern nation building, which was a strong aspiration for Koreans at the turn of the twentieth century. The Chosŏn kingdom (1392–1910) was decaying in the nineteenth century and became a Japanese colony despite strenuous efforts by Koreans to achieve modernization and independence. Nobody blamed the Protestant Christians, for they in fact actively participated in these nation-building projects. Working against invading foreign powers, they introduced democratic ideals and practices through their mission schools, debate clubs, pulpits, books and tracts, newspapers, and the like.

"Christian nationalism" was not an oxymoron but a self-defensive means of survival for Koreans when Western (including and especially Russian Orthodox) Christian expansionism and Japanese Shinto imperialism (pan-Asianism) were competing for the colonization of Korea. In contrast, Protestantism kept its status as a foreign religion in both China and Japan, where its missionaries were often despised as "foreign devils" of Western imperialism; many in fact were killed in China. In Korea, however, the colonizer was Japan, a non-Christian empire. The Protestant missionaries were respectfully called *yang-daein* ("great Westerner") and *yang-daebuin* ("great Western lady") because they possessed cultural and moral authority among the people, as well as political influence at the court.

Thus, Protestant Christian nationalism in Korea combined the modernization movement with the anti-Japanese colonial movement. When Queen Min was assassinated by Japanese terrorists, who were supported by the Japanese legation in October 1895, King Kojong asked the Protestant missionaries to guard his bedroom chamber at night, for he could not trust anyone else in the court. American and Canadian missionaries, armed with pistols, safeguarded his rooms every night and tasted the king's food for fear of poisoning. When King Kojong fled to the Russian Legation in February 1896, and purged the pro-Japanese high officials from the cabinet, the Russians plundered Korea through forced concessions. In July 1896, Protestant Christians—including Philip Jaisohn (1864–1951), Yun Ch'iho (1864–1945), and Yi Sangjae (1850–1927)—and reform-minded Confucianists organized the Independence Club, seeking independence of the nation and enlightenment of its people. In 1897 they built the Independence Gate as a symbol of Korea's independence from China, and they held weekly debates about political and civil rights, proposed reform laws for the liberation of slaves, advocated for the establishment of a congress, and urged universal enfranchisement. Kil Sŏnju (1869–1935) also participated in the Independence Club in Pyongyang, and went on to lead the revival movement that began in 1907.

When Japan defeated Russia in 1905, and began to rule Korea through military force and secular modernizing projects, Christian nationalism had been split in three directions: military resistance, an enlightenment movement, and revivalism. These three movements were not disconnected; they worked together for national independence. Many Korean nationalists experienced a conversion or spiritual awakening during these revivals, held between 1903 and 1907, and then they joined in the various anti-Japanese movements.[15] The chief difference between what was happening in Korea during the early twentieth century and what had happened almost three centuries earlier in Europe is in the levers of power. In Europe, the new Protestant nationalisms came to power officially, whereas in Korea the new nationalism operated for several decades beneath the structures of government.

When Korea had become a semi-colony of Japan in 1905, some Protestant Christians engaged in radical anti-Japanese activity. The militant resistance included the assassination of pro-Japanese traitors; the Korean Righteous Army's three-year war against the Japanese (1907 to 1909); and the establishment of a military academy. Ahn Ch'angho (1878–1938), who became a Christian at the Presbyterian school in Seoul in 1895, had participated in the Independence Club in Pyongyang in 1897, went on to form the Korean National Association in San Francisco in 1905, and then organized the Sinminhoe (New People Society), a secret association for the independence movement, in Korea in 1907.

By 1910, the Protestant mission schools had 22,967 students, whereas the government's public schools had only 15,774. The Japanese colonial government sought to strengthen their control of the Protestant schools by introducing new oversights. These schools were often regarded by the Japanese as breeding grounds for Korean nationalism.

The Sinminhoe, or New People Society, not only promoted education and business in Korea but also planned a military academy in Manchuria in 1910 for armed resistance against Japan. In 1911, the Japanese government fabricated the "Conspiracy Case" to oppress the Christian nationalists and imprisoned 105 people, most of them Christian students, teachers, and leaders. A few Methodist evangelists voluntarily joined in the Korean Righteous Army against Japan; others attempted to assassinate pro-Japanese Korean politicians and American advisers. Still other Christian leaders devoted themselves to the cause of national independence among the Korean diaspora communities. Beginning in 1919, some of the Christian leaders served as presidents of the Korean Provisional Government in Shanghai. One of them, Syngman Rhee (1875–1965), became the first president of the Republic of Korea in 1948.

Cultural Transformation: Christian Civilization

Protestant institutions were one of the main venues for transmission of modern Western civilization (science, technology, education, printing culture, democracy, and so on) in early modern Korea, whereas governmental initiatives and secular institutions had been the main means by which these were introduced in Japan and China. The gospel of "Christian civilization" promoted Western education, technology, and secular ideas through modern hospitals, schools, and printing presses—almost direct parallels with the social transformations that characterized many areas of sixteenth-century Protestant Europe. When James S. Dennis published the first volume of *Christian Missions and Social Progress: A Sociological Study of Foreign Missions* in 1897, Methodist missionaries in Korea applauded it wholeheartedly, for they had adopted a progressive, social mission policy for building the "kingdom" of God by Christianizing "heathen" Korea. They wanted to transform society, not just plant churches. This resonated with Dennis's twofold focus on individual salvation (or "personal holiness") as the starting point of the missions and on social salvation (or "social sanctification") as the long-term goal of the missions, or what we might call today "development."[16]

Some Korean intellectuals regarded "Christian civilization" as an alternative way for Korea to survive in the age of competitive imperialism. The culpability of Christianity in the destruction of local culture—a common claim of postcolonial criticism today—was not a major worry for them. They generally embraced Protestantism as a religion of advanced civilization for the modernization of the "semi-civilized" Korean kingdom. Progressive Korean Protestant Christians participated in the reform movements for the modernization (usually called the "enlightenment and civilization") of Korea.

Western missionaries and Korean Christians who sought modernization focused on several chief items: (1) social welfare, by establishing diakonia institutions; (2) vernacular literature, through the rediscovery of the Korean alphabet, *hangŭl*, and by enhancing the literacy of ordinary people; (3) social equality, by elevating the lowest class—those involved in butchering animals, to commoner status; (4) greater gender equality, by uplifting women's status and advocating girls' education; and (5) a concept of vocation, by insisting on the dignity of all labor and industrial education.

Diakonia, which might be briefly defined as disinterested Christian love for nonbelievers, was offered for those who were outcasts, as defined by the strictures of neo-Confucian society. Missionaries built orphanages for homeless children, schools for the blind, asylums and self-supporting colonies for lepers, and libraries for the imprisoned, as well as hospitals for the poor in major cities.

The Protestant missions emancipated the Korean vernacular characters, *hangŭl*, from the scorn of the literary classes and made it a sacred language of the Bible. This helped promote literacy and greater social and political involvement among the lower classes. Presbyterians and Methodists organized the Permanent Executive Bible Committee in Korea and the Board of Translators in 1887 for Bible translation and publication, and in 1890 the Religious Tract Society began publishing Korean Christian books and evangelistic tracts. The Trilingual Press of Paejae School, the first modern press in Korea, printed millions of pages a year, beginning in 1889. When the Independence Club published the first Korean newspaper in 1896 to enlighten the people with modern ideas and concepts, it was printed at the Trilingual Press. Missionary Henry Appenzeller and the Methodists published the weekly *Korean Christian Advocate,* and missionary Henry Underwood and the Presbyterians produced the weekly *Christian Newspaper.* Both papers were in vernacular Korean. Korean Christian gospels and tracts were often used as textbooks for language learning.

Rev. Samuel F. Moore and Dr. Oliver R. Avison helped liberate the butchers from the lowest class, moving them from the near equivalent of slavery to the common class in 1895. For example, Dr. Avison, the head doctor of the government hospital, offered medical treatment to the king and to butchers alike. Mr. Moore did away with a separate section of pews designated for the outcast butchers, although he kept the curtain between the sexes for cultural reasons. Moore's revolutionary mixed seating of the *yangban* (elite class) with the butchers seemed at first to be a failure because, in reaction, the *yangban* Christians organized a separate church for themselves. Pak Sŏngch'un, a butcher deacon (later elder) of the "butchers' church," visited the butchers' villages for evangelism and participated in social reform actions by the All People's Joint Association. Eventually, the separate *yangban* church was united with the butchers' church.[17]

Scholars of gender studies sometimes see the late nineteenth-century evangelical missions as preaching a Victorian idea of womanhood, and say that the cult of domesticity prevailed in the mission schools for girls. This is certainly true, but most Korean women were expected to live primarily as mothers and wives. In contrast the missions provided them with identities and agency that extended outside the domestic sphere. Indeed, Korean women used the mission schools, mission hospitals, local churches, vernacular mission newspapers, and their own homes to find their way and voice, even if limited.

Here, we need more nuanced investigations of the interactions between female missionaries and Korean women, as well as their hierarchical relationships at the mission institutions. Without losing sight of either the gender studies critiques of cultural imperialism or the recent mission studies emphasis on "native" agency, we must recognize the various levels of freedom that existed for Christian women before the 1920s emergence of the "new women." And we must differentiate between the new type of Christian woman (who pioneered modern professional jobs like doctors, teachers, nurses, and "Bible women"—a non-ordained female minister) and the most ordinary Christian housewives (who mediated the modern and traditional understandings of female education, identity, and family life).[18]

Furthermore, Protestants across the board at this time had strict prohibitions on concubinage, ancestor worship, and early marriage. All three of these practices traditionally worked against the status of Korean women. Men took concubines to conceive a son who would serve as priest at the ancestor-veneration ceremony. Then they married off their sons at an early age to beget children. By rejecting these traditions, the Protestant missionaries fostered better family life. The Protestants also condemned drinking, smoking, gambling, and adultery among men, all of which negatively affected women.

Outreach to workers figured importantly in the growth of Protestantism in Korea. Often this was not through the agency of the churches but, rather, through the YMCA. For instance, Syngman Rhee was imprisoned in the Seoul Prison from 1899 to 1904 for his radical political activities. Rhee was converted to Protestant Christianity in prison and he guided many former high officials, then also imprisoned, to Christian belief. When they were released in 1904–05, they joined the Seoul YMCA and Rev. James S. Gale's church, and campaigned for the enlightenment of urban youth and intellectuals. Likewise, the industrial classes of the YMCA trained many young men for vocations as urban workers. After participating in the protests against the Protectorate Treaty in 1905, many Christians, including Kim Ku (1876–1949), engaged in this educational movement. Even Yu Kiljun (1856–1914), who remained an atheist Confucian scholar after studying in the United States in 1884–85, joined the Presbyterian Church in 1907 and participated in the YMCA's educational movement and Bible study classes.

Indigenous Church: The Nevius-Ross Method and Fulfillment Theory

Many missionary methods and policies contributed to the development of the indigenous Korean Protestantism. The main ones, however, were itineration, the use of vernacular literature (complemented by Chinese Christian literature), the so-called Nevius-Ross Method, and a fulfillment theory toward traditional religions. These often appeared as unique Korean developments, even though they replicated earlier Protestant efforts toward the local indigenization of Christian faith and practice.

Extensive itineration by missionaries and Korean workers not only formed new groups of believers that developed into local churches but also fostered partnerships between missionaries and Korean leaders. A clerical missionary would be responsible for fifty or sixty churches in rural areas, and he would visit them at least once a year. These missionaries walked hundreds of miles together with Korean helpers, ate Korean food together, and slept together at small Korean inns. Walking, talking, and eating proved good means for discipleship.

As already mentioned, adoption of the vernacular character *hangŭl* (that is, not the Chinese and Sino-Korean scripts of the educated classes) in Bible translations and Christian literature contributed to the development of the indigenous churches. This enhanced the status of the people's language, promoted literacy, and thus ultimately led to democracy. People loved to read and memorize the vernacular Korean scriptures. Based on the principle of *sola scriptura*, Korean Protestantism became "Bible Christianity" and Korean Christians became a community of the Book, which adopted a Korean vernacular term, *Hanănim*, as the term for God.

John Livingston Nevius, a nineteenth-century American missionary to China, advocated what became known as the "three-self method," encouraging churches to be self-propagating, self-governing, and self-supporting. Nevius's three-self method was officially adopted by the Korea Mission of the PCUSA in October 1891, and soon was employed by the other three Presbyterian missions and the Southern Methodist mission. The Scottish Presbyterian missionary John Ross had adapted the three-self method for use in Manchuria; he employed more paid helpers, built Daoist-style churches, used Confucian classics to illustrate Christian theological points in his preaching, and allowed for more Chinese leadership. Thereafter, Samuel A. Moffett adopted this approach, the "Nevius-Ross" method, and applied it at the Pyongyang station beginning in 1895.

In Pyongyang, the Nevius-Ross method proved very effective. A "self-supporting" church aimed to achieve financial independence from missionary support. Individual Christians remained at their old occupations, and only a limited number of members were employed by the missionaries; rural churches were encouraged to build small native-style chapels using their own resources. This first principle targeted the so-called rice Christians, who often wanted to join the church simply for pecuniary benefits. A "self-propagating" church emphasized voluntarism and discipleship for all members. Bible training classes for leaders and the Sunday school program for all church members were educational tools for self-propagation. Evening evangelistic meetings of the Bible training classes became the sites of Presbyterian revivals. Evangelism was designated not as the missionaries' job but, rather, the task of all Korean converts. Poor Korean Christians invented a unique system of "day offering" (dedicating days or weeks to evangelistic work) for personal evangelism and "rice offering" (daily collection of spoonful of rice before cooking) for the support of full-time evangelists.

Nevertheless, the self-governing churches required Korean leadership. In the case of the Presbyterian Church, they ordained the first seven Korean ministers in 1907, and organized an independent Korean presbytery. After five years, they organized a General Assembly composed of 44 missionaries, 52 Korean ministers, and 125 Korean elders from seven presbyteries. Koreans occupied 80 percent of the delegates of the first General Assembly, which proved a major step toward self-government. On the local level, an unordained "leader" (one who was ordained as an elder later) ministered to the congregation. Because there were not enough ministers until the early 1910s, leaders and elders preached at services and recommended candidates for baptism to itinerating missionaries. So-called Bible women (unordained female ministers) worked among the women in urban churches.

Thus, in the process of indigenization, Anglo-American Christianity was gradually transformed into Korean Christianity. And in this process, the role of "fulfillment theory" cannot be overemphasized. Simply put, this meant that missionaries and early Korean Christian worked hard not to impose Western ideas if they could find parallels within the traditional Korean culture, and they often interpreted Christian novelties in continuity with older practices. One example of this, as already mentioned, was the use of a Korean term for God, *Hanănim,* taken from the traditional name for the sky god of shamanism. Other examples include the interpretation of the advent of Christianity as the fulfillment of popular prophecies, understanding Christian exorcism and healing of the possessed victims in traditional categories of thought, development of a Korean Christian memorial service from the Confucian ancestor-veneration ceremony, and formation of the Christian dawn prayer meeting and adoption of audible prayer from Daoist practices.[19]

Recent Decades, 1984–2013

Before discussing recent decades, permit me to call attention to a few statistics that may help give a brief review of the colonial generation (1910–1945) and the post-liberation generation (1945–1984). The colonial years brought a period of suffering and fluctuation (see figure 10.2). The church declined sharply in 1924–27, and again in 1938–45. Roughly speaking, Protestantism in Korea grew from 170,000 in 1910 to 350,000 in 1938. The general population of Korea doubled during that period, probably owing to the imperial government's efforts to improve sanitation for general well-being and ultimate exploitation of human resources for labor and wars.

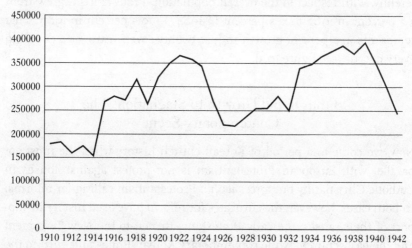

FIGURE 10.2 Protestant Adherents in South Korea, 1910–1942.

See *Han'guk Kidoggyo ŭi Yŏksa* [A History of Christianity in Korea] II (Seoul: Kidoggyomunsa, 1990), 260–61. The author drew the chart based on the statistics of the Japanese Governor General Government.

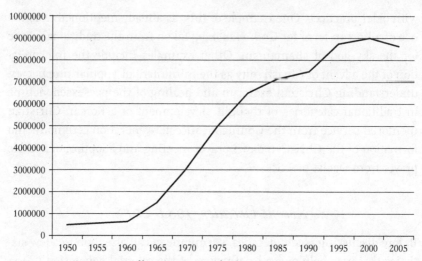

FIGURE 10.3 Protestant Adherents in South Korea, 1950–2005.
See *Han'guk Kidoggyo ŭi Yŏksa* [A History of Christianity in Korea] III (Seoul: Han'guk Kidoggyo *Yŏksa yŏnguso*, 2009), 116. The author drew the chart with a slight adjustment.

During the last decade of Japanese militarism, the church had lost a large number of the gains that had been achieved earlier. By contrast, then, Protestantism made record-breaking growth from the 1960s on, expanding from 1 million people in 1966 to 8.5 million in 1995. To put it differently, with respect to the overall population, Protestantism grew from 4.3 percent in 1962 to 13.5 percent in 1984, to 19.5 percent in 1989. That represents 450 percent growth in just twenty-seven years, or a doubling every decade (see figure 10.3).

From Rapid Growth to Stagnation: The Contemporary Scene

Now, we come to a period of Korean church history when the most apt parallel with European Protestantism is not protest against abuses in Catholic Christianity but forces *within* Protestantism calling for reforms. In both cases, however, the advocates for reform have used history in support of their causes; the early Protestants turned to the New Testament and the early church, while contemporary Korean Protestants turn to the New Testament and what they see as faithful service to God.

When we consider the fact that, in 1962, only about 3 percent of the population in South Korea identified as Protestant Christians, then growth to

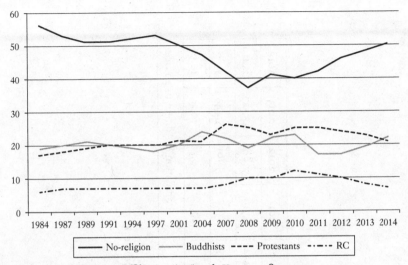

FIGURE 10.4 Religious Affiliation in South Korea, 1984–2014.
Han'gugin ŭi Chonggyo 1984–2014 [Religions of Koreans, 1984–2014] (Seoul: Korea Gallup, 2015). http://www.gallup.co.kr/gallupdb/reportContent.asp?seqNo=630.

20 percent of the population by 1995 represents a truly impressive expansion. One factor to consider is a general increase in religious affiliation in Korea during that period (see figure 10.4), owing to fervent evangelistic efforts by all religious groups. For example, Buddhism (or Buddhist affiliation) grew from 4.5 percent in 1962 to 19 percent by 1997, while Roman Catholicism grew from about 1.5 percent to 9 percent in the same period. Relatedly, the number of people claiming no religious affiliation dropped considerably.

In the past three decades, as South Korea has changed from an industrial, autocratic society to a postindustrial, democratic society, Protestantism has grown from 17 to 21 percent (about 11 million) of the population. Roman Catholicism made a record increase from 5.5 to 10 percent of the population in the same period. Protestantism's growth has slowed in the past decade (see figure 10.5), and it counts about 5.5 million adherents at present. Buddhism rivaled Protestantism in terms of religious identification from the late 1980s to 2005, but then dropped from 25 percent of the population in 2004 to 23 percent in 2010, and to a record low of 17 percent in 2012. Interestingly, the percentages of the nonreligious decreased until 2008, but since then have moved up to constitute 46 percent. This is all in part due no doubt to stiff competition and interreligious conflicts among the major religions and sectarian groups

Year	2003	2004	2005	2006	2007	2008	2009	2010	2011	2012	2013	2014
Population	48,823	49,052	49,267	49,624	50,034	50,349	50,643	51,434	51,716	51,881	52,127	52,419
Adherents	4,430	4,537	4,667	4,768	4,873	5,004	5,120	5,205	5,309	5,361	5,443	5,560
%	9.1	9.3	9.56	9.6	9.7	9.9	10.1	10.1	10.3	10.3	10.4	10.6

Population & Adherents x 1,000

FIGURE 10.5 Adherents of the Roman Catholic Church in South Korea, 2003–2014.*

*Catholic Bishops' Council of Korea, "Statistics of the Korean Catholic Church," April 2014 & April 2014.

in what is generally a limited religious market. The growth of the non-religious reflects a loss of trust in religious institutions in general and a weariness of religious leaders, who often in untoward ways expand and aggrandize their institutions. Therefore, we can conclude that the number of atheists has been rising in Korea while the number of the religious has been stagnating.

In short, the last three decades of Protestantism can be described as a slow-growth period (1984–2007), followed by seven years of stagnation and slow decline (2008–2014). The peak in expansion was 2007, when Protestants made up 26 percent of the population. But since 2007 there has been a significant decline, dropping from 26 percent in 2007 to 21 percent in 2014. However, it seems that Christianity in Korea is still doing fine, at least in term of the numerical growth, considering the low growth rate of its population. Nevertheless, the atmosphere has shifted from one of triumphalism in 1984 and 1995 to one of pessimism and a sense of crisis in recent years. A bellwether for documenting this is the T'onghap Presbyterian Church. One of the most influential denominations, whose reports are quite reliable, this church began to report a decline in adherents, including its Sunday school attendance in 2011 (-0.001%) and 2012 (-1.46%).

Losing Social Accountability

Year by year, people have lost trust in the Protestant churches and clergy, and particularly in ministers of the mega-churches. Many of these ministers have made the headlines for sex scandals, plagiarism, or the nepotistic practice of pastoral inheritance from father to son. According to a 2010 poll of the Christian Ethics Movement in Korea, only 17.6 percent of those polled trusted Protestant churches. Significantly, the rate drops to 8.2 percent among non-Christians and is even lower among the poor and socially marginal.[20]

Public confidence in religious organizations in general has declined, whereas individual religiosity remains relatively high. This may not be a uniquely Korean pattern. But the low credibility comes from the deteriorated "ecology of ministry," in which cooperation and interdependence among mega-churches, large churches, mid-size churches, small churches, and newly opened churches is disappearing. Koreans continue to value religion in their daily lives, yet they have little confidence or trust in religious institutions.

When the same poll asked people about what kind of changes were most needed for these churches, popular concerns included the integrity of church leaders (38.8%), greater religious tolerance (29.7%), financial transparency (13.0%), and increased social service (12.3%).[21] Other surveys show that unethical behaviors and the apparent hypocrisy of ministers are the most serious problems. Often, people see a vicious cycle: as ministers want bigger churches, their church programs focus on aggressive proselytism, and then on constructing large buildings beyond the means of the congregation to attract people. For example, more than 200 churches are put up for auction sale each year.[22] The asking price for one such church in 2012 was 200 million dollars and another in 2013 was 500 million dollars. But these church buildings have sold for much less. As ministers spend the money squeezed from their congregations for buildings and high salaries, their churches have had less money for providing social services. Additionally, many megachurch ministers have refused to pay income taxes; some have made explicit comparisons to the practices of Catholic bishops in the days of Martin Luther.[23]

Neo-Pentecostalism and the Prosperity Gospel

Many scholars have discussed not only the phenomenal success of Pentecostal Christianity in the 1970s and 1980s, but also various problems of its "prosperity theology" in the 1990s and 2010s. This form of Christianity emphasizes physical healing, spiritual warfare and exorcism, material blessings, secular success, and personal achievement.[24] Supporters argue that this Pentecostalism blends individualism and spirituality, promoting self-betterment, meritocracy, and economic advancement by empowering the self through mystical religious experience in a new, globalized economic system. They point out that Pentecostal churches are also doing various social welfare works.[25]

But critics have faulted the Pentecostals for syncretic experientialism and excessive accommodation to "the world" by emphasizing prosperity over Christian discipleship.[26] To use Martin Luther's terms, their theology of glory has little space for a theology of the cross. Rev. Cho Yonggi, now the emeritus pastor of Yoido Full Gospel Church, preached prosperity theology while he and his family accumulated wealth and power; they also engaged in tax evasion totaling $14 million. In this respect, some Korean church leaders bear unfortunate resemblance to some scandalous evangelical leaders in the United States. The Heavenly Touch Ministry of Elder Son Kich'ŏl, influenced by the New Apostolic Movement, has gained large audiences from the middle class and young people, but it, too, emphasizes prosperity and power.[27]

Pentecostal leaders have been quick to accommodate the changing cultural norms and political situations. They reflect more than they challenge the dominant value system of mainstream society. According to their critics, they have not paid sufficient attention to ethics, social justice, democracy, and economic justice; instead, they have demonstrated some similarity to a Korean shamanism that claims secular blessing with the help of various spirits of prosperity in the precarious economy of millennial capitalism.[28] "Mammonism," bad theology, anti-rationalism, cheap grace, commercial spiritualism, and spiritual egoism—these, critics claim, are now the dominant "spiritual grammar" of Korean Protestant Christians.

Aging Churches

According to a 2013 report of the Presbyterian Church in Korea (T'onghap), its adherents dropped from 2,852,311 (in 2010) to 2,852,125 (in 2011) to 2,819,531 (in 2012). This rate of decrease is accelerating from 0.01 percent (in 2011) to 1.46 percent (in 2012). Membership in the Roman Catholic Church shows the same decline. That is, the number of younger members is decreasing more rapidly than decreases in other age groups. The current birth rate in South Korea (1.3%) is the lowest among the OECD countries. This reflects partly the demographic changes in Korea (see figure 10.6). For instance, in 2002, people in their twenties and thirties constituted about 48.3 percent of the country's population. In 2016, they are only 35.7 percent, a decrease of 12.5 percent in fifteen years. At that point, people over fifty will make up 45 percent of the population. As a matter of course,

Year/ Age	20s	30s	40s	50s	60s+
2002	23.21	25.1	22.4	12.9	16.4
2007	21.1	22.9	22.5	15.4	18.1
2012	18.1	20.1	21.8	19.2	20.8
2016	17.9	17.8	19.9	19.8	24.6

FIGURE 10.6 Demographic Change (Age Group) in Korea.

churches are doing ministry among older people. Yet they would do well to pay more attention to the younger generations, among whom their influence is slackening.

In fact, many young people are leaving the churches altogether. In some quarters, this may be a reaction to those churches' uniformity and rigidity in theology, liturgy, and message. That is, most ministers are conservative in their theology and focus on church growth, whereas laypeople are quite syncretistic and seek secular blessings. Many churches introduce contemporary music to appeal to young people; some give ethical sermons on relevant topics. But the younger generations, often facing unemployment and a precarious job market, do not seem to be listening as they did in the past.

Innovative Missional Churches and the Decline of Ecumenism

In the 1980s, Minjung theology and the Minjung church movement contributed to the democratization of Korean society and the enhancement of human rights. Since the launch of Korea's civil government in 1987, however, these liberal Christians have participated in government and became part of the ruling power, often losing their prophetic voice in the process. Therefore, an "alternative church" movement emerged to transform Korean society by appealing to the marginalized.

Since South Korea's financial crisis in the late 1990s, the country has rapidly become a "mission field"—arguably less Christian and more a postmodern society of multiculturalism, religious pluralism, and racial diversity. Over 1 million foreign workers from many other Asian countries, who are Muslims, Hindus, and Buddhists, have immigrated to South Korea in the recent past.[29] Rapidly increasing numbers of foreign brides have married Korean bachelors. What is more, the South has thousands of defectors from North Korea. For example, in 2009, 2,929 North Koreans entered the country. But this number is declining owing to North Korea's stricter border controls, among other factors. More than 70 percent of these defectors are young women in their twenties and thirties.[30] The churches' efforts to minister to these foreigners have often been deemed wanting.

The switch of religious affiliation to Protestantism has been at a low rate since the late 1990s, but is gradually improving compared to other groups. Roman Catholics and Buddhists attracted people in the 1990s and early 2000s, but their popularity has decreased.

Looking at these two facts together—growing migrant populations and shrinking religious mobility—might suggest that Protestant churches should scrutinize their paradigm of evangelism and foreign missions, and transform themselves once again into missional churches. Advocates of reform in Korean Protestantism might seek out migrant workers and North Korean refugees, study their religions and background in communist ideology, and embrace them as a basis for Asian missions and the reunification of Korea. This is happening, but to a limited degree.

Ecumenical ties, along with new divisions, also have shaped Protestantism in Korea. There are about 300 main Protestant denominations in the country, the splits initially caused by issues relating to Shinto shrine worship, the World Council of Churches (WCC), and the liberal theology of the 1950s. The Korean National Council of Churches (KNCC), organized in 1924, was the main force for "liberal ecumenism" and it fought for the democratization of South Korea from the 1960s to the 1980s. In 1989, evangelical denominations formed the Christian Council of Korea (CCK), and this "conservative ecumenism" increased its influence in Korean politics and religion in the 1990s. But in the past decade, the CCK, too, has suffered from infighting. Major denominations (including T'onghap, Koryŏ, and Haptong of the Presbyterian Churches) finally left the CCK in 2012 and 2013, causing it almost to collapse. The T'onghap Presbyterian Church organized a new association, and the Haptong and Koshin Presbyterian Churches continue to search for a way to form another ecumenical organization. In reaction, the CCK accepted some "sectarian" churches as members to make up for its losses.

In this milieu, the tenth Assembly of the World Council of Churches was held in Busan, from October 30 to November 8, 2013. Ironically, the meeting deepened divisions among the Protestant churches in Korea. In May 2013, about forty denominations, including some major Presbyterian Churches (Haptong, Koryŏ, Koryŏ, Hapshin), raised a protest against the WCC. Some of their main arguments were that the WCC denies Jesus Christ as the unique mediator of salvation, it leans heavily in a socialist direction, and it condones homosexuality. At present, the KNCC has nine member churches: the Korean Church of Korea (T'onghap), the Korean Methodist Church, the Presbyterian Church in the Republic of Korea, the Salvation Army Korean Territory, the Korean Anglican Church, the Korea Evangelical Church, the Assembly of God of Korea, the Korean Orthodox Church, and the Lutheran Church in Korea. As Pentecostal leaders have been in the KNCC since around 1995, it cannot be considered in a "liberal ecumenical camp" any longer.

The ebbing of ecumenism among Korean Protestants has brought unfortunate consequences, both in the mushrooming of sectarian groups and in the way these denominational divisions have complicated pastoral care. That is, pastors sometimes perceive themselves as defending their flocks from wolves, while the flock often perceives their troubles as coming from shepherds themselves!

Conclusion

When Protestant Christians occupied less than 1 percent of the Korean population at the turn of the twentieth century, they transformed Korean politics, the social order, personal morality, and spiritual life. They actively participated in the "civilization and enlightenment" of Korea and the "anti-Japanese imperialism" movement for the independence of Korea. They produced leaders for the nation, churches, and families. In equal parts comparable to and contrasting with sixteenth-century Europe, Korea's indigenous nationally-oriented Protestantism was created. Pundits, scholars, and journalists alike felt that the future of Korea resided to a significant degree in Protestantism.

Today, membership in the Protestant churches is around 20 percent of the South Korean population, yet only 15 percent of the Korean people place their trust in the Protestant church and its leaders. Many prognosticate that the decline of the Protestant churches in Korea is at hand, that their adherents will shrink in the coming decades. But such predictions might be premature, for crises, real or perceived, often occasion reform and renewal.

Indeed, the situation confronting today's Korean churches is not without opportunities for growth and change. Luther's Reformation was arguably needed for the millennium-old churches of Europe, and another reformation sometimes is bidden for the 500-year-old Protestant churches in the West. Perhaps it is time for a reformation in Korea, too, for a 130-year-old church that has become part of the mainstream. It may be time to engage in self-examination and develop new purpose. Discipleship training for church members; reaching out to young people, foreign workers, and migrants and North Korean refugees; overcoming materialism and its prosperity theology; and diminishing the polarization between conservative and liberal groups are some, among many, possible avenues for renewal.

Notes

1. For broad treatment of this theme, see Hugh McLeod, *Religion and the People of Western Europe, 1789–1989* (Oxford: Oxford University Press, 1998); W. R. Ward, *Christianity under the Ancien Régime, 1648–1789* (Cambridge: Cambridge University Press, 1999), 71–104; and David Hempton, *Religion and Political Culture in Britain and Ireland: From the Glorious Revolution to the Decline of Empire* (Cambridge: Cambridge University Press, 1996).

2. The history of Korean Protestantism can be broken down into five periods, as follows: (1) Initial Contacts, 1832–1883; (2) Founding Missions and Churches, 1884–1910; (3) Struggles under Colonialism, 1910–1945; (4) Rapid Growth and Contribution to the Nation Building, 1945–1994; (5) Global Missions and Stagnation, 1995–2014.

3. See Martha Huntley, *To Start a Work: The Foundations of Protestant Mission in Korea, 1884–1919* (Seoul: Presbyterian Church in Korea, 1987).

4. Harry A. Rhodes, *History of the Korean Mission Presbyterian Church USA*, vol. 1: *1884–1934* (Seoul: Chosen Mission, PCUSA, 1934), 563.

5. Sung-Deuk Oak, *Sources of Korean Christianity* (Seoul: IKCH, 2004), appendices.

6. James S. Gale, *Korea in Transition* (New York: Eaton & Mains, 1909), 258–59.

7. Mark A. Noll, *The New Shape of World Christianity: How American Experience Reflects Global Faith* (Downers Grove, IL: IVP Academic, 2009), 154–61, 168.

8. H. G. Underwood to F. F. Ellinwood, January 22, 1887. Presbyterian Historical Society Microfilm Reel# 174, Vol. 2, Letter #5.

9. Minjung church historians attempted to present the Minjung perspective—which emphasizes liberation of suffering people and their subjectivity in salvation history—but these historians have failed to produce any monograph on the history of Korean Protestantism so far. The fourth perspective is emerging by postcolonialist and postmodernist scholars, who also have published no noticeable monographs yet.

10. Andrew F. Walls, *The Missionary Movement in Christian History: Studies in the Transmission of Faith* (Maryknoll, NY: Orbis Books, 1996), 3–15.

11. Tim Stafford, "Historian Ahead of His Time," *Christianity Today* 51, no. 2 (February 2007): 87.

12. Sung-Deuk Oak, *The Making of Korean Christianity: Protestant Encounters with Korean Religions, 1876–1915* (Waco, TX: Baylor University Press, 2013), xvi.

13. Robert E. Speer, *Report on the Korean Missions of the PCUSA* (New York: Board of Foreign Missions of the Presbyterian Church in USA, 1897), 7.

14. The following dissertations, books, and articles discuss the factors of early church growth in Korea: George L. Paik, *The History of Protestant Missions in Korea, 1832–1910* (Pyongyang: Union Christian College Press, 1929); Charles A. Clark, *The Korean Church and the Nevius Methods* (New York: Fleming H. Revell, 1930); Rhodes, *History of the Korean Mission*; Alfred W. Wasson, *Church Growth in Korea* (Concord, NH: International Missionary Council, 1934); Spencer J. Palmer, *Korea and Christianity: The Problem of Identification with Tradition* (Seoul: Royal Asiatic Society Korea Branch, 1967); David Chung, *Syncretism: The Religious Context of Christian Beginnings in Korea* (Albany: State University of New York Press, 2001); Andrew Eungi Kim, "Protestantism in Korea and Japan from the 1880s to the 1940s: A Comparative Study of Differential Cultural Reception and Social Impact," *Korea Journal* (Winter 2005): 276–82.

15. The American nationalism of evangelical missionaries embraced American colonization of the Philippines in 1897 and consequently supported Japanese colonization of Korea in 1905–1910 in the name of civilization. Korean Christian nationalism fought against Japanese colonialism, yet Korean Christians were not so much aware of U.S. pro-Japanese foreign policy and the secret Taft-Katsura Agreement of 1905, which allowed the Japanese colonization of Korea.

16. James S. Dennis, *Christian Missions and Social Progress: A Sociological Study of Foreign Missions*, 3 vols. (New York: Revell, 1897, 1899, 1906).

17. On outcast groups in Korea and efforts to improve their plight, see Joong-Seop Kim, "In Search of Human Rights: The Paekchŏng Movement in Colonial Korea," in *Colonial Modernity in Korea*, ed. Gi-Wook Shin and Michael Robinson (Cambridge, MA: Harvard University Asia Center, 1999), 311–35.

18. See Hyaeweol Choi, *Gender and Mission Encounters in Korea: New Women, Old Ways* (Berkeley: University of California Press, 2009).

19. See Sun-Deuk Oak, *The Making of Korean Christianity*.

20. Christian Ethics Movement in Korea, 2010 Poll of Social Credibility of the Korean Church, December 15, 2010. (http://trusti.tistory.com/657)

21. Christian Ethics Movement, 2010 Poll. The census is conducted every three years.

22. *Christian Nocut News*, July 3, 2013.

23. Sung-Deuk Oak, "Luther and Clergy Tax: Who are Anti-Christ today?" *Newsnjoy*, February. 16, 2013.

24. See Kim Sung-Gun, "Korean Pentecostal Christianity: Reasons for Success and Challenges for Future Research," *Bulletin* 37 (2013): 27–34.

25. Peter Berger, "Faith and Development," *Society* 46 (2008): 69–75.

26. Council of Pastors for Church Renewal, "Report of the Survey of the Religious Life and Consciousness of Koreans," 2012, www.churchr.or.kr/news/articleView.html?idxno=3767; Yi Sanghwa, ed. *Han'guk Kidoggyo Pusŏk Report* (Analytical Report of Korean Protestantism) (Seoul: URD, 2013), 57.

27. Kim Sung-Gun, "'The Heavenly Touch Ministry' in the Age of Millennial Capitalism: A Phenomenological Perspective," *Nova Religio* 15, no. 3 (2012): 51–64.

28. See Laurel Kendall, "Korean Shamans and the Spirits of Capitalism," *American Anthropologist* 98, no. 3 (September 1996): 512–27.

29. According to the first survey on foreigners in Korea by the government, June 2012, there were 1,114,000 foreigners (over age 15) and 791,000 were employed. There are also many undocumented laborers.

30. Ministry of Unification, "Statistics of the North Korean Defectors," October 2015. (http://www.unikorea.go.kr/content.do?cmsid=1440)

II

Chaotic Coherence

SOLA SCRIPTURA AND THE TWENTIETH-CENTURY SPREAD OF CHRISTIANITY

Mark A. Noll

FROM THE VERY beginning of the Reformation, Protestants proclaimed *sola scriptura* as their foundational principle of God-given authority; from the very beginning of the Reformation, Catholics responded that *sola scriptura* could only lead to self-exalting disorder, disaster, and despair. The latter judgment received a classic early formulation in the monumental polemic of a Jesuit, Robert Cardinal Bellarmine, published in several parts during the 1580s as *Disputations on the Controversies Over Christian Faith Against the Heretics of the Day*. If, wrote Bellarmine, the Protestant "makes individual persons the judges in matters of faith, not only of the Fathers but also of the councils, he leaves almost nothing to the common judgment of the Church." In his view, this Protestant insistence doomed the Bible for captivity "to the spirit of individual persons."[1]

The paradox of *sola scriptura* in our own time might be considered through the case of modern Mongolia. The history of scripture translation in modern Mongolia seems at first to be yet another sad Protestant instance of biblicism run amuck. If we understand "biblicism" in its most negative sense as a denunciation of every religious authority except my own grasp of the scriptures, then recent controversies over Mongolian Bible translations would seem to be the inevitable fruit of a misguided idea.[2] In Mongolia the disorder that Bellarmine saw as inevitable for the Protestant attachment to scripture appears to characterize efforts at providing the Bible for native speakers of the Khalka or Halh dialect, the language spoken by the great majority of Mongolia's 2.7 million inhabitants.[3] Bible translation in Mongolia may have begun with Nestorian efforts in the thirteenth century, but firm documentation exists only for the late nineteenth century, when representatives of the London Missionary Society published a New Testament in the literary Mongolian language. This version was then revised several times under very difficult conditions, including the murder of a Scandinavian missionary-translator during the Boxer Rebellion of 1900. These earlier translations, however, did not catch on, probably because they used an overly formal version of the language.

By contrast, a translation by the Englishman John Gibbens and his Mongolian wife, Altaa, did catch on late in the twentieth century. Gibbens had been a student at the Mongolian National University in Ulaanbaatar when, in 1972, he began translating the New Testament. Then in 1980, after he and Altaa were expelled by the Soviet-dominated communist government, they continued their work at the University of Leeds in England, along with assistance from many Mongolian ex-patriots, as well as representatives of the United Bible Societies and Wycliffe Bible Translators. Under the auspices of the United Bible Society, Gibbens published a complete New Testament in 1990, only one month before the collapse of Mongolia's communist government. That collapse led to unprecedented religious freedom, but also to a strong resurgence of Lamaistic Buddhism, the main religion of pre-communist Mongolia. In 1993, the new government passed a law defining Tibetan Buddhism, Shamanism, and Islam as Mongolia's official state religions, but also offering substantial toleration to other faiths so long as foreign influence remained minimal.

Bible wars began shortly after 1990, when missionaries from the United States, Germany, Korea, and Japan questioned the Gibbens's translation of names for God. They had used neologisms to differentiate Christianity from Buddhism. The critics, however, complained that these neologisms were meaningless to native speakers; they also contended that the Gibbens's thought-for-thought translation resulted in an insufficiently biblical Bible. To correct those mistakes, an ad hoc Mongolian Bible Translation Committee started work on a second translation. Its members followed a word-for-word model. They also used the common Mongolian term for Buddha (*Borhan*) to translate the biblical name of "God," which the Gibbens considered a dangerous invitation to syncretism. Working hastily, the second set of translators short-circuited standard linguistic protocols. Their procedure was to translate into Mongolian from whatever language the translators knew best, often English, then to have missionaries,

former missionaries, and Mongolians check the manuscripts before publication. The Gibbens and their allies sharply criticized this new translation as much inferior to their own, which had been rendered from the
up-to-date Greek text of the United Bible Society. (When the Mongolian
Bible Translation Committee had consulted a Greek text, it was the older
Textus Receptus that New Testament scholars now overwhelmingly consider a much-inferior original.) As heated exchanges escalated, confusion
grew as both groups produced revisions of their original work—and as
two additional mission societies, the German Missionswerk Unerreichte
Völker, e.V., and the Wycliffe Bible Translators, sponsored their own translations in closely related Mongolian dialects. The result, within fifteen
years of when the Mongolian change of government made possible a new
degree of religious freedom, was at least six or seven Protestant-sponsored
versions of the New Testament or the entire Bible circulating in Mongolia
and competing for the support of that landlocked Asian nation's Christian
community. What Christopher Hill had once labeled the "individualist
anarchy" characterizing "the essence of Protestantism" during the period
of the English Civil Wars seemed to have re-emerged, this time literally on
the other side of the world.[4]

We will return to Mongolia after an extended historical detour into the
early Reformation and then a conceptual effort to nuance the debate over
what Protestant attachment to scripture has, and has not, entailed for the
history of Christianity over the last five hundred years. To provide that
nuance, I would like to distinguish among different applications of *sola
scriptura* that explain why it operates both cohesively and chaotically, then
illustrate those differences with a brief excursus on hymnody, and finally
probe more deeply into the pre-Reformation history of *sola scriptura* itself.
But first it is important to return to the beginning, even though the history of that beginning is very well known.[5]

The Reformation and the Bible

The furor over Martin Luther's 95 Theses of 1517 is properly regarded
as the flash point that instigated the Protestant Reformation. In light of
later Protestant insistence on scripture as the defining norm for doctrine
and life, however, it is noteworthy that the 95 Theses contained very little
direct appeal to the Bible as such. Instead, the theses mostly attended to
questions about the theology and practice of indulgences.

When, however, Luther's proposal for an in-house academic debate was translated into German and republished by several enterprising printers, it is well known that a wide populace responded with enthusiasm, even as the pope and his associates responded with outrage. The ensuing controversy witnessed an almost immediate explosion of publication. What the Gutenberg revolution would mean for Western society became much clearer when Luther's theses precipitated a blizzard of print. But this publicity also led to another almost immediate consequence: a shift in the controversy's center of gravity.

Specific questions of Christian doctrine certainly remained important, but almost immediately they were joined by first-order questions concerning Christian authority: How could faithful believers know what was true, and who could guide them in finding out? The 95 Theses were likely posted in Wittenberg on October 31, 1517; less than a year later, Luther was called to meet a representative of the pope, Cardinal Thomas Cajetan, in the imperial city of Augsburg. At Augsburg, the controversy over the doctrine and practice of indulgences almost instantly expanded into controversy over the use and authority of scripture. Luther wanted to cite the Bible to defend his positions, but Cajetan never took this bait; he insisted instead that Luther must return to follow the established teachings of the church.

Since the spheres of religion and society were so intimately conjoined in early modern Europe, Luther's challenge to religious authority was quickly perceived as a challenge to authority in general. That broader challenge took center stage when, in April 1521, Luther traveled to an imperial Diet convened by the Holy Roman Emperor, Charles V. If Charles lacked experience as emperor, and if everything spoken in German had to be translated for him into Latin, he nonetheless represented at Worms the personal embodiment of Christendom. The "Christendom ideal," built up over the previous millennium and more, took for granted that the interests of religion and society could be harmonized in one integrated whole. Before such an august personage representing such a well-established ideal, Martin Luther appeared as a solitary monk who in his private spiritual journey had become convinced that scripture taught much that the pope, the emperor, and of all Christendom had tragically misconstrued.

When Luther came before the imperial court, he said he would recant what he had written, but only upon one condition. That condition amounted to a quintessentially Protestant challenge: "Therefore, I ask by the mercy of God, may your most serene majesty, most illustrious lordships, or anyone at all who is able, either high or low, bear witness, expose my errors, *overthrowing them by the writings of the prophets and the evangelists.*"[6]

But that statement did not satisfy the emperor, who asked Luther to say more. In response to the emperor's urging came Luther's memorable words:

> Since then your serene majesty and your lordships seek a simple answer, I will give it ... : Unless I am convinced by the testimony of the Scriptures or by clear reason (for I do not trust either in the pope or in councils alone, since it is well known that they have often erred and contradicted themselves), *I am bound by the Scriptures* I have quoted and *my conscience is captive to the Word of God.* I cannot and I will not retract anything, since it is neither safe nor right to go against conscience.[7]

This dramatic statement in this most auspicious setting established a baseline for later Protestants. They would follow the Bible before all other authorities—even when, as many of them later concluded, the Bible taught truths at considerable variance from what Luther found in scripture. The statement also defined a second landmark that has exerted almost as much influence: "my conscience"; or the individual Bible reader, aware of standing before God, would be the principal guide for interpreting the supremely authoritative scripture.

Immediately after Luther had finished speaking his piece, the emperor's spokesman called him to account for setting himself up as superior to the historical councils of the Catholic church that had already ruled on many of the issues he was addressing. "In this," the imperial secretary told Luther, "you are completely mad." Then he went on with words that forecast any number of controversies to come: "For what purpose does it serve to raise a new dispute about matters condemned through so many centuries by church and council? Unless perhaps a reason must be given to just anyone about anything whatsoever. But if it were granted that whoever contradicts the councils and the common understanding of the church must be overcome by Scripture passages, we will have nothing in Christianity that is certain or decided."[8]

Further reflection on Luther's profession to follow the Bible above all other authorities came the next day from the emperor himself. In words written out with his own hand, Charles V reminded his German nobles about the inheritance of Christendom: he was descended from the "most

Christian" monarchs of Germany, Spain, Austria, and Burgundy who, "to the honor of God, the strengthening of the faith, and the salvation of souls," had everyone "remained up to death faithful sons of the church." Charles, to say the least, was not impressed with what he had heard the day before from Luther. "It is certain," he concluded, "that a single friar errs in his opinion which is against all of Christendom and according to which all of Christianity will be and will always have been in error both in the past thousand years and even more in the present."[9]

Yet Charles and the pope's representatives dawdled after Luther's dramatic appearance. By the time they figured out what they wanted to do with him, he had long since left Worms. Luther's prince, the elector Friederich of Saxony, was torn between a desire to protect the theologian who was bringing renown to his principality and his need to show proper deference to the emperor. Friederich's creative response was to maintain a public position of noncommittal impartiality while arranging, under strictest secrecy, for Luther to be "kidnapped" and spirited away to a secret retreat, the Wartburg Castle near Eisenach.

As soon as Luther was settled in the Wartburg, he turned his energy to preparing a German-language translation of the New Testament. As with all such efforts, much was at stake both implicitly and explicitly in Luther's path-breaking translation. His 1522 German New Testament was immediately noteworthy for the chance it gave Luther to accentuate the themes of scripture that most directly fueled his reforming fire. A much-noticed instance was his translation of a key passage about faith and justification found toward the end of the third chapter of Paul's Epistle to the Romans. Luther added the world "alone" to the apostle's statement that believers are "justified without the works of the law by faith."[10]

A second noteworthy feature of Luther's momentous New Testament was its annotations, which came in two forms. In slender margins alongside the translated text of scripture, Luther inserted quotations from what he considered pertinent Old Testament texts and also explained what he felt the New Testament authors were trying to say. He also supplied prefaces, first to the New Testament as a whole and then to each of the individual books.

In his general introduction to the entire New Testament, Luther told why there needed to be a preface at all. His very first sentences explained that, "It would be right and proper for this book to go forth without any prefaces or extraneous names attached and simply have its own say under its own name." Yet Luther did provide an introductory preface because "many unfounded [*wilde*] interpretations ... prefaces have scattered the thought of Christians to a point where no one any longer knows what is gospel or law, New Testament or Old." It was, therefore, a "necessity" for Luther to give some "notice ... by which the ordinary man can be rescued from his former delusions, set on the right track, and taught what he is to look for in this book, so that he may not seek laws and commandments where he ought to be seeking the gospel and promises of God."[11]

This very first Protestant Bible translation, thus, mingled the ideal and the real as they would be consistently mingled in Protestant history. The ideal was biblical authority alone; the real was constant effort by those with standing or authority to make sure that others were carefully guided so that they could understand "the Bible alone" aright.

Two more incidents in Luther's early reforming career are pertinent. While Luther was hidden away in the Wartburg Castle, colleagues who shared his desire for reform got to work in Wittenberg. They were led by an older university professor and cleric, Andreas Bodenstein von Karlstadt, who believed that a right interpretation of scripture demanded more and faster changes than Luther had ever desired. In short order Karlstadt drastically simplified the ritual of the Mass, led his followers to destroy artistic images in Wittenberg churches, and took many other radical steps. Luther and the elector Friedrich were furious. To bring an end to what they saw not as reform but a rush into anarchy, Friedrich called Luther back to Wittenberg to deliver a series of sermons during Lent 1522. And then the prince, with Luther's full backing, banished Karlstadt from Saxony because Karlstadt's interpretations of scripture seemed so dangerous to both the Elector Friederich and the theologian Luther.

The last incident involves Luther's famous debate with Desiderius Erasmus in 1525 over the theological question of the freedom of the human will. The key matter for our purposes is that Erasmus in this debate argued that the Bible was obscure on this point and so allowed for a great deal of theological latitude. Luther, by contrast, insisted that the Bible on this issue was entirely clear. It was perspicacious; and this perspicacity justified Luther in defending the opinion he felt he had taken from the scriptures.[12] Yet because Erasmus resided in Basel, Switzerland, far beyond the authority of any Saxon prince, Luther had no means to compel Erasmus to agree with his interpretation of scripture.

At roughly the same time a similar story was playing out in Zurich, Switzerland, where reforming ideas had advanced under the leadership of Ulrich Zwingli. Zwingli's biography shared much with Luther's, including inspiration by Erasmus's edition of the Greek New Testament, opposition to the indulgence traffic, bold preaching from the New Testament, and a dramatic experience of God's grace from his personal encounter with scripture. Zwingli also shared with Luther a partnership with governing officials, in his case the town councils of Zurich, as they sought to implement reform.

Zwingli's battle cry echoed Luther's. When in 1523, he drew up a series of 67 Theses directed toward clarifying obscured doctrines and reforming corrupt practices, he affirmed "I have preached in the worthy city of Zurich these sixty-seven articles ... on the basis of Scripture." He stood ready "to defend and vindicate these articles with Scripture." And he desired, "if I have not understood Scripture correctly," to be instructed, "but only from the same Scripture."[13] If, however, Luther had his Karlstadt, so Zwingli had his Anabaptists.

Zwingli's arguments convinced the Zurich town fathers to renounce their Catholic bishop and to establish a reformed church order. Yet there were also other reformers in Zurich, equal in zeal to Zwingli and eager with him to be guided by the Bible, but who interpreted scripture more radically. As they read the Bible, they did not find any justification for the church to be supported by government, they did not see any instruction for Christians to wage war, and they did not believe any biblical passage taught that the state could punish deviance in religious beliefs. These erstwhile followers of Zwingli became known as Anabaptists (or "rebaptizers") when they concluded that scripture did not authorize the baptism of infants but, rather, that baptism should be offered only to adults who made a personal profession of faith.

The Zurich council was even harsher in constraining these interpretations of scripture than Friederich of Saxony had been with Karlstadt. Felix Manz, once an ardent disciple of Zwingli, became the first Anabaptist martyr when he was executed by his fellow Zurich Protestants on January 5, 1527. The mode of execution, drowning in Lake Zurich, was chosen to mock his stance on baptism.

So, here is how things stood with scripture before the Reformation was even ten years old. Leading Protestants held that the Bible as God's definitive written revelation was being corrupted by self-seeking church officials, yet all the more they insisted that scripture still deserved to be honored as the first authority for all of life's important questions. Moreover, the individual standing humbly before God could follow his own conscience (and, though much later, her own conscience) in grasping the message of scripture. In turn, that clear perception purified Christian teaching, cleaned up church corruption, and brought new life in the Holy Spirit to individuals and Christian communities alike. The Reformation reliance on scripture made a real difference in Europe, and then throughout the world, because it first made a life-or-death difference *coram deo* for countless individuals.

But, of course, that is not all. Since few could read the Bible's original Greek and Hebrew for themselves, it was necessary for translations to be prepared so that all could apprehend scripture in their vernacular languages. Inevitably, as has become a commonplace observation, all Bible translations "are, by their very nature, partisan."[14] "*Traduttore, Traditore*," say the Italians with characteristic overstatement: a translation is a traitor (to the original). If it is really not that bad, still wherever translation takes place, the translators shade the final product. For scripture, a translated text is no longer "the Bible alone."

And there is more. As soon as there was a Protestant movement appealing to scripture as ultimate authority, there were Protestant *movements* differing on how best to interpret the supremely authoritative scripture. Some of those differences were minor, others were literally deadly in the effect they had on those who maintained them. And so began the Protestant swinging to and fro that has gone on since late 1517, to this very day. On the one side we hear credible testimonies of lives transformed, piety strengthened, and societies reformed because consciences have been made captive to the Word of God. These testimonies, moreover, have ranged and continue to range across time, gender, age, social class, and place. Yet on the other side, we find individual biblical interpretations restrained by authoritative directives from religious, intellectual, or political leaders about what your conscience is supposed to find when you open the scriptures. For most of the first three centuries of Protestant history that restraint was statist and coercive—occasionally with deadly violence directed at those who persisted in what the authorities considered erroneous views of scripture. For the last two hundred years the restraint has been more informal, but still no less real as voluntary organizations have erected democratic forms of coercion to define what is and what is not a proper understanding of scripture.

As a Protestant historian, I want to insist that Martin Luther's appeal to a conscience captive to the Word of God solved some very important problems. In particular, "captivity to the Word of God" has meant life-transforming liberation in Christ for countless believers throughout the world. Yet even as it solved some problems, this same Protestant doctrine created other and quite serious problems as well. It is important—perhaps especially as a Protestant historian—to look at these difficulties directly and to realize that what Catholic and secular critics have said about Protestant use of *sola scriptura* is not at all beside the point.

So, already at the Council of Trent in 1546, the Catholic Church complained about "that boldness whereby the words and sentences of the holy Scriptures are turned and twisted to all kinds of profane usages ... to things scurrilous, fabulous, vain" and much more. The Tridentine solution was to "command" and "enjoin" all people to "be restrained by the bishops as violators and profaners of the Word of God, with the penalties of law and other penalties that they may deem fit to impose."[15] As any number of scholarly accounts have documented, the situation that Trent defined polemically for the sixteenth century continued to define the entire course of Protestant history.[16]

Protestant Cohesion and Hymnody

Despite a steady chorus of understandable criticism aimed at the consequences of *sola scriptura*, my own conclusion is that the positive results from this Protestant principle have been as remarkable as the negative results. Much chaos has in fact resulted from Protestant appeal to "the Bible alone." Yet that chaos has been constrained; it has not been unlimited. Thus, after 457 years of fissiparous Protestant history, over 2,700 representatives of hundreds of Protestant organizations could gather at Lausanne, Switzerland, in 1974 and voluntarily affirm an expansive Covenant of agreed-upon Christian doctrines and agreed-upon standards of Christian practice—all based on a strongly Protestant conception of scripture: "We affirm the divine inspiration, truthfulness and authority of both Old and New Testament Scriptures in their entirety as the only written Word of God, without error in all that it affirms, and the only infallible rule of faith and practice. We also affirm the power of God's Word to accomplish his purpose of salvation."[17]

An even more broadly representative range of Protestant churches and organizations has always agreed on an array of truths that they affirm, as it were independently, by pursuing "the Bible alone." These truths include that God should be worshiped as Trinity, that reconciliation with God results from God's own gracious initiative in Jesus Christ, and that the ministry of the Holy Spirit enables believers to lead lives of loving service to others. Of course, there are nearly infinite variations in how Protestants affirm such basic Christian teachings. But despite the chaos of individual biblical interpretation, there also exists an unquestioned measure of cohesion. The questions addressed in the rest of this chapter are these: Where does that cohesion come from? and How can it be explained?

The Protestant theological answer for why individual reliance on scripture can be coherent has always been clear: the same Holy Spirit who inspired the sacred text communicates the truth of that written revelation to those who turn in faith to God. Since the triune God is perfect coherence, so too does the presence of God through Word and Spirit produce coherent Christian existence. John Calvin provided a classic statement in *The Institutes of the Christian Religion*: "the highest proof of Scripture derives in general from the fact that God in person speaks it. . . . If we desire to provide in the best way for our consciences . . . we ought to seek our conviction in a higher plane than human reasons, judgments, or conjectures, that is, in the secret testimony of the Spirit."[18]

Yet how, then, to explain what appears among Protestants as so many contradictory differences over what the Spirit is saying in and through the scripture? Although Protestants have repeatedly answered this question with a theological appeal to the Holy Spirit, the question can be approached historically. A clue to recognizing that the situation involves several discernible layers, or subquestions, provided by C. S. Lewis's argument in *Mere Christianity*. (Incidentally, this book's phenomenal worldwide popularity since its publication in 1952 testifies to the possibility of Christian spiritual cohesion existing apart from visible institutional authority.[19]) In discussing the manifold divisions among Christian believers, Lewis found it "curiously consoling" that at what he called the "centre" of the Christian faith "where her truest children dwell . . . each communion is really closest to every other in spirit, if not in doctrine. And this suggests at the centre of each there is something, or a Someone, who against all divergences of belief, all differences of temperament, all memories of mutual persuasion, speaks with the same voice."[20]

The point I take from Lewis is that *sola scriptura* has always operated most coherently when it defines the path by which individuals are led to faith in Jesus Christ. While it is never possible to prove such an assertion, even when piling up examples, testimonies exist almost without number to describe how direct, personal encounter with the Bible has led readers or hearers to Christ. The following come from a nearly inexhaustible store.

There was Thomas Bilney, a Cambridge priest in the 1520s, whose life was transformed when he began to study newly published Greek and Latin editions of the New Testament. Bilney reported that he had not "heard speak of Jesus" until he read Erasmus's Latin and Greek text. There, although he had purchased that edition because of its literary reputation, he was almost immediately transfixed by its spiritual message: "at the first reading … I chanced upon this sentence of St. Paul (O most sweet and comfortable sentence to my soul) in I Tim. i: 'It is a true saying and worthy of all men to be embraced that Christ Jesus came into the world to save sinners, of whom I am the chief and principal.'" By means of this biblical source, Bilney "through God's instruction and inward working" was "wounded with the guilt of my sins." But then from this same scriptural source, he experienced "a marvelous comfort and quietness, insomuch that my bruised bones leaped for joy."[21]

There was Jupiter Hammon, who in 1760 began one of the very first publications by an African American by conjoining faith in Christ and the message of scripture:

> SALVATION comes by Jesus Christ alone
> The only Son of God;
> Redemption now to every one,
> That love his holy Word.[22]

There was Hammon's near contemporary, Olaudah Equiano, who in his *Interesting Narrative* of 1789 described the biblical path that led him to Christ. Here is his much-abridged account phrased in almost entirely biblical language, including Equiano's own citation of chapter and verse:

In the evening of the same day, as I was reading and meditating on the fourth chapter of the Acts, twelfth verse ["Neither is there salvation in any other: for there is none other name under heaven given among men, whereby we must be saved"], under the solemn apprehensions of eternity.… [I]n this deep consternation the Lord was pleased to break in upon my soul with his bright beams of heavenly light; and in an instant, as it were, removing the veil, and letting light into a dark place, Isa[iah] xxv. 7. [T]he Scriptures became an unsealed book, I saw myself a condemned criminal under the law, which came with its full force to my conscience, and when 'the commandment came sin revived and I died.' … I then clearly

perceived, that by the deed of the law no flesh living could be justified.... I was then convinced, that by the first Adam sin came, and
by the second Adam (the Lord Jesus Christ) all that are saved must
be made alive.... It was given me at that time to know what it was
to be born again, John iii. 5.[23]

Then there is Zhao Xiao, a rising Chinese economist of the early
twenty-first century who, after visiting churches in trips to America,
began to read the Bible in order to verify his convictions that God did
not exist. "Three months later," he has written, "I admitted defeat....
[Scripture] talks about the history of the relationship between God and
human beings, and this kind of book does not exist in China." Zhao's
Christian encounter has led to widely recognized publications about the
necessity for personal morality to undergird productive economic life.[24]

These biographical vignettes are varied, but they all describe the capacity of scripture to draw individuals from diverse paths to a unifying
point around Jesus Christ. Of course, it is far from the case that all who
attend to scripture with an interest in its depiction of Jesus come away as
Christian believers. Some have received that depiction as nonsense, others
as primitive myth, still others with complete indifference. But where a
Christian understanding of the Bible does take hold, that understanding
has often proved surprisingly coherent.

From such examples, I conclude that if *sola scriptura* meant only that
the Bible preserves the definitive account of Jesus's life and work, that
principle would be seen as producing coherent convictions about the liberating, consoling, humbling, and transformative message of reconciliation
with God through Christ. Hymnody, which for Protestants long exercised
some of the functions that the sacraments fulfilled for Catholics, supports
the notion that focus on the biblical Christ draws otherwise fragmented
communities together.

It has long been the case that churches separated by their particular
biblical interpretations come together through hymns that praise the
Christ revealed in scripture as redeemer. Baptists sing heartily "When
I survey the wondrous cross on which the prince of glory died" by the
paedo-Baptist Isaac Watts. Calvinists join Wesleyans in singing together
Augustus Toplady's "Rock of ages, cleft for me" and Charles Wesley's
"And can it be that I should gain an interest in the Saviour's blood"—despite the fact that Wesley and Toplady hammered each other on what each
thought was the other's near-demonic interpretation of biblical teaching

on the human will. Reserved believers sing boisterously "Jesus thy blood and righteousness" by the eccentric Count von Zinzendorf, and those who regard church order as an evil chime in on "Blessing and honor and glory and power" by the divine-right Presbyterian Horatius Bonar. Churches where the Bible is read to exclude women from ordained ministry are nonetheless led in song by Anne Steel's "Here the redeemer's welcome voice," Charlotte Eliot's "Just as I am without one plea, but that thy blood was shed for me," Cecil Frances Alexander's "There is a green hill far away," Fanny Crosby's "Rescue the perishing," Margaret Clarkson's "We come, O Christ, to you," and many more. Most remarkably, Protestants of all sorts, even as they score Catholicism for disregarding fundamental biblical truth, have sung any number of Christ-centered hymns from the Western Catholic tradition: Prudentius ("Of the Father's love begotten") and Bede ("A hymn of glory let us sing"); Thomas Aquinas ("Zion, to thy Savior singing") and Bernard of Clairvaux ("Jesus, the very thought of thee"); and in recent decades a cornucopia of worship music from Catholic publishers like GIA and many others.

In 1870, the noted Protestant church historian Philip Schaff published *Christ in Song: Hymns of Immanuel Selected from All Ages*. In the preface to this unusual collection, made up entirely of hymns about the person and work of Christ, Schaff explained why he could fill its almost 600 pages with representatives from every era and every denominational tradition: "The hymns of Jesus are the Holy of holies in the temple of sacred poetry. . . . [H]ere the dissensions of rival churches and theological schools are hushed into silence; here the hymnists of ancient, medieval, and modern times, from every section of Christendom—profound divines, stately bishops, humble monks, faithful pastors, devout laymen, holy women—unite with one voice in the common adoration of a common Saviour."[25] In a word, the extensive ecumenical reach of classic Christian hymnody demonstrates that reliance on the Bible's central theme can work cohesively—without institutional support and beyond even informal coercion.

Yet this cohesive effect is admittedly only part of the story. When Protestants extrapolate from what they have experienced in the scriptural message of Christ—when they move on to implement in doctrine, practice, or church order what they consider the necessary implications of the Bible's message of salvation in Christ—pluralism if not chaos is regularly the result. This move—from relative cohesion in apprehending scripture's message of a redeeming Christ to relative chaos in following Christ according to scriptural norms—is the great engine of Protestant history. *Sola scriptura* draws people to Christ; *sola scriptura* drives Christians apart.

It is not all that difficult to explain what appears to be a paradox, or at least a conundrum. To experience the biblical message of redemption in Christ is to be pulled out of the self, to be overcome by an emotion of gratitude, and to be focused on what God has done for fallen humans. Despite endless Protestant debate over how much human will or exertion contributes to salvation, there is considerable Protestant unity, shared with Christians of all traditions, that God-in-Christ is the primary agent of salvation.

The perspective shifts, however, when it comes to formulating doctrine, defining proper Christian behavior, or determining God-honoring church order. To engage in these tasks, which flow inevitably from the experience of salvation, is to rely on scripture interpreted for concrete particular circumstances, to be driven by emotions related to protection, and to focus by necessity on the exercise of human authority. Over-simplifying perhaps, Protestants join virtually all other Christians in believing that reconciliation with God entails powerlessness, while all Protestant efforts to shape ecclesiastical or personal Christian life require the exercise of power—and power, however portrayed in altruistic terms, always entails self-exertion.

Catholic Christianity, which is neither blessed nor burdened with *sola scriptura*, acknowledges that the powerlessness of Christian redemption ineluctably entails the power of doctrine, discipline, and ecclesiastical order, but treats the church's exercise of that power as organically connected to the powerlessness of salvation. Protestantism, which arose from the conviction that church power was making it impossible to experience the powerlessness of redemption, substituted *sola scriptura* for the Catholic understanding of God-given institutional authority. The Protestant gain was to liberate scripture and so liberate the scriptural message of salvation; the Protestant loss was to consign scriptural interpretation to personal whim and so discredit the whole idea of God-given scriptural authority.

In my own view, the last fifty years have witnessed a remarkable period of mutual instruction between Catholics and Protestants. [26] Catholicism, without abandoning the belief that the institutional church plays an intrinsic role in the gift of salvation, proclaims much more clearly the scriptural message of salvation in Christ alone. Many Protestants, without abandoning the belief that *sola scriptura* remains imperative for communicating salvation in Christ, realize that fidelity to scripture requires respectful deference to tradition. A Catholic writer has recently described the situation with these hopeful words: "It has become part of our Christian experience, on the one hand, that a critical attitude to scripture and a re-discovery of tradition, have much to contribute towards the solution of the crisis of the scripture principle in Protestantism and, on the other, that a critical attitude to tradition and a re-discovery of scripture, are able to dispel any fears that the Roman Catholic Church ignores or down-grades scripture."[27]

If Protestants after nearly five hundred years of maintaining *sola scriptura* can now both justify this principle and realize that it must be restrained, what practical guidance can assist in preserving the virtues of the concept while curtailing its drawbacks?

In Protestant terms, there is no simple way forward. Any effort to confer absolute authority on any institutional arbiter of the scriptural message must raise fears that the biblical message of salvation is being imperiled. But continuing to act as if *sola scriptura* involves only inconsequential weaknesses means continued undermining of the very notion of scriptural authority, and hence also of Scripture's central message of salvation in Christ.

Sola Scriptura *Before Luther*

It does not solve the enigma of Protestantism to examine more closely the history of the term *sola scriptura*, but such a closer look is nonetheless helpful. The phrase, along with attacks on corrupt church authority with which it was always linked, enjoyed a well-established career centuries before Martin Luther. Without pretending mastery of the intricate theological and intellectual history of the late Middle Ages, it is nonetheless striking to find this phrase, or equivalents, at use from the fourteenth century onward among both philosophical nominalists and philosophical realists, among both supporters of church councils against the Roman curia and supporters of the curia against church councils.[28]

Two points are most obvious from the labors of acknowledged experts on the complicated history of the pre-Reformation period. First is that the notion of *sola scriptura* was already functioning in two ways as early as the fourteenth century. John Wycliffe, a chief example, excoriated the institutional church of his day for what he considered its sinful imposition of false teaching concerning the Lord's Supper and for its blithe disregard of widespread corruption in religious orders. As his standard for judgment, he appealed to *sola scriptura*, but *sola scriptura* deployed in two ways. Sometimes he used it in what might be called "a catholic and traditional sense" as the main trajectory of scriptural interpretation to which early church fathers, popes, the ecumenical councils, bishops, theologians, and the lay faithful had all made important contributions.[29] In other words, it was the consensus of historical church teaching that he thought condemned dangerous innovations with respect to the Eucharist and corrupt degeneration among the religious orders. At other times Wycliffe seems to have used *sola scriptura* in what might be called "a literal sense."[30] Here, he was willing, as one historian has put it, "to drive a coach and four through the testimony of any of these [other authorities] insofar as it [did] not harmonize with his own views; so that in a very true sense it can be said that he [did] not in fact accept Tradition."[31]

To borrow helpful terms of differentiation from Heiko Oberman and Alister McGrath, Wycliffe's first sense of *sola scriptura* can be called Tradition 1; it regards scripture as the supreme, comprehensive authority, but with interpretation guided by self-conscious reference to historical church consensus.[32] Wycliffe's second sense of *sola scriptura* can be called Tradition 0; it comes close to the extreme biblicism sometimes still visible where my own interpretation trumps all others absolutely.

It is intriguing that students of the nominalist tradition, focusing on William of Occam and Gabriel Biel, present conclusions about scripture parallel to what students of Wycliffe, a passionate philosophical realist, also say. Thus, in his study of that nominalist tradition, Heiko Oberman differentiated between Tradition 1 (understood as scripture uniquely supreme but interpreted with the guidance of historical church teaching) and Tradition 2 (understood as positing two coordinated sources of God-given authority, one in the scriptures and one through the institutional church).

Pre-Reformation reformers often attacked Tradition 2 by referring to *sola scriptura* or equivalent terms. Usually those attacks employed *sola scriptura* in the sense of Tradition 1, the Bible as supreme authority but supreme because it embodied a historical consensus of interpretation. In fact, in one of the few times where Wycliffe cited the actual phrase *sola scriptura*, he listed many ways in which appeal to biblical authority could be abused: "They all presume to mutilate and teach it [*sola scriptura*] before having learnt it, whether it be the chattering old woman, the delirious old man, or the verbose sophist."[33] More often, late medieval reformers meant, in Heiko Oberman's summary, "not *sola scriptura* in the sense that it would exclude Tradition understood as the ongoing interpretation of Scripture. The *sola* is only restrictive in that the law of God is sovereign and sufficient to determine alone—*without ecclesiastical law*—all cases that have to be tried in the Church."[34]

Yet in practice, appeal to scripture as Tradition 1 could easily slip into appeal to scripture as Tradition 0. The key historical observation is that when the excesses, errors, and enormities of the late medieval institutional church became most threatening, reformers easily slipped from the nuance of Tradition 1 to the full-throated outrage of Tradition 0. Yet taken in its most common usage, *sola scriptura* was almost never intended as a radical biblicism excluding the guidance of history and tradition. In short, the most consistent meaning has been well summarized by G. C. Berkouwer: "The phrase ... expressed a certain way of reading Scripture, implying a continual turning towards the gospel as the saving message of Scripture."[35]

As many have shown, this broader sense of *sola scriptura* has been the standard usage in most Protestant circles since the sixteenth century. As only one example, Gerald McDermott has pointed out that Jonathan Edwards did occasionally deploy scripture as Tradition 0, "especially when plotting the course of Protestant progress against Catholic persecution." But much more often—"in his reflections on the history of revelation, the history of theology, the history of his own theological development, and his remarks on church practice"—Edwards "showed in a number of ways that theology and practice must look outside the bible to know what the Bible means"—in other words, scripture deployed as Tradition 1.[36]

It remains all too evident, however, that even when considering *sola scriptura* as Tradition 1, the chaos that attends the concept is bounded rather than banished. From one angle, the pressing question becomes more involved when Tradition 1 comes into view: who is to say which part of, or which voices in, the church's long history of biblical usage are normative for Bible believers now? This question marks the furthest point that nuancing of *sola scriptura* can go. In the same way that the concept has facilitated more unity than seems possible, especially unity around the Bible's message of Christ, so also historical investigation of the concept involves much more respect for tradition than facile stereotyping recognizes. Yet the weight of criticism remains. *Sola scriptura* does often yield chaotic results; it does regularly divide those who say the same thing about the Bible being their sufficient and ultimate authority. The *blessing* of *sola scriptura* is also the *bane* of *sola scriptura*.

Nonetheless, as the contemporary history of Bible translation in Mongolia attests, the mixture of blessing and bane makes it impossible to render a simple or preemptive judgment about *sola scriptura*. The clash among Protestants over which Mongolian translation is most faithful to the best understanding of scripture seems irresolvable except by appeal to techniques of persuasion—techniques that do not necessarily entail coercive violence but ones that also rarely produce peace, unity, or cohesion. So, once again chaos descends when Protestants trumpet *sola scriptura*.

To be sure. But so also does Christianity advance. In 1990, when Mongolia's communist government fell, knowledgeable observers concluded that there were not even ten Christian believers in the entire country. Today, with the scriptures unleashed, there are over 330 individual Christian congregations with close to 50,000 adherents, most of whom are students or young adults.[37] Serious questions continue about the religion that these new Christians practice: Is it authentic Christianity or merely ancestral Buddhism repackaged with a Christian patina? Mongolian believers and missionaries argue earnestly over these difficult questions. But amid the chaos caused by these intense debates, observers from afar can see that where only shortly before there had been no Christianity, now there exists a multitude of Christian churches. Where the Mongolians had not been able to read the scriptures for themselves, the Bible is now widely available and numerous Mongolian consciences have come into contact with the Word of God. *Sola scriptura* is doing its work once again—yes, with a considerable degree of chaos, but not without cohesive effect as well.

Notes

1. Robert Bellarmine, *Disputations*, as excerpted in app. III, in Richard J. Blackwell, *Galileo, Bellarmine, and the Bible* (Notre Dame, IN: University of Notre Dame Press, 1991), 193.
2. For the negative connotation, see Christian Smith, *The Bible Made Impossible: Why Biblicism Is Not a Truly Evangelical Reading of Scripture* (Grand Rapids, MI: Brazos, 2012); for more neutral usage, see James S. Bielo, *Words upon the Word: An Ethnography of Evangelical Group Bible Study* (New York: New York University Press, 2009); and Brian Malley, *How the Bible Works: An Anthropological Study of Evangelical Biblicism* (Walnut Creek, CA: Altamira, 2004).

3. I am relying on a superb student paper, Grace Gerber, "New Testament Translations in Mongolia, 1990–2000," Wheaton College, 2004; and a very helpful account by veteran missionaries to Mongolia, Tom and Lynn Suchy, "Our Position and Perspective on a Critical Commentary" (privately printed, April 2005).

4. Christopher Hill, "The Problem of Authority," in *Collected Essays of Christopher Hill* (Amherst: University of Massachusetts Press, 1986), 2:38.

5. Standard accounts that treat the incidents described below include Roland H. Bainton, *Here I Stand: A Life of Martin Luther* (New York: Abingdon, 1950); and Diarmaid MacCulloch, *The Reformation: A History* (New York: Viking, 2003).

6. "Luther at the Diet of Worms" (orig. 1521), trans. Roger A. Hornsby, in *Luther's Works*, vol. 32: *Career of the Reformer II*, ed. George W. Forell (Philadelphia: Fortress, 1958), 111 (emphasis added).

7. "Luther at the Diet of Worms," 112 (emphasis added).

8. "Luther at the Diet of Worms," 113. The spokesman was Johann Eck, but not the Eck famous for exchanging polemical pamphlets with Luther.

9. "Luther at the Diet of Worms," 114n9.

10. Kenneth A. Strand, *Facsimiles from Early Luther Bibles*, vol. II: *Romans* (Ann Arbor: Ann Arbor Publishers, 1972), 10 ("alleyn durch den glawben").

11. "Prefaces to the New Testament," trans. Charles M. Jacobs and E. Theodore Bachman, in *Luther's Works*, vol. 35: *World and Sacrament* I, ed. E. Theodore Bachman (Philadelphia: Fortress, 1960), 357.

12. A superb edition of the two main books in this exchange is E. Gordon Rupp and Philip S. Watson, eds., *Luther and Erasmus: Free Will and Salvation* (Philadelphia: Westminster, 1969); see 109–12 for Luther on the perscipacity or clarity of scripture.

13. "The Sixty-Seven Articles of Ulrich Zwingli," trans. Mark Noll, in *Confessions and Catechisms of the Reformation*, ed. Mark Noll (Vancouver: Regent College Publishing, 2004 [orig. 1991]), 39.

14. Robert Carroll and Stephen Prickett, "Preface," in *The Bible Authorized King James Version with Apocrypha* (New York: Oxford University Press, 1997), v.

15. "Canons and Decrees of the Council of Trent," excerpted in *Confessions and Catechisms of the Reformation*, ed. Mark Noll (Vancouver: Regent College Publishing, 2004), 172–73 (from *Canons and Decrees of the Council of Trent*, ed. H. J. Schroeder (Rockford, IL: TAN Books, 1978).

16. As only a sampling, see Christopher Hill, *The English Bible and the Seventeenth-Century Revolution* (London: Penguin, 1973); Hans Frei, *The Eclipse of Biblical Narrative: A Study in Eighteenth and Nineteenth Century Hermeneutics* (New Haven, CT: Yale University Press, 1974); Jonathan Sheehan, *The Enlightenment Bible: Translation, Scholarship, Culture* (Princeton, NJ: Princeton University Press, 2005); Michael C. Legaspi, *The Death of Scripture and the Rise of Biblical Studies* (New York: Oxford University Press, 2010); and Brad S. Gregory,

The Unintended Reformation: How a Religious Revolution Secularized Society (Cambridge, MA: Harvard University Press, 2010).

17. John Stott, *The Lausanne Covenant: An Exposition and Commentary* (Minneapolis: World Wide Publications, 1975), 10.

18. John Calvin, *Institutes of the Christian Religion*, trans. Ford Lewis Battles, ed. John T. McNeill (Philadelphia: Westminster, 1960), 1:78 (I.vii.4).

19. For an insightful account of that popularity, see George Marsden, *C. S. Lewis's Mere Christianity: A Biography* (Princeton: Princeton University Press, 2016).

20. C. S. Lewis, *Mere Christianity* (New York: Macmillan, 1952), 9.

21. E. G. Rupp, *Studies in the Making of the English Protestant Tradition* (New York: Cambridge University Press, 1966 [orig. 1946]), 23, quoting from John Foxe's *Acts and Monuments*.

22. Jupiter Hammon, "An Evening Thought. Salvation by Christ, with Penitential Cries ..." (orig. 1760), in *Unchained Voices: An Anthology of Black Authors in the English-Speaking World of the Eighteenth Century*, ed. Vincent Carretta (Lexington: University Press of Kentucky, 1996), 26.

23. Olaudah Equiano, *The Interesting Narrative and Other Writings*, ed. Vincent Carretta (New York: Penguin, 1995), 189–90.

24. Luis Bush with Brent Fulton, "China's Next Generation: New Church, New China, New World," *Global Missiology* 2, no. 14 (January 24, 2014); http://ojs.globalmissiology.org/index.php/english/article/view/1635/3627.

25. Philip Schaff, "Preface," in *Christ in Song: Hymns of Immanuel Selected from All Ages* (London: S. Low, Son, and Marston, 1870), v–vi.

26. As an instance, see the positive assessment by a Reformed Protestant, Hans Boersma, "The Real Presence of Hope & Love: The Christocentric Legacy of Benedict XVI," *Books & Culture*, September/October 2013, 11–14. Cf. Mark A. Noll and James Turner, *The Future of Christian Learning: An Evangelical and Catholic Dialogue*, ed. Thomas Albert Howard (Grand Rapids, MI: Brazos, 2008).

27. Eric Doyle O.F.M., "William Woodford on Scripture and Tradition," in *Studia Historico-Ecclesiastica: Festgabe für Prof. Luchesius G. Spätling O.F.M.*, ed. Isaac Vázquez O.F.M. (Rome: Pontificium Athenaeum Antonianum, 1977), 481–502 (quotation on 501).

28. I have benefited especially from Michael Hurley, *Scriptura Sola: Wyclif and his Critics* (New York: Fordham University Press, 1960); Heiko Augustinus Oberman, *The Harvest of Medieval Theology: Gabriel Biel and Late Medieval Nominalism* (Durham, NC: Labyrinth, 1983 [orig. 1963]), esp. 371–98; G. C. Berkouwer, *Holy Scripture* (Grand Rapids, MI: Eerdmans, 1975); Doyle, "William Woodford"; and Keith A. Mathisen, *The Shape of Sola Scriptura* (Moscow, ID: Canon, 2001).

29. The phrase is from Doyle, "Woodford," 502.

30. Doyle, "Woodford."

31. Hurley, *Scriptura Sola*, 25.

32. Oberman, *Harvest*, 371–78;. Alister E. McGrath, *Historical Theology: An Introduction to the History of Christian Thought*, 2nd ed. (Chichester, West Sussex: Wiley-Blackwell, 2102), 151–52.

33. John Wyclif,*On the Truth of Holy Scripture*, trans. and ed. Ian Christopher Levy (Kalamazoo, MI: TEAMS by Medieval Institute Publications, 2001), 80; translating *John Wyclif's De Veritate Sacrae Scripturae Now First Edited from the Manuscripts with Critical and Historical Notes*, ed. Rudolf Buddensieg (London: Wyclif Society, 1905), 80.

34. Oberman, *Harvest*, 377.

35. Berkouwer, *Holy Scripture*, 306.

36. Gerald R. McDermott, "Is *Sola Scriptura* Really *Sola?* Edwards, Newman, Bultmann, and Wright on the Bible as Religious Authority," in *By What Authority: The Vital Questions of Religious Authority in Christianity*, ed. Robert L. Millet (Macon, GA: Mercer University Press, 2010), 72.

37. See "Mongolia," in Jason Mandryk, *Operation World*, 7th ed. (Downers Grove, IL: InterVarsity Press, 2010), 594–97.

PART III

Theological Considerations

12

Martin Luther at 500 and the State of Global Lutheranism

Sarah Hinlicky Wilson

WHEN I WAS NINE years old, my fourth-grade class did a unit on Martin Luther King Jr. for Black History Month. Kicking off the activities on a Monday morning, my teacher asked the class to tell her anything we knew about Martin Luther King Jr.—anything at all. My hand immediately shot into the air. The teacher called my name, and I relayed what was, to me, a Lutheran, clearly the most interesting and relevant detail about him: "He was named after Martin Luther." The teacher, rather stunned by my response, replied after a pause, "That's right, Sarah. He was named after his father, Martin Luther King Sr."[1] The conversation moved on—undoubtedly to the *genuinely* relevant details of the life of the great civil rights leader—before I could protest the misunderstanding.

Meeting people who don't know the difference between Martin Luther and Martin Luther King Jr. is a pretty routine experience for Lutherans in America. But at least that mistake is easy to correct. The much more difficult problem is separating what people *think* they know about the sixteenth-century Martin Luther and what is actually the case about the sixteenth-century Martin Luther. I don't mean to suggest a naïve confidence in our ability to reproduce a flawless, historically accurate Luther in our day and age, one that is not subject to later revision and enhanced understanding. But I do mean to call attention to the mythology that surrounds Luther like an obfuscating fog—a fog that clings to self-professed Lutherans as much as to the casual student of Western civilization or the prolific Internet commentator.

So, depending on whom you consult, you might get any one of the following Luthers. There's the Luther who was, above all, a champion of conscience and forever set us free from the heavy hand of authority. He is probably the most popular mythological Luther. A close second is the strident reformer Luther who knowingly and intentionally tore down the Catholic religious hierarchy in order to replace it with universal equality of access to and knowledge about God, everyone the priest of his or her own private religion. These two depictions of Luther are generally meant to be laudatory, although not always. Then there are the bad-guy Luthers, such as the Luther-who-couldn't-keep-his-pants-on[2] and the Luther-who-ultimately-caused-the-Holocaust.[3] This last is the one most likely to be known and despised by those who reject Christianity altogether.

Such Luthers are broadly and sloppily painted, and they can be refuted if those holding to such mythological portraits are willing to listen to countervailing evidence. But then there are the more sophisticated mythological Luthers, the ones fleshed out and defended by those most heavily invested in maintaining the status quo of religious division—in other words, theologians. So, you will find a Catholic account of Luther that modestly admits that maybe some things were out of order in the late medieval church, but Luther's "subjectivism" and "individualism" unfortunately put him beyond the pale of legitimate Christianity. You'll find a Reformed or Baptist or Pentecostal version of Luther that appreciates the good start he got on cleaning up a messy house, but unfortunately, he did not go quite far enough, remaining stuck in the old Catholic thought-world. You'll find a Lutheran version of Luther that sees him as the apex of church history, a solitary genius, an innovator, the creator of a structure of Christian thought incompatible with any other form, to be accepted in whole or rejected in whole. And you'll even find an ecumenical version of Luther that renders him entirely unproblematic for anyone—barring, of course, his demonization of Jews, Turks, Papists, and Anabaptists. Albert Schweitzer said that the quest for the historical Jesus ended in scholars beholding their own faces reflected back in Jesus'. In the quest for the historical Luther, we see not so much our own faces reflected as we see the state of the church we want to promote or reject. That both Jesus and Luther become invisible in this process is not surprising.

By now I have nicely set myself up for an impossible task: to present the real, pure, untrammeled, unideologized Luther. I don't pretend to be able to do that any better than anyone else can. Even if ideology were not a problem, systematizing would be: as countless scholars have noted, Luther never composed a systematic theology in the style of Thomas Aquinas or John Calvin. Rather, he worked his way intuitively from one theological locus or pastoral-care challenge or ecclesiastical problem to the next, and as the pace of events picked up, he was forced to engage with what lay right in front of him.[4] Any attempt to summarize Luther's theology loses the setting and much of the excitement that characterized the unfolding of his career and the development of his thought over the course of four decades.

What I can offer here is a brief portrait of what Luther believed was at the heart of the Christian faith, the bone-deep conviction that motivated everything else. Because whatever else he may have supported or decried, in church or in society, the source of it all, for Luther, was the gospel of Jesus Christ.

Real Presence in Luther's Theology

There are many excellent shorthand approaches to Luther's theology. Two particularly commendable ones are Johann Anselm Steiger's use of the *communicatio idiomatum*[5] and Risto Saarinen's application of the giver-and-gift motif.[6] My point of entry is not far from either: the real presence. This term is most familiar as relating to Luther's sacramental theology, and with good reason. He insisted that the whole gospel is summed up in the real presence: whether Christ, who is God, is there for you in the bread and the cup or not. If Christ the Lord, the divine and incarnate Son, is not there where he says his body and blood are in their lowly humanity, then everything else falls apart, the promise is void, the incarnation is a fake, the resurrection avails nothing, and your sins are not forgiven. There is no good news if the good news is not precisely the real presence of God in what appears to be a godless and godforsaken world.

Far from being a nostalgic hangover of medieval metaphysics— as later Protestants often accused Luther—the real presence in the Lord's Supper is for Luther the consistent and coherent outcome of his Christology.[7] Jesus is the man in whom God is so really and truly present that he is in fact God Himself,[8] God in the flesh. There is no good news about the crucified itinerant teacher of Galilee and Judea if he is not God, too. For this reason Luther insisted so strongly on the full communication of attributes and the unity of the person of Christ.[9] All that is human is given to the divine—so God truly suffers and dies on the cross in this Jesus. And all that is divine is given to the human—so we can identify that poor little baby lying in the manger as the creator of the universe. Luther writes: "Wherever this person is, it is the single, indivisible person, and if you can say, 'Here is God,' then you must also say, 'Christ the man is present too.' And if you could show me one place where God is and not the man, then the person is already divided and I could at once say truthfully, 'Here is God who is not man and has never become man.' But no God like that for me!"[10] It is no accident that this and many other Christological assertions are found in Luther's treatise "Confession Concerning Christ's Supper": Christology and sacramentology are tightly interwoven.

The real presence that is the incarnation extends to the Lord's Supper, as I have already noted, but it is by no means restricted to it. The church's whole ministry of reconciliation requires and depends on the real presence. Thus of baptism Luther says, in the *Large Catechism*, "To be baptized in God's name is to be baptized not by human beings but by God himself. Although it is performed by human hands, it is nevertheless truly God's own act."[11] Likewise, pastors and preachers never speak on their own authority, out of their own religious convictions or compassionate hearts (though we generally prefer it when those qualities are present, too). As Luther wrote, "[T]he office of preaching is not our office but God's. But whatever is God's, that we do not do ourselves; but He does it Himself, through the Word and the office, as His own gift and business."[12] The task of the ministers of the gospel is to speak God's own words directly to the sinner: "Your sins are forgiven." In fact, the German Luther scholar Oswald Bayer argues that the "real" Reformation breakthrough was not the 95 Theses of 1517 but the 50 Theses on the Remission of Sins from 1518,[13] where Luther argued strongly that the promise of Christ to forgive through absolution is the decisive reality, not the contrition of the sinner or the authority of the priest.[14] If Bayer is right, then we'll all be commemorating the Reformation a year too early! That aside, the point is that the real presence of Christ in the word of forgiveness is the reason and lifeblood of the Christian ministry.

And further, what the presence of Christ in preaching, absolution, baptism, and the Lord's Supper all intend is justification by faith. Here especially, a corrective to misunderstandings about Luther's teaching on faith is badly needed.[15] Is having faith something we human beings do, for God, as our offering to Him, a mental trick indifferent to our hearts or ensuing behavior, an assent to historic facts that even the demons share, which in turn earns us the Holy Spirit? If that is the case, then Lutherans are the worst Pelagians of them all. But that is most certainly not what Luther meant. Quite the contrary, it is the really present Christ in faith who does the believing that justifies us; it is the really present Holy Spirit Who hears the Word for us and in us.[16] Faith is the presence of Christ and the Spirit in us—clinging to the promises of the Father despite all appearances to the contrary, fighting off the sin and death and devil that continue to afflict us. Christ himself is our righteousness, present in faith, and that is why we are declared righteous.

And because our justification by faith always includes the renewal of the heart, it should be no surprise that God is and must be present in sanctification as well; this is the real continuity between justification and sanctification, which an absent-God theology will always try to tear apart. As Luther wrote in his early treatise, "The Freedom of a Christian":

> Who then can comprehend the riches and the glory of the Christian life? It can do all things and has all things and lacks nothing. It is lord over sin, death, and hell, and yet at the same time it serves, ministers to, and benefits all men. But ... we are altogether ignorant of our own name and do not know why we are Christians or bear the name of Christians. Surely we are named after Christ, not because he is absent from us, but because he dwells in us, that is, because we believe in him and are Christs one to another and do to our neighbors as Christ does to us.[17]

The fitting counterpart to the truly present Christ working sanctification in us is the real presence of Christ in the neighbor whom we are commanded to serve. The most basic diaconal text of the New Testament is "as you did it to one of the least of these ... you did it to me" (Matt. 25:40, ESV). Christ is truly present in our neighbors, and in serving them we serve him, in honoring them we honor him. As Gustav Wingren has observed, the neighbor is at the center of Luther's ethics.[18] The ecclesial, social, and political implications of this are enormous.[19] And here at last we begin to see the unfolding of the massive social and diaconal project of the Lutheran reformers. For if Christ is truly present everywhere—as Luther's doctrine of ubiquity argued, consistent with his Christology— and if it is Christ who animates our faith and service, then the Christian need not hide from the world, fearing infection, but must turn outward, seeking the neighbor just as God sought us. God does not need our good works, but our neighbor certainly does.[20] God intends to serve our neighbor through us, masking Himself in our ordinary lives of work and family,[21] and honoring us when we join Him in the service of others.[22]

The real presence of Christ is *a* dominating if not *the* dominating theme of Luther's theology, but it has a fearful counterpart. The real presence of Christ is always dogged and persecuted by the real presence of the devil. Luther's conviction regarding demonic presence is rejected by many today, and partly with good reason: Luther at times became entirely too confident about identifying the devil's work with a particular group of people—one of the most dangerous and destructive habits of the human race, at which Luther unfortunately excelled. As we commemorate 2017, that piece of his legacy certainly should be cast aside, once and for all. But the misuse of his own conviction ought not blind us to the real intuitions he had. Remember that Luther's doctrine of God starts from the cross: whatever else we know about human beings and about God, their intersection lies on the cross. One of the reasons Luther would not tolerate optimistic anthropologies in the form of, most famously, justification by works is that they could never do justice to the unfathomable horror and metaphysical trauma of God nailed to a tree.

Likewise, if Luther gave way at times to an excessive apocalyptic fervor—a recurring theme in Christianity that the reformer also eagerly took up and made his own—it was due to a painfully realistic assessment of the evils human beings inflict on one another. It is surprising, in the wake of the last bloody century, that we still either dismiss or sensationalize the demonic, neither of which approach is capable of dealing with the reality of evil. In Luther's perspective, the course of human history is neither decline nor progress but, instead, a struggle between Christ and the powers and principalities that will continue until the Last Day. Even the best of human institutions, movements, and ideas cannot remain immune to the devil's active perversion of them in the course of history.[23] The battle for civic righteousness in this world—and how much more the battle toward holiness!—can only be carried out, can only be survived, in the perspective of eschatological hope.

The picture we should have of Luther's thought by now is that the real presence is never generic, not a pious affirmation nor a silent accompaniment of the sort advocated under the rubric "ministry of presence." It's more like an invasion. Emmanuel, God with us, seizes His own creation back from its distortion at the hands of sin, death, and the devil by suffusing it with His presence, empowering every good act, from a mother breastfeeding her infant to the gentle words of forgiveness spoken to an exhausted sinner. Luther would not consider evil to be a deal breaker for faith; quite the contrary, it is the good that is the deal breaker for unbelief.

Global Lutheranism, 500 Years Later

It is with this perspective—the real presence of Christ in His creation as Luther's foundational teaching—that I turn to the matter of Lutheranism five hundred years after the start of the Reformation. The struggle between God and the devil for the public space of creation was why Lutherans contended that such a thing as the Reformation was necessary in its time: for also the church—in fact, *supremely* the church, as the very conduit of God's forgiveness—is prey to the assaults of the devil. The same is the reason for the Protestant slogan *ecclesia semper reformanda*, the church always reforming. Whether this vision with its full metaphysical consequences is still the determining one in Lutheran churches today, especially the older ones, is rather more in question. Generally it is the sheer fact of change, not the perversion of the good and the gospel's determination to reclaim what has been subjected to sin, that animates contemporary language regarding reform.

That makes popular and ecclesial attempts to advertise the Reformation as something generally good for society naïve at best. My impression of much of the build-up to 2017 in European Lutheranism—admittedly, as an American with a particular set of cultural lenses—is that the Reformation is being touted as that which gave the Europeans of today many of the social and civilizational benefits they enjoy. The subtext is: therefore, ye masses who have deserted Christianity, give the church another chance, but if not, at least do us the honor of recognizing all the gifts we have given you.

I have to say, this appears to me as a real failure of nerve, if not of faith altogether. Again in the words of Gustav Wingren, "It is hard to avoid the suspicion that the present enormous interest in the good moral and social consequences of Christian faith arose simultaneously with the loss of the simple belief in actual life after death."[24] Can Christ's benefits be enjoyed without Christ? Luther certainly didn't think so, nor did he think that Christ's benefits held a candle to Christ himself. As Luther wrote in his early commentary on the Magnificat, "In giving us the gifts He gives only what is His, but in His grace and His regard of us He gives His very self.

In the gifts we touch His hand; but in His gracious regard we receive His heart, spirit, mind, and will."[25] And again, in the Large Catechism: "[T]he Creed brings pure grace and makes us righteous and acceptable to God. Through this knowledge we come to love and delight in all the commandments of God because we see here in the Creed how God gives himself completely to us, with all his gifts and power, to help us keep the Ten Commandments: the Father gives us all creation, Christ all his works, the Holy Spirit all his gifts."[26] To desire the gifts of God without desiring the real presence of God is to insult the giver and ultimately to endanger the gifts. If Lutheranism and Christianity more broadly have done society any good such that this good should continue, they will only succeed insofar as they bring people into contact with the real presence of Christ. It is Christ-clinging faith that gives rise to devil-defeating love. The secondary approach is not only doomed to failure but it also smacks of the desperate propaganda of a dying movement.

This, of course, is not a problem restricted to the old Lutheran churches of Europe, nor the middle-aged ones of North America that in many ways mimic their elders, though in the setting of fierce religious competition instead of folk- or state-church privilege. All the historic churches of the North Atlantic world are coping with the loss of voice, nerve, and faith, as has been amply documented. And like other Christians, northern Lutherans are discovering the almost unnerving vitality of their younger sister Lutheran churches in the Global South—among them the million-member Lutheran church in Papua New Guinea, the dozen Lutheran churches of Indonesia that range in size from twelve thousand to over 4 million, and the truly massive churches in Ethiopia and Tanzania, both of them hovering around 6 million members.[27]

Over the past five years I have had the honor of teaching an annual two-week intensive course on Luther's theology in Wittenberg, Germany, with my colleague Theodor Dieter. The seminar is for pastors of churches belonging to the Lutheran World Federation (LWF), an organization whose two tasks are to practice diakonia toward all in need and to foster communion among the 95 percent of the world's Lutherans whose churches belong to LWF. The participants in our seminar are deliberately drawn from all regions of the world—some facility in English is the only real prerequisite—with the idea that study of our common theological ancestor in his own city of action can build up our communion and create spiritual friendships across the planet. Theodor and I went into this project with some trepidation. We had no real idea how Luther would "play" outside of the cultures that bear some direct relationship to his sixteenth-century Germany. It was a live question whether Luther's theology was as universal as we hoped and believed, or if that was only a matter of our own wishful thinking and narrow horizons.

As it turns out, our hopes were confirmed beyond our wildest dreams. Most of our Global South participants have never encountered any Luther texts directly, owing to limited resources, lack of translations, or little opportunity at ecumenical seminaries. Yet their response is powerful and sustained. I have never worked a group of students so hard as the ones who come to these annual seminars. I have also never before encountered students who never complained and even asked for more; some have started up Luther reading groups for other pastors back home. They all get caught up in the immediacy and applicability of Luther to the diverse situations they find themselves in. I do not think it is overstating the situation to say that the seminar functions like a conversion experience for them—and, I should add, for most of those coming from older Lutheran churches also, to whom Luther is such a constant companion that he has been rendered invisible and uninteresting.[28]

I had much the same experience in the summer of 2012, teaching a shorter course on Luther for charismatic preachers of the Ethiopian Evangelical (Lutheran) Church Mekane Yesus, which has about 2,600 ordained clergy, 8,000 congregations, and 300,000 lay preachers; clearly, this was a church that has finally managed to take Luther's teaching on the priesthood of all believers seriously! My hundred or so students were not only extraordinarily attentive but they also pushed for more and asked questions that stretched me to the limits of my own theological knowledge.[29] A massive project of translating Luther into Amharic is under way in Ethiopia at present, as is happening in Brazil, where Luther is being translated into Portuguese and into Spanish in other Latin American countries. Luther appeared in Estonian for the first time last year. We are just now beginning to see the first fruits of a globally interpreted Luther.[30]

Division, Correction, and Commemoration

But a global Lutheranism also implies the exportation of 500-year-old controversies to the rest of the world. That is, tragically, unavoidable. All new Christians are baptized into Christ, but they are also baptized into Lutheranism, Catholicism, Pentecostalism, Evangelicalism, Methodism, or whatever other -ism is now an unavoidable part of Christian identity—even, and ironically, "Nondenominationalism." It was a timely rebuke to the comfortable status quo of division that the modern ecumenical movement arose directly in response to the mission movement, officially at the Edinburgh Missionary Conference of 1910, where "Old World" Christians were forced to acknowledge that their competition for converts, and their own internecine polemics, was not a very convincing display of the love that is supposed to characterize Jesus's disciples.

At the same time, church divisions are ancient—the New Testament is peppered with them—and the issues disputed, even if laced and laden with plain old unrepented sin, usually touch on real and pressing issues of interpretation. Ecumenism invites us not to a suppression of differences but, rather, to an open-minded, open-hearted, and open-ended reckoning with them. Disputes will not go away but division might, as long as we recognize that such can happen only through the fruit of the Spirit. It is easy to practice tribal love, joy, and peace once we have driven out the intruders, but even the Gentiles can do that (Matt. 5:47). Christian divisions are the testing ground for the genuineness of the Spirit's fruit among us.

For this reason there is a special burden on the 2017 commemoration of the Reformation: not only is it the nice round number 500, but it is the first commemoration since Lutherans and Catholics—the seminal actors in the radical transformation of the Western church that started in 1517—have started talking to each other again.[31] Both the regional and the international dialogues between these churches have produced studies of exceptional depth and quality, clearing away a host of misunderstandings and recognizing new possibilities for rapprochement. The apex of this process was the 1999 Joint Declaration on the Doctrine of Justification, the first and only time the Catholic Church has promulgated a binding doctrinal statement together with a Protestant church.[32]

Although the Joint Declaration has not been without its naysayers on both sides for its common formulations, perhaps the more remarkable thing about it is that it did not require either church to stop being itself or to abandon its specific emphases. Both Catholics and Lutherans were granted their theological particularities. These particularities were explained in such a way as to remove confusion and offense at the other's typical misinterpretations of them, but not to deny the importance of the particularity in the shaping and ethos of each church's theology.[33]

The ability to grant the legitimacy of the other's formulation is itself a recognition of a deeper reality: that Lutheran theology and Catholic theology did not develop in isolation from one another, much less as pure and unmediated responses to the Word of God but, rather, in a definite state of controversy and mutual opposition that has left a permanent mark on both. There is, in fact, no such thing as either Catholic or Lutheran theology today without the presence of the other lurking in the background, whether as a mere annoyance or as an outright threat.[34] As the 1983 dialogue statement, "Martin Luther: Witness to Jesus Christ," describes it:

> For centuries opinions about Luther were diametrically opposed to one another. Catholics saw him as the personification of heresy and blamed him as the fundamental cause of schism between the Western churches. Already in the sixteenth century, the Protestants began to glorify Luther as a religious hero and not infrequently also as a national hero. Above all, however, Luther was often regarded as the founder of a new church. The judgment of Luther was closely connected with each church's view of the other: they accused one another of abandoning the true faith and the true church. (§I.2–3)[35]

The statement then goes on to specify the distortions that took place in each church. One important admission is how the Lutheran churches "have tried over the centuries to conserve Luther's theological and spiritual insights. Not all his writings, however, have influenced the Lutheran churches to the same degree. There has often been a tendency to give more importance to his polemical works than to his pastoral and theological writings. ... Luther's heritage has suffered various losses and distortions in the course of history" (§IV.18–19). In turn, Catholics admit: "A defensive attitude toward Luther and his thinking was in some respects determinative for the Roman Catholic Church and its development since the Reformation. Fear of the distribution of editions of the Bible unauthorized by the church, a centralizing over-emphasis on the papacy, and a one-sidedness in sacramental theology and practice were deliberately developed features of Counter-Reformation Catholicism" (§IV.21).[36]

Many self-corrections have taken place in both churches, partly as a result of ecumenical dialogue itself, partly as a recognition of the radical social changes taking place in the world that have shifted the pieces of the puzzle and heightened the urgency of making a united witness. And that means it is no longer possible for Lutherans to contemplate a celebration of 2017 in a way that requires today's Catholic Church to be the same old bad guy of ages past. Nor is it possible for today's Catholic Church to maintain the line that Luther is the heresiarch of heresiarchs and so stonily ignore the date. Neither one-sided triumph nor other-directed denunciation is an option anymore. So what could 2017 mean for them?

The international Lutheran-Catholic dialogue has taken up the issue again with its 2013 statement, "From Conflict to Communion."[37] Meant as a study guide from the lay to the leadership level, the text starts out by analyzing the changed situation between Lutherans and Catholics and what factors on both sides led to the change. It then lays out the characteristic theology of both sides in a way that is meant to be mutually accessible: first Luther's theology in the setting of the sixteenth-century Reformation—with a great deal of attention given to the political and military pressures on both sides that cut short any hope of real dialogue—followed by a careful setting of his theology within the Catholic thought-world, taking into account the Council of Trent but clearly treating the Second Vatican Council as the decisive touchstone. Finally, it draws the consequences for a mutual commemoration of 2017, which is remarkable in itself: the very idea that mutual commemoration is possible!

But commemoration can be a dodge. It is one thing to acknowledge that something very big and important happened five hundred years ago. It is another thing to evaluate it conscientiously and then, as a result, either repent or celebrate as appropriate. It will be a mark of the maturity of the ecumenical movement if, in 2017, Lutherans prove able to repent and celebrate in equal measure—not just one or the other—and likewise if Catholics prove able to celebrate at all. To further this possibility, I would like to conclude by suggesting a two-part task for all parties concerned to take up in light of the 2017 commemoration.

Recognizing the aforementioned reality that hostility shapes confessional theology,[38] I would like to see theologians on all sides take up the reconstructive task of disentangling the hostility from the churches' respective theologies and reimagining, counterfactually and optatively, what these might be like without the hostility written into them. This is not so much a request for an ecumenical "super-theology" or a lowest-common-denominator theology as it is for a multiplicity of purged confessional theologies, maintaining the particular gifts and insights on all sides while remaining open to the truly Christian insight of the other, even of the old enemy.

At the same time, I would like to see deep and careful historical work examining just how the politics and personalities of the Reformation led to such explosive and enduring results. Why, after all, did this reformer in a line of so many Western Christian reformers earn himself such a dire response? How did his counter-response set the conditions for later developments? To what extent did state violence and individual martyrdom close down possibilities for reconciliation? Interested historians could do no better than to follow the path laid down by the Lutheran-Mennonite dialogue, whose first-ever, jointly written history of Lutheran-Anabaptist relations in the sixteenth century paved the way for a public declaration of repentance and request for forgiveness on the part of the Lutheran World Federation in 2010, which was met with a full declaration of forgiveness on the part of the Mennonite World Conference.[39] The same project undertaken by Lutherans and Catholics would, I am convinced, break down many barriers and open up new possibilities for unity that will remain invisible to us as long as we refuse to confess our sins openly and in detail.

Neither task can be undertaken on human steam alone. Freeing ourselves from the burden of our guilt-laden pasts can be accomplished only by the power of the one Who takes away the sin of the world. Half a millennium has passed since 1517 and in the intervening years we have seen how the presence of Christ is working itself into the far corners of the world, bringing His grace and peace. At the same time, his "adversary the devil prowls around like a roaring lion" (1 Pet. 5:8). So it will be until the final enemy is defeated and Christ is all in all.

In the meanwhile, what lies before us is simply the task of clinging to the really present Christ in faith and turning to our neighbors, near and far, in love. If the church needs to be reformed along the way for the sake of this faith and love, so be it. Insofar as Luther can be of service in these tasks, I hope Lutherans will continue to turn to him for insight and guidance. But we do not retain the copyright on the reformer, and we have not always been the best ambassadors for his witness. Luther at five hundred is not primarily for Lutherans but for all who hunger for the real presence of Christ. The best anniversary that I can imagine for the Reformation at five hundred is a prodigal distribution of Christ to the hungry, as well as to those who have not yet realized that they are starving. In such a celebration, I expect Luther will be only one—a conspicuous one, no doubt—but only one of the many saints of the church present at the table.

Notes

1. To be precise, both Sr. and Jr. originally were named Michael Luther King. King Sr. changed both of their first names to Martin when King Jr. was five years old, in honor of the reformer, after a visit to Berlin for a congress of the Baptist World Alliance.

2. King Henry VIII of England promoted this view—ironically, in view of later events in his own life. See Martin Treu, "Katharina von Bora, the Woman at Luther's Side," *Lutheran Quarterly* 13 (1999): 162. Luther, in fact, believed he had received the divine gift of chastity; it was because of others' struggles, not his own, that he argued in favor of married clergy (that, and the Bible). Initially his marriage to Katharina von Bora appears to have been an act of faith, not desire, though the desire followed.

3. I have no interest in defending Luther's unconscionable statements about and against the Jews. The only remark worth making is the contextual one: Luther said what his fellow Christians had been saying for nearly 1,500 years; he only said it with greater rhetorical skill and with his own fame to back it up. To their credit, his friends tried to suppress the worst of his writings and they were forgotten by everyone, including Jews, until the twentieth century. Among other recent Lutheran rejections of Luther's destructive words, see "Declaration of ELCA to Jewish Community," available online at www.elca.org/Who-We-Are/ Our-Three-Expressions/Churchwide-Organization/Office-of-the-Presiding-Bishop/Ecumenical-and-Inter-Religious-Relations/Inter-Religious-Relations/ Christian-Jewish-Relations/Declaration-of-ELCA-to-Jewish-Community.aspx. See also the critical study by Lutheran theologian Paul R. Hinlicky, *Before Auschwitz: What Christian Theology Must Learn from the Rise of Nazism* (Eugene, OR: Cascade, 2013), and the excellent chapter by John Witte Jr. in this volume.

4. However, he did recognize the importance of returning ever afresh to the scripture and other theological sources so as not to be controlled by the battle of the moment. As he remarked in the preface to the German version of his Jonah commentary, "For some time I have entered the lists and fought against these spirits and factions. Now that others have joined the fray, I have decided to take Scripture in hand again to feast our hearts, to strengthen, to comfort, and to arm them, lest fatigue and lassitude subdue us in our daily struggle." In *Luther's Works*, American ed., ed. J. Pelikan and H. Lehmann (St. Louis and Philadelphia: Concordia and Fortress, 1955ff.) [hereafter, *LW*], 19:35.

5. The *communicatio idiomatum*—literally, the "communication of properties"—is a Christological confession that all the human properties of Jesus Christ are also "communicated" to his divine nature, and all his divine properties are communicated to his human nature. Luther strongly held to the full exchange in both directions. See Anselm Steiger, "The *communicatio idiomatum* as the Axle and Motor of Luther's Theology," trans. Carolyn Schneider, *Lutheran Quarterly* 14 (2000): 125–58.

6. Risto Saarinen, "Theology of Giving as a Comprehensive Lutheran Theology," in *Transformations in Luther's Theology: Historical and Contemporary Reflections*, ed. Christine Helmer and Bo Kristian Holm (Leipzig: Evangelische Verlagsanstalt, 2011), 141–59. See also Walther von Löwenich's classic study, *Luther's Theology of the Cross* (Minneapolis, MN: Augsburg, 1976 [1929]), though it should be noted that "the theology of the cross" as found in the Heidelberg Disputation is an emphasis of Luther's early career. While the cross was always central to his understanding of the Christian faith, "the theology of the cross" as a method or interpretive lens did not stay the course in his thought.

7. See the wonderful study by Marc Lienhard, *Luther: Witness to Jesus Christ: Stages and Themes of the Reformer's Christology* (Minneapolis, MN: Augsburg, 1982).

8. I use grammatically masculine pronouns when referring to God in the third person, following the biblical pattern. However, mindful of the fact that this does not mean that God is male the way biological creatures are male—also a strong biblical claim—I capitalize these, as well as all other pronouns for God, to emphasize the distinction. I generally use the lowercase when referring to Jesus, since his maleness is a matter of human biology. In quotations I retain the format of the original.

9. Like Cyril of Alexandria, Luther started from the unity of Christ rather than from the two natures and their respective capacities, which then would somehow have to be harmonized. It would not be wrong to say that Luther demonstrates an appreciation for the lost witness of the Miaphysites against the Tome of Leo, the latter of which reached its apex in Zwingli, demonstrating the odd similarity in Reformed and Catholic Christology despite their differing sacramental conclusions.

10. Martin Luther, "Confession Concerning Christ's Supper," *LW* 37:218–19. I am persuaded by Luther's christological argument in this treatise. At the same time, I find his deliberately offensive mockery of Zwingli to be a real failure. Certainly it was part of the rhetoric of the time, and certainly Luther realized how much was at stake for us and for our salvation. Nevertheless, if he had really hoped to draw Zwingli to the truth, could he have expected to do so with such disrespectful attacks on Zwingli's person, thought, and even his Swiss German language? Luther's style closed down any possibility of growth in understanding on Zwingli's part instead of fostering it. Even when we can accept Luther's arguments today, we should reject his insulting strategies of (non) communication.

11. Martin Luther, "The Large Catechism," in *The Book of Concord: The Confessions of the Evangelical Lutheran Church*, ed. Robert Kolb and Timothy J. Wengert (Minneapolis, MN: Fortress, 2000) [hereafter, *BC*], 457.

12. Luther's commentary on the Sermon on the Mount (1530/32), *LW* 21:119.

13. I have published a translation entitled "For the Sake of Investigating the Truth and Comforting Terrified Consciences," *Lutheran Forum* 44, no. 4 (2010): 34–35.

A slightly revised translation of the same will appear in the forthcoming vol. 72 of *Luther's Works*.

14. Oswald Bayer, *Promissio: Geschichte der reformatorischen Wende in Luthers Theologie* (Göttingen: Vandenhoeck & Ruprecht, 1971), 182–202.

15. The Finnish school of research on Luther has famously brought these issues to wider attention. In English, see Tuomo Mannermaa, *Christ Present in Faith: Luther's View of Justification*, ed. Kirsi Stjerna (Minneapolis, MN: Fortress, 2005); and Kirsi Stjerna, ed., *Two Kinds of Love: Martin Luther's Religious World* (Minneapolis, MN: Fortress, 2010); also Carl E. Braaten and Robert W. Jenson, eds., *Union with Christ: The New Finnish Interpretation of Luther* (Grand Rapids, MI: Eerdmans, 1998).

16. Thus Gustav Wingren: "[F]aith is simply the presence of Christ." In *Luther on Vocation*, trans. Carl C. Rasmussen (Eugene, OR: Wipf and Stock, 2004 [1957]), 31.

17. Again, Wingren: "Christ is present with men in these works, since they serve others. And he is also present there bringing forth faith. Faith and works are never to be divorced. If a person begins in faith, works immediately leap forth, for faith is Christ." Wingren, *Luther on Vocation*, 32. Luther also expresses the faith-works relationship nicely in his treatise "On What to Look for and Expect in the Gospels": "Now when you have Christ as the foundation and chief blessing of your salvation, then the other part follows: that you take him as your example, giving yourself in service to your neighbor just as you see that Christ has given himself for you. See, there faith and love move forward, God's commandment is fulfilled, and a person is happy and fearless to do and to suffer all things. Therefore make note of this, that Christ as a gift nourishes your faith and makes you a Christian. But Christ as an example exercises your works. These do not make you a Christian. Actually they come forth from you because you have already been made a Christian. As widely as a gift differs from an example, so widely does faith differ from works, for faith possesses nothing of its own, only the deeds and life of Christ. Works have something of your own in them, yet they should not belong to you but to your neighbor." *LW* 35:120.

18. Wingren, *Luther on Vocation*, 46. Unfortunately if not surprisingly, Wingren shares the mild antinomianism of many Lutherans who insist on understanding "the law" only in the sense of accusing power or legalism, never as Torah or instruction, which is not faithful to Luther and certainly not to the scripture. One cannot discover "what is of greatest benefit to a neighbor" (49) apart from the teaching of God's law, though Wingren is right to point out that a strictly rule-based fulfillment of the law lacks both the motivation of love and attention to the particularity of the neighbor. See my article that tries to offer a corrective interpretation of Luther on this point: "The Law of God," *Lutheran Quarterly* 27, no. 4 (2013): 373–98.

19. But note: "Luther takes it as a matter of fact that to be a Christian implies the renewing of the earthly realm, where the Christian is. But the same is true of every able and intelligent person who is faithful to his position. Luther does not compare the Christian and the non-Christian in their works on earth, or contentedly affirm that the Christian is foremost. That would be a blow at Christianity's character as pure grace, and an infraction of the spontaneous gladness of the child of God. Luther recognizes two kingdoms, not just one. There is in him no apologetic tendency to argue for Christianity on the claim that its 'contributions' to earthly matters are indispensable." Wingren, *Luther on Vocation*, 144–45.

20. This aphorism is usually attributed to Luther; it's actually Wingren's summary of Luther, in *Luther on Vocation*, 10. But see Luther's commentary on 1 Pet. 1:15–16: "Now when I have given God this honor, then whatever life I live, I live for my neighbor, to serve and help him. The greatest work that comes from faith is this, that I confess Christ with my mouth and, if it has to be, bear testimony with my blood and risk my life. Yet God does not need the work; but I should do it to prove and confess my faith, in order that others, too, may be brought to faith. Then other works will follow. They must all tend to serve my neighbor. All this God must bring about in us." *LW* 30:32–33.

21. In Luther's exposition of Psalm 147:13 from 1532: "God could easily give you grain and fruit without your plowing and planting. But He does not want to do so. Neither does He want your plowing and planting alone to give you grain and fruit; but you are to plow and plant and then ask His blessing. . . . What else is all our work to God—whether in the fields, in the garden, in the city, in the house, in war, or in government—but just such a child's performance, by which He wants to give His gifts in the fields, at home, and everywhere else? These are the masks of God, behind which He wants to remain concealed and do all things." *LW* 14:114.

22. "If you ask why God does not undertake these good works himself since God obviously knows how to help every person, here is the answer. God certainly can do them but prefers not to do them alone. God wants us to work together with him, and God does us the honor of accomplishing his work with and through us. If we decline to accept this honor, then God will do it alone and help the poor. Those people, however, who did not wish to help God and scorned that great honor will be damned along with the doers of injustice and be considered with their confreres. In like manner, God alone is blessed, but he will also give us the honor and not be blessed by himself. The commandments would be given to us in vain if only God were active, because no one would have cause to exercise themselves in the great works of these commandments." Martin Luther, *Treatise on Good Works*, trans. Scott H. Hendrix (Minneapolis, MN: Fortress, 2012), 54–55.

23. Luther "is convinced that the devil is still present as change for the better is made; and his concept of sin proclaims that there are no sinful orders apart from sinful people." Wingren, *Luther on Vocation*, 48.

24. Wingren, *Luther on Vocation*, 144.

25. Luther's Magnificat commentary (1521), in *LW* 21:324–25.

26. BC 440.69.

27. In his own way, Luther foresaw this change. "Let us remember our former misery, and the darkness in which we dwelt. Germany, I am sure, has never before heard so much of God's word as it is hearing today; certainly we read nothing of it in history. If we let it just slip by without thanks and honor, I fear we shall suffer a still more dreadful darkness and plague. O my beloved Germans, buy while the market is at your door; gather in the harvest while there is sunshine and fair weather; make use of God's grace and word while it is there! For you should know that God's word and grace is like a passing shower of rain which does not return where it has once been. It has been with the Jews, but when it's gone it's gone, and now they have nothing. Paul brought it to the Greeks; but again when it's gone it's gone, and now they have the Turk. Rome and the Latins also had it; but when it's gone it's gone, and now they have the pope. And you Germans need not think that you will have it forever, for ingratitude and contempt will not make it stay. Therefore, seize it and hold it fast, whoever can; for lazy hands are bound to have a lean year." *To the Councilmen of All Cities in Germany That They Establish and Maintain Christian Schools* (1524), in *LW* 45:352–53.

28. But based on my experiences with the North Atlantic participants, I will formulate a Law of Luther Reception: the greater the importance attached to Luther in a given culture, the more difficult it is for members of that culture actually to hear him.

29. Some of the memorable questions were: If Christ is divine, why does 1 Cor. 15 speak of his subjection to the Father? Why is God not mentioned at all in Mark 16:1–8? and Will Christ keep both of his natures after Judgment Day?

30. On this theme, see Christine Helmer, ed., *The Global Luther: A Theologian for Modern Times* (Minneapolis, MN: Fortress, 2009).

31. Most mainline Protestants got involved in ecumenism right at the start; in the early 1920s, the Eastern Orthodox joined in; after some very harsh words against ecumenism in the first part of the twentieth century, the Catholic Church turned an about-face during the Second Vatican Council, and since then has been one of the most devoted and persistent actors in the ecumenical realm. The past ten years have seen some new openness to ecumenism on the part of Evangelicals and Pentecostals, who had hitherto usually denounced it, if they paid any attention to it at all.

32. This is what distinguishes the Joint Declaration from other statements issued by the international Lutheran-Catholic dialogue. In those cases, the statements

are simply the work of the Catholic dialogue commission under the auspices of the Pontifical Council for Promoting Christian Unity, but they have no further binding character on the Catholic conscience. The Joint Declaration, however, is actually Catholic teaching. Analogously, the churches of the Lutheran World Federation receive the results of the dialogues and do what they want with them, but in the case of the Joint Declaration, every member church studied it and the Assembly of LWF ratified it.

33. For example: "20. When Catholics say that persons 'cooperate' in preparing for and accepting justification by consenting to God's justifying action, they see such personal consent as itself an effect of grace, not as an action arising from innate human abilities. 21. According to Lutheran teaching, human beings are incapable of cooperating in their salvation, because as sinners they actively oppose God and his saving action. Lutherans do not deny that a person can reject the working of grace. When they emphasize that a person can only receive (*mere passive*) justification, they mean thereby to exclude any possibility of contributing to one's own justification, but do not deny that believers are fully involved personally in their faith, which is effected by God's Word." The complete text of the Joint Declaration can be found on the Vatican website at www.vatican.va/roman_curia/pontifical_councils/chrstuni/documents/rc_pc_chrstuni_doc_31101999_cath-luth-joint-declaration_en.html.

34. And this extends to all Christian theologies of all times and places. The New Testament is a Christian theology in the setting of Jewish opposition and gradual Gentile interest; early church theology is dealing with heresies and sects; Orthodox theology inherits this and then gives it a new twist in its gradual separation first from the Near Eastern (Oriental) Orthodox churches and later the Western (Roman) church; and on and on forever after. There is no Christian theology without an adversary in view. When the adversary is discovered to be a fellow Christian after all, then ecumenism begins.

35. The statement is available online at www.prounione.urbe.it/dia-int/l-rc/doc/e_l-rc_luther.html.

36. See also the Lutheran-Catholic statement from 2007 on *The Apostolicity of the Church*: "Trent did not present a dogmatic ecclesiology, but left this area open. Theologians responded to the immediate needs of controversy by developing an apologetical treatment of apostolicity, that is, a presentation of evidence to prove that the Roman Church is alone the *vera ecclesia* ('true church'), with rightful authority in teaching and a legitimate corps of bishops and presbyters. .... Post-Tridentine Catholic theology was narrowed by constraints of argument to give practically no place to the ecclesial endowments of Scripture, creeds, worship, spirituality, and discipline of life, which in fact shaped the lives of Catholics but which were also shared in different ways with Christians of the separated churches. Ecclesiology was dominated by concern with the formal issue of legitimacy in holding these and other gifts. Interior gifts appeared less

important than the verifiable marks employed by an apologetics drawing on
history" (2.4.2., §104–05).

37. Available online at www.lutheranworld.org/sites/default/files/From%20
Conflict%20to%20Communion.pdf.

38. The hostility behind confessional theology is treated in fascinating length
and even given its own term, "eristology," in Ephraim Radner, *A Brutal
Unity: The Spiritual Politics of the Christian Church* (Waco, TX: Baylor University
Press, 2012).

39. The study is *Healing Memories: Reconciling in Christ*, Report of the
Lutheran-Mennonite International Study Commission (Geneva and
Strasbourg: Lutheran World Federation and Mennonite World Conference,
2010). See also my article, "Six Ways Ecumenical Progress Is Possible,"
Concordia Journal 39, no. 4 (2013): 310–32; John D. Roth, "Mennonites and
Lutherans Re-Remembering the Past," *Lutheran Forum* 44, no. 1 (2010): 38–
42; and Mennonite theologian Jeremy Bergen's book *Ecclesial Repentance: The
Churches Confront Their Sinful Pasts* (London: T & T Clark, 2011) on the
broader question of church apologies.

13

Looking Ahead by Glancing Back

JOHN CALVIN AND THOMAS AQUINAS ON THE CHURCH

Matthew Levering

THE 500TH ANNIVERSARY of the Reformation provides a welcome opportunity not only for Protestant and Catholic historians to take stock of
the Reformation's legacy but also for theologians on both sides of the confessional divide to discern and carry forward the best ecumenical impulses
in recent decades—and especially since the Second Vatican Council. This
chapter, on the holiness of the church in the thought of John Calvin and
Thomas Aquinas, is an effort toward such constructive, ecumenical theology. Looking back at two theological titans, I'm persuaded, helps us
think well and wisely about the mission of the church in the twenty-first
century.

Can Catholics and Protestants together affirm the Nicene Creed's confession that the Church is holy? At first glance, it hardly seems right to talk
about Christian holiness when there is so much evidence to the contrary.
The Reformation-era divisions might seem to be a perfect instance of this.
The present chapter will compare John Calvin and Thomas Aquinas on
this topic, which has risen to new prominence in recent years, considering
the perceived and real failures of the "institutional" Church, including terrible failures with respect to Christian unity.[1] Given the obvious evidence
of lack of holiness on the part of Christian believers, is it possible to affirm
the Church's holiness without making a historically ridiculous and dangerously prideful claim about the Church?

I will argue that it is important to appreciate that for both Calvin and
Aquinas, the answer is yes. As we will see, Calvin and Aquinas hold views

that are divergent in some significant respects. But they both argue that the missions of Christ and the Holy Spirit for the sanctification of the members of the Church justifies calling the Church holy. For both theologians, what is at stake in terms of Christian witness is our ability to proclaim with gratitude the sanctification that the Holy Spirit is accomplishing in and through the "body of Christ" (1 Cor. 12:27). The divisions that persist among Protestant and Catholic Christians should not prevent us from gratefully proclaiming—together—God's sanctifying work in Christ's Church.

John Calvin on the Holiness of the Church

In the first chapter of Book III of the *Institutes*, Calvin develops his theology of the Holy Spirit's activity. He states that it is due to "the secret efficacy of the Spirit . . . that we enjoy Christ and all his blessings."[2] Citing 1 Corinthians 6:11, he argues that our justification and sanctification come in Christ and by the Spirit. He describes the Spirit as "the bond by which Christ effectually bonds us to himself" (1:463). We have to be cleansed and made holy in order to be truly united to Christ. Christ, says Calvin, came for this very purpose. The prophets promised that in "the kingdom of Christ . . . the Spirit would be poured out in richer abundance" (1:463). Now that Christ has inaugurated his kingdom, the "Spirit of sanctification" has been given to us to be "the seed and root of heavenly life in us" (1:463).

In this vein, Calvin underscores that the "energy of the Holy Spirit" is "the special life that Christ breathes into his people" (1:464). The emphasis here is not simply on sanctification but on *communal* sanctification. Christ's "people," his "kingdom," is filled with the Holy Spirit. God does this freely, and our righteousness is God's free work. Calvin states that it is the Spirit's "secret irrigation that makes us bud forth and produce the fruits of righteousness" (1:465). When we receive the Spirit, we "are restored to the full vigour of life" (1:465). The Spirit purifies us from sin and inflames us with desire for God. Calvin describes our individual and communal sanctification in powerful terms: we receive "all heavenly riches," God "exerts his power" and rules us "by his motion and agency," Christ accomplishes a "sacred marriage" with us so that "we become bone of his bone, and flesh of his flesh," and Christ "keeps us under him" (1:465) so that the Church is truly his body (obedient to the commands of the Head).

We receive all this, Calvin notes, by faith, which itself is the Holy Spirit's gift in us. Through the Holy Spirit, Christ enlightens us and regenerates us: we become "new creatures," "cleansed from all pollution," "holy temples to the Lord" (1:466).

It would seem clear, then, that for Calvin, the Holy Spirit makes the Church holy. In the first chapter of Book IV of the *Institutes*, Calvin clarifies this point. On the one hand, when the Church lacks truth and holiness, it cannot be the Church. Truth and holiness come to the Church from Christ's and the Spirit's work in "the ministry of the word and sacraments" (2:304). Wherever this ministry is lacking in its proper form, we must speak of "the death of the Church" (2:305). In Calvin's view, such a death has happened in the Church that remains under the jurisdiction of Rome: "if the true Church is 'the pillar and ground of the truth' [1 Tim. 3:15], it is certain that there is no Church where lying and falsehood have usurped the ascendancy. Since this is the state of matters under the Papacy, we can understand how much of the Church there survives."[3] Calvin goes on to specify that under the Papacy the ministry of the word has been replaced by "a perverted government, compounded of lies" and that the ministry of the sacraments (especially the Eucharist) has been replaced by "the foulest sacrilege" and "intolerable superstitions" (2:305). The true Church, therefore, is indeed holy; without sufficient holiness, the Church will die.

But on the other hand, Calvin makes clear that he is not suggesting that the Church requires a perfect holiness in order to exist. Certainly, so long as the ministry of the word and sacraments "exists entire and unimpaired," the Church exists even despite other defects (2:304). Even when the ministry of the word and sacraments is itself infected by minor defects, the Church still exists. Against the radical Reformers, Calvin cautions that "we arrogate too much to ourselves, if we presume forthwith to withdraw from the communion of the Church, because the lives of all accord not with our judgment, or even with the Christian profession" (2:296). After all, the holy prophets did not withdraw from the Church ("the Israel of God" [Gal. 6:16]) despite the terrible corruption and idolatry that they found. Christ himself, along with the apostles, did not withdraw from the religion of the Temple of Jerusalem, despite "the desperate impiety of the Pharisees" and "the dissolute licentiousness of manners which everywhere prevailed" (2:296). Those who reject the Church because of even a "minutest blemish," therefore, are wrongly expecting the Church on earth to be the eschatological Jerusalem (2:297). So long as "the word of God is preached and the sacraments are administered," we have no right to leave the Church even if a large number of our fellows—even of our pastors—are unworthy (2:297). Calvin states that the "sacred rites are not less pure and salutary to a man who is holy and upright, from being at the same time handled by the impure" (2:297).

Thus we should not expect the Church to be perfect, even though too much imperfection results in the death of the Church. It is noteworthy, too, that Calvin follows Augustine in holding that "the Scriptures speak of the Church in two ways" (2:288). The first way consists in "the Church as it really is before God" (2:288). The Church known to God contains all the elect, and more particularly, all "who by the gift of adoption are sons of God, and by the sanctification of the Spirit true members of Christ" (2:288). The second way consists in the Church as it appears to our limited vision. The Church known to us contains many who profess to be members of Christ but who in fact are not, and these persons cause scandal by their false witness. The one Church is both visible and invisible. The true Church is the invisible Church (which God alone sees), but this Church is in fact the same Church as the visible Church, even if some of the members differ.

Calvin affirms that God has willed that for the duration of human history, the elect and the reprobate are to be mingled in the one visible Church. With respect to this visible Church (which is the one Church), Calvin states that this Church is our "Mother" and observes that being able to recognize the visible Church is crucial because "there is no other means of entering into life unless she conceive us in the womb and give us birth, unless she nourish us at her breasts, and, in short, keep us under her charge and government" until we die and enter into eternal life (2:283). Citing numerous biblical texts from both Testaments, Calvin is quite clear that "beyond the pale of the Church no forgiveness of sins, no salvation, can be hoped for" (2:283).

As we have seen, Calvin considers that the true visible Church of his day is not the Church under papal jurisdiction, which was the Church in which he was raised. That false Church is dead and deadly, owing to the work of Satan. Rather, the true visible Church of his day is the reformed Church in which, at long last, the true ministry of the word and the sacraments can again be observed. This Church is present in all the local congregations that truly "have the ministry of the word, and honour the administration of the sacraments."[4] As Calvin puts it, "Wherever we see the word of God sincerely preached and heard, wherever we see the sacraments administered according to the institution of Christ, there we cannot have any doubt that the Church of God has some existence, since his promise cannot fail, 'Where two or three are gathered together in my name, there am I in the midst of them' [Matt. 18:20]" (2:289). No one can be justified in separating themselves from this Church in its local instantiation. Calvin insists that we must acknowledge as our fellow Christians not only those who appear most worthy to our eyes, but also all "who by confession of faith, regularity of conduct, and participation in the sacraments, unite with us in acknowledging the same God and Christ" (2:288–89).

In this regard, Calvin remarks that the way in which Paul handled his churches should instruct us. So long as they retained the true ministry of the word and sacraments, he did not separate from them. Calvin points out, for instance, that "[a]mong the Corinthians it was not a few that erred, but almost the whole body had become tainted" by a variety of grave sins; yet Paul still "acknowledges and heralds them as a Church of Christ, and a society of saints" (2:293). The radical Reformers are thus mistaken to think that since the true Church is holy, "there is no church where there is not complete purity and integrity of conduct" (2:292). Calvin cites various parables of Jesus that make clear that "the Church will labour under the defect of being burdened with a multitude of wicked until the day of judgment" (2:292). Those who deny this burden—for example, Donatists and "Anabaptists"—have failed to listen to Jesus. Calvin explains that "there always have been persons who, imbued with a false persuasion of absolute holiness, as if they had already become a kind of aerial spirits, spurn the society of all in whom they see that something human still remains" (2:292). In fact, as Calvin says, "the holiest sometimes make the most grievous fall," (2:295) whereas open sinners often repent and seek amendment.

Delving yet deeper into the sense in which the Church is "holy," Calvin notes that we must not deny the truth of Paul's statement that "Christ loved the church and gave himself up for her, that he might sanctify her, having cleansed her by the washing of water with the word, that he might present the church to himself in splendor, without spot or wrinkle or any such thing, that she might be holy and without blemish" (2:295). That said, Christ is today in the process of sanctifying the Church by the Holy Spirit. The Church on earth still has both "spot" and "wrinkle"; the Church on earth is not perfect.

In what sense, then, can the Church be said to be holy? Have prophecies such as Joel 3:17 ("Jerusalem shall be holy") and Isaiah 35:8 ("it shall be called the Holy Way") not in fact been fulfilled by Christ? Calvin argues that they have been fulfilled, but not yet perfectly fulfilled. Their perfect fulfillment awaits the eschaton. The Church "daily advances, but as yet has not reached the goal" (2:295). The Church is "holy" because the hearts of its true members cry out for perfect holiness. Calvin here has recourse to the legal imagery that he uses also for justification. The Church is holy not only because the Holy Spirit is sanctifying believers but also because God imputes holiness to the Church. In this case, however, the free imputation is based on the Church's striving toward holiness under the sanctifying power of the Holy Spirit, which Calvin does not wish to deny or undermine. As Calvin explains regarding the members of the Church, "with their whole heart they aspire after holiness and perfect purity: and hence, that purity which they have not yet fully attained is, by the kindness of God, attributed to them" (2:295). Calvin admits that the instances of Christians truly seeking holiness have, over the centuries, been "too rare" (2:295). But it is in these instances that the holy Church is found. The holy Church is present where, under the impulse of the Holy Spirit, believers eagerly seek perfect holiness; God imputes the attribute "holy" to the Church on this basis. In every time and place, furthermore, there have been (and will be) such believers: "at no period since the world began has the Lord been without his Church, nor ever shall be till the final consummation of all things" (2:296).

How does Calvin know that in every age God raises up his true Church, which strives for holiness and to which God imputes the attribute of holiness? In Pauline language, Calvin emphasizes that despite our terrible fallenness, God "always sanctifies some vessels to honour, that no age may be left without experience of his mercy" (2:296). We know this because of God's covenantal promises. Calvin cites in particular God's covenants with Israel and with David (as recorded in Ps. 132:13–14 and 89:3–4 and in Jer. 31:35–36), but Calvin's point extends to the beginning of the world, since otherwise there would have been a time when there was no holy Church in the world. Despite the Fall, God's free covenantal love has always been mercifully present.

Thomas Aquinas on the Holiness of the Church

Thomas Aquinas has a short sermon-commentary on the Apostles' Creed, which he delivered during Lent of 1273, the year before his death.[5]

When he turns to the creed's affirmation of the "holy catholic church," Aquinas discusses the characteristics of the Church, including its unity and holiness. At the outset of his discussion, he compares the Church to a body-soul organism: the Church's "body" is its many members, and the Church's soul, which gives life and operation to the body, is the Holy Spirit. The Church is guided and governed by the Holy Spirit. Aquinas also describes the Church as "the congregation of the faithful."[6] He conceives of this assembly as an assembly for learning God's ways. In this regard, he quotes Sirach 51:23, "Draw near to me, you who are untaught, and lodge in my school."

With respect to the creed's description of the Church as "holy," Aquinas first remarks that the Church is a holy congregation. Aquinas is aware, of course, that the visible Church includes wicked persons. But scripture makes clear that the Church possesses a real sanctity through the indwelling of the Holy Spirit in believers. In this regard, Aquinas quotes 1 Corinthians 3:17, "For God's temple is holy, and that temple you are." Although we are imperfect, insofar as the Holy Spirit dwells in us, we truly possess holiness (even if not perfectly); otherwise, we could not be described as God's holy temple. Since this is the case, the Church of believers must be holy. Paul does not mean simply that some individuals are God's holy temple. Rather, the Holy Spirit indwells individuals precisely as members of Christ, united to him by faith and love: "Now you are the body of Christ and individually members of it" (1 Cor. 12:27). This "body of Christ" is the Church.

Aquinas also points out that if the Church were not holy, then it could not be contrasted with wicked assemblies. The Church would merely be yet another congregation of sinners. Aquinas quotes the Psalmist's statement, "I hate the company of evildoers, and I will not sit with the wicked" (Ps. 26:5). As Aquinas knew, the Psalmist proceeds to describe his love for the Temple worship, "I wash my hands in innocence, and go about your altar, O Lord, singing aloud a song of thanksgiving, and telling all your wondrous deeds. O Lord, I love the habitation of your house, and the place where your glory dwells" (Ps. 26:6–8). The Temple is characterized by the presence of God's glory and by true worship of God, unlike the "company of evildoers" that lacks God's presence and is antithetical to God's goodness. Christ's Church, too, is characterized by the indwelling Holy Spirit and by true worship in Christ, and so it differs profoundly from the "company [or assembly] of evildoers." This is so even though the members of

Christ's Church are still venial sinners, and even though there are false Christians who are outwardly, but not inwardly, members of the Church.

In addition to defending the holiness of the Church by these arguments, Aquinas holds that the Church is holy because the Church is the place of our sanctification. If the Church were not holy, then we would not need the Church for sanctification. But in fact, by God's will, our sanctification is inseparable from the Church. In the Church, Aquinas observes, believers are sanctified by the washing in the blood of Christ, by the anointing of the Holy Spirit, by the indwelling Trinity, and by the invoking of God's name for our salvation. The washing and anointing suggest the sacrament of baptism (and the sacrament of confirmation); the indwelling Trinity and invoking of God's name suggest the basis and pattern of Christian worship.

Aquinas first remarks that just as a church building is consecrated (by being cleansed), so also the members of the Church are "washed in the blood of Christ."[7] The reference here is to the sacrament of baptism, which unites us to Christ's Passion and takes away original sin. It may seem a stretch to connect what happens to believers with what happens to the church building, as if the latter had anything to do with the Church's holiness. But for Aquinas, the church building itself has iconographic significance.[8] The church building suggests, by its structure and the direction of its altar, both the Church's communal participation in Christ's Pasch and the Church's eschatological expectation of Christ's return in glory. The symbolism present in the consecration of a church building indicates the basis for the real sanctity of the Church—namely, Christ's sanctifying us through his blood.

Regarding our being washed in the blood of Christ, Aquinas cites Ephesians 5:25–27 (which Calvin also quoted) and Hebrews 13:12, "Jesus also suffered outside the gate in order to sanctify the people through his own blood." Ephesians 5:25–27 explicitly depicts the Church as sanctified by Christ. While Hebrews 13:12 does not explicitly describe the Church, it does refer to Jesus's having suffered to "sanctify the people." Hebrews 13:14–15 goes on to say that "here we have no lasting city, but we seek the city which is to come. Through him then let us continually offer up a sacrifice of praise to God." Lest this talk of two cities and of "a sacrifice of praise" seem to depict individuals praising God and awaiting the eschatological Jerusalem (with no need of a Church on earth), recall that Hebrews 13:17 adds, "Obey your leaders and submit to them; for they are keeping watch over your souls, as men who will have to give account." Jesus died in order "to sanctify the people"; the Church is that people, and its members are called to "offer up a sacrifice of praise to God." We do so as a sanctified people that must obey its leaders. Jesus does not merely sanctify individuals. Rather, he sanctifies a "people," and this sanctified people possesses a hierarchical form as the Church.

The second way in which the members of the Church are sanctified, according to Aquinas, is by "a spiritual anointing."[9] Here, Aquinas points out that when a church building is being consecrated, it is anointed with holy oil. Similarly, the sacramental anointing of the members of the Church consecrates the Church as holy. By this anointing, the members of the Church become like Christ who was anointed by the Holy Spirit. To be "Christ" means to be "anointed." Aquinas remarks that if we did not receive this anointing that makes us holy, we "would not be Christians," since we would not be like the anointed one, Christ (127). In support of the role of the anointing in making us holy, Aquinas cites 1 Corinthians 6:11 ("you were washed, you were sanctified, you were justified in the name of the Lord Jesus Christ and in the Spirit of our God") and 2 Corinthians 1:21 ("It is God who establishes us with you in Christ, and has commissioned [Vulgate "*unxit*," anointed] us"). For Aquinas, 1 Corinthians 6:11 suggests that the baptismal washing is followed by sanctification through anointing. Similarly, 2 Corinthians 1:21 appears to give a central role to anointing.

The contexts of these two verses are also worth noting, although Aquinas does not comment on them here. In 1 Corinthians 6, Paul is urging the Corinthians not to take their legal cases "before the unrighteous instead of the saints" (1 Cor. 6:1), and indeed to entirely avoid legal cases against each other. The Church consists of the "saints," but they are still prone to acting in the ways of the world. In 2 Corinthians 1, Paul is speaking of his apostolic commission to teach and govern; he says of himself that God "has put his seal upon us and given us his Spirit in our hearts as a guarantee" (2 Cor. 1:22). Both passages refer to the anointing or sanctifying work of the Holy Spirit and show that it pertains not solely to individuals but also to the Church as an interconnected and hierarchical body. In addition, in both passages, Paul discusses the Holy Spirit's sanctifying or anointing work in the context of his criticisms of the Corinthians' notable lack of holiness. The holiness of the Church does not depend on the perfect sanctity of the members of the Church, and indeed, some of them are members in name only (see 1 Cor. 5:2).

The third way that the Church is made holy is through the indwelling Trinity. Aquinas has already argued, as we have seen, that the congregation of the faithful is washed in Christ's blood and anointed by his Spirit so as to be the temple of God. Connecting this with the indwelling Trinity, he now observes that "wherever God dwells, that place is holy" (127). Again, he gives two biblical citations, this time both from the Old Testament: Genesis 28:17, in which Jacob, having dreamt of a ladder reaching from earth to heaven and having received YHWH's covenantal blessing, proclaims that this place is "none other than the house of God" and "the gate of heaven"; and Psalms 93:5, "Your decrees are very sure; holiness befits your house, O Lord, for evermore." Jacob's awed proclamation comes as he is leaving Canaan, the Promised Land where God will dwell with his people. Psalm 93 describes the glorious sovereignty of the Creator God and concludes by suggesting that a people with such a powerful and wise sovereign will be holy. God dwells in his people as a sanctifying power, not as a passive inhabitant. Furthermore, the indwelling of the Trinity is not simply an individual experience but, rather, is the fulfillment of God's covenantal promises to his people.

The fourth and final aspect noted by Aquinas is that the Church sanctifies its members by invoking the name of God. Why does the invocation of God add anything? Aquinas cites a prophecy that Jeremiah received during a period of terrible drought in Judah. The prophecy begins with the mourning of Judah, with a lament that pleads with God to act. God is committed to punishing his rebellious people, but Jeremiah intercedes for the people and begs God, "We acknowledge our wickedness, O Lord, and the iniquity of our fathers, for we have sinned against you. Do not spurn us, for your name's sake; do not dishonor your glorious throne; remember and do not break your covenant with us" (Jer. 14:20–21). The verse that Aquinas quotes comes earlier, at the end of the prophecy's first lament: "Yet you, O Lord, are in the midst of us, and we are called by your name; leave us not" (Jer. 14:9). The point is that the people of Israel are "called by your name"; God has placed his "name" upon this people by associating them so intimately with himself and by making himself present to them in true worship. Even though they are sinners, God has united himself to them in the sense of making them the bearers of his holy "name." Christians, too, have been baptized and anointed in God's name, now revealed as Father, Son, and Holy Spirit. God has placed his "name" on us and has made us (both individually and as the Church) his temple. In Christ, we bear the saving name of God. On this basis, Aquinas warns against sin: "we should be careful, lest after such a sanctification we soil through sin our soul, which is the temple of God" (129). The consequences of rebelling against the holy God are spiritually fatal. Aquinas quotes Paul's admonition, "Do you not know that you are God's temple and that God's Spirit dwells in you? If any one destroys God's temple, God will destroy him" (1 Cor. 3:16–17).

Aquinas thus defends the holiness of the Church by attending to the Church's sources: "the blood of Christ" and "the grace of the Holy Spirit." Baptism enables the members of the Church to receive the saving power of Christ's Passion and to be filled with the grace of the Holy Spirit. God the Trinity dwells in the Church, and wherever he dwells is holy. Just as God placed his name on the Temple in Jerusalem (see 1 Kings 8), so also God has placed his name upon the Church, which is the true holy temple. In this discussion, Aquinas does not advert to the sinfulness of the members of the Church. He focuses simply on the reasons we must hold that the Church is holy, reasons that have to do with Christ's mission to sanctify his people, with the sending of the Holy Spirit, with the Trinitarian indwelling, and with the Church's status as God's temple.

We can understand something more of Aquinas's position from his commentary on Ephesians 5:25–27. Aquinas makes clear that the Church that lacks "spot or wrinkle" (Eph. 5:27) is primarily the eschatological Church, the perfected Church as it will be at the consummation of all things. When Christ presents to himself the Church "in splendor," this refers, says Aquinas, to the Church comprising members whose bodies and souls have been glorified. He cites Philippians 3:21 (to which I add verse 20), "Our commonwealth is in heaven, and from it we await a Savior, the Lord Jesus Christ, who will change our lowly body to be like his glorious body." The blessed in heaven will be perfect, and will have no "spot"; in this regard, Aquinas applies two psalms that describe the blameless person who walks with God (Ps. 101:6 and Ps. 119:1). Neither will the blessed in heaven have any "wrinkle"—that is, any suffering.

Yet Aquinas also thinks that the passage can refer to the Church of grace, the Church on earth that is not yet perfect. From this perspective, the Church has no "spot," not in the sense of having no sin at all, but in the sense that the true members of the Church on earth are not in a state of mortal sin. The Church on earth is already "in splendor" (Eph. 5:27) because of the dignity of following God by the grace of the Holy Spirit. The Church also already lacks any "wrinkle," if by wrinkle one means "duplicity of purpose," which would be a mortal sin and thus would be far from "those who are rightly united with Christ and the Church."[10] The Church even now is "holy" by its "aspiration [*intentionem*],"[11] even if the members of the Church still suffer from venial sin (and keeping in view those who profess to belong to the Church, but who in fact have separated themselves from the Church by mortal sin). Can the Church even now be "without blemish"? Aquinas suggests that the Church can be without blemish, insofar as the members of the Church manifest a real sanctity and "every kind of purity," even though not in a perfect way (220). Even now, Christ presents the Church "to himself in an immaculate state," through the grace of the indwelling Holy Spirit (219).

Aquinas connects this gift of real holiness with the sacrament of baptism, in accord with the logic of Ephesians 5:25–27. Regarding the cleansing that Christ brings "by the washing of water" (Eph. 5:26), Aquinas explains that Paul is here speaking of baptism, which has its "power from the passion of Christ" (219). In this respect, Aquinas cites two prophetic texts about the day of the Lord: Ezekiel 36:25 ("I will sprinkle clean water upon you, and you shall be clean from all your uncleannesses") and Zechariah 13:1 ("On that day there shall be a fountain opened for the house of David and the inhabitants of Jerusalem to cleanse them sin and uncleanness"). Christ's Passion is the day of God's triumph over sin, although this day awaits its perfection at the end of time and the final judgment. Baptism constitutes the "fountain" or sprinkling "of clean water" that, by enabling us to share in Christ's Passion, causes our cleansing from sin. Aquinas quotes Paul in this regard: "Do you not know that all of us who have been baptized into Christ Jesus were baptized into his death? We were buried therefore with him by baptism into death" (Rom. 6:3–4). The role of baptism in this work of salvation is made even clearer by the risen Christ's commanding his disciples to baptize all nations "in the name of the Father and of the Son and of the Holy Spirit" (Matt. 28:19).

In this way, Christ's Passion makes the people of God fit for marriage with God, since "[i]t would be highly improper for the immaculate bridegroom to wed a soiled bride" (219). Aquinas emphasizes that Christ came for the purpose of bringing about "the Church's purity."[12] As we have seen, he argues that even now, by the grace of the Holy Spirit and through the sacrament of baptism, Christ is already able to present the Church "to himself in an immaculate state."[13] On the one hand, Aquinas agrees with Calvin that the Church can be called holy, in its "appearance through faith [*exhibitione per fidem*]," through its "aspiration" or "intention," its single-mindedness of purpose and striving in the process of sanctification (220).

Like Calvin, Aquinas recognizes the sinfulness of the Church's members, even though he distinguishes these sins as venial. But on the other hand, Aquinas insists that the Church already, by the grace of the Holy Spirit, is "immaculate." How can this be? Arguably, the Church even now is "immaculate" because it is able faithfully to mediate the sanctifying work of Christ and the Spirit.

Lest this position seem to idealize the Church, let me underscore that Aquinas recognizes that the sins of the Church's members mar the face of the Church and make it difficult to perceive the Church's holiness. Almost any of the *Summa theologiae*'s questions on the vices would suffice to show that Aquinas is hardly naïve about human nature after baptism. He displays a large acquaintance with the contours of the sin of simony that especially plagued the wealthy medieval Church. He notes that "[t]he Pope can be guilty of the vice of simony, like any other man," and he warns that the Pope would commit simony by accepting "money from the income of any church in exchange for a spiritual thing" or "by accepting from a layman moneys not belonging to the goods of the Church."[14] He knows that "it happens sometimes that someone maliciously hinders a person from obtaining a bishopric or some like dignity," and he knows that there are priests who are "unwilling to baptize without being paid."[15] Likewise, Aquinas speaks of fraternal correction as a most important virtue for Christians; this would hardly be the case if the Church were holy in an undifferentiated or empirically verifiable sense. He expects that people will have to correct their prelates, although he encourages them "to do so in a becoming manner, not with impudence and harshness, but with gentleness and respect."[16] The pope may need to be corrected publicly, as Paul corrected Peter. Even though we are sinners, we can still rightly correct our sinful brethren, so long as we do so humbly. Aquinas's view of the visible Church, in other words, is not rose-colored. He recognizes the extent of sin among baptized persons, and thus among the human agents of the Church.

Conclusion

For Calvin, the holy word and sacraments are given to the Church so as to enable the Church's members to look in faith toward the Savior Christ. God's word and sacraments do not constitute a holy interior dimension of the Church, although they do help to sanctify the members of the Church by establishing the Church in a posture of dependent faith. Because the true members of the Church are in fact imperfect, despite their striving for holiness, it follows that the holiness of the Church—which Calvin certainly affirms—depends on God's imputation. In this sense, Calvin considers that there has always been a holy Church. At all times and places, even when the visible Church has been at its most wicked (mired in an idolatrous worship and false teaching, in the pre-Reformation period), God has always ensured the existence of a remnant of believers who strive for holiness, and thus the true proclamation of God's word and the true celebration of the sacraments (baptism and the Eucharist) has never completely ceased. God imputes the attribute "holiness" to this remnant Church. For Calvin, of course, "all sin is mortal, because it is rebellion against the will of God, and necessarily provokes his anger; and because it is a violation of the Law, against every violation of which, without exception, the judgment of God has been pronounced."[17]

Aquinas agrees that the members of the Church are sinners, although the distinction between venial and mortal sin makes it possible for him truly to call the members of the Church "holy." Like Calvin, Aquinas holds that the members of the Church possess charity and are being sanctified by the Spirit. Yet Aquinas also teaches that the Church on earth is already, in a real sense, "immaculate." He highlights the New Testament teaching that the Church is the body of Christ and the true temple of God, guided by the Holy Spirit in such a way as to manifest the real marriage of God and his people. In its sacraments and definitive teachings, the Church not only mediates Christ's holiness but also truly shares in it as Christ's "body." The Church, therefore, is not merely an extrinsic conduit of the holy gifts that flow through the Church, because these gifts are constitutive of the Church.

While Calvin and Aquinas thus hold different positions, they both affirm that the Church is correctly called "holy" despite the ongoing sinfulness of the Church's members. The Church's holiness, then, does not depend on us; it can withstand our failures and conflicts. In this light, Catholic and Protestant Christians need not give up on the creedal confession that the Church is holy, despite the ongoing and painful evidence of Christian sinfulness. For both Calvin and Aquinas, the Church is holy because of the sanctifying power of Christ's Passion and Resurrection, and because of the Pentecostal outpouring of the Holy Spirit and his gifts upon the community of believers. The divine Trinity dwells in believers not simply individually, but in the Church as the body of Christ.

Five hundred years after the Reformation era's sadly enduring divisions about where and how to locate the Church, it would be a victory indeed if Catholics and Protestants today were able to stand together in proclaiming to the world our ongoing gratitude for Christ's Passion, Resurrection, and sending of his Spirit upon his eschatological people. With Calvin, Aquinas, and the ancient Creeds, we can do this today by praising God for the gift of holy Church.

Notes

1. See, for example, Ephraim Radner's *A Brutal Unity: The Spiritual Politics of the Christian Church* (Waco, TX: Baylor University Press, 2012).

2. John Calvin, *Institutes of the Christian Religion*, trans. Henry Beveridge (Grand Rapids, MI: Eerdmans, 1989), 1:463.

3. Calvin, *Institutes*. When treating the unity and catholicity of the Church, Calvin observes, "For although the sad devastation which everywhere meets our view may proclaim that no Church remains, let us know that the death of Christ produces fruit, and that God wondrously preserves his Church, while placing it as it were in concealment. Thus it was said to Elijah, 'Yet I have left me seven thousand in Israel' [1 Kings 19:18]"; Calvin, *Institutes*, 2:282.

4. Calvin, *Institutes*, 2:289. See Kilian McDonnell, *John Calvin, the Church, and the Eucharist* (Princeton, NJ: Princeton University Press, 1967).

5. Herwi Rikhof has rightly observed that this sermon-commentary "contains a wealth of theological insights and can therefore serve well as a frame and a starting point for examining Thomas' views on the Church"; Rikhof, "Thomas on the Church: Reflections on a Sermon," in *Aquinas on Doctrine: A Critical Introduction*, ed. Thomas G. Weinandy, Daniel A. Keating, and John P. Yocum (London: T. & T. Clark, 2004), 199–223, 199. For discussion of this sermon-commentary, see also Jean-Pierre Torrell, "La pratique pastorale," in *Recherches Thomasiennes* (Paris: J. Vrin, 2000), 282–314.

6. Thomas Aquinas, *The Sermon-Conferences of St. Thomas Aquinas on the Apostles' Creed*, trans. and ed. Nicholas Ayo (Notre Dame, IN: University of Notre Dame Press, 1988), 125.

7. Aquinas, *Sermon-Conferences on the Apostles' Creed*, 127.

8. See Thomas Aquinas, *Summa theologiae* III, q. 83, a. 3. Aquinas explains in ad 2: "The house in which this sacrament [the Eucharist] is celebrated denotes the Church, and is termed a church; and so it is fittingly consecrated, both to represent the holiness which the Church acquired from the Passion, as well as to denote the holiness required of them who have to receive this sacrament."

9. Aquinas, *Sermon-Conferences on the Apostles' Creed*, 127.

10. Thomas Aquinas, *Commentary on Saint Paul's Epistle to the Ephesians*, trans. Matthew L. Lamb (Albany, NY: Magi Books, 1966), ch. 5, lect. 8, 220.

11. Aquinas, *Commentary on Epistle to the Ephesians*, 220.

12. Aquinas, *Commentary on Epistle to the Ephesians*, 219. See also Joseph Ratzinger's comment on the relationship of the Church and the Kingdom: "the gathering and cleansing of men for the Kingdom of God is part of this Kingdom"; Ratzinger, *Called to Communion: Understanding the Church Today*, trans. Adrian Walker (San Francisco: Ignatius Press, 1996), 21–22.

13. Aquinas, *Commentary on Epistle to the Ephesians*, 219.

14. Thomas Aquinas, *Summa theologiae*, II-II, q. 100, a. 1, ad 7, trans. Fathers of the English Dominican Province (Westminster, MD: Christian Classics, 1981).

15. II-II, q. 100, a. 2, obj. 5 and ad 1.

16. II-II, q. 33, a. 4.

17. Calvin, *Institutes*, 1:362.

14

The Reformation and the New Ecumenism

Timothy George

AS WE APPROACH the 500th anniversary of the Protestant Reformation, we might find it instructive to glance back at the four centennial commemorations of the Reformation preceding the one we are preparing for in 2017. While Thomas Albert Howard has sketched some of this history more fully in chapter 1, permit me, too, to briefly take stock.

The 100th anniversary of the Reformation was celebrated in 1617, during the age of confessionalization. The Council of Trent had done its work, and Lutheran and Reformed polemics were in high gear. It was also one year before the beginning of the Thirty Years' War. The 200th anniversary of the Reformation in 1717 took place in the age of pietism and deism, of Hobbes and Locke, and of Johann Sebastian Bach. In 1817, the smoke of the Napoleonic Wars was still in the air, and what we call the modern missionary movement was beginning to change the global map of Christianity. The Enlightenment was in full swing, and its reactionary cousin, romanticism, had begun to rise. It was the age of Emerson, Hegel, and Schleiermacher. By 1917, the ecumenical embers, stirred at the World Missionary Conference at Edinburgh seven years before, were still glowing in the midst of the most savage war humankind had known up to that point.

Now, here we are again, at the half-millennial benchmark of the Reformation, at another key symbolic moment in the life of both the church and the world. We find ourselves wondering again what, if anything, the messy theological business of the sixteenth century has to do with our lives today.

My contribution to this discussion consists of three parts. First, I offer a brief autobiographical reflection, highlighting some turning points that have led me to church history, historical theology, and ecumenical concerns. Second, I reflect on a "Reformation intuition" about Christian unity based on the statement by Catholic historian Donald Nugent: "Contemporary ecumenism is only a renaissance of a Reformation ideal."[1] Finally, I offer a word about what I, following the theologian Thomas Oden, am calling "the New Ecumenism" and provide a few examples of what I take to be hopeful indicators of it.

Becoming a Church Historian

I understand church history to be a theological discipline, the purpose of which is to illuminate that article of the Nicene Creed confessed by all Christians: "I believe in the one, holy, catholic, and apostolic church": *Credo unam, sanctam, catholicam, et apostolicam ecclesiam.* I understand my vocation as that of a church historian, not merely a historian of the church, although I acknowledge that there is a proper role for the latter. And, I understand the church in its widest configuration to be nothing less than, in the formulation of Orthodox theologian Georges Florovsky, the Body of Christ extended throughout time as well as space.

How did I come to these convictions? Not easily, and not by any predictable line of progression. to be sure. Growing up in the American South, I was nurtured in a community of faith that was part of the one, holy, catholic, and apostolic church, but that had no idea that this was so. We were separatistic, biblicistic, and baptistic. In my youth, I remember hearing a number of very bad jokes about theologically liberal "ecumaniacs" and the need to avoid them at all costs.

There was a small Unitarian church in my neighborhood—the South is a pioneer mission field for Unitarians—and one day, as a ten- or eleven-year-old, I stopped by to challenge the Unitarian minister on why he did not baptize in the name of the Father, the Son, and the Holy Ghost. To my surprise, I discovered that he did not practice baptism of any kind at all. Around the same time, I also contacted the local Catholic priest to ask several impertinent questions as to why the Catholic Church was so unbiblical in its teachings about Mary and the Mass. He was not as friendly as the Unitarian minister, but took my questions seriously and tried to answer them.

More important than either of these isolated encounters was my great-uncle Willie Nash, a dyed-in-the-wool convert to the Church of Jesus Christ of Latter-day Saints. His life's mission was to convert me to becoming a Mormon. He failed in that project, but in the process he did turn me into a Christian theologian, as I spent many hours debating Uncle Willie and the Mormon missionaries about the authenticity of the golden plates, marriage in the temple, celestial underwear, and where the Baptist church came from.

I attended a state university in Tennessee, where I majored in history and philosophy and was introduced to Reformation studies by a wonderful teacher named Bill Wright, a devout Missouri Synod Lutheran and former student of the Reformation historian Harold J. Grimm. However, my real entrée into ecumenical theology began during the seven years I spent at Harvard Divinity School. Among my teachers there were John Booty, an Anglican church historian; Krister Stendahl, our dean and sometime Bishop of Stockholm who introduced me to Lutheran liturgical life; and Heiko A. Oberman (Dutch Reformed) and David C. Steinmetz (Methodist), both of whom were visiting professors at Harvard in my day. But above all, there was my major professor and academic mentor, George Huntston Williams.

Williams is best remembered for *The Radical Reformation*, a monumental overview of Anabaptists and other sixteenth-century religious dissenters, first published in 1962 and still in print today.[2] But he never considered this his principal work. It was, he said, only a "fresh trench" or irrigation ditch—he borrowed this image from Thomas Mann, who referred to such motifs as *coulisses*—in the landscape of the wider Christian tradition. His true *magnum opus*, he envisaged, would be titled *The New Testament People: An Ecumenical History of Christianity with Attention to Its Relations at All Important Nodal Points with Judaism and Islam*. Like the unfinished cathedrals of Thomas Aquinas's and Karl Barth's life work, Williams's projected covenantal history of the people of God was never completed. But, as a determined generalist in church history, he was always alive to the subtle and complex interconnectedness of the events he studied—events he saw not as isolated, opaque moments in the history of religion but, rather, as translucent windows opening to a whole pattern of Christian experience.

Williams was a medievalist with a deep knowledge of the patristic tradition, West and East. He also studied and wrote about Celtic monasticism, New England puritanism, modern American evangelicalism, Pentecostalism, and much, much more. A fourth-generation Unitarian minister who nonetheless steadfastly affirmed the doctrine of the Holy Trinity, Williams was one of the few official Protestant observers at all four sessions of the Second Vatican Council. There he met and developed a fast friendship with Karol Wojtyła, a young bishop from Poland. In 1981, Williams published one of the first books in English about the new pope, *The Mind of John Paul II: Origins of His Thought and Action.*[3]

The Reformation as both Tragic and Necessary

From Williams, Oberman, and others, I came to appreciate, as do the editors of this volume, what Jaroslav Pelikan once called "the tragic necessity of the Reformation."[4] Both of these aspects—the necessity of reform and the tragedy of scandalous division—are important for understanding the New Ecumenism—even as we continue to groan for the fulfillment of Jesus's prayer that his disciples would be one, as he and the Father are one, so that the world might believe (John 17:21).

It is not hard to find champions of only one side of this antinomy. The tragic side of the Reformation is obvious to those who care deeply about the unity of the church and who feel keenly the *dys*-evangelical impact of a fractured Christian community and its muted witness in our world today. All Christians repeat Jesus's prayer for the unity of his church, and yet who can deny the open scandal of the followers of Jesus excluding one another from the Lord's Table, all the while proclaiming "one Lord, one faith, one baptism" (Eph. 4:5)?

But the necessity of the Reformation is also evident to those who hear in the teaching of Luther, Zwingli, Calvin, and Cranmer and others the good news of God's free and unfettered grace, and the message of justification by faith alone. One ought to rejoice in the recovery of Bible-based proclamation at the heart of the church's worship, for as the Second Helvetic Confession of 1566 puts it, "The preaching of the Word of God is the Word of God."[5]

Perhaps we cannot quite say with the great church historian Philip Schaff that the Protestant Reformation was the greatest event in the history of the church since the day of Pentecost, but we can nonetheless give thanks for the spiritual and ecclesial renewal that took place in the great upheavals of the sixteenth century. Perhaps *simul iustus et pecator* applies not only to individuals, as Luther taught, but also to particular epochs and episodes in the history of the church. The New Ecumenism will be deeper, richer, and more conducive to genuine renewal if it recognizes both the *tragic* and the *necessary* dimensions of the Reformation.

This perspective, however, is not shared by all. In some ecumenical discussions it is tempting to pass over the Reformation altogether. Many want to get back as quickly as possible to the early church to reclaim a common patrimony for all Christians in the fathers and mothers of the church of the first few centuries. But this is a luxury that Christians, especially in the West, cannot afford. It reflects the same reductionist impulse of those Christians who transmute the cherished principle of *sola scriptura* (scripture as highest authority) into *nuda scriptura* (scripture as only authority), and accordingly read the Bible as though the ancient councils of Nicaea, Ephesus, or Chalcedon had never happened—"no creed but the Bible" is their slogan.[6] However well-intentioned this impulse might be, an ecumenism that proceeds on the basis of forgetting earlier periods of church history must be regarded as theologically suspect. We must have an ecumenism of remembrance, not an ecumenism of amnesia.

This approach ignores the fact that the Reformation itself was an age of great patristic *ressourcement*, to use a phrase often associated with the Second Vatican Council. In that first age of printing, not only do we have the first critical edition of the Bible, Erasmus's Greek New Testament of 1516, but we also have the first critical and printed editions of the church fathers. These include the magisterial editions of Augustine, Jerome, and Origen, edited by Erasmus himself, as well as numerous other editions by Protestant and Catholic scholars alike. Philip Melanchthon was one of the great patristic scholars of the age, and John Calvin was not far behind him. In fact, the Reformation was as much a debate about the church fathers as it was about the Bible itself: "Whose Cyprian?" "Which Augustine?" "My Chrysostom, not yours!"[7]

This retrieval of patristic sources in the sixteenth century was not merely the happy product of Renaissance humanist learning, although of course it was that as well, but it also shaped the way in which the great tradition of Christian believing was received, repackaged, and reformulated in the confessions and liturgies of the Reformation itself. Jaroslav Pelikan summarized the Protestant way of putting the argument like this: "If the Holy Trinity was just as holy as the Trinitarian dogma taught, and if original sin was as virulent as the Augustinian tradition said it was, and if Christ was as necessary as the Christological dogma implied, then the only way to treat justification in a manner faithful to the Catholic tradition was to teach justification by faith."[8]

In John 4, which depicts Jesus traveling from Judea to Galilee, we read: "And he must needs go through Samaria" (John 4:4, KJV). Today, in our desire to recover what the seventeenth-century Puritan divine John Owen called "the old glorious beautiful face of primitive Christianity," we must go through Wittenberg, Strasbourg, Geneva, and Canterbury, not to mention Louvain, Avila, and Rome.[9]

In the fall of 2013, Pope Francis spoke with members of the Lutheran World Federation, and he made a similar point in the following words: "I believe that it is truly important for everyone to confront in dialogue the historical reality of the Reformation, its consequences, and the responses it elicited. Catholics and Lutherans can ask forgiveness for the harm they have caused one another and for their offenses committed in the sight of God. Together we can rejoice in the longing for unity which the Lord has awakened in our hearts, which makes us look with hope to the future."[10]

Understanding the New Ecumenism

I have proceeded this far without attempting to define the New Ecumenism, and it is indeed a very difficult term to define. It is not something static, contained, or crystallized in a particular institution or movement. Rather, it is pluriform, multivalent, and elusive. As a term, New Ecumenism is used in many ways all across the ecclesial spectrum. For example, the Orthodox scholar and philosopher Christos Yannaras has said that we need a New Ecumenism, not one tied to the old structures and tired debates of the past, but "an ecumenism of concrete encounter among those who share a thirst for the life that can conquer death—people who are looking for real answers to the dead ends of the civilization in which we live today."[11]

In the West, Thomas C. Oden is among the most prominent theologians to make use of the phrase. In his view, the New Ecumenism is a recent expression of what is in fact a very old ecumenism, one grounded in the scriptures and the apostolic tradition. The "old" bureaucratic ecumenism of late (or ultra-) modernity, often called "conciliar ecumenism," is in serious decline, Oden claims. It is, in some ways, like the phone booth or a transistor radio. Those were once handy devices and useful in their time, but we do not use them very much anymore.[12]

According to Oden and others, this older ecumenical ideal has pretty much had its day. Its utopian dreams, its revolutionary pretenses, and its uncritical accommodations of modernity have left it financially vexed and bereft of a constituency. What remains of this old bureaucratic ecumenism is largely a liberal Protestant artifact, with Roman Catholicism never fully engaged and with Orthodoxy always a frustrated and, here lately, a near-rebellious minority partner.

Lesslie Newbigin, one of the great framers of ecumenism in our time, was present in 1948 at the formation of the World Council of Churches (WCC). He was also the person most responsible for integrating the International Missionary Council into the WCC in 1961. But in his later years, Newbigin declared that the WCC was in danger of becoming a global sectarian phenomenon lacking a strong focus on world missionary and evangelistic outreach. At the same time, however, he never gave up completely on those conciliar structures. Some years ago, when I was invited to become a member of the Faith and Order Commission, I asked Newbigin's advice about whether to participate. He strongly encouraged me to do so, saying that evangelical Christians needed to be at that table. It is important, he said, not to give up on the conversation.[13]

But the conversation is changing. Permit me to return to Thomas Oden and offer his distinction between the old and the new ecumenism. In his own words:

> The new ecumenism is already widely dispersed among Protestant, Catholic and Orthodox believers, not as an organizational expression of institutional union, but a movement of the Spirit. The old ecumenism was largely a liberal Protestant artifact.... The new ecumenism is above all committed to ancient classic ecumenical teaching. That means that it has a high doctrine of scripture, and a long term view of cumulative historical consensus, a Chalcedonian Christology, and a classic ecumenical view of God the Father, God the Son, and God the Holy Spirit.... In the old ecumenism the institutional manipulators were trying to create unity by negotiation. In the new ecumenism all territorial claims are less relevant, and proprietary ownership concerns subordinated. Within the old

ecumenism, Christian unity appeared to be based more on negoti-
ation skills, tolerant expression of feelings, and the sharing of political goals. In the new ecumenism, Christian unity is based on
Christian truth, not deliberative compromise.[14]

Three Encounters

Evangelical Christians have played a significant role in the emergence
of the New Ecumenism. I have been privileged to be involved in several of these ventures. Three encounters in particular stand out: first,
Evangelicals and Catholics Together (ECT); second, the recent bilateral dialogue between the Baptist World Alliance and the Pontifical Council for
Promoting Christian Unity; and, third, the 2012 Vatican Synod of Bishops
for the New Evangelization. Permit me to reflect on each.

1. The founding of Evangelicals and Catholics Together in the early 1990s
would not have been possible without a long pre-history that included the
catalytic ministries of evangelical stalwarts such as Harold John Ockenga
and Billy Graham.[15] In 1942, Ockenga, the pastor of Boston's Park Street
Church, brought together a group of neo-evangelical reformers to organize
the National Association of Evangelicals (NAE). Representing a variety of
denominations, Ockenga and his friends were pioneers. They were intent
on forging a new way in American Protestant life—over against their separatist, fundamentalist, and somewhat obscurantist co-religionists whom
they had known and grown up with and whose theological views they
substantially shared.

The "New Evangelicalism," or "Neo-Evangelicalism," as it came to be
called, found itself engaged in a struggle on two fronts. One was against
modernism, a leftover term from the 1920s and 1930s. Modernism, liberalism, or mainline Protestantism—it is referred to in various ways—was
still dominant in the early 1940s and well into the 1950s. The other front
was known by the pejorative term *Romanism*. "Romanists" were those
who belonged to the Roman Catholic Church. The post-World War II reformers hoped that a reinvigorated evangelical church, shorn of its fundamentalist trappings, would both restore true Christianity and rescue
American society by resisting the forces of modernism/secularism, on the
one hand, and Romanism, on the other.

Today, both of those fronts look completely different from how they
would have to Ockenga and the founders of the NAE in the 1940s. On the
one hand, there are very few diehard modernists anymore. While once

enjoying near hegemony in American religious life, practically all forms of mainline Protestantism are in decline—terminal decline, many would argue. On the Catholic side, of course, there is the revolution that began on January 26, 1959, when Pope John XXIII called for a new ecumenical council, the first one held in almost one hundred years (since Vatican I, in 1869–70).[16] The new council was undertaken with the express purpose of promoting Christian unity as a priority for the church. Both of these developments, the waning of modernism and the renewal of the Roman Catholic Church, have radically changed the ecumenical landscape for us today. The New Ecumenism represents, therefore, the opportunity to provide stewardship for a fresh beginning.

The year 2014 marked the twentieth anniversary of Evangelicals and Catholics Together, an initiative launched by the late Father Richard John Neuhaus and his close friend, the late Charles W. Colson. ECT has always been an ad hoc ecumenical venture; it has neither sought nor received official approval from any ecclesial body. It was, at least initially, what I once called an "ecumenism of the trenches." This term was first used in an editorial that I wrote for *Christianity Today* in 1994, soon after the release of the first ECT document, "Evangelicals and Catholics Together: The Christian Mission in the Third Millennium toward a Common Mission."[17] By "ecumenism of the trenches" I meant the fact that Catholics and Evangelicals had been brought together at a particular moment in our history to bear witness and to be allies in a struggle too easily caricatured as a "culture war." The struggle had to do with issues of moral concern, family life, civic life, and with life itself, in terms of the welcome and protection owed to those children still waiting to be born.[18]

Having met and developed a comradely friendship, we Evangelicals and Catholics alike recognized one another as partners in a common spiritual and moral struggle. But we also began to look at one another in the trenches, standing together, shoulder to shoulder, side by side, heart to heart; and we discovered the reality of what was said in the first ECT statement: that we are, and recognize one another to be, brothers and sisters in the Lord. Thus, the initial "ecumenism of the trenches" led to a deeper spiritual ecumenism, to a process of collaboration, dialogue, and common witness. The closer we came to unity in Jesus Christ, the freer we were to explore with honesty both our commonalities and our differences. Since the initial document, many others have followed as we have explored together such issues as Marian theology and the relationship between scripture and tradition.

While only God can read anyone's heart, surely there are countless Roman Catholics who, in evangelical parlance, know Jesus Christ as their personal Savior and Lord. By the same token, there are, no doubt, in my denomination many Southern Baptists who have been "duly dunked" but are still spiritually moribund. There is no place for either Catholic bashing or Baptist berating among true believers in Jesus. Without ignoring the serious and substantial differences that remain between our two faith communities, it behooves all of us to work and pray for genuine reformation within our own ranks before throwing stones at others.

2. Allow me now to turn to a recent bilateral dialogue between the Baptist World Alliance and the Pontifical Council for Promoting Christian Unity. This encounter involved five years of serious ecumenical discussion on the theme of "The Word of God in the Life of the Church," published in 2012.[19] A number of major issues are covered in this report. Some new ground was broken in the section on the Blessed Virgin Mary. For the first time in our history, we Baptists openly embraced and confessed that Mary is the Mother of God. This is not a new doctrine, of course, but simply the necessary corollary of believing that Jesus Christ is the Son of God. The declaration of Mary as Theotokos at the Council of Ephesus in 431 was more a Christological affirmation than a Mariological one.[20] The deity of Christ is really what is at stake here. But, for the first time in any kind of official Baptist-Catholic statement that I know about, a group of Baptists came together with Catholic dialogue partners to confess this fundamental truth about Jesus Christ, the divine Son of God, and his mother, Mary.

One of the Baptist theologians on the dialogue team, Elizabeth Newman, a professor at the Baptist Theological Seminary in Richmond, Virginia, has published a book that shows ecumenical theology at its best. *Attending the Wounds on Christ's Body: Teresa's Scriptural Vision* is a study of St. Teresa of Avila and Christian unity. To my knowledge, this is the first book ever published by any Baptist theologian on this saint, who is officially recognized as one of the doctors of the Catholic Church.[21] Newman has gathered amazing ecumenical fruit by taking this Catholic mystic and saint seriously and attempting to think *with*, not *against*, her theological outlook. Here is another example of the New Ecumenism.

3. A final example comes from an experience that I will never forget: the Synod of Bishops for the New Evangelization that met in October 2012. At the invitation of Pope Benedict XVI, 375 Catholic bishops from around the world came together with a number of fraternal delegates assembled

in the Vatican to deliberate on the theme of evangelization. I was asked to represent the Baptist World Alliance. There were also fraternal delegates from many other ecclesial communities, including the World Evangelical Alliance, the Lutheran World Federation, the World Methodist Council, the World Alliance of Reformed Churches, and the Anglican Communion, along with representatives from the Eastern Orthodox communities.

The synod revealed in surprising ways the complementary relationship, indeed the dovetailing of purpose, between the New Evangelization and the New Ecumenism. Much of the renewal work taking place inside the Catholic Church involves ministries committed to Christian unity and with a distinctive evangelical focus on conversion and the new birth. For what else can you call something like Alpha? Alpha is a remarkable worldwide teaching, evangelistic, and discipleship network that originated in 1977 at Holy Trinity Brompton, an Anglican church in London, but has since spread to many denominations in some two hundred countries throughout the world.[22] At the synod, I met Marc and Florence de Leyritz, a Catholic lay couple, husband and wife, who are the directors of Alpha for the entire country of France. They were asked to make a speech about their work and to talk about Alpha as a means of evangelization in one of the most secularized countries of Europe today. Also present at the synod was Brother Alois, the successor to Brother Roger as the prior of Taizé. Taizé is a small hillside town in Burgundy that sheltered persecuted Jews in World War II, and now houses a vibrant ecumenical community dedicated to contemplation, hospitality, and compassion. Thousands of young people are attracted to the distinctive music, liturgy, and worldwide ministry of Taizé.[23]

At the synod we also heard representatives from renewal movements within the Catholic Church, each of which has a distinctive ecumenical charism or mission. One of these was the movement of Sant'Egidio, which attracts large numbers of Italian young people to sing, pray, read the scriptures, and serve others through acts of mercy. Sant'Egidio is a Spirit-anointed, charismatic, and evangelistic movement among Catholic and other youth, and it reaches out to those who have no religious commitment whatsoever.[24] The Focolare Movement represents yet another renewal stream within contemporary Catholicism. This movement, with more than 100,000 followers, adheres to an explicitly ecumenical mission derived from its founder, Chiara Lubich.[25] The coalescence of evangelical activism and Catholic spirituality, shared by these groups, is also a mark of the New Ecumenism.

For me, the highlight of the synod was a visit, shared with other fraternal delegates, to the Basilica of St. Bartholomew. This beautiful basilica sits on a tiny island in the Tiber River. It is named after the Apostle Bartholomew because, according to tradition, the basilica possesses one of his thumbs. However, the centerpiece of the basilica is not an ancient relic but a recent painting, the *Icon of the New Martyrs*, which was commissioned by John Paul II for the Catholic jubilee year in 2000. This remarkable work of art shows martyrs from many places around the world in the act of being killed. Some of them are being hanged while others are slaughtered by bayonets or machine-guns. The *Icon of the New Martyrs* is a gruesome thing to look at, and yet there is a splendor about it. There is something transcendent about that large and striking icon with the heavenly host depicted above a banner with this biblical text: "These are they who have come through the great tribulation" (Rev. 7:14). The icon portrays martyrs of recent memory from many ecclesial contexts—Orthodox, Protestants, and Catholics, none of whom considered their own lives dear but gave them up for the sake of Jesus Christ.

I stood in front of that icon, reading from the guidebook as my limited Italian allowed me, about the figures depicted there. I was surprised and delighted to find among the martyrs two Baptists, one of them being Martin Luther King Jr. and the other a Romanian pastor who was put to death under the regime of the tyrant Nicolae Ceauşescu. The Baptist pastor represented there is shown with a Catholic and an Orthodox priest in the same prison. They are each holding a portion of the Bible so they can all be nourished by the Word of God as they await execution together.

I came away thinking to myself that *this* is really the New Ecumenism. Whatever we might say as theologians gathered in a synod or engaged in a dialogue, it is actually those called to give their life for Jesus Christ who, in the final analysis, are doing the most to advance the Christian faith in our time. As Pope Francis has said, the ecumenism of the future will likely be an ecumenism of blood, for the church of the future, like that of the past, will be built upon the blood of martyrs. But whether facing persecution or not, I am persuaded that as we consider the Reformation's quincentenary in 2017. it is the duty of all Christians to learn to behave, not as seventeenth-century polemicists, but as the Catholic, Orthodox, and Baptist clergy in this Romanian prison.

Notes

1. Donald Nugent, *Ecumenism in the Age of the Reformation: The Colloquy of Poissy* (Cambridge, MA: Harvard University Press, 1974), 229.

2. George Huntston Williams, *The Radical Reformation*, 3rd ed. (Kirksville, MO: Truman State University Press, 2000). See also Timothy George, "Keeping Truth Alive as a Holy Calling," *Harvard Divinity Bulletin* 29, no. 4 (Winter 2001): 4–6; and "George Huntston Williams: A Historian for All Seasons," *American Journal of Theology and Philosophy* 7, no. 2 (1986): 75–93.

3. George Huntston Williams, *The Mind of John Paul II: Origins of His Thought and Action* (New York: Seabury Press, 1981).

4. Jaroslav Pelikan, *The Riddle of Roman Catholicism* (Nashville, TN: Abingdon Press, 1959), 45.

5. Arthur C. Cochrane, ed., *Reformed Confessions of the Sixteenth Century* (Louisville, KY: Westminster John Knox Press, 2003), 225.

6. See Timothy George, "An Evangelical Reflection on Scripture and Tradition," *Pro Ecclesia* 9, no. 2 (2000): 184–207.

7. See Arnoud Visser, *Reading Augustine in the Reformation* (New York: Oxford University Press, 2011).

8. Jaroslav Pelikan, *Obedient Rebels* (New York: Harper and Row, 1964), 50–51.

9. John Owen, *A vindication of the animadversions on Fiat Lux: Wherein the principles of the Roman Church, as to moderation, unity and truth are examined and sundry important controversies* (1664; reprint, London: Banner of Truth Trust, 1967), 207.

10. Pope Francis, "To the President and Delegation of the Lutheran World Federation," October 21, 2013, www.news.va/en/news/to-the-president-and-delegation-of-the-lutheran-wo.

11. John A. Jillions, "Orthodox Christianity in the West: the Ecumenical Challenge," in *The Cambridge Companion to Orthodox Christian Theology*, ed. Mary B. Cunningham and Elizabeth Theokritoff (Cambridge: Cambridge University Press, 2008), 289.

12. Thomas C. Oden, "The New Ecumenism and Christian Witness to Society," www.ucmpage.org/articles/toden3.html. See also his chapter titled "New Ecumenism," in *The Rebirth of Orthodoxy: New Signs of Life in Christianity* (San Francisco: HarperOne, 2003), 55–81.

13. See David J. Bosch, "'Ecumenicals' and 'Evangelicals': A Growing Relationship?" *Ecumenical Review* 40 (1998): 461; and M. E. Brinkman, *Progress in Unity? Fifty Years of Theology Within the World Council of Churches, 1945–1995* (Louvain: Peeters Press, 1995), 145–66.

14. Oden, "The New Ecumenism and Christian Witness to Society."

15. See William M. Shea, *The Lion and the Lamb: Evangelicals and Catholics in America* (New York, Oxford University Press, 2004); Timothy George, "Evangelicals and Others," *First Things* 160 (February 2006): 15–23.

16. John W. O'Malley, *What Happened at Vatican II* (Cambridge, MA: Harvard University Press, 2010).

17. Charles Colson and Richard John Neuhaus, eds., *Evangelicals & Catholics Together: Toward a Common Mission* (Nashville, TN: Thomas Nelson, 1995). See Mark A. Noll and Carolyn Nystrom, *Is the Reformation Over? An Evangelical Assessment of Contemporary Roman Catholicism* (Grand Rapids, MI: Baker Academic, 2008).

18. Timothy George, "Catholics and Evangelicals in the Trenches," *Christianity Today* 38, no. 6 (May 1994): 16. See also "That They May Have Life," *First Things* 166 (October 2006): 18–25.

19. "The Word of God in the Life of the Church," *American Baptist Quarterly* 31, no. 1 (Spring 2012): 28–122.

20. Jaroslav Pelikan, *Mary Through the Centuries: Her Place in the History of Culture* (New Haven, CT: Yale University Press, 1996), 55–65.

21. Elizabeth Newman, *Attending the Wounds on Christ's Body: Teresa's Scriptural Vision* (Eugene, OR: Wipf & Stock, 2012).

22. Graham Tomlin, "Evangelism as Catechesis, Hospitality and Anticipation: A Study of the Alpha Course," *Christian Education Journal* 10 (Fall 2013): 91–103.

23. Jason Brian Santos, *A Community Called Taizé: A Story of Prayer, Worship, and Reconciliation* (Downers Grove, IL: IVP Books, 2008).

24. See the Sant'Egidio website at www.santegidio.org/.

25. Thomas Masters and Amy Uelmen, *Focolare: Living a Spirituality of Unity in the United States* (Hyde Park, NY: New City Press, 2011).

Afterword

Ronald K. Rittgers

THE CHAPTERS IN this volume combine both historical and theological reflection. This presents a dilemma for someone writing an afterword. Should I comment in a theological or a historical register—or both? Prudence probably counsels one of the latter two—historical or "both." Permit me, however, to "sin boldly," and following in the direction of the book's last three chapters, engage in a no-holds-barred theological reflection.

I appreciate the straightforward title of the book, but I can't help but wonder if it should have included a question mark at the end: hence *Protestantism after 500 Years*? What might an inserted question mark have signified? In the introduction, editors Thomas Albert Howard and Mark A. Noll explain that they have invited the contributors to engage a whole host of questions, most of which have to do with the origins and nature of Protestantism, its historical significance, and how its 500th anniversary should be observed. A question mark might thus have pointed to the importance of these questions for the shape of the volume. But a question mark also could have signified something more radical. It could have indicated that the subject of the book, Protestantism, can itself be questioned. A question mark could have placed Protestantism in the dock, suggesting that an additional cluster of questions may be asked of it: Should there *still* be Protestantism after five hundred years? Should it *still* exist? Should the centuries-long "protest" finally cease? Should the Reformation finally be over?[1]

In light of the numerous dire problems created by Protestantism for both church and society, many of which are detailed in this volume, this proposed radical questioning of Protestantism may not be as far-fetched as it might seem. Especially owing to the violence done to Christ's body, the church, through endless Protestant schism,[2] perhaps a volume like this should have concluded with a prayer for Protestantism finally to come to an end, so that Christ's prayer "that they may be one as we are one" (John 17:11, 22) may finally be realized. According to Christ, Christians are to imitate and participate in the unity that he enjoys with the Father, a unity of love, so that believers may know this love and share it with others until he returns: Christian unity-in-love is central to Christian mission (John 13:35). While Protestants have been very active in Christian mission, they have also done great harm to this mission through their interminable and sometimes bloody feuds, which they have exported around the world. Perhaps it is therefore time for Protestants to come home to Mother Church, especially given the genuine reforms that have occurred in Catholicism over the last fifty years and the progress that has been made in Protestant-Catholic relations.[3] Perhaps the theological differences that still separate Protestants and Catholics are not of sufficient weight to warrant ongoing schism and its ongoing dire consequences. Perhaps we have now come to a point where we can see that the good Protestantism has brought to the church and the world has been outweighed by the harm it has brought in its wake (whether intentionally or unintentionally) in the form of endless conflicts, schisms, warfare, secularism, and so on. Perhaps Protestantism is simply too dangerous to justify its continued existence.[4]

This more radical read of the proposed question mark may seem a bit preposterous, for Protestantism will of course continue, and in its evangelical and charismatic expressions has never been more successful in terms of numerical adherence, especially when viewed on a global scale. For many Christians, there is also reason to hope that God in his mercy will continue to accomplish much that will be good for both the spiritual and the temporal realms through Protestantism in the future. But I think the proposed question mark in its more radical guise still would have made sense, because it would have drawn attention to a challenge that Protestantism, owing to its sharp rupture with tradition on the basis of "the Bible alone" or "conscience," has faced ever since its inception— namely, the challenge of legitimacy. "Are you alone wise?" This is the question with which thoughtful Protestants have always struggled.[5] Despite his confident assertiveness, Martin Luther wrestled with this question,[6] as did other Protestant reformers. A good deal of early Protestant apology was designed to respond to this question;[7] one important explanation for the vicious nature of much early Protestant invective was that Protestants felt its sting. The legitimacy question, in short, is a good one and also a potentially lethal one: it challenges the very existence of Protestantism, implicitly asserting that Protestantism is a deficient form of Christianity at odds with or forgetful of much in the church's Spirit-inspired tradition.

I believe that this legitimacy question and Protestant responses to it are also present in a number of the chapters in this volume, albeit below the surface. No contributor openly states that Protestantism was a mistake, and no one openly seeks to refute such a claim; but the question, its challenge, and the Protestant responses to it still lurk beneath the surface. Even though most of the chapters in this volume are largely descriptive in form, and most seek to strike a conciliatory tone, one may discern in several of them a value judgment about Protestantism: it has been a basically positive development in the history of church and society; or, it has been a primarily negative one.

Most Protestants will remain Protestant in 2017 and beyond, of course. Many will do so for largely cultural reasons. Others will continue to respond to the centuries-old legitimacy challenge much as their forbears did, by pointing out alleged deficiencies in Catholicism, even in its reformed post-Vatican II incarnation. Most will thankfully not do so with the same invective as the first Protestants, and many may even possess a genuine desire for healing the Roman-Protestant schism. But they will still claim that Catholic Christianity has an insufficient supply of the Word, or grace, or faith, or the Spirit, or lay ministry; or, that it remains too hierarchical, too rigid, too clerical, too papal, too rich, or too beholden to mere human teaching (e.g., indulgences). The Reformation's 500th will be an occasion for these Christians to give thanks to God for the gift of Protestantism, or at least for their version of it.

Yet there is another way of responding to the legitimacy challenge, another way of facing the proposed question mark, that avoids triumphalism and still seeks to render humble yet penitent thanks to God for Protestantism, even as it longs for and seeks to effect full communion among Christians in the future. This alternative perspective suggests, ironically, that Protestantism may function as a safe and necessary haven from the storms of Christian schism that it did nothing to create. In developing this idea it is essential to place Protestantism within the larger context not just of Western Christianity, or even of world Christianity—by which we usually mean Christianity in the Global South—but of a world Christianity that also includes Eastern Orthodoxy. I recognize that this volume cannot treat all topics, but assessments of Protestantism, this book included, almost always leave out the Orthodox, and this is unfortunate. Viewed within this larger pan-Christian context it becomes clear that schismatic Protestants are not the original or perhaps even the most destructive schismatics in Christendom. The first Protestants split from the Latin church that had, of course, already been in schism with the Orthodox church for almost five hundred years. In light of this reality, all Christians must be considered schismatics; no Christian church is immune from this accusation, including Catholics and the Orthodox. All Christian churches can be placed in the dock and found wanting.

At their best, Protestant churches acknowledge this fact; at their best, Protestant churches possess what one might call an ecclesiology of brokenness—they accept and lament the fact that the church is broken by human sin, including their own, although not to the despair of salvation. Unlike both Catholics and the Orthodox, most Protestant churches do not claim to be *the* one, holy, catholic, and apostolic Church;[8] they are simply imperfect expressions of this church. They content themselves with a rather minimalistic (perhaps too minimalistic) ecclesiology—the preaching of the Word and proper administration of the sacraments, or, simply, the presence of the resurrected Christ.[9] Therefore, they do not confront one with the impossible choice between two mothers, both of whom have important, compelling, and yet contradictory claims to being *the* church.[10] Protestantism protects from this double bind even as it protests this double bind, and this protest should not cease until the original schismatics are reconciled. Then it might be time to declare the Reformation over. In the meantime, the protest should continue, but in such a way that it helps to promote Christian reconciliation by welcoming others to its safe haven for seasons of honest self-examination, penitence, and restoration.

At their best, Protestants believe that God works through the earthen vessels (2 Cor. 4:7) that they know themselves to be as he continues to strengthen and spread his kingdom until Christ returns. With Mark Noll, they find evidence of this divine activity in the chaotic coherence that repeatedly emerges when human beings are caught up in the redemptive story about Christ and sinners in the Word that Protestant churches preach.[11] With C. S. Lewis, they believe that at the "centre" of the faith there is an unimpeachable "mere Christianity," a personal, loving someone who despite their sad divisions "speaks with the same voice" and continues to call lost sinners home to himself.[12] They believe that this divine mission will not finally be frustrated by Christian schism, even as they confess, lament, and seek to repair the same. (Remarkably, most Protestant churches also hew to the ancient rule of faith as they seek to be conduits for this divine mission, which is no doubt owing to the fact that the version of Christianity against which they have traditionally defined themselves, Catholicism, is still part of their DNA, protecting them in most cases from making a complete shipwreck of the faith. Protestants regularly fail to acknowledge this reality.)

How, then, shall we mark 2017? As a tragic necessity, as has been suggested in this volume? The Reformation was certainly tragic, for all the reasons that have been cited by my colleagues. Was it necessary? Nearly every sincere Christian believer in the early sixteenth century, including several popes, would have said that a reformation of church and society was necessary, but they did not agree that the Reformation that actually occurred was necessary. So, there is no historical consensus on the necessity of the Reformation. Today, in addition to being grateful for the ecclesiology of brokenness that Protestantism provides, and the good it can achieve, one should also certainly give heartfelt thanks for the recovery of the ministry of the Word and the strong emphasis on divine love and generosity that were essential features of early Protestantism; one could also mention in this connection the renewed emphasis on the ministry of the laity. Each of these may be seen as salutary developments in the history of Christianity, although it should be stressed that each had important precedents in late medieval Christianity. But it seems unwarranted to assert that the Reformation was necessary, for the simple fact that we cannot know if evangelical-style reforms would have triumphed within Catholicism in the course of time even if Luther, Calvin, Cranmer, and Menno Simons had never appeared on the scene, or if they had behaved differently from how they did. The historical evidence suggests that such reforms, even those that were already under way and were promoted by reform-minded Catholics, faced serious challenges, but this fact does not justify statements of historical necessity. We ought not to introduce necessity into our interpretations of the past; the past is always the land of contingency. Beyond this, appeals to necessity too easily excuse Protestants from facing the darker side of their origins and the missteps of their history by supplying a convenient *Deus vult* that effectively silences or mollifies all criticisms and accusations. Perhaps it would be better to speak of the Reformation as tragic but salutary, or as simultaneously tragic and salutary (*simul tragicus et salutaris*), for it was certainly both.

But 2017 should not be about Protestants only, or Protestants and Catholics only. It should be about Christianity as a whole, for Christians are finally members of one Body, the Church, and what happens or has happened to one member affects the others (1 Cor. 12:12–31). Therefore, perhaps the larger goal of 2017 should be to prepare the way for 2054 when Christians will observe the millennial anniversary of the tragic, unnecessary schism between Catholics and the Orthodox. The Reformation will not be over in 2017, but perhaps, if Protestants observe their 500th in the proper spirit, by 2054—should the Lord tarry—they will have taken up their place in a new fellowship of churches that no longer invites accusing question marks.

Notes

1. See Mark A. Noll and Carolyn Nystrom, *Is the Reformation Over? An Evangelical Assessment of Contemporary Roman Catholicism* (Grand Rapids, MI: Baker Academic and Paternoster, 2005).

2. On this subject, see Ephraim Radner, *The End of the Church: A Pneumatology of Christian Division in the West* (Grand Rapids, MI: Eerdmans, 1998); and Ephraim Radner, *A Brutal Unity: The Spiritual Politics of the Christian Church* (Waco, TX: Baylor University Press, 2012).

3. For a recent, engaging account of one such homecoming, see chs. 1, 3, and 6 in Mickey L. Mattox and A. G. Roeber, *Changing Churches: An Orthodox, Catholic, and Lutheran Theological Conversation* (Grand Rapids, MI: Eerdmans, 2012).

4. See Alister McGrath, *Christianity's Dangerous Idea: The Protestant Revolution—A History from the Sixteenth to the Twenty-First* (New York: Harper One, 2007). McGrath argues that the Protestant revolution, while dangerous, should continue.

5. See Susan E. Schreiner's *Are You Alone Wise? The Search for Certainty in the Early Modern Era* (Oxford: Oxford University Press, 2010).

6. *WA* 8: 483.2; *LW* 34: 136.

7. For example, see John C. Olin, ed., *A Reformation Debate: John Calvin and Jacopo Sadoleto* (Grand Rapids, MI: Baker Books, 1966).

8. This statement should not be read as denying the important ecumenical progress that has been made between Catholics and the Orthodox in the modern period. Pope John Paul II readily conceded that the Catholic Church breathes with one lung while it remains separated from the Orthodox. Still, the longed-for reunion between West and East has not yet occurred, and the Catholic and Orthodox churches continue to make strong claims about being the Church, even if no longer insisting as in the past on the categorical exclusion of all others.

9. Radner asserts, "The one true Church is where Jesus is." *Brutal Unity*, 443.

10. I am fully aware of the fact that many Protestants have converted to either Catholicism or Orthodoxy, but in my experience it is rare to find among these converts someone who has studied deeply the competing ecclesiological claims of both the Catholic and Orthodox churches. I am also aware that some have studied both Catholicism and Orthodoxy, and have found the decision between the two possible, if difficult, to make. See, for example, Mattox and Roeber, *Changing Churches*. (Mattox converted from Lutheranism to Catholicism; Roeber, from Lutheranism to Orthodoxy.)

11. See pp. 269–70. One source of this chaos is the kind of cultural diversity that delights God; the other source, it must be stated, is human sin, which grieves God.

12. C. S. Lewis, *Mere Christianity* (New York: Macmillan, 1952), 9.

Index